RISC OS 5
User Guide

Published by RISC OS Open Ltd.

Issue 1, April 2018 (updates by RISC OS Open Ltd).
Issue 2, October 2020 (updates by RISC OS Open Ltd).

Contents

Chapter 11: Changing the computer's configuration 81

Chapter 12: The Boot application 111

Chapter 13: Using discs 121

Introduction

T his Guide describes the RISC OS 5 operating system. If you are new to your
computer, you should first read its *Welcome Guide*, which tells you how to set it
up and start using it.

About this Guide

This book is divided into the following parts and appendices:

Part 1 – Beginner's concepts starts out describing some of the terms used throughout
this Guide, alongside using the keyboard and mouse to interact with your
computer. You can skip this part if you've used RISC OS before, as you're not a
beginner.

Part 2 – Managing the desktop tells you more about manipulating files, directories and
applications. It shows you how to use the Filer and the pinboard, and how to select
the colours and resolutions used on the desktop. There's information on changing
the way the desktop behaves and changing the start-up procedure so that the most
frequently-used applications are started automatically. There's also help if things
go wrong. Finally there's a description of the filing and storage systems.

Part 3 – Networking describes how to get connected to a network of other computers
on the same site as you and how to exchange files with them. It also covers the
settings needed to connect to a wide area network – the internet.

Part 4 – Printing shows you how to set up your printer correctly, and how to
configure your printer to make the most of the computer's capabilities.

Part 5 – RISC OS applications introduces you to the applications supplied with your
computer, and describes how to use different colours and fonts. It gives tutorial
information on how to use the painting, drawing and editing applications, and
follows this with detailed reference material about the other RISC OS applications
provided.

Part 6 – RISC OS diversions takes a look at some of the more fun applications
supplied with your computer including games and puzzles that you can play.

Part 7 – RISC OS utilities describes applications designed to assist with specific
tasks, such as formatting a new hard disc, file conversion to RISC OS native formats
for use with the main applications, and updating existing applications.

The *Appendices* tell you about the Command Line Interface. This provides you with an additional way of communicating with the computer, one which programmers and experienced users will find especially useful. They also contain reference material on subjects such as BBC BASIC, file-types, character sets and error messages.

At the end you'll find a *Reader's Comment Form* to return with your comments or suggestions for this Guide.

The RISC OS operating system

RISC OS stands for **R**educed **I**nstruction **S**et **C**omputer **O**perating **S**ystem. RISC OS consists of three layers:

- The *core*, containing the programs that actually make the computer work.

- The *command line interface*, which is a text-based interface used to write programs and scripts. Most people never need to use the command line.

- The *desktop*, which is the outermost layer. This manual is mostly about the desktop, which uses icons to represent files, directories and applications, and runs applications in windows. You can have many windows on the screen at once.

RISC OS allows you to load an application from a disc, for example, and then determines how that program is run, using your input from the mouse and keyboard. When you've finished, it lets you save your work back to a disc, in a file.

In some places this Guide assumes your computer has a hard disc. If you're using a network machine, your network manager or IT coordinator will help you out.

Conventions used in this manual

The following conventions are used in this Guide:

Mouse techniques

Usually, you'll perform the following techniques with the Select (lefthand) mouse button, unless instructed otherwise in the text:

- *clicking* – pressing a button just once and then releasing it immediately.

- *double-clicking* – pressing and releasing twice in quick succession. This is most commonly used to load an application.

- *dragging* – moving an object from one place to another whilst holding down a button.

Often, you'll be told to 'press Menu over' an object. This means move the pointer over the object and press the Menu (middle) mouse button.

Menu names and options are shown in bold type. The path you need to take through a series of submenus to reach an option is described like this:

'Choose **Filer/Options/Newer**' means:

'Press Menu to display the **Filer** menu and choose **Newer** from the **Options** submenu'

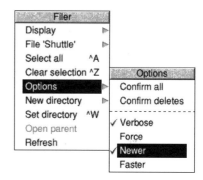

These techniques are covered in greater depth in the chapter *Using the mouse* on page 7, and the chapter *Menus and dialogue boxes* on page 23.

Other conventions

- Often you'll be told to *'press Return'* (to enter a command, or confirm an action). This is the key marked with the following symbol: ↵
- The Shift key is marked with this symbol: ⇧
- Sometimes you will need to press one key while holding down another. For example, *'press Ctrl-F9'* means hold down the Control (Ctrl) key and press the function key F9. Your keyboard may have two Control keys, one on each side, either can be used in these situations.

Important tips

Freeing up more disc space

If you require more hard disc space, you can free up space by deleting directories that you don't often use; refer to the section *Deleting files and directories* on page 38 for details of how to do this. Before deleting them, you should always take a backup of any files, directories or applications that you may wish to keep (see *Backing up hard discs* on page 128).

If your computer halts at the command line when you switch it on (the screen is blank except for a * prompt and a flashing cursor), it may be because your hard disc is full. Type *Desktop to display the desktop. Free up some space on your disc then reboot the computer.

Unexpected behaviour

If the screen goes blank

If your screen goes blank while you are not using it, it's probably because the screen saver has automatically switched off the display to save electricity and wear on the screen. You can restore the display by moving the mouse or pressing any key on the keyboard (e.g. the Shift key).

Check that the computer and monitor are connected to the mains supply and that the connectors between the monitor and the computer are tight.

Pointer won't move

If moving the mouse does not move the pointer, check that

- the mouse is firmly connected to the socket on the computer

- the surface you are using the mouse on is not shiny or covered in a pattern that would confuse the position sensor if the mouse is an optical type

- the surface you are using the mouse on is firm enough to allow the mouse ball to move if the mouse is a roller ball type.

The pointer is not visible on the RISC OS desktop

If the pointer is not visible at all, check whether the command line (with * prompt) is at the bottom of the screen (you might have accidentally pressed F12):

Star
prompt

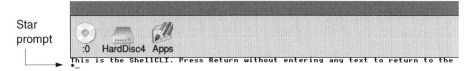

If it is, press ↵ (Return) to get back to the Desktop.

If the computer powers up in Supervisor mode

If the computer powers up in Supervisor mode (the word Supervisor will appear near the top of a black screen), it is possible that the configuration settings in !Boot are incorrect. You will need to restore !Boot from a known good backup copy, created by following the steps in the section *Getting out of a mess* on page 111.

Type Desktop after the star (*), then press ↵ (Return). This will start the desktop, although you will find that many things will not work correctly. Locate your copy of !Boot (ignore any error messages you see when opening directory displays), and copy it back to the root directory of your hard disc (making sure it is called !Boot). Shut down the machine and switch it back on.

If this does not work, performing a Delete power on (switching the computer on while holding down the Delete key) will restore the configuration settings to their factory default values.

If this still does not cure the problem, ask your supplier for help.

Getting out of a mess (resetting the computer)

Very occasionally your computer may 'hang up' – where pressing a key or mouse button has no effect. You can normally cure this by resetting the computer. To do this, first try pressing Alt-Break or, if that fails, Ctrl-Break. If this fails, press the Reset button. Alternatively, turn the computer off, wait a short while (20 seconds) and turn on again. When you reset the computer, any unsaved data is lost.

Getting help

The Help application

The Help application provides on-screen information as you use your computer. You can use this to get help on the desktop and most applications. For information refer to *Help* on page 401.

This is what a typical help message looks like:

> • *Click SELECT to select a file, directory or application.*
> • *Drag SELECT to copy (or drag ⇑SELECT to move) a file, directory or application.*
> • *Double-click SELECT to open a directory, or to run a file or application.*

The Help option on the Filer menu

You can get help on some applications by clicking Menu over an application's icon in a directory display and choosing **App./Help**. For example, here is the help text for the Alarm application (for more information, see *Information and help* on page 54).

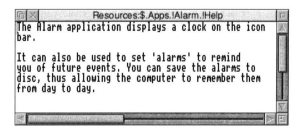

Additional documentation

Your supplier should have the following products available:

BBC BASIC *Reference Manual*
A reference manual for BBC BASIC V and VI. The BBC BASIC programming language is provided with RISC OS. If you plan to write BASIC programs on your computer, you will find the BBC BASIC *Reference Manual* invaluable.

RISC OS *Programmer's Reference Manual*
A multi-volume reference manual for the RISC OS operating system. Essential reading for all serious RISC OS programmers explaining all of the programmer interfaces to communicate with the operating system.

RISC OS *Style Guide*
This sets out any user interface design guidelines application authors should follow.

User Interface Toolbox
Information for application authors on writing powerful desktop applications, using the Toolbox to perform much of the work for you.

Technical Reference Manuals
These are available for most RISC OS computers. They give the technical specifications of all interfaces used in the computer. These manuals are essential if you are developing hardware add-ons and enhancements for the computer.

Desktop Development Environment
If you are developing desktop applications for RISC OS, you'll need the DDE. This contains the *Acorn C/C++*, *Acorn Assembler*, and *Desktop Tools* books.

Part 1 –
Beginner's concepts

1   The RISC OS desktop

This chapter introduces some of the basic concepts behind the RISC OS desktop, what they are for, and how they are used. These terms will be referred to throughout the rest of this Guide.

What is the RISC OS desktop?

RISC OS is the name of the *operating system* of your computer. It controls the way the computer screen appears, and how the computer performs various actions and tasks.

Having turned the computer on, you should be able to see the RISC OS *desktop* on your screen.

The icon bar   Icon bar icons

The desktop is your working area. At first it is clear, except for the bar across the bottom of the screen. As you perform tasks and use applications, things will be added to the desktop. You can move them around, change their size, hide and remove them to make room for others.

The desktop is a graphical user interface which uses **W**indows, **I**cons, **M**enus and a **P**ointer – or WIMP.

Windows

A *window* is an area of the screen displaying an activity or application. It shows only the portion of the information that you choose to view, like looking through a window to a larger scene outside.

Icons

The small pictures at the bottom of the screen represent the tools, applications and storage devices available. The pictures are called *icons*. The area they occupy is called the *icon bar*.

Device icons

The icons on the left of the icon bar represent the *devices* which are available – that is, the discs and other places where you can load information from, and save it to:

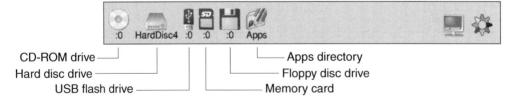

You will see a combination of the following icons, depending on which devices are available on your computer.

CD-ROM drive. If your computer has a CD-ROM drive installed, you will see the icon shown on the left. This gives you access to information on any CD-ROMs placed in the drive.

Hard disc drive. The hard disc drive, if one is fitted, is where you can store all of your work.

USB flash drive. If there are USB sockets on your computer, you can put a flash drive in any USB socket and it will appear here.

Memory card. If your computer has a memory card socket then you will see an icon here. The shape of the socket determines which types of card can be used to store your work.

Floppy disc drive. The floppy disc drive, if one is fitted, stores your work on removable 3.5" plastic discs which you put into the slot in the front of the computer.

Apps. Gives you quick access to some useful applications which are available on the computer.

Battery Manager. This icon will only be present if your computer is powered from a rechargeable battery.

If your computer is fitted with a *network* interface, there may also be a **Discs** icon or **Net** icon shown. These are used to let you share information or equipment connected to other computers on the network. You'll find more information about networking later on in the chapter *Local networks* on page 149.

Discs icon (Access)   Net icon (Econet)

Application icons

On the righthand side are the *application icons*. These represent things you can do, such as word-processing and drawing programs. Initially there are only two or three:

Display Manager ⏤⏐
Task Manager

Display Manager. This enables you to change the screen resolution (the amount of data you can display) and the numbers of colours or grey scales displayed on the screen.

Task Manager. This enables you to look at and control your computer's memory, amongst other things. You don't need to worry about this for now since the chapter *Managing the desktop* on page 73 explains its facilities in full. It is always the rightmost application icon, though it may look very different to a coloured cog.

Any other applications which you load will normally be represented by icons displayed on the righthand side of the icon bar.

Menus

A menu on the desktop is similar to a menu in a restaurant: it's a list of things to choose from. In a foreign restaurant, if you can't actually speak the language, you can point at the menu with your finger to tell the waiter which dish you want (assuming that you know what the menu means!). On the computer, you move the mouse to point at your choice from the menu.

This is the main way of doing things on the RISC OS desktop.

Menu options shown in grey (like **Clear selection** above) are not available at that time. Often you must perform another action before the option becomes available.

The pointer

The arrow on the screen is the *pointer*. It is used to point at things you want to use or move, and is itself moved by sliding the mouse around on the desk with your hand. The pointer can have a number of different shapes, which you will come across as you become more familiar with your computer.

2   Using the mouse

T his chapter tells you how to use the mouse to select and move things displayed on the screen.

What is a mouse?

The mouse is the main way of interacting with the computer, apart from the keyboard (see page 11 for an introduction to the keyboard). As you move the mouse on a flat surface, so the pointer moves around on the screen. Using the mouse and its three buttons you control much of what the computer does.

Holding the mouse

Hold the mouse so that your fingers rest easily on the three buttons. For example, if you are right-handed, you should hold it like this:

Move the mouse around and watch the pointer move around the screen. If you run out of space to move the mouse, lift it up and put it down again in a more convenient position. While the mouse is lifted, the pointer will not move, and when you put it down again you can carry on where you left off.

Use the mouse on a smooth but non-slippery surface such as a mouse mat (available from your supplier). Other surfaces on which the mouse works well are wood and coarse paper.

The mouse will not work well on painted metal or highly polished surfaces, and optical mice in particular will not work well on regularly patterned surfaces.

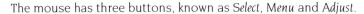

The mouse buttons

The mouse has three buttons, known as *Select*, *Menu* and *Adjust*.

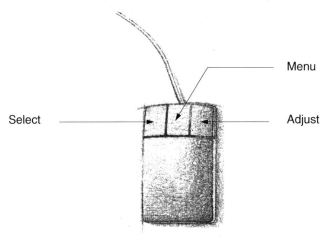

Menu

Select

Adjust

You use the **Select** button to select and move icons displayed on the screen, or to choose from *menus*.

You use the **Menu** button to make a menu appear. Menus are described in the chapter *Menus and dialogue boxes* on page 23. Some mice incorporate a scroll wheel in the centre position to give a third axis of movement to the user; pressing the wheel down will emit an audible click as the button is built into the wheel mechanism.

The **Adjust** button does a variety of things. It is most often used to choose from menus without removing the menu from the screen. *Keeping a menu on the screen* on page 24 shows you this. The Adjust button is also sometimes used to perform the opposite action to the Select button. See *Practising scrolling* on page 21 for an example of this.

Basic mouse techniques

The following mouse techniques are all you need to know to start using your computer:

clicking – pressing a mouse button just once and then releasing it immediately.

double-clicking – pressing and releasing twice in quick succession. This is most commonly used to load an application.

dragging – moving an object from one place to another whilst holding down the Select (or Adjust) mouse button.

Clicking and dragging techniques are summarised on the following pages. You can try out the examples in *italic text*.

Clicking

This is used, for example, to choose a menu option, select an object, or open an application window.

1 Point at the object

Move the mouse so that the pointer is over the object you want to select.

For example, point at the Apps icon on the icon bar.

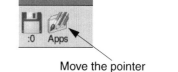

Move the pointer over this icon and click

2 Click Select

Press and release the Select (lefthand) button of the mouse.

The Apps directory display will appear.

Note: from now on, 'clicking' means clicking with the Select button, unless otherwise stated.

Double-clicking

You usually use double-clicking to initiate an action, such as loading an application.

1 Point at the object

Move the mouse so that the pointer is over the object you want to double-click on.

For example, point at the !Edit icon in the Apps directory display.

Move the pointer over this icon

2 Double-click on the object

Press and release the Select (lefthand) mouse button twice in quick succession.

 You have to make the second click while the pointer's arrowhead is still illuminated after the first click. If the item is highlighted but nothing else happens, try again, but double-click a little faster. Try not to move the mouse while you're doing this.

Double-click on the !Edit icon. The Edit icon will appear on the icon bar, showing that the Edit application has been loaded ready for use.

Dragging

You usually use dragging to move an object to a different place on the screen.

1 Point at the object

Move the mouse so that the pointer is over the object you want to move.

For example, to move a window, point at the title bar along the top of the Apps directory display. (The title bar is the part of the directory display containing the words Resources:$.Apps)

2 Select it with the mouse

Press **and hold down** the Select (lefthand) button of the mouse.

3 Move the mouse and drag the object

Move the mouse to drag the object across the screen. Release the Select button when the object is where you want it to be.

Drag the Apps directory display to a different position on the desktop.

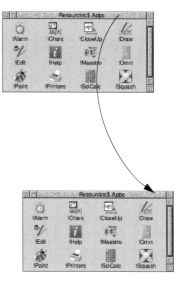

3 Using the keyboard

This chapter describes the main features of the keyboard, and tells you how to use the different groups of keys.

A quick tour of the keyboard

The illustration on this page shows how the keys are laid out on a typical keyboard.

The keyboard is divided into the following major blocks:

The *typewriter keys* are in the main block, and are similar to a typewriter keyboard.

The *function keys* (marked F1 to F12) are in a row above the typewriter keys. The function of these keys in a particular piece of software is often marked on a card supplied with the software. You don't need to use these keys at the moment.

The *numeric keypad* is at the far right, laid out like a calculator. These keys can be used either to type numbers (when the **Num Lock** key is on) or to perform special functions, depending on the program or application you are using.

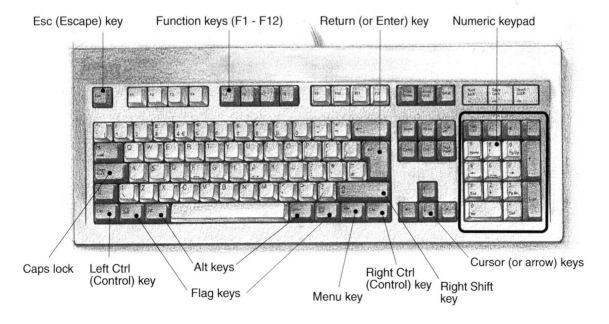

Esc (Escape) key   Function keys (F1 - F12)   Return (or Enter) key   Numeric keypad

Caps lock   Left Ctrl (Control) key   Alt keys   Flag keys   Menu key   Right Ctrl (Control) key   Right Shift key   Cursor (or arrow) keys

When to use the keyboard

You will need to use the keyboard for many tasks, such as

● supplying answers to questions the computer asks in writable menu boxes (including giving names for files and documents you create)

● using a word processor, or a text editor like Edit (for an example of this, see *Using applications* on page 29)

● choosing some menu options using keyboard shortcuts (for example pressing F3 from many applications to **Save** a file)

● entering data in a spreadsheet or database.

The caret
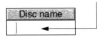

Whenever you need to use the keyboard within the desktop, a vertical bar appears. This is called the *caret*. Any characters you type will appear to the left of the caret, which will move to the right. The caret may only appear when you click in a window.

The computer control keys

The *computer control keys* are those keys which do not produce visible characters when pressed. They therefore exclude most of the typewriter keys, and the numeric keypad, but they include all the function keys. Computer control keys sometimes have different functions, depending on the software they are being used with, although some of the more common keys are used as follows:

Esc (*Escape*)	at the top left of the keyboard cancels an operation (e.g. printing).
F1, F2, ..., F12 (*Function keys*)	as mentioned above, the function of these keys in a particular piece of software is often marked beside a menu option, or on a keycard.
↵ (*Return*)	completes a line, either starting a new line of text, or sending a name or instruction to the computer.
← (*Backspace*)	above the ↵ key deletes a character to the left of the caret.
Delete	deletes a character to the right of the caret.
Caps Lock	makes everything you type appear in capitals (when on). If you don't want this, press the key once to turn the lock off.
⇧ (*Shift*)	changes the meaning of a key, when held down while that key is pressed. For example, holding down ⇧ (Shift) and pressing a letter causes that letter to appear in upper case. There are two of these keys.
Ctrl (*Control*)	changes the meaning of a key, when held down while that key is pressed. There are two of these keys.

12

Alt	changes the meaning of a key, when held down while that key is pressed. There are two of these keys.
Print Screen	normally displays the print option box when used in conjunction with an application.
Break	used in conjunction with the Control key to force the computer to restart itself. **All unsaved work is lost when you do this.**
↑, ↓, ←, → (*Cursor keys*)	move the cursor (when it is visible) around the screen in the direction of the arrow on the key. These are also known as arrow keys.
Flag and **Menu** (*Macro keys*)	these optional keys can be programmed to perform custom actions if your keyboard has them. There is a Flag key next to each Alt key. The Menu key is next to the righthand Control key.

Special key combinations

Sometimes you need to press more than one key. In such cases:

1   Press **and hold down** all except the last key in the sequence.

2   Press and release the last key in the sequence.

3   Release all the other keys.

For example:

- 'Press Shift F1' means press and hold down the ⇧ (Shift) key, then press and release F1, then release Shift.

- 'Press Ctrl Shift F1' means press and hold down the Ctrl and ⇧ (Shift) keys, then press and release F1, then release Ctrl and Shift.

Moving around a document

Some other keys allow you to move around long documents. Try these out when you are using an Edit document.

Home	moves the caret to the start of the document
End	moves the caret to the end of the document
Page up	moves to the previous 'windowful' of the document
Page down	moves to the next 'windowful' of the document

These keys have no effect in some applications (Paint, for example).

Typing special characters

Sometimes you need to be able to type special characters that are not apparently on the keyboard, such as accented characters, or symbols like ©. Many of these symbols are accessible via the standard keyboard. Here's how to type them:

Typing accented characters

Some of the keys on the figure below are marked with a triangle in the lower right corner adjacent to an accent. These keys allow you to type accent characters.

For example, to type an 'e' with an acute accent (é):

1 Whilst holding down the Alt key, press and release the | key.

2 Release the Alt key.

3 Press and release the E key.

Typing other special characters

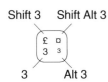

Shift 3   Shift Alt 3

3   Alt 3

You can type the other special characters shown in the keyboard map using the instructions shown on the left.

For example, to type a ¤ symbol:

1 Hold down the ⇧ (Shift) and Alt keys, press and release the 3 key.

2 Release the ⇧ (Shift) and Alt keys.

The Chars application also lets you insert many special characters and symbols into your document. For more information, refer to the chapter *Chars* on page 403.

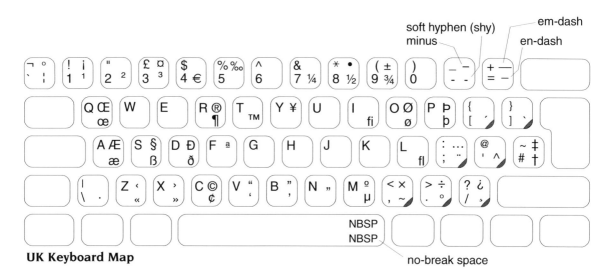

UK Keyboard Map

4 Windows

T his chapter describes windows and explains how you can move, resize, hide and close them. It also describes how to move through the contents of a document too large to display in one window all at once.

Features of windows

You can move windows around the screen, hide them behind other windows, close them to a small icon on the desktop, or close them completely. Icons on the window borders allow you to do these things. Most windows also have icons which allow you to change their size.

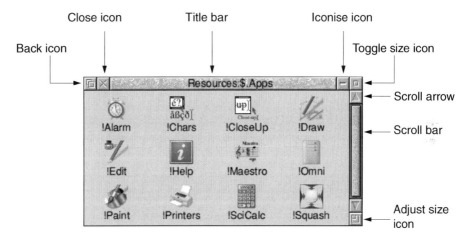

Title bar

The *title bar* displays the title of a window. This may be the name of an application, directory, or a document you're editing. Here's the title bar from the Apps directory display, which you can get by clicking on the Apps icon on the icon bar:

Back icon

 Clicking on the *back icon* has the effect of putting a window to the back of the pile of windows on the screen. If you click on this, the window will be hidden behind any windows which overlap the area it occupies.

Close icon

 Clicking on the *close icon* closes a window. If you click on this, the window will be removed from the screen.

Iconise icon

 Clicking on the *iconise icon* reduces the window to a miniature version of itself stuck to the desktop background, behind all the other windows.

Toggle size icon

  Clicking on the *toggle size icon* switches a window between full size and the last non-full size displayed. (Full size is either large enough to display everything in the window, or such that the window fills the whole screen.)

This alternating action is called *toggling*.

Adjust size icon

 Dragging the *adjust size icon* lets you alter the size and shape of a window. Clicking the Select button on it also brings a window to the front of a stack of windows.

Practising manipulating windows

Practise using the window icons to do the things described on the following pages. You can use the Apps directory display to practise most of this.

Changing a window's size

1 Point at the adjust size icon

Move the pointer to the adjust size icon.

2 Drag the adjust size icon

Press and hold down the Select button. Move the mouse and drag the icon to change the size of the window.

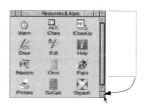

3 Release the mouse button

Release the button when the window is the size you want it to be.

Moving a window

You move a window by dragging its title bar – follow the steps in D*ragging* on page 10.

Off the screen

You can drag windows almost off the screen if you want to. Be careful if you do this – you can forget that you've dragged a window off screen, and think you've "lost" it.

Over the icon bar

If you've dragged a window so that it obscures the icon bar, hold down either of the ⇧ (Shift) keys on the keyboard and press the F12 key. This will bring the icon bar to the front. (Press the same key combination again to send it to the back – this is another instance of toggling).

Toggling window size

1 Click on the Toggle size icon

Move the pointer over the Toggle size icon and click the Select button.

The window size will snap to nearly the width of the screen.

2 Click on the Toggle size icon again

Clicking on the icon again will reverse the process (note the changing toggle size icon).

Bringing windows to the front

When you have a stack of windows on the screen, you can get at the one you want by sending windows to the back or bringing them to the front.

First, click on the Display Manager icon on the icon bar to bring up another window. Drag it on top of the Apps directory display.

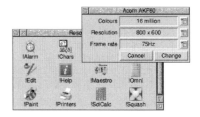

Bring a window to the front

Click on the title bar (or the Adjust size icon) to bring a window to the front.

Send a window to the back

Click on the Back icon to send a window to the back again.

Note: Not all windows have Adjust size or Back icons (for instance, the Display Manager window has no Adjust size icon).

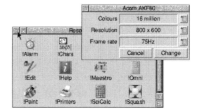

Closing windows

Click on the Close icon

Position the pointer on the Close icon and click Select.

For example, close the Apps directory display, and the window will disappear from the screen.

When you start using applications, you will find that most of them will ask whether you want to save your changes if you close a window containing unsaved work. *Saving a file* on page 35 tells you more about this.

Click on the Close icon

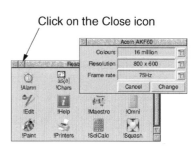

Scrolling

A window is so named because it allows you to see all or part of a file, application or whatever you've displayed on the screen. If a file is too large to display all at once, the window will only show a section of it. The proportion of the file visible depends on the size and shape of the window. The part of the file you can see alters as you move the window around the file:

A window onto an area of a document

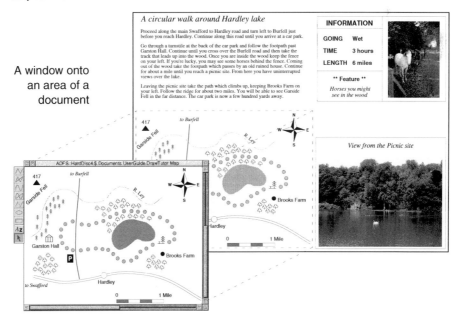

The technique of moving around a large display inside a window is called *scrolling*. Try out the techniques on the following pages, and you'll soon get used to doing this.

Windows usually have scroll bars and scroll arrows to enable you to move around a display:

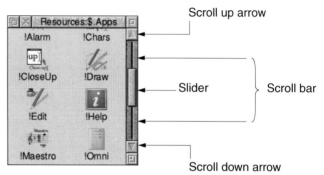

Scroll bars

The *scroll bars* allow you to scroll the window over the file, directory or picture you are viewing.

Slider

The size of the *slider* shows what proportion of the file is visible: if the slider occupies half the length of the scroll bar, half the file is visible. To display a different area of the file, drag the slider along the scroll bar. This technique is useful for moving quickly around a large file.

Scroll arrows

The *scroll arrows* are at each end of the scroll bar. Click on the arrow showing the direction you want to move the window in – left, right, up or down. This technique allows you a finer control over scrolling than dragging the slider.

Some windows (like the one above) only have vertical scroll bars, sliders and scroll arrows. Others have horizontal scroll bars, sliders and scroll arrows as well (they're along the bottom edge of the window).

Practising scrolling

In the examples in the rest of this chapter you are going to use the Map example file provided in the Documents.UserGuide.DrawTutor directory on your hard disc or network.

To find the file, click on the disc or network icon. Double-click on the Documents *directory; this displays the contents of the directory. Now double-click on the* UserGuide *directory, and finally double-click on the* DrawTutor *directory.*

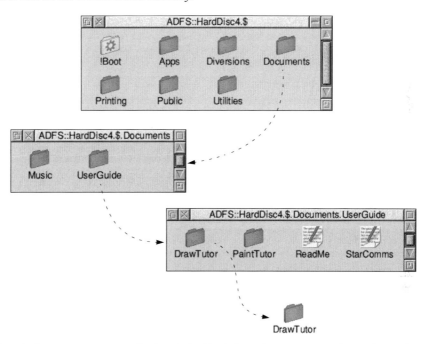

When the directory contents are displayed, double-click on the Map *icon, and a window with scroll bars appears, containing some drawings and text.*

If you are having problems with clicking and double-clicking, go back to page 8 and review your mouse techniques first, then come back to this point.

There are three main ways of scrolling around a window:

● Using the scroll arrows to scroll step by step.

● Using the scroll bars to scroll by a screenful at a time.

● Using the slider to move directly to a position in the window.

These techniques are described in the rest of this chapter so that you can practise them.

Scrolling step by step

Click on the scroll arrow for small steps

Position the pointer on the scroll up arrow and click the Select button to scroll by small steps at a time.

Keep the Select button held down to continue scrolling.

Click Select on the scroll down arrow to scroll downwards in small steps.

Use the horizontal scroll bar (on windows which have one) to scroll left or right in the same way.

Click above or below the slider for large steps

Position the pointer above or below the slider (above the slider to scroll up, below the slider to scroll down) and click Select.

The next screen of the document will appear.

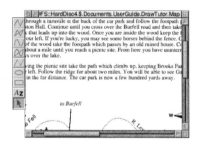

Moving through a file

1 Select the slider

Position the pointer on the slider, press Select and keep it pressed down.

2 Drag the slider

Drag the slider to display the part of the file you want to view.

Move from one side of a document to the other by using the horizontal scroll bar (if the window has one) instead.

Note: If you drag either slider with Adjust, you can move both from side to side and up and down at the same time. The pointer disappears while you're dragging then reappears when you release Adjust.

5   Menus and dialogue boxes

T his chapter tells you what menus and dialogue boxes are, how to display
them and choose things from them, and how to supply information when the
computer asks you to be more specific about what you want.

Menu basics

Using menus

To display a menu, click the Menu (middle) mouse button over a window, over an
icon on the icon bar, or over a blank area of the desktop (the latter will display the
Pinboard menu – see the section *Pinboard* on page 39).

The menu displayed will depend on where the pointer is on the screen at the time,
whether you have previously selected an icon, and on the application you're using.

Cancelling an unwanted menu

If you press Menu by mistake, or decide you don't want a particular menu after all,
you can make a menu disappear by clicking on a blank area of the desktop or icon
bar.

Displaying a menu

1   Point to the relevant icon

Move the pointer over the window or icon
you're interested in.

*For example, click on the Apps icon on the icon bar and
move the pointer over the Apps directory display.*

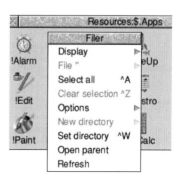

2   Click Menu

A menu will be displayed (in this example, the
Filer menu).

If the pointer is over a file icon when you click the Menu button (or if you had previously selected an icon by clicking on it) the menu will apply to that individual file.

You can make the menu apply to more than one icon in a window by clicking on each icon in turn with Adjust (not Select) before you bring the menu up. Use Adjust to deselect icons, too.

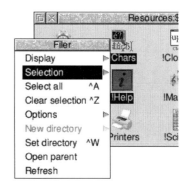

You can make the menu apply to all the icons in a window by choosing **Select all** from the menu – see below.

Choosing from a menu

With a menu displayed, click on the option you want (notice that menu options are highlighted as you move the pointer over them).

For example, on the Filer menu you displayed above, point at the **Select all** *option and click Select. All the file icons in the directory display will be highlighted and the menu will disappear.*

To reverse this, repeat the above process, choosing **Clear selection** *instead. Alternatively, click on a blank area of the directory display.*

Keeping a menu on the screen

You'll notice that after you click Select to choose a menu option, the menu disappears.

If you click with Adjust instead of Select, the menu will stay on the screen, and you can choose another option.

Choosing from a submenu

1 Highlight the main menu item

Move the pointer onto a main menu item with an arrow. An arrow to the right indicates that a *submenu* is available.

For example, point at the **Display** *option on the Filer menu.*

2 Display the submenu

Move the pointer onto the arrow.

The Display submenu will appear on the screen.

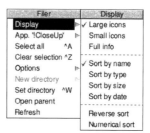

3 Click on the submenu item

Highlight and make your submenu choice by moving the pointer over it and clicking on it.

Click on **Small icons**. *The icons in the directory display will change size.*

Note: If a menu is on the righthand side of the screen, it may become partially obscured by a submenu. To prevent this, move the menu towards the left of the screen by dragging on its title bar **before** displaying the submenu.

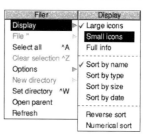

Choosing menu options – conventions in this Guide

Now that you know about menus, here are the conventions we'll use in the rest of this Guide to tell you how to choose menu options and fill in writable menu boxes.

What the manual says	What you actually do
Move the pointer over the Tutorials directory display, click Menu and choose **Display/Small icons**.	1 Move the pointer over the Tutorial directory display. 2 Click the Menu (middle) button. 3 Move the pointer to the right of the **Display** option. This opens the **Display** submenu. 4 Move the pointer over the **Small icons** option. 5 Click Select to choose the **Small icons** option.
Move the pointer over the drive icon, click Menu and type `Letters` into the **Disc name** writable menu box.	1 Move the pointer over the drive icon. 2 Click the Menu (middle) button. 3 Move the pointer to the right of the **Name disc** option. 4 Use the Backspace key to erase any existing default name. 5 Type in the name `Letters` for your new disc. 6 Click Select over the **Disc name** writable menu box (or press ↵) to enter the name.

What is a dialogue box?

A *dialogue box* is a window which contains a number of related options from which you can make choices. You can think of it as like filling out a form – you need to supply answers to the questions being put to you. Once you have done that, applying your choices will perform an appropriate action. Dialogue boxes can appear in two circumstances:

● Instead of a submenu, you will sometimes see a dialogue box.

● If you choose a menu item whose name ends in an ellipsis (**...**), you will see a dialogue box.

Components in dialogue boxes

Here are the different components you'll come across:

Writable icon

This is a field, containing a *caret*. A caret shows where you can type text. Some fields are blank. Others include a default name, which you can change if you want.

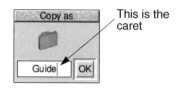

This is the caret

To erase the default name, press Backspace until it has gone. (A quicker way is to hold down the Ctrl key and press U.)

Option icon

This is a 'switch' that can either be on or off. You may have more than one switch on at once.

Radio icon

This is one of a group of 'buttons', only **one** of which may be selected at once (like the waveband selection buttons on a radio).

Adjuster arrow icon

This is an arrow you click on to increase or decrease any progressive series, such as numeric values, dates, or sliders.

Pop-up menu icon

This is a button which displays a menu list when you click on it. Choose an option from the menu list and the choice is reflected in the dialogue box.

Applying the changes you've made

The way you apply the changes you've specified depends on the type of dialogue box. Some dialogue boxes have one or more buttons at the bottom for you to click on (such as **Save** and **Cancel**); others take effect as soon as you click on an arrow or radio icon.

Dialogue boxes with several buttons may have a *default action button*. This is a button with a thicker border (like the **Save** button shown above), and can usually be found in the bottom righthand side of the dialogue box. As well as clicking on this button, you can apply the changes you've made by pressing ↵ (Return) on the keyboard.

Some dialogue boxes (usually **Save as** boxes) have a writable icon which you should type in (to supply a filename, for instance). There are three ways of applying the name you supply in such a dialogue box:

● press ↵ (Return)

● click on **OK**

● drag the file's icon from the dialogue box to a directory display

You'll find out more about this in *Files and directories* on page 33.

Cancelling a dialogue box

You can cancel a dialogue box by clicking on the Close icon (if it has one) or the **Cancel** button. Any choices you made in the dialogue box prior to cancelling it will be ignored.

Transferring between writable icons in dialogue boxes

When you are editing text at the caret in a writable icon there are some shortcuts available if you want to transfer that text between writable icons. Using the mouse, drag a selection starting at the caret to highlight some (or all) of the text.

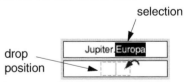

This selection can now be dragged and dropped into another writable icon. This **moves** the selected text from the original icon and places it at the caret where you dropped it.

Rather than moving the selection you can leave the original behind and make a **copy** instead. To do this:

1   Hold down the Ctrl key and press C to copy it.

2   Place the caret in the other icon using the mouse.

3   Hold down the Ctrl key and press V to paste it.

Text can also be transferred to and from many applications in this way by *cutting*, *copying*, and *pasting*. See page 255 for an example of how Edit does just that.

6   Using applications

This chapter tells you how to load and run applications on your computer. It uses the Edit application as an example.

What are applications?

 Applications, like Edit or Draw, are the tools that you use to produce your letters, drawings, music and so on. In a directory display application names always start with an exclamation mark (!) – for example, !Draw.

Some applications (such as Edit) are provided in the Apps directory on the icon bar. There are other applications on your hard disc or network. Many other applications and games are available from other suppliers.

Starting an application

There are three main ways you can start an application:

- Double-clicking – move the pointer over the application's icon, and double-click.

- Dragging – move the pointer over the application's icon, then drag it onto the icon bar, and release.

- Double-clicking on an associated file – e.g. double-click on a Draw file to start Draw. This only works if the computer knows where to find the application (i.e. if it is in the Apps directory, like Draw or Edit, or if the directory containing its icon has been displayed since you last switched on).

1   Open the directory display containing the application directory

To use an application that is on removable media such as a USB flash drive, memory card, or floppy disc, put the disc in the appropriate socket or drive then click on the drive icon. This will open the *root directory* display for the disc.

To use one of the computer's own applications, like Edit, click on the Apps icon on the icon bar to show the Apps directory display.

Try this now as an example.

2 Start the application

Double-click on the application's icon. It will appear on the righthand side of the icon bar, ready for you to use.

For example, double click on !Edit. Its icon will appear on the icon bar, indicating that it has been loaded into the computer's memory, and is waiting for you to use it.

Some applications (like Configure) or games (like Meteors) open a window as soon as you double-click on their icon, instead of appearing on the icon bar.

Using applications

Once you have started an application, you can usually begin using it by clicking on its icon on the icon bar. An *application window* will open on the desktop.

To use Edit, click on its icon on the icon bar: an empty Edit window will appear, ready for you to start writing.

Type in some text. Any text you type using the keyboard appears in the window. Text appears to the left of the vertical bar – the caret. The caret moves to the right, to make room for the text.

Press ↵ (Return) to start a new line, and press it again to leave a blank line.

Once you have typed a few lines of text, move the caret around the text by moving the pointer with the mouse and clicking Select – the caret will jump to the position of the pointer. You can insert (or delete) text at the new position.

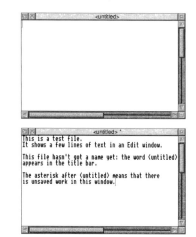

After you've finished using an application, you will need to *save* any work you've done in a *file* on a disc (otherwise your work will be lost when you switch the computer off). The next chapter, *Files and directories*, tells you how to save the text file you've just created, so you can leave its window on the screen for now.

Using more than one application window

Often you'll have more than one application window open on the desktop. You can only enter information (e.g. write some text, or draw a picture) in one window at a time. To change the window you are working in, move the pointer over your chosen window and click Select. You'll notice that the title bar will change to a light shade of yellow, indicating that it is now active, and you can type into it.

For example, click on Edit's icon on the icon bar to bring up a second Edit window. The second window will be active.

Now click on some text in the first Edit window to make it active.

Close the second (empty) window. You don't need it now.

Quitting applications

When you've finished using an application, you'll usually want to *quit* it. To quit an application:

1 Display the application's icon bar menu

Click Menu over the application's icon on the icon bar.

For example, try this on Edit's icon.

2 Choose Quit

Click on the **Quit** option.

If you've already saved everything you've done in the application, its icon will disappear from the icon bar.

If you've forgotten to save any work, the computer will remind you, and ask if you really want to quit, discarding any changes.

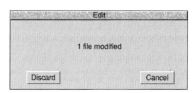

In this case, you have not yet saved your work in Edit. So, click on **Cancel** *to leave Edit running. You'll find out how to save your work in the next chapter.*

The Boot application

!Boot

If you were writing a letter by hand, you would need to know where to find the resources to write it (paper, envelope, pen etc). The computer uses different types of resources, and also needs to know where to find them. They are contained in the *boot application*.

Normally you can ignore the Boot application; it just contains the resources required and controls the applications and the fonts that you use.

Note: Never try to delete the Boot application. It is one of the most important applications on your computer; without it your computer will not operate correctly.

Locating the Boot application

The Boot application is usually held in the root directory of your hard disc in an application directory called !Boot. If the computer is set to boot from a network file server instead it will be called one of !ArmBoot, !NFSBoot, or !ShareBoot depending on the type of file server.

Throughout this Guide the term Boot application means whichever one was used to boot from, unless the context requires the specific name to be used.

7 Files and directories

This chapter explains how you can store information in an organised way, copy it, and delete it when you no longer need it.

What are files and directories?

Everything you create using an application can be saved as a file, whether it consists of text, graphics or a program. Each file has a name – you have to provide one when you save a new file.

 File icons are usually square shaped overall, but what's in the box depends on what sort of file it is. Double-clicking on a file's icon will load the file (if the application to display it is available).

 Files are stored in *directories*. A directory can contain many files, and also other directories (*subdirectories*) and applications. Directory icons usually look like folders, to indicate that they can contain files or other directories.

 There is a special sort of directory called an *application directory*. Its name always begins with a '!', and it contains an application, such as a word-processor, or a drawing package. Applications usually have their own individual icons; the icon shown here is the icon for !Draw.

Opening directory displays

1 Open a directory display

For example, double-clicking on the UserGuide *directory opens the directory and the* UserGuide *directory icon changes to the open directory icon.*

The resulting directory display shows various contents, including a directory called DrawTutor.

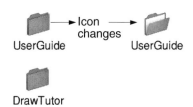

2 Open a subdirectory

Double-click on the DrawTutor *directory, and the* DrawTutor *directory display will appear. This contains files (in this case, drawings used with the Draw application).*

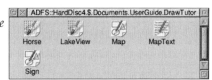

Double-clicking on an application

Double-clicking on an application directory loads the application, usually onto the icon bar ready for use. See the previous chapter for more on this.

Three refinements you might find useful later on:

● Double-clicking Adjust on a sub-directory icon opens the sub-directory display and simultaneously closes the directory display it came from (the *parent*). This can help to reduce the number of windows that will gather on the desktop during a work session.

● Double-clicking Adjust on an application icon will simultaneously load the application and close its directory display.

● Clicking Adjust on the close icon closes a directory display and simultaneously opens its parent directory.

See chapter RISC OS *applications* on page 235 for more examples of this.

Building a file structure

You need to organise your files carefully. If you leave them all in the root directory on the disc, it will soon become large and unwieldy.

Build up a file structure with files of similar types grouped in directories. For instance, the file structure of a disc for a newsletter might look something like this:

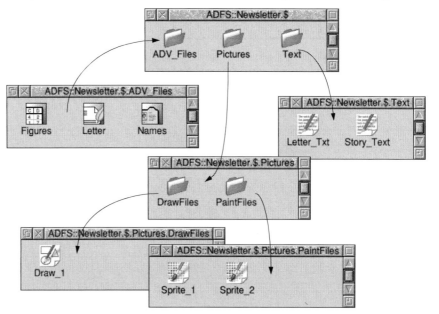

To create a structure like this, you'll need to create directories, and save, copy or move files into them. You'll be able to do this by creating a new directory on the hard disc and saving your files there.

A fuller description of the *filing system* is given in the chapter *The desktop* on page 47.

Creating a new directory

1 Open a directory display

Decide where you want to create the new directory, and open a directory display.

For example, click on the hard disc or network icon on the icon bar.

2 Enter a name for your new directory

Move the pointer over the directory display and click Menu to display the Filer menu.

Type in a name for your new directory in the **New directory** dialogue box and click on OK (or press ↵).

Call it TestFiles1, *for example.*

An icon for the new directory will appear in the directory display.

Saving a file

1 Open the directory display

Decide on the directory in which you want to save your file, and double-click on its icon to open a display for it.

For example, double-click on the TestFiles1 *directory you've just created.*

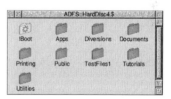

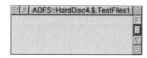

2 Give your file a name

Move the pointer over the work you want to save and press Menu to display the application menu. Type a name in the **Save as** dialogue box.

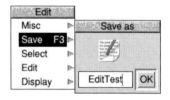

For example, try this on the text file you created in the last chapter.

Click Menu and type the name EditTest *in the* **Save/Save as** *dialogue box (you'll need to erase the default name* TextFile *using Backspace).*

Filenames and directory names on disc cannot contain the characters $ & % @ \ ^ : . # * " |.

You can use upper-case (capitals) and lower-case letters wherever you like in the name – the computer makes no distinction between them. The only reason for calling your file EditTest instead of edittest is that it's easier for you to read.

If you've saved this file before (the correct filename will appear on the box if you have) you can miss out the next step – just press ⏎ (Return).

3 Save your file

To save your file, drag the file icon in the dialogue box into the directory display and release the Select button.

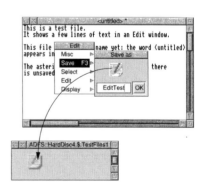

For example, save your file EditTest *in your* TestFiles1 *directory. Then close the file* EditTest *(click on the Close icon).*

Loading a file

You can **load** a file by double-clicking on its icon, as long as the relevant application is either in the Apps directory, or the application icon has been displayed on the screen since you last switched on the computer (the application has been 'seen').

Copying a file to another directory

1 Open the destination directory display

If you haven't already done it, open the directory you want to copy the file into.

For example, create another new directory called TestFiles2 *(follow the instructions in Creating a new directory on page 35). Open the new directory, so both* TestFiles1 *and* TestFiles2 *are displayed.*

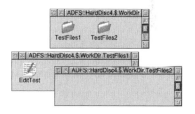

2 Select the file to be copied

Click on the icon of the file you want to copy.

You can select two or more files in the same directory display by clicking on their icons with Adjust (or by choosing **Select all** from the menu). Use Adjust to deselect icons, too.

3 Copy the file to the new directory

Drag the file's icon into the new directory display.

For example, drag the file EditTest *onto the directory* TestFiles2.

The file will be copied into the new directory. A copy of the icon will appear in the directory display when this has been done.

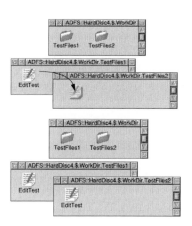

Moving a file

To *move* a file (so that the original is not retained in its original location), repeat the steps in the previous section, but hold down ⇑ (Shift) between steps 2 and 3.

Deleting files and directories

Warning: once you have deleted a file or directory, you can't get it back again, so use this option with caution!

1 Select the file or directory to be deleted

Click on the icon of the file you want to delete.

For example, select the copy of EditTest *in directory* TestFiles2.

(You can select multiple files by clicking on their icons with Adjust, or by choosing **Select all** from the Filer menu.)

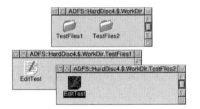

2 Delete the file or directory

Keeping the pointer over the same directory display, click Menu to display the Filer menu and choose the **File/Delete** option (this might be **App**, **Dir** or **Selection** instead of **File**, depending on what you've selected).

Delete the copy of file EditTest *from the* TestFiles2 *directory.*

Note: Deleting a directory also deletes all the files in that directory, so use this option with caution!

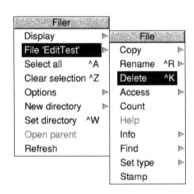

If any files (or directories) have been *locked* against deletion, they will not, in fact, be deleted. See the section *Advanced Filer operations* on page 55 for information on *file access* and removing *file locks*.

Pinboard

If you click Menu over an empty area of the desktop, you will see a menu called **Pinboard**.

Don't worry too much about the pinboard at the moment. It's explained further on page 67, and enables you to do things like

- changing the whole background of the desktop into a picture

- leaving file or application icons 'stuck' to the desktop background, so you can see and use them, even when the directory they came from is closed

- miniaturising a window down to an icon on the background.

You might come across one use of the pinboard when you are dragging files (for example) from one directory to another. If you let go of the Select button accidentally while the file you are dragging is over a blank portion of the desktop, its icon will stay on the background.

You can remove the 'dropped' icon from the background as follows:

1 Display the Pinboard menu

Move the pointer over the dropped icon and click Menu.

2 Remove the icon

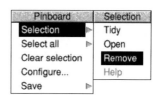

Choose **Selection/Remove** from the menu. If that option is greyed out, it means that the pointer wasn't quite over the icon when you clicked Menu. Try again.

This action does **not** delete the file itself – the icon stuck to the pinboard is merely a 'pointer' to the real file on your disc.

8   Switching off the computer

This chapter describes the correct procedure to follow before switching off your computer. Do this at the end of the day, or if you're not intending to use the computer for a few days.

Normal shut down procedure

When you've been doing some work on the computer and want to switch it off, it is generally inadvisable to just switch off using the On/Off power button: you will lose any unsaved work this way, and you **may** cause damage to the files on your hard disc.

By following the instructions in this chapter, you can switch off the computer more 'gracefully'. This will ensure that you don't lose any work, because the computer is in a state which makes it OK to turn off at the switch.

1 Save your work

Make sure that you save any work you have been doing, or you might lose it (see *Files and directories* on page 33).

2 Shut the computer down

Move the pointer over the Task Manager icon and click Menu, then choose **Shutdown** from the menu.

The computer checks to see whether you have left any work unsaved. If you have, a window will appear for each application with unsaved work, prompting you if you really want to quit the relevant application.

If you're sure you want to quit, click on **Discard** (to discard any changes). If you want to save your work before you switch off, click on **Cancel**, save the work, then choose **Shutdown** again.

41

The computer will perform any 'tidying-up' operations necessary, such as quitting any applications, logging off any networks to which you may be connected, and parking the hard disc drive heads.

A window will appear when this has happened, telling you that the computer is ready to be switched off.

Note: when the window appears telling you shutdown has completed, you can restart the computer instead of switching off. Click on **Restart** to do this.

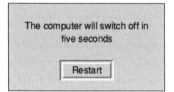

The computer is now ready to be switched off.

Restart

3 Switch off the computer and peripherals

If your computer supports *soft off*, allowing it to turn itself off by software control, this will cause a modified message to be used in the window.

To switch off the computer either wait for the time to elapse, or where soft off is not available use the manual On/Off button instead.

The computer will switch off in five seconds

Restart

It is now safe to eject any removable discs from their drives because all the files are now closed.

If you have any other peripherals connected to your computer, check in the manuals supplied with them to see whether they will switch off automatically every time you switch off the computer. If any do not, switch them off now.

Should you intend to leave your computer unused for a long period of time you should switch off the mains at the wall socket, and similarly switch off the monitor. This will save electricity and extend the lifetime of the equipment which might otherwise be left in a low power (standby) mode.

Part 2 –
Managing the desktop

9   The desktop

The *Beginner's concepts* covered an introduction to the desktop, and to the basic tasks of loading, saving, copying, moving and deleting files, etc. This chapter expands on those concepts by covering the desktop and Filer in much more detail.

Manipulating windows

Firstly, here's a reminder of the various window icons:

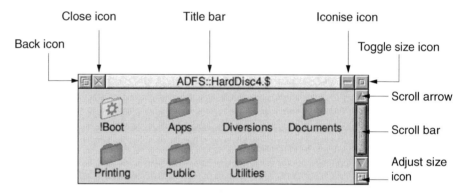

The chapter *Windows* on page 15 introduced the most common ways you will manipulate windows. The following table repeats those techniques and builds on them with other, more advanced ways to manipulate windows.

	Action with Select	Action with Adjust	Notes
	Moves a window to the back of the stack.	Moves a window to the front of the stack.	Hold down Shift to move by one position in the stack.
	Picks up the window for moving by dragging.	Picks up the window for moving by dragging without affecting the window order.	Click Select, but don't drag, to only bring the window to the front.

	Action with Select	Action with Adjust	Notes
⊠	Closes a window.	Closes a window and opens its parent at the front.	Shift-Select-click to iconise the window (see page 68). Shift-Adjust-click to open its parent without closing it. Ctrl-Alt-Select-click to close all currently open windows.
⊟	Iconises a window to the pinboard.	Iconises a window to the pinboard.	The Windows setup plug-in (see page 109) controls whether this icon is present or not.
⊡	Toggles between full size at the front and stack previous size.	Toggle between full size and previous size without changing the window order.	Hold down shift to maximise without covering the icon bar.
▽	Scrolls through a file step by step in the direction of the arrow.	Scrolls through a file step by step in the opposite direction to the arrow.	
▬	Scrolls through a file by dragging in the orientation of the Scroll bar.	Scrolls around in both axes by dragging. Either Scroll bar can be used for this.	When scrolling in both axes the pointer is temporarily hidden.
▬	Scrolls through a file screen by screen.	Scrolls through a file screen by screen in the opposite direction.	
⊡	Changes a window's size, bringing it to the front.	Changes a window's size without changing the window order.	Click Select, but don't drag, to only bring the window to the front.

46

Windows obscuring the icon bar

After moving windows around for a while the icon bar may be hidden. To temporarily reveal it, for example to save a file from a **Save as** box to a drive icon, hover the mouse at the bottom edge of the screen. The icon bar pops to the top.

Alternatively, press Shift-F12 to toggle the icon bar to the top. Press Shift-F12 once more to toggle it to the back again.

Directory displays

HardDisc4

Information stored on the computer is shown on the screen in directory displays. Clicking on the icon for a particular information storage device (such as a disc drive) opens the root directory display for that device. For example, here's the root directory display for a hard disc:

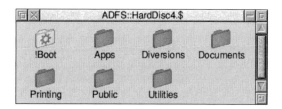

The basic techniques used to move around the files and directories have already been introduced in the chapter *Files and directories* on page 33. This section recaps on those techniques, and describes some more advanced operations.

Opening and closing directory displays

Here's a summary of how to open and close directory displays on the desktop:

To		Do this	Notes	
Open a directory display		Double-click on the directory icon.		
Open a directory display without running internal files of applications		Hold down Ctrl and double-click on the directory icon.	This speeds up the opening of large directories, and saves memory. Application icons are replaced by the generic RISC OS application icon.	

47

To		Do this	Notes
Open a subdirectory, and simultaneously close its parent		Double-click Adjust on the subdirectory icon.	
Close a directory display and open its parent		Click Adjust on the Close icon.	This option is not available from the root directory, or from the user root directory of a file server (in this case, use **Open '$'** from the icon bar menu of the file server icon).
Open an application directory		Shift double-click on the application directory icon.	This opens the application directory without actually running the application.
Bring an open directory display to the front		Double-click on the icon for the directory.	You can Shift double-click to close any subdirectories.
Close a directory display		Click on the Close icon.	You can also Shift double-click on the directory icon
Close a directory display, leaving its icon on the pinboard		Shift click on the Close icon.	See *Using the pinboard* on page 68.

Note: If a subdirectory is 'buried' too deeply in the overall directory structure, you may not be able to open it. See *Pathnames* on page 61.

The Apps directory

Apps

When you click on the Apps icon on the icon bar you see a directory display containing some of the most frequently used applications (these are described starting at *Part 5 – RISC OS applications* on page 233).

Changing information in directory displays

You can change the way file and directory information is shown in directory displays using the Display menu. The new display choices will be applied to the current directory display and any you open afterwards. The default directory display style can be set using the Filer setup plug-in (see page 89).

Changing the icon size and displaying file information

To	Do this
Show files etc. in directories with large icons (but no file information)	Choose **Display/Large icons**.
Show files etc. with small icons (but no file information)	Choose **Display/Small icons**.
Show all information on files in a directory display	Choose **Display/Full info**.

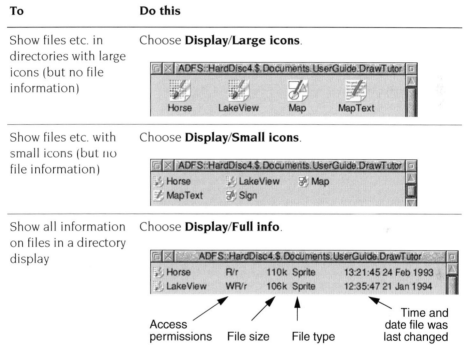

Full info gives you lots of information about a file:

● Access permissions are described in *Access* on page 55.

● File sizes are shown in bytes, kilobytes, megabytes and so on. See *Information and help* on page 54.

● File types are described in *Setting a file's type* on page 59 and appendix *RISC OS file types* on page 529.

● The time and date used is that provided by the computer's real-time clock, which you can set by following the section *Time and date setup plug-in* on page 107. For application directories containing a !RunImage, the directory will show the time and date from the !RunImage.

Changing the sort order of files in a directory display

To	Do this	Notes
Sort files in alphabetical order	Choose **Display/Sort by name**. 	Files are sorted by name, in ascending alphabetical order.
Group files according to type	Choose **Display/Sort by type**. 	Undated files appear first, then dated files in numerical order of file type, then applications, and finally directories.
Sort files according to size	Choose **Display/Sort by size**. 	Files appear first sorted in descending size order, followed by applications then directories. (Directories are only in alphabetical order.)
Sort files in order of creation	Choose **Display/Sort by date**. 	The most recent appear first.
Sort files in the opposite order	Choose the modifier **Display/Reverse sort**.	Ascending order sorting becomes descending, and vice versa.
Sort files in numerical order	Choose the modifier **Display/Numerical sort**.	Names containing numerals are sorted naturally (e.g. File9 is next to File10). Type, size, and date sort order is unaffected.

Selecting files and directories

Here's how to select or deselect icons in a directory display:

To		Do this	Notes
Select a single icon		Click on it.	
Select a group of icons		Click Select or Adjust on the first icon, and Adjust on each of the others in turn.	You can also drag a box round a group of icons to select them. Dragging a box with Adjust inverts the selected state of any icons within the box.
Select all icons in a directory display		Press Menu, choose **Filer/Select all** or press Ctrl-A.	There's more on the Filer menu on page 52.
Deselect an icon		Click Adjust on it.	Useful for selecting many icons in a display: choose **Select all** then click Adjust on unwanted icons.
Deselect a group of icons		Press Menu, choose **Filer/ Clear selection** or press Ctrl-Z.	You can also click over a blank part of the directory display.

Once you've selected an icon, or a group of icons, you can perform various Filer operations on that selection. See *The File, Dir., App. or Selection submenu* on page 52.

Creating a new directory

To create a new directory:

1 Open a directory display within which you want to create the new directory.

2 Press Menu and type the new directory name into the **New directory** box.

3 Click on **OK** or press Return (↵).

The name must contain at least one printing character, and must not contain any of the following reserved characters:

$ & % @ \ ^ : . , # * " |

The Filer

The Filer is the part of the desktop that handles operations on files and directories, such as selecting, copying, deleting, moving and so on. This section tells you how to use the Filer to manipulate files and directories, and how you can modify its behaviour.

Filer operations normally run 'in the background', so that you can carry out other desktop activities while copying, searching, deleting and so on.

A typical background
Filer copy operation
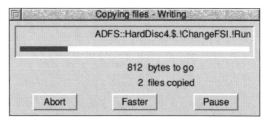

The blue progress bar shows an estimate of how much of the operation has completed so far.

The Filer menu

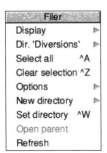

Click Menu anywhere over a directory display to show the Filer menu.

Some operations when applied to a directory (such as copying and deleting) apply recursively to all objects within that directory. If any of those objects are themselves directories, the operation applies to their contents as well (and so on). Moving an application, for example, will move all of it: its directory and all its contents. So think, especially before you delete a directory!

Although you can run several Filer operations simultaneously, you should not run more than one operation on the same file or directory at the same time. For example, don't copy or move files into a directory while at the same time deleting existing files from the same directory – you may lose files or data.

The File, Dir., App. or Selection submenu

Once you've selected an icon or icons (see *Selecting files and directories* on page 51) you can use the Filer menu to perform various operations on your selection.

- If you select a directory icon, the **File** option changes to **Dir**.
- If you select an application icon, the **File** option changes to **App**.
- If you select more than one icon, the **File** option changes to **Selection**.

Copying, moving and deleting files

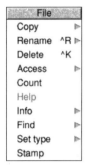

This section tells you how to manipulate your files, directories and applications using the Filer.

Note: For simplicity, this section refers to operations on a **File**, but most of the operations apply equally to a directory, an application, or a selection.

To	Do this	Notes
Copy a file	Drag the file's icon to the destination directory.	
Copy a file with a different name	Change the name in the **File/Copy/Copy as** writable menu box and click on **OK**.	To copy to a different directory, drag the **Copy as** icon to the destination directory display.
Move a file	Hold down Shift while dragging the file's icon to the destination directory.	This will copy the file and delete the original from the source directory.
Rename a file	Type the new name in the **File/Rename/Name** writable menu box. You can also click on the file's name while pressing the Alt key, or pressing Ctrl-R, to rename the file in the directory display.	Filenames mustn't contain any of these reserved characters: $ & % @ \ ^ : . , # * " | Most filing systems are not case sensitive (the NFS filer **is** case sensitive).
Delete a file	Choose **File/Delete** or press Ctrl-K.	You can't retrieve deleted files!
Delete a locked file	Choose **File/Access/Unprotected** before deleting the file.	You can override file locks permanently by choosing **Options/Force**; see page 59.

53

Note: During copying you'll see a partially drawn icon to represent the partially copied file. With a 'Full info' directory display the word 'DEADDEAD' will be displayed on the line as well. When the file copying completes, the correct icon is filled in the file type set.

Copying and moving to another device

Files can be dropped directly onto device icons on the lefthand side of the icon bar; the Filer will open a directory display and proceed to copy or move those files to the default directory for that device, usually the root directory. This only works for devices that are writable, so you cannot drop files onto the Apps icon for example.

Information and help

You can use the Filer menu to find out more information about your selection, or get help on an application:

To	Do this	Notes
Find the total size of a file or selection	Choose **File/Count** to see the number of files and their total size.	There are 1024 bytes in a kilobyte, 1024 kilobytes in a megabyte, and 1024 megabytes in a gigabyte. A one megabyte file is therefore 1,048,576 bytes.
See information about a file	Choose **File/Info**.	This displays the file type, size, access details and date last modified – information similar to that shown when you choose **Display/Full Info** (see page 49).
Get help on an application	Select the application and choose **App./Help**. Not all applications support this.	You can also use the Help application – see page 401.

Advanced Filer operations

This section describes some of the more advanced Filer operations.

Setting file access permissions

A file's access permission settings define who is permitted to read it, write to it or delete it.

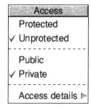

Simple access permissions

To	Do this	Notes
Allow a file to be read and altered only by **you**	Choose **Access/Private** and **Access/Unprotected**.	This is the default setting.
Allow a file to be read but not altered by **anyone** on a network (including you)	Choose **Access/Public** and **Access/Protected**.	This is a good way of protecting finished files. The **Force** option (see page 59) overrides this.

If you change the access to a directory, all the files in the directory are affected.

Detailed access permissions

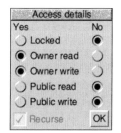

Most of the time you'll use the simple method above to set access permissions. However, you can also set access using the **File/Access/Access details** dialogue box:

- **Locked** – the file cannot be deleted (off by default). You can override this with **Force** (see page 59).

- **Owner read** –the file's owner can read it (on by default).

- **Owner write** – the file's owner can write to it (on by default).

- **Public read** – other network users can load your files or run an application in your network space (off by default).

- **Public write** – other network users can write to the file (off by default).

To apply access permissions recursively to the contents of a directory, switch the **Recurse** option on (this only works with applications and directories).

If you use a Level 4 Fileserver, take care when you set directories on it to **Locked**: this may make these directories invisible to other users on the network.

How to identify file access permissions

There are several ways to find out the access permissions for a file.

● You can display the **File/Access/Access details** dialogue box.

● You can display the files using the **Display/Full info** menu option.

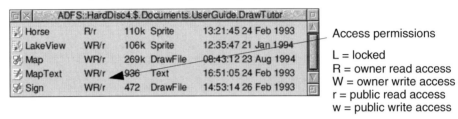

Access permissions

L = locked
R = owner read access
W = owner write access
r = public read access
w = public write access

● You can use the **File/Info** option; see *Information and help* on page 54.

Setting the currently selected directory

Sometimes, to save typing when using the command line, it is convenient to set the *currently selected directory*. Choose **Set directory** to make the directory display on which the menu was opened the working directory, or press Ctrl-W having clicked on the directory display first.

The command line is described in the appendix *The command line* on page 495.

Finding files

If you've saved a file somewhere in your directory structure, but can't remember where, **Find** will help you locate it:

1 Select the directory or directories you want to search.

2 Press Menu and type the name of the file you want to find into the **Dir./Find/Find file** writable icon.

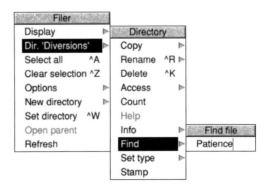

3 Click on the name, or press Return (⏎).

If the object is found, you'll see one of two dialogue boxes:

Finding an object - Found	Finding an object - Found
ADFS::HardDisc4.$.Diversions.!Patience	ADFS::HardDisc4.$.finder.Documents
2 directories checked	2 directories checked
0 files checked	0 files checked
Abort Run View Continue	Abort Open Continue

If the object found is a file, you can

- **Abort** the search
- **Run** the file (if the file is a program, it will be run; if it is a file, it will be loaded into the appropriate application, if one can be found)
- **View** the directory containing the file
- **Continue** to search for another object with the same name.

If the object found is a directory, you can

- **Abort** the search
- **Open** the directory
- **Continue** to search for another object with the same name.

Using wildcard characters

You can use *wildcards* to represent unknown characters in the search string:

*	represents zero or more characters of any sort.
#	represents one character of any sort.

For example:

aeo*	would match aeo, aeon and aeons, and any name that begins aeo.
a*o	would match any name beginning with an a which ends with an o.
aeo#	would match aeon, and any four letter name that begins aeo.
aeo##	would match aeons, and any five letter name that begins aeo.

All **Find** parameters are case-insensitive; AEO# is the same as aeo# or Aeo# etc.

Modifying Filer operations

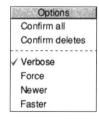

Six settings in the **Options** submenu provide finer control over most of the filing system operations invoked. These options apply to all subsequent Filer operations, as well as the current one.

Confirm all

This prompts you before performing an action. This helps safeguard against the accidental deletion of files, for example. It is off by default.

When this option is switched on, you can

- choose **Abort** to abandon an entire operation
- choose **No** to skip the present object and go to the next
- choose **Yes** to carry out the operation on the present object and go to the next
- choose **Quiet** to continue with the operation without asking for further confirmation (in cases where the operation affects more than one object).

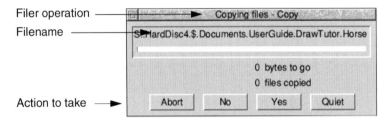

Confirm deletes

This is similar to **Confirm all**, but prompts you only when deleting files. It is off by default.

Verbose

This tells you about the progress of an operation. It is switched on by default.

Information about the current operation is displayed in a dialogue box. You can

- choose **Abort** to abandon the entire operation
- choose **Faster** to speed up the operation, see *Faster* on page 59
- choose **Pause** to interrupt it temporarily. The button will change to **Continue** (click on **Continue** to proceed with the operation, or on **Abort** to stop).

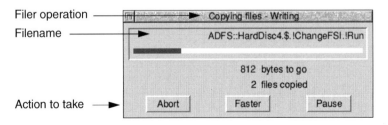

If **Verbose** is switched on, you can click Menu on any of the standard Filer dialogue boxes, such as those you get with copying, finding, deleting and moving. You will then be able to choose options for that Filer operation to override any that were set from the **Filer/Options** menu, and those options will only apply to the selected operation.

Force

This enables you to delete files and directories even if they are locked (unless they are stored on a network server with different ownership). It is off by default.

This is particularly useful if you want to delete a directory containing a lot of files, some of which may be locked. However, use this option with great care, as it overrides all file protection (see *Setting file access permissions* on page 55).

Newer

This applies only to copying, and is designed to ensure that you don't overwrite a file by an older version of the same file. It is off by default.

If you set out to copy a file to a directory where there is already a file of that name, the file will only be copied if it is newer than the file in the destination directory.

Note: This slows down copying operations over networks, since the destination must be checked for a newer file of the same name before each copy.

Faster

This option makes file operations faster, at the expense of the responsiveness of the desktop. Normally during file operations, keeping the look of the desktop up-to-date takes priority over speed. If you choose the Faster option, speed takes priority: files and windows aren't updated until the current operation has finished.

Setting a file's type

Every file has a file type, which determines what happens when you double-click on a file icon. For example, files of the type Text are loaded into Edit, files of the type Obey are interpreted as lists of commands to be carried out, etc.

To change a file's type:

1   Select the file whose type you want to change.

2   Press Menu and go to the **File/Set type** writable icon.

3   Enter the file type, in normal text or as a hexadecimal number.

For a list of file types, see appendix RISC OS *file types* on page 529.

Date/time stamping

Files are marked with the date when they were last altered, and directories when they were first created. Applications show the date of the !RunImage file (or, if one is not present, of the directory). This information is shown when you display **Full info**, or when you select a specific file or directory and choose **File/Info** (see page 54).

Stamp enables you to update the date and time stamping on files and directories to the current date and time. To do this:

1   Select the object(s) you wish to stamp.

2   Choose **File/Stamp**. The date stamp will be updated. You can check this using the **Info** menu option.

Correcting problems

If a problem arises during a Filer operation, you'll see an error box displayed:

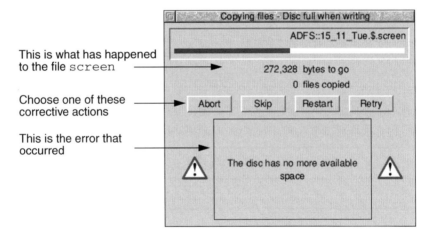

This is what has happened to the file screen

Choose one of these corrective actions

This is the error that occurred

- **Abort** lets you cancel the file operation completely.
- **Skip** skips the current file operation and starts afresh on the next file.
- **Restart** starts the operation on the current file from the beginning.
- **Retry** tries to start the operation again from where the error occurred.

Once you've cleared a problem, you'll find that clicking on **Retry** normally allows you to continue with the operation.

Pathnames

The full name of a file or directory appears in the title bar at the top of the file window or directory display:

The *pathname* is the complete 'address' of a file or directory.

Usually just the filename is sufficient, but sometimes you need to specify the whole pathname.

Technically, a pathname has the following general form:

`filing-system::disc-name.[directory-names.]filename`

So, in the above example:

This text	Points to
`ADFS:`	the filing system name (note the trailing colon). If you omit the filing system name, the current filing system is assumed (see below). On a network, the filing system name is followed by the network name.
`:HardDisc4`	the name of the hard disc, floppy disc or other storage device (note the preceding colon).
`.$`	the 'root' directory, usually the directory you first open when you click on a storage device icon. On network file servers, this will be replaced by &, your 'user root directory' (which may be one or more directories away from the root). If you omit this, and the filing system name and disc name, the path is taken relative to the current directory.
`.Images` `.00-49`	directories nested within the root directory (note the preceding full stops).
`.key00-24`	a file or directory within the `00-49` directory.

Note: If the pathname of a directory exceeds around 250 characters in total, you may not be able to open it. If this is the case, move the directory higher up the overall directory structure (it's unusual to have such a deeply-nested structure, and you should avoid it if possible).

Current filing system

The default current filing system is that used by your hard disc drive (if fitted), usually ADFS. The current disc is also usually your hard disc drive.

Desktop colours and resolution

You can change the number of colours displayed, and the size of the desktop, using the Display Manager. The Display Manager icon is on the righthand side of the icon bar, next to the Task Manager (see page 73).

The 'resolution' is amount of information displayed on the computer screen:

- The higher the resolution, the more information on the screen, so the better the displayed quality of the applications and pictures on your computer.

- The higher the resolution, the more of an application or picture that can be viewed in the same screen space.

(Don't confuse resolution with the dot pitch of the monitor, which is fixed.)

The more colours that are available, the more faithfully images will be displayed. For example, you will see a difference if you display a photograph in 256 colours rather than 16 million colours.

The following pictures show the same desktop at different resolutions:

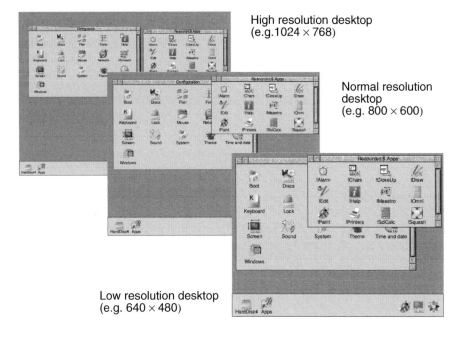

High resolution desktop
(e.g.1024 × 768)

Normal resolution desktop
(e.g. 800 × 600)

Low resolution desktop
(e.g. 640 × 480)

Changing the desktop display characteristics

 Clicking on the Display Manager icon on the icon bar shows the Screen display window, which shows the current settings of the desktop. Use this to alter the current resolution, number of colours, and frame rate, then click **Change**.

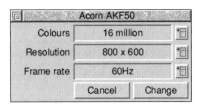

To	Do this	Notes
Change the number of colours or greyscales used in the desktop display	Click on the **Colours** menu icon, choose a number from the list. Colours: Black/white, 4 greys, 16 greys, 16 colours, 256 greys, 256 colours, 4096 colours, 32 thousand, 64 thousand, ✓ 16 million	There may be colour options that are greyed out if your computer doesn't offer all of the options that RISC OS can use.
Change the resolution	Click on the **Resolution** menu icon, choose the resolution you want. Resolution: 1280 x 480, 1600 x 600, 480 x 352, 640 x 480, ✓ 800 x 600	The resolutions you can select depend on the type of monitor you are using.
Change the frame rate	Click on the **Frame rate** menu icon, choose the rate you want. Frame rate: ✓ 60Hz, 56Hz	To reduce eye strain, choose a higher frame rate as that will flicker less.

How colour and resolution interact

As you experiment with the Display Manager, you'll find that you can only display certain combinations of colours and resolutions. These combinations are limited by the computer, the amount of video memory it can use, and the capabilities of your monitor.

The Display Manager assumes that the most recent change you make is the most important. If you choose a higher resolution, the Display Manager may have to reduce the number of colours correspondingly. If this happens, it will try to pick the maximum number of colours possible at that resolution.

Similarly, if you choose a large number of colours, the Display Manager may have to reduce the resolution at which it can display these colours. If this happens, it finds the highest resolution at which this number of colours is possible. The Display Manager does not always pick the optimum resolution and you may have to change to a more appropriate resolution for the desktop.

Note: Every time you switch on, the default display characteristics will be used which are set by the *Screen setup plug-in* on page 101. The Display Manager only changes the screen for the current session.

Advanced display options

Normally you won't need to use the information given in this section.

Mode string

The mode string defines the current screen display mode:

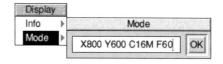

The mode string is made up of

X	horizontal resolution
Y	vertical resolution
C	number of colours (2, 4, 16, 256, 4k, 32k, 64k or 16M)
G	number of greyscales (2, 4, 16 or 256)
EX	horizontal eigen factor
EY	vertical eigen factor
F	frame rate (optional)
L	pixel layout (optional)

You can edit the existing mode string, or you can replace the whole string with one of your own creation.

Using eigen factors to improve the display detail

The *eigen factors* determine the scaling between the operating system's coordinates and pixels on the screen.

You can use the eigen factors to change the level of detail of the desktop, as appropriate for your screen. Increasing the level of detail will decrease the amount of usable space. Conversely, you can decrease the level of detail to increase the available space.

For example, with eigen factors of 2 (EX2 EY2 present in the mode string) a monitor set to display 800 × 600 will be considered as 3200 × 2400 in operating system coordinates. This will give an apparently large desktop work area to use, but with much less display detail.

The eigen factor sets the number of *dots per inch* when viewed on screen:

Scaling from OS coordinates to pixels	Eigen factor	Equivalent level of display detail
÷1	0	180 dpi (highest)
÷2	1	90 dpi (default)
÷4	2	45 dpi
÷8	3	22.5 dpi

To show the highest possible detail set the eigen factors to 0. For example, change from X800 Y600 C16M F60 to X1600 Y1200 C16M F60 EX0 EY0 and the desktop will be at the same relative size on screen but at twice the detail:

1 Click Menu over the Display Manager and move to the **Mode** dialogue box.

2 Move the cursor to the mode string and change the EX and EY eigen values (or add them if they are not already present).

3 Click on **OK** for the new eigen values to take effect.

Note: The eigen values are changed back to their default values whenever you use the Display Manager to change display modes.

Using old type mode numbers

You can still display screen modes using the old type mode numbers by typing the mode number directly into the mode box on the icon bar:

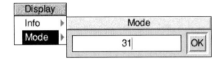

A list of old type numbers is given in the table *List of screen modes* on page 535. Some of these modes may not be available if the resolution is outside of the range that your monitor can display, or the number of colours required are not one of the combinations that the computer's hardware can output.

Note: If your monitor cannot display a given mode, the Display Manager will automatically choose a mode with the same number of colours. If the mode is supported by your hardware but not the desktop, you'll see an error message.

Displayed pixel shape

Square pixel modes are the most useful for everyday use; they maintain the correct proportions of images on the desktop. Some examples of these are:

- 800×600
- 1024×768
- 1280×1024
- 1920×1080

Rectangular modes do not maintain the correct proportions of the desktop; they have a width which is more than twice their height. Some examples of these are:

- 640×256
- 1056×256
- 1280×480

The rectangular pixel modes are common with some types of game that were originally intended to be played on a television set; a standard definition television's picture is scanned as two interlaced frames, giving it half the vertical detail.

When you select a rectangular pixel mode from the Display Manager the desktop will have its eigen factors set to EX1 EY2 to keep the proportions of images true, even though there is only half the normal vertical detail available.

The pinboard

This section shows you another useful part of the Filer: the *pinboard*. The pinboard area adds another dimension to the desktop and the Filer. For example, you can

● pin file, directory and application icons to the pinboard, to save having lots of directory displays open

● double-click on these pinned items to activate them just as you would if they were in a directory display

● move files around on the pinboard

● display a picture on the background (a backdrop)

● shrink application windows and directory displays to icons to save space on the desktop.

Directory pinned

File pinned

Picture displayed as backdrop

Iconised application windows

Using the pinboard

This section shows you how to use the pinboard. The techniques you'll need are much the same as those used in normal file operations.

To		Do this	Notes	
Pin an icon to the pinboard		Drag the icon from a directory display and drop it on the background (not the icon bar).	You can pin icons for files, directories and applications. Drag icons to reposition them.	
Open a directory display from a pinned directory icon		Double-click on the pinned directory icon.	The pinned icon will stay on the pinboard.	
Start an application from its pinned icon		Double-click on the pinned application icon.		
Load a file from its pinned icon		Double-click on the pinned file icon.	This also starts the application, if it's been seen by the Filer.	
Select a group of icons on the pinboard		Use the same technique as for selecting files and directories. See page 51.	You can also use **Select all** from the Pinboard menu. See page 69.	
Copy a selection from the pinboard to an open directory display		Drag and drop the selection onto the destination directory display.	Your selection can include icons from different parent directories. You can't **move** files from the pinboard to a directory display.	
Iconise an open directory display or active application window to an icon on the pinboard		Shift-click on Close to iconise at the pointer. Click on Iconise to use the pinboard's **Iconise to** rules instead (see page 100).	This saves cluttering the desktop with open windows. When you reopen an iconised window, the icon disappears from the pinboard.	

Pinboard menu options

Like the Filer, Pinboard is controlled by a menu. To display the menu options, press Menu anywhere over the desktop background. To see the options available for a particular icon on the background, select the icon and press Menu (or press Menu over the icon when there is no other selection).

To	Do this	Notes
Arrange icons neatly on the pinboard	Select the icons and choose **Selection/Tidy**.	Changing screen display resolution may cause icons to disappear off the edge of the screen; **Select all** followed by **Selection/Tidy** brings them back.
Lock icons onto an invisible grid on the pinboard	Choose **Configure...**, then switch **Arrange pinned objects on a grid** on and click on **Set**.	
Remove an icon or selection from the pinboard	Select the icon and choose **Selection/Remove**.	This doesn't actually delete files. It simply removes icons from the pinboard.
Remove an iconised window	Double-click on the icon to open the window, then click on its Close icon.	
Select all icons on the pinboard	Choose **Select all**.	The Select all submenu can be used if you only wish to select files or windows. Choose **Clear selection** to de-select icons.
Save the current pinboard layout	Use the **Save/Save as** box.	Double-clicking on this file restores Pinboard to its saved state. You can't save information about iconised application windows.

Using backdrop images

You can display any sprite file or JPEG (see *Paint* on page 353) as a backdrop image on the desktop. For best results, use a screen mode that can display at least the same number of colours as there are in the backdrop image.

To display an image, click Menu over the pinboard and choose **Configure...** then drag the sprite or JPEG file icon to the **Custom image** icon.

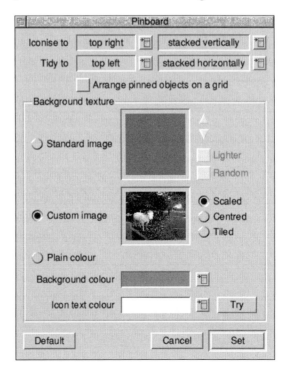

Custom image also has options for finer control of the image's display:

- **Scaled** has the effect of scaling the image to fill the whole screen.

- **Centred** has the effect of centring the image on the background. The correct proportions are maintained, but may leave plain space around the edges of your backdrop image if the picture is smaller than the size of the desktop.

- **Tiled** makes multiple copies of the image and repeats them so that the backdrop fills your screen.

Note: Each time you use the Display Manager to change the resolution or colours used by the desktop, the original picture is read in again. This may take some time if the image file is large or held on a slow disc.

Having made your image selections, click **Set** to change the backdrop.

Removing a backdrop

You can remove a backdrop picture by choosing **Standard image** or **Plain colour**. This does not delete any files, or remove any icons from the backdrop.

Textured desktop backdrops

The computer contains a number of built-in textured desktop backdrops.

You can change these using the **Standard image** option; see page 101 for more information.

For a little variety, enable the **Random** option to have the computer pick a different one at the start of each session.

The adjacent picture shows a marbled backdrop being used.

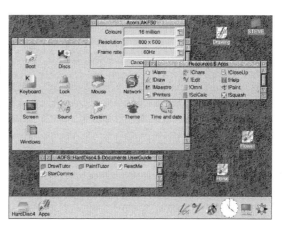

Iconised application menu options

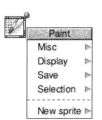

Hold down Shift and press Menu over an iconised application window to display the **application** menu for that window (instead of the usual Pinboard menu).

This can be useful if you want to save a file without actually opening its window to full size.

10 Managing the desktop

This chapter tells you about the day-to-day running of your computer. It shows you how to control the desktop using the Task Manager, how to shut the computer down, and how to get the most out of your computer's memory.

Introducing the Task Manager

The Task Manager is the rightmost icon situated on the icon bar. Throughout this Guide it's shown as a coloured cog wheel, though the exact icon used depends on which theme is being used. You'll learn how to change the theme later on in the chapter *Changing the computer's configuration*.

The Task Manager controls all the 'tasks' running on the computer. Think of it as a control panel, with which you can monitor and control the computer system.

You'll mostly use the Task Manager for three things

- monitoring and controlling tasks and memory;
- launching Configure to change the computer's settings;
- shutting the computer down, prior to switching off or resetting.

You can also use the Task Manager to access the RISC OS command line in various ways – see *The command line* on page 495, and to save the state of the desktop in a Desktop settings file.

Controlling tasks and memory

Click on the Task Manager icon to see a window containing details of the current tasks and the use of the computer's memory as a whole:

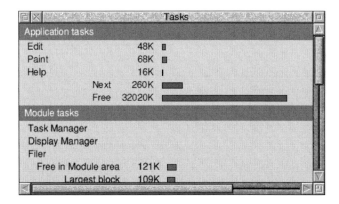

Tasks window areas

The Tasks window is divided into four areas:

- application tasks
- module tasks
- dynamic areas
- system memory allocation

You can alter values shown with red bars by dragging the end of the bar. The Tasks window is updated as applications are running. This allows you to monitor the state of the system.

Any changes you make with the Task Manager are forgotten when you reset the computer. If you need to change system settings often, you may find it more convenient to change them permanently using the Configure application (see *Changing the computer's configuration* on page 81).

Application tasks

This area shows how much memory current applications are using. The bars marked **Next** and **Free** show how much memory is allocated by default to an application when it starts up, and how much free memory is remaining in the system; you can change these values. However, most applications override the value allocated to **Next**, and take as much memory as they need (assuming it is available).

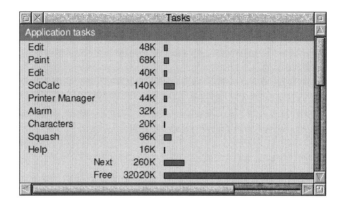

Module tasks

This section lists all tasks which are running as relocatable modules (extensions to the operating system) and the amount of free memory in the module area.

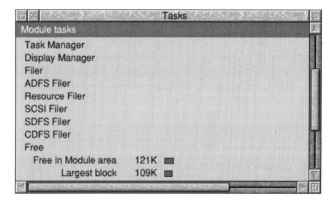

Dynamic areas

This section contains the entry **Wimp sprite pool**, a special memory area reserved for the sprites used by the Window Manager. There may be other entries here too for filing system buffers and similar shared workspace.

System memory allocation

This section summarises how the areas of the computer's memory are being used overall.

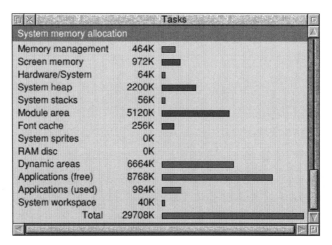

You can change some of the values in this section:

To	Do this	Notes
Create a RAM disc*	Drag a red bar to the right until the RAM disc is the size you want.	You can only change an existing RAM disc's size if it's empty.
Change the font cache†	Drag the red bar to the left or right.	See page 250 for more information.
Change the System sprites memory	Drag the red bar to the left or right.	If you're running short of memory, you can reduce this – it's not often used.

* The RAM disc size is limited to a maximum of 512MB.
† You can't reduce the cache to less than 32kB.

You may notice, when trying to resize a task slot size in the Tasks window, that you just can't select the amount of memory you want. Don't worry; this is a side effect of the way the Tasks window scales the mouse movement to enable computers with a lot of memory to be usable. For small amounts in a slot you have accurate control, but as the slot gets larger the changes in the amount of memory get coarser and coarser.

Forcing tasks and applications to quit

Quitting tasks from the Task Manager

You can use the Task Manager to force any of the tasks from the first two sections of the Tasks window to quit:

1   Click Menu over the entry for the task you want to quit.

2   Choose **Task/Quit**.

The task will quit, and the memory it was using will be freed. Although some programs (including Edit, Draw and Paint) warn you if there is some work you have not saved, not all programs do so; use this command with caution, as a last resort to force a program to quit.

Quitting tasks using the system monitor (emergency use only)

Very occasionally the computer will lock up (pressing keys has no effect) or the hourglass will stay on the screen for much longer than is normal. The key combination Alt-Break activates the system monitor. This displays a dialogue box from which you can selectively quit current tasks.

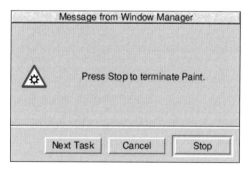

You can **Stop** a particular task (quit it), go on to the **Next Task** running, or **Cancel** the system monitor window.

Note 1: This is really a last resort, if you're having problems. Should the system monitor also not respond either, try these methods in order: press Ctrl-Break, **or** press the Reset button, **or** switch off and on again.

Note 2: You can also stop some tasks (e.g. printing a file) in a less permanent way by pressing Escape.

Note 3: Stopping a task with the system monitor may leave the desktop in an indeterminate state. Save any work and restart the computer when possible.

Warning: Don't stop the internal desktop tasks (Task Manager, Pinboard, Filer, Display Manager, Free) unless you know what you're doing.

Controlling tasks from the command line

Choose **Task window** from the Task Manager menu to start a RISC OS command line session within the desktop. The command line is described in detail in *The command line* on page 495.

The menu displayed from the main Tasks window also provides two ways to access the command line from outside of the desktop. Choose ***Commands** to start a command shell (press Return on an empty line to get back to the desktop) or **Exit** to finish using the desktop permanently. When you exit the desktop there will be more memory to run any commands you enter because the Window Manager is no longer keeping other applications you have run suspended in memory.

To start a task using a command line from within the desktop, type the command into the **New task** writable menu box. The command will be run without leaving the desktop, so can be used to issue commands that are only possible when the Window Manager is running such as starting new tasks.

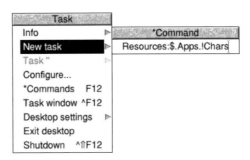

A full alphabetical list of star commands is given in the file `StarComms` in the directory `Documents.UserGuide` on your hard disc or network.

Managing memory

This section gives some suggestions for getting the best out of the memory fitted to your computer.

Some models of computer can have the amount of RAM (Random Access Memory) or VRAM (video RAM) expanded. If you find that you are frequently running out of memory the easiest way to resolve this is by fitting more. Ask your supplier for details.

Choice of screen display

You can save some memory by using a screen display that does not use much memory. To do this you should choose fewer colours or a lower resolution. For example, 640×480×16 colours uses 152kB, and 800×600×32k colours uses 940kB.

Opening directory displays

When you open a display for a directory containing applications, the computer loads the applications' sprite files, which occupy some of the computer's memory. If you are very short of memory, you cannot afford to waste this space.

Hold down Ctrl when opening a directory by double-clicking, the sprites used by any applications are not loaded into the sprite pool. This tip is also useful when opening application directories using a slow network connection, when the memory used is less of a concern than the time spent transferring the sprites.

Optimising memory usage

Use the Task Manager to display the computer's current memory usage. You can reduce any of the red bars to release as much memory as possible for applications.

Launching Configure

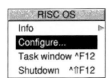

To easily access the Configure application, choose **Configure...** from the Task Manager's menu. The Configure application is covered in more detail in the chapter *Changing the computer's configuration* on page 81.

The same menu option is also in the extended Task menu.

Saving a Desktop settings file

Once you have a desktop layout on your screen that you would like to use each time you start your computer, you can save the layout:

1   Press Menu over the Tasks window and display the **Desktop settings/Save settings** dialogue box:

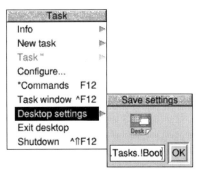

2   Save the file by clicking on **OK.**
    Don't change the path name given in the Save box.

Now, each time you switch on or reset your computer it will restore the desktop to the way it looked when you saved the Desktop settings file. There are more details on exactly what is saved in this file in the section *Desktop settings file* on page 116.

Shutting the computer down

You should **always** shut down your computer prior to switching it off with the On/Off switch. This

● quits all applications and ensures all your work is saved

● runs any post desktop Obey scripts

● logs you off any networks and file servers

● parks any disc drives.

Refer to the chapter *Switching off the computer* on page 41 for instructions on how to shut down RISC OS.

11 Changing the computer's configuration

This chapter tells you all about changing your computer's default configuration by using the Configuration window to change the settings to suit your individual requirements.

Introduction

There are two ways of customising your computer to suit your own way of working:

● Changing the default hardware and software configuration settings (this chapter).

● Changing the actions the computer performs, and hence the way the desktop looks when you first switch on (see *The Boot application* on page 111).

Changes to the configuration mostly take effect as soon as you make them, and are maintained even when you switch the computer off.

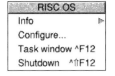

To open the Configuration window, click Menu on the Task Manager icon and choose **Configure...** from the menu. The main Configuration window will open with one icon for each aspect that can be configured.

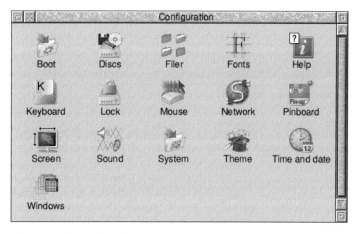

The Network setup plug-in leads to a further network configuration windows. These are explained in the chapter *Setting up networking* on page 167.

Configuration held in CMOS RAM

One term you'll come across many times in this chapter is **CMOS RAM**. This is part of the computer's memory where many essential configuration settings are stored which set up the computer prior to running the Boot application. Unlike ordinary RAM, they are retained when the main power is turned off.

With such essential configuration being held in CMOS RAM the computer may not start up properly if there is a problem with the settings. This can occur on those machines where the CMOS RAM is powered by a battery and the battery is exhausted, or if you have made manual changes to the configuration which are incorrect.

One possible symptom of a CMOS RAM problem is no picture on the monitor because the configured monitor type has been forgotten or mis-configured, so you will need to perform a CMOS RAM reset.

There are several types of CMOS RAM reset, each is performed by holding down a single key when the power is turned on:

- Delete key

  Sets **all** of the CMOS RAM locations to their factory defaults. The Econet station number is protected; ask your network manager if this needs to be changed too.

- End key

  This is similar to Delete-Power on, except that the monitor sync type is set to drive a monitor with separate horizontal and vertical sync signals.

- R key

  Sets the operating system CMOS RAM locations to their factory defaults. The user CMOS RAM locations, expansion card information, number of enabled ADFS drives, and country code are all left unchanged. The Econet station number is protected, as described under Delete-Power on.

- T key

  This is similar to R-Power on, except that the monitor sync type is set to drive a monitor with separate horizontal and vertical sync signals.

You may not be able to alter the CMOS RAM at all if there is a configuration protection link inside the computer and it's set to the 'protected' position, these resets will have no effect: see your *Welcome Guide*.

Whenever the CMOS RAM is reset, the computer will pause to show a message at the top of the screen acknowledging that the requested operation worked. Press Escape to confirm the message. Once you have a usable desktop, use Configure to restore the remaining settings by working through each of the following sections in this chapter.

Planning ahead

Before you change the computer's configuration in any way, it's a very good idea to save all the default settings. Similarly, when you've got the computer set up exactly as you want it, save the current settings. That way, if you ever change something you don't mean to, you'll always be able to get back to a known state!

Here are the files you'll need to save:

● a backup copy of the CMOS RAM

● a backup copy of the Choices directory (see page 113)

To save a backup copy of the CMOS RAM on disc click Menu anywhere in the main Configuration window and choose **CMOS/Save**.

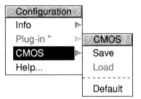

To restore the CMOS RAM by loading it from the backup copy on disc choose **CMOS/Load** instead (this option will be greyed out if no backup was previously saved). There is no undo facility for this operation, so take care only to load the CMOS RAM from a known good backup copy.

To restore the CMOS RAM to the factory default settings for the current version of RISC OS, choose **CMOS/Default** from the menu.

Changing configuration settings with Configure

Your computer will function well with the default settings that were set up when it was manufactured. However you can change many of these settings to suit your own way of working using the plug-ins in the Configuration window.

To		Do this	Notes
Open one of the Configure plug-ins	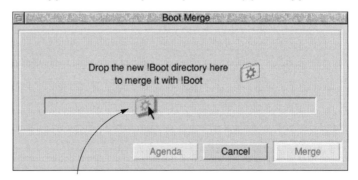 Sound	Click on the relevant icon in the main window (e.g. Sound).	
Close the plug-in window and configure each of the settings		Click on **Set**.	Click with Adjust to keep the plug-in window open too.
Close the plug-in window and restore the settings to those before you made any changes		Click on **Cancel**.	Click with Adjust to keep the plug-in window open too.
Restore the values in the plug-in back to their factory settings		Click on **Default**.	

Merging updates using Configure

The Boot, Font, Theme, and System setup plug-ins can each be used to update files within the Boot application with updates provided by your supplier.

Drop the update on to the merge window. Click the **Agenda** button to review the files that the merge will update, then click **Merge** to go ahead with the updates.

Boot setup plug-in

The Boot setup plug-in changes aspects of the Boot application that are user editable.

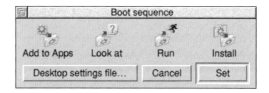

Warning: If a mistake is found when the Boot application is run, your computer may fail to start up correctly. See *Getting out of a mess* on page 111 for details of how to backup your current working configuration.

The first three icons perform the following actions:

● **Add to Apps**

Applications listed here will be added to the Apps directory on the left of the icon bar.

● **Look at**

Applications listed here will be Filer_Booted so that they are known to the Filer and any file types that they can open are noted.

● **Run**

Applications listed here will be run when the desktop starts.

The dialogue boxes for Add to Apps, Look at, and Run all behave in the same way so only the latter is described in detail. Most of the space in the dialogue box is used to display a scrollable list of applications, and the place where they are installed.

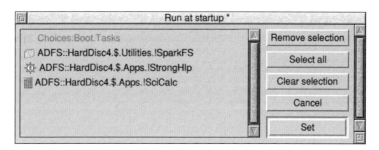

Any entries shown in grey at the top of the list are built-in entries which you cannot edit or remove.

To	Do this	Notes
Add an application to the list	Drag the application from a directory display and drop it onto the scrollable list.	
Remove one application from the list	Click on the application in the list, then click on **Remove selection**.	Click with Adjust to change which applications are in the selection one at a time.
Remove all of the applications from the list	Click on **Select all** then **Remove selection**.	

Unsaved changes will be shown in the title bar with an asterisk. Click **Set** to save the changes made, or **Cancel** to discard them.

The Boot setup window allows two further aspects of the Boot application to be edited:

- **Install**

  Opens a dialogue box where updates to the Boot application can be installed. If your supplier issues an update for !Boot, use this dialogue to merge the update by following the steps described in *Merging updates using Configure* on page 84.

- **Desktop settings file...**

  Opens the settings in a text editor. Should you wish to edit the lines in the file its contents are described in the chapter *The Boot application* on page 111. If there is no Desktop settings file saved, the button will be greyed out.

Discs setup plug-in

Use this plug-in to change the size of the RAM disc or number of installed disc drives you have in your computer.

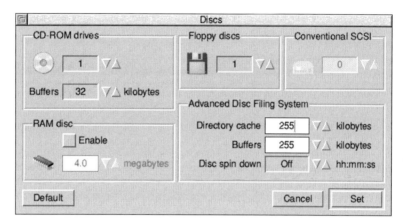

Warning: If you set an incorrect number of discs, your computer may fail to start up correctly. In this case, see *Configuration held in* CMOS RAM on page 82.

Your computer is supplied with several different filing systems used to support different types of disc drive. Not all computers support all types of interface as standard; you may need to fit a suitable expansion card from your supplier first.

One such expansion card is for SCSI, and permanently attached SCSI drives are called *Conventional* SCSI in this context. Other drive types also use the SCSI communications protocol but do not need to be manually configured as they are automatically detected when plugged in; one such example is a drive connected to a USB socket.

To	Do this	Notes
Define the number of CD-ROM drives, floppy disc drives, or permanently attached SCSI drives connected to your computer	Click on the arrows to reflect the number of drives fitted, then click on **Set**.	Do **not** select a larger number of discs than are in your computer.
Change the memory set aside for buffering CD-ROM operations	Click on the arrows to set the buffer memory amount, then click on **Set**.	Larger values will improve performance on slow CD-ROM drives.
Create a RAM disc on start-up	Select **Enable**, click on the arrows to choose the size you want, then click on **Set**.	You can only change an existing RAM disc's size if it's empty. The RAM disc size is limited to a maximum of 512MB.
Change the memory set aside for directory data and buffering ADFS operations	Click on the arrows to set the directory cache or buffer memory amount, then click on **Set**.	These settings only apply to automatically detected hard discs used by the ADFS.
Power down hard discs when not in use	Click on the arrows to set the **Spindown delay**, then click on **Set**.	These settings only apply to automatically detected hard discs used by the ADFS.

After altering the disc settings it is necessary to restart the respective filing system in order for the changes to take effect. This may cause the computer to pause while the discs are re-mounted.

Filer setup plug-in

Use this plug-in to set up the Filer configuration.

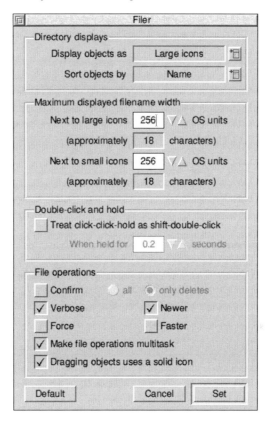

The window is split into four sections, concerning:

- display of directories
- display of filenames
- special mouse behaviour while using the Filer's directory displays
- default actions when the Filer is performing an operation

To	Do this	Notes
Configure the default view and sort order for a directory display	Choose from the **Display objects as** and **Sort objects by** menus.	These are the same options presented in the Filer's **Display** menu.
Configure the maximum width of filenames	Click on the arrows to choose the width when **Next to large icons** and when **Next to small icons**.	The approximate width in characters will be shown.
Make the Filer treat *double-click* and hold as *shift-double-click*	Switch **Treat click-click-hold as shift-double-click** on.	With the option turned on, anywhere this Guide instructs you to *shift double-click* on a file or directory you can instead *double-click* and hold.
Configure the default Filer operation options	Switch **Confirm**, **Verbose**, **Force**, **Newer**, **Faster** on or off as desired.	For an explanation of how these modify operations see *Modifying Filer operations* on page 57.
Enable multi-tasking Filer operations	Switch **Make file operations multitask** on.	When disabled, operations will complete more quickly, but you can't use the desktop at the same time.
Show a file's icon when a selection is dragged	Switch **Dragging objects uses a solid icon** on.	If this is not selected then files will be shown as a dotted outline.

Fonts setup plug-in

Use this plug-in to change the font configuration.

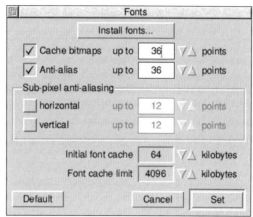

To	Do this	Notes
Merge a new !Fonts with the existing !Fonts in your computer	Click on **Install fonts** then merge the new !Fonts as described in *Merging updates using Configure* on page 84.	**Never use a !Fonts designed for use with RISC OS 2**. Transfer any fonts you want into a current version of !Fonts before merging.
Specify the largest bitmap font size to be cached	Use the arrows to set the **Cache bitmaps up to** limit.	Set to the size of text you usually use in documents (e.g. 12pt).
Place an upper limit on the size of anti-aliased fonts	Use the arrows to set the **Anti-alias up to** limit.	Never set to less than 12pt (the desktop font size). Larger fonts are usually printed with no anti-aliasing.
Have more control over anti-aliasing	Use the arrows to set the **Sub-pixel anti-aliasing** limits.	If you use this option, you will need to increase your font cache. You should normally leave this **Off** if your computer has limited spare memory.

Allowing the font cache to grow

If the font cache is too small, the Font Manager attempts to increase its size up to the **Font cache limit**. If this happens, it shrinks back to the normal current size as soon as any fonts can be discarded. The Font Manager decides to do this rather than throw away cached blocks of fonts currently displayed.

If the Font cache limit is zero, or smaller than the **Initial font cache**, the cache will not expand. If you are using several fonts you may want to set this to a higher value (e.g. 512kB) up to the maximum of 16MB supported.

If you want to know more about these options, see *Using fonts in applications* on page 245.

Help setup plug-in

Use this plug-in to set up interactive help.

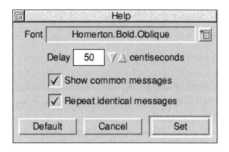

To	Do this	Notes
Configure the character style used to display help messages	Choose from the **Font** menu.	
Change the time between positioning the mouse and a help message being shown	Use the arrows to set the **Delay**.	
Reduce the amount of interactive help that is shown	Turn off **Show common messages** to suppress help from the desktop itself, and turn off **Repeat identical messages** to show help only once when moving the mouse between areas of the screen which would otherwise offer the same help text.	

Keyboard setup plug-in

Use this plug-in to set up the computer's keyboard layout, Auto repeat, macro keys, capitals and number lock.

The *macro keys* are six special control key combinations which can be used to run a command of your choosing when pressed, for example you might use a calculator frequently and want to run SciCalc without having to double click on it from the Apps directory. The location of these keys is illustrated on page 11.

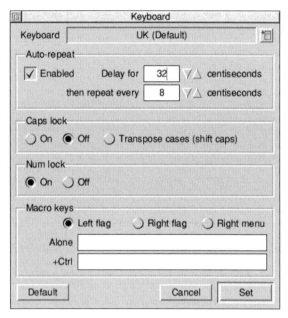

To	Do this	Notes
Configure the keyboard layout	Choose from the **Keyboard** menu icon to reflect the they of keyboard in use.	The default layout for your territory is indicated by the suffix (Default).
Control how quickly characters repeat when you hold down a key on the keyboard	Tick **Enabled**, set the **Delay for** and **then repeat every** intervals.	

To	Do this	Notes
Configure the state of the Caps Lock key on start-up	Choose **On** (all caps), or **Off** (all lower case), or **Transpose cases** (Caps Lock on, Shift gives lower-case).	In normal use Caps lock should be **Off**. Shift caps is like the reverse of Caps Lock.
Configure the state of the Num Lock key on start-up	Choose **On** (numeric keypad enabled) or **Off** (numeric keypad disabled).	
Assign a command to a macro key	Choose **Left flag**, **Right flag**, or **Right menu**, then type the command in the field beside **Alone**.	Put the command into the **+Ctrl** box to run the command when those two keys are pressed together.

Lock setup plug-in

Use this plug-in to set a password to protect your hard disc and computer configuration against unwanted changes.

The computer can be in one of three states:

- permanently unlocked – no password is set (the computer is supplied this way)

- locked

- temporarily unlocked – a password has been set to lock the computer, but the password was entered while in the locked state to temporarily unlock

When unlocked, you can change files on the hard disc and modify the computer's CMOS RAM configuration settings using !Boot.

When locked, only the **Public** directory in the root directory of the hard disc and the **Scrap** directory are writable, but all of the hard disc is readable. You can **not** modify the computer's configuration when it is locked.

Note: Unlocking the computer does not override any individual file access permissions already in force (see page 55).

To	Do this	Notes
Set a password and lock the computer	Select **Lock**, type the password in the two **New password** boxes (use the arrow keys to move between them) then click on **Set**.	Passwords must be at least five characters long. The Configuration window changes so you can only use the **Lock** window.
Change an existing password	Select **Change password**, then type in the **Old password**. Type the **New password** twice, then click on **Set**.	
Temporarily remove password-protection	Select **Unlock**, type the password in the **Old password** box then click on **Set**.	Next time you switch on, the computer reverts to being locked.
Lock the computer	Select **Lock** then click on **Set**.	This assumes you've previously set a password.
Unlock the computer permanently	Select **Change password**, type in the **Old password** then click on **Set**.	In effect, you're supplying a blank new password.
Restart the computer if you've forgotten the password	Reset the computer's CMOS RAM configuration to the default settings – see page 82.	

Using applications with a locked computer

Some applications automatically write information to the hard disc during use. If your computer is locked, this cannot occur. For example:

● Alarm usually saves its alarm files onto the disc. You can't do this with a locked disc so you'll see an error message. However, you can explicitly save your alarm file to the Public directory (see *Save as alarms* on page 396).

● You can't modify Printers while the disc is locked.

● You can't change applications that save configuration details using a **Save choices** option (such as Puzzle).

Mouse setup plug-in

Use this plug-in to set up the mouse configuration options.

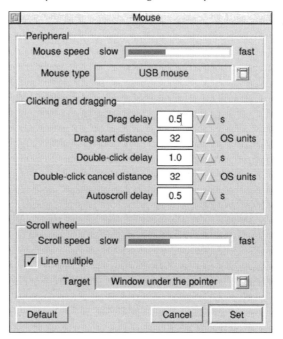

To	Do this	Notes
Set the mouse/pointer sensitivity	Drag the **Mouse speed** slider.	The faster the speed, the quicker the pointer moves around on the screen.
Define the type of mouse you're using	Choose from the **Mouse type** menu icon to reflect the type of mouse fitted.	The first item in the menu is the default mouse type for your machine. Your computer will not work properly if you select the wrong type[*].
Change the timings for a mouse 'drag'	Set the **Drag delay** and **Drag start distance** using the arrows.	Delay default: 0.5 seconds. Start distance default: 32 OS units.

To	Do this	Notes
Change the timings for a 'double-click'	Set the **Double-click delay** and **Double-click cancel distance** using the arrows.	Delay default: 1 second. Cancel default: 32 OS units.
Change the timings for scrolling within a window during a mouse 'drag'	Use the arrows to set the **Autoscroll delay**.	Delay default: 0.5 seconds.

* If you do set the wrong mouse type by mistake, you'll need to reset it from the command line. See page 495.

Some mouse types include a scroll wheel as part of the Menu button mechanism. This can be used to scroll windows as though the windows' scroll arrow had been pressed when the wheel is 'nudged'. The **Scroll wheel** section of the plug-in configures this behaviour.

To	Do this	Notes
Set the speed of scrolling	Drag the **Scroll speed** slider.	The faster the speed, the further each nudge of the wheel scrolls the window.
Ensure windows with fixed line heights, such as text editors, to scroll one line at a time	Switch **Line multiple** on.	
Define whether the window under the pointer, or the one with input focus, is to be scrolled	Choose from the **Target** menu.	You can alternatively scroll either type of window (if one has the input focus, but is not under the pointer), or even the one at the top of the stack of windows.

Pinboard setup plug-in

Use this plug-in to configure the pinboard.

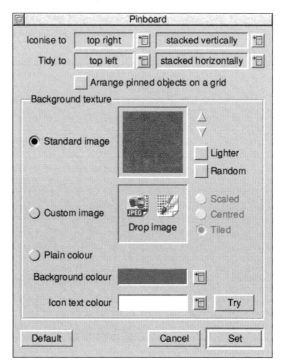

To	Do this	Notes
Choose where to place iconised window icons	Choose from the **Iconise to** menu.	You can also configure the direction in which to stack icons.
Choose where to place tidied file and directory icons	Choose from the **Tidy to** menu.	You can also configure the direction in which to stack icons.
Lock items to a regular grid	Switch **Arrange pinned objects on a grid** on.	
Change the background texture	Choose a **Standard image** by using the arrows. Turn on **Lighter** to pick a brightened variant	Turn on **Random** to have the computer choose a random image for you each time it is turned on.

To	Do this	Notes
Use an image of your own as the background	Drag the image file to the **Custom image** icon. Choose to display it **Scaled**, **Centred**, or **Tiled** to fill the available space as best as possible.	The file must be stored somewhere that is still available when the computer is next turned on.
Use a flat colour for the background	Choose a **Background colour** by selecting from the colour picker dialogue.	
Change the colour of text under icons on the pinboard	Choose an **Icon text colour** by selecting from the colour picker dialogue.	

To test the current background texture without saving the configuration click on **Try.**

Screen setup plug-in

Use this plug-in to set up the display and screen saver parameters.

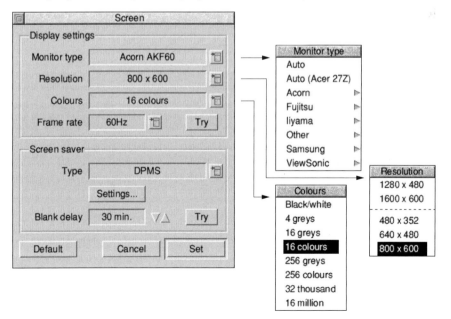

Display settings

These determine how the display is set up when the computer is turned on.

To	Do this	Notes
Define the type of monitor you're using	Choose from the **Monitor type** menu. If yours isn't listed, try the **Auto** option.	If you can't get a picture at all, see page 82.
Configure the default resolution used on start-up	Choose from the **Resolution** menu. Resolution 1280 x 480 1600 x 600 - - - - - - - - - 480 x 352 640 x 480 800 x 600	Resolutions above the dotted line will use rectangular pixels, those below will use square pixels (preferred).
Configure the default number of colours used on start-up	Choose from the **Colours** menu.	If you find you always work with more colours you can change this.
Configure how often the screen is refreshed	Choose from the **Frame rate** menu.	The manual provided with your monitor will indicate its optimal frame rate.

Automatic monitor type

Some monitors are able to provide *extended display identification data* (EDID) to the computer automatically, which includes the monitor's full capabilities. Look in the **Monitor type** menu for an extra entry with the specific model or name of your monitor listed, and choose that in preference to manually searching through the manufacturer submenus.

Within the EDID is the *native resolution* of the screen, when the image is at its best. Choose **Native** from the **Resolution** menu to use this facility. The best colours and frame rate will be automatically selected for you.

Testing the settings

To test the current monitor settings without saving the configuration click on **Try**. Don't worry if this results in no image, for example because the settings are incompatible with the monitor, the plug-in will prompt to confirm they have worked; if you can't see the prompt it will time out and return the computer to the previous settings.

Screen saver settings

You can also set up a screen saver when the computer is left unused for a period of time. Using a screen saver will make the monitor last longer.

To	Do this	Notes
Activate the screen saver after an idle period elapses	Set the **Blank delay** using the arrows.	
Configure the type of screen saver to use	Choose from the **Type** menu. The DPMS screen saver turns off the power to the screen as well.	Some screen savers can be further configured by clicking on **Settings...**.

Testing the settings

To test the current screen saver settings without saving the configuration click on **Try**. Move the mouse to restore the display.

Sound setup plug-in

Use this plug-in to set the Sound configuration.

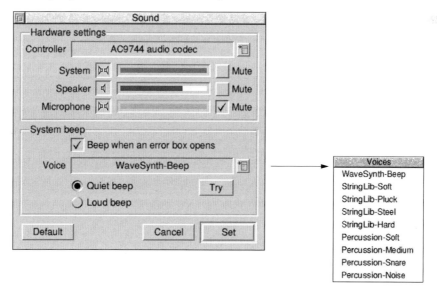

To	Do this	Notes
Select the controller to use for system sound output	Choose from the **Controller** menu. There may only be one to choose from – the one internal to the computer.	Not all computers support changing the controller, so this menu may be replaced by options to enable 16-bit sound output and software oversampling instead.
		☑ 16-bit sound system ☑ Oversampling
		Consult the *Welcome Guide* supplied with your computer to learn whether there is 16-bit sound hardware installed.
Set the volume of contributors to the system sound output	Drag the slider for that contributor, or click **Mute** to disable its contribution completely.	The number of sliders will depend on how many contributors your computer supports.
Change the system beep sound	Click on the **Voice** menu icon to display a list of installed voices and choose a voice.	This sets the voice used by the first of the computer's eight sound channels.
Change the system beep level	Choose **Quiet** or **Loud**.	The value of **Quiet** and **Loud** is determined by the volume sliders.
Cause a beep to sound when an error box is displayed	Turn on **Beep when an error box opens**.	

System setup plug-in

Use this dialogue box to update your computer system with replacement parts of the operating system or additional extensions required by applications.

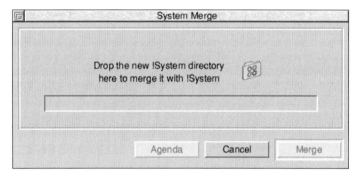

Merge the new !System as described in *Merging updates using Configure* on page 84.

Theme setup plug-in

Use this plug-in to configure the appearance of the desktop.

To change the behaviour of windows in the desktop rather than their appearance, use the *Windows setup plug-in* on page 109.

To	Do this	Notes
Set the desktop to use an outline font	Turn on **Desktop text uses outline font**, then click on the menu icon and choose an outline font.	Text in menus and directories is displayed at 12pt. The standard desktop font is Homerton Medium. If an outline font is not used then the System font will be used instead.

Font List
Corpus ▷
✓ Homerton ▷
NewHall
Sassoon
Selwyn
Sidney
System
Trinity ▷
WIMPSymbol

Homerton
Bold
Bold.Oblique
✓ Medium
Medium.Oblique

To	Do this	Notes
Configure a desktop theme	Turn **Load extra theme resources on startup** on, then choose a theme from the menu.	The theme change will not apply until you shut down and restart the computer.
Install a new desktop theme	Click on **Install themes**, then merge the new !Boot as described in *Merging updates using Configure* on page 84.	
Stop applications from overriding your themed icons	Turn **Protect theme icons from being modified** on.	
Add texturing to the background of desktop windows or menus	Turn on **Textured window backgrounds** for windows, or **Textured menu backgrounds** respectively.	You can also use a different background for menus than for windows.
Use a raised depth effect for windows	Switch **Windows have 3D borders** on.	You can also apply this effect to the icon bar edges.

Time and date setup plug-in

Use this plug-in to configure the computer's time and date.

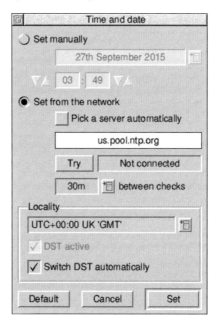

To	Do this	Notes
Set the time and date manually	Select **Set manually**, then set the time using the arrows and the date using the calendar pop-up menu.	
Set the time and date from a network time server	Select **Set from the network** then enter the address of your internet service provider's time server in the address field.	Turn on **Pick a server automatically** if you do not know the address of your provider's time server.
Test the connection to the network time server	Click the **Try** button.	It may take several seconds to make contact. Check the address carefully if the test is unsuccessful.

To	Do this	Notes
Configure how often the clock is resynchronised to the network time	Choose a time period **between checks** from the menu.	Default: 30 minutes
Tell the computer which time zone you live in	Choose from the **Locality** menu.	
Adjust the clock to account for daylight saving	Turn on **DST active** to add I hour to the time. The computer can update this setting for you twice per year if **Switch DST automatically** is enabled.	Automatic DST correction is only available for territories which are currently loaded.

Time servers

The option to **Pick a server automatically** will be greyed out if a definitive time server address was received at the same time that the network address was obtained via DHCP - the chapter *Setting up networking* explains how enable this method.

Time keeping

When the time and date is configured to be **Set from the network**, an attempt is made to contact the time server every time the computer is turned on. If the server can't be contacted then the *hardware real time clock* is used temporarily, and the computer will try again later to contact the server. Once a reply is received, this latest information is used to correct any errors found in the current time and date.

Your computer may be fitted with a hardware real time clock which is powered by a backup battery while the computer is switched off. Good time keeping can only be achieved if the battery has charge. The hardware real time clock will be taken to be the current time and date if you chose that they are to be **Set manually**, and the information appears valid.

RISC OS will use a default time and date should there be no hardware real time clock. This will lead to bad time keeping because the default is not incremented while the computer is turned off, so could differ from the current time and date considerably.

Windows setup plug-in

Use this plug-in to configure the way that desktop windows behave.

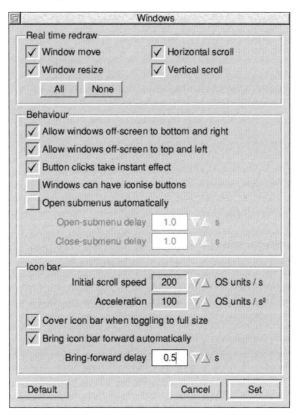

To	Do this	Notes
Update the screen as you drag, resize or scroll a window	Switch on any or all of the **Real time redraw** options.	When disabled, only a dotted outline moves until you have finished the drag.
Allow windows to be dragged off-screen	Choose **Allow windows off-screen to bottom and right** and/or **Allow windows off-screen to top and left**.	You can't 'lose' a window, since part of the Title bar is always visible on screen[*].

To	Do this	Notes
Make window border icons act as soon as you click on them	Turn **Button clicks take instant effect** on.	When off, the action occurs on releasing the mouse button.
Configure windows to have an Iconise icon	Turn **Windows can have iconise button** on.	When off, windows can still be iconised by clicking on the close icon while holding the Shift key.
Display submenus automatically	Choose **Open submenus automatically**. Use the arrows to set the **Open-submenu delay** and **Close-submenu delay**.	If you point at a menu option that has an arrow next to it, the submenu will open automatically after a short time.
Change how fast the icon bar scrolls when the mouse is at the screen edge	Use the arrows to set the **Initial scroll speed** and **Acceleration**.	
Allow windows to cover the icon bar when toggled to their maximum size	Turn on **Cover icon bar when toggling to full size**.	
Automatically make the icon bar visible when the mouse is at the bottom of the screen	Turn on **Bring icon bar forward automatically**. Use the arrows to set the **Bring-forward delay** before this happens.	

* It can be difficult to see a window right at the bottom of the screen. Changing to a larger screen mode will 'find' any lost windows.

12   The Boot application

The Boot application is a part of the operating system which adds to the software supplied inside the ROM. This chapter describes the resources contained inside the Boot application.

Introduction

The Boot application, called !Boot, is always kept in the root directory of the hard disc (or, if you are using a network, kept on the network file server under a similar name).

Your computer is supplied with a working copy of the Boot application.

Save a copy of the Boot application before you make any changes within it (follow the directions given in *Backing up hard discs* on page 128, but only copying !Boot). Then, should a problem occur, you've a known-good copy to go back to.

Never move or delete the Boot application; your computer may not work if you do!

Getting out of a mess

The main day to day changes occur in the Choices directory, this is where the Configure plug-ins described in the chapter *Changing the computer's configuration* write all of their settings. In case of a problem, restoring the Choices from an earlier backup will resolve most problems.

To restore an earlier copy of Choices:

1   Hold down Shift when the computer boots so that the problematic Boot application is skipped before starting the desktop.

2   Rename !Boot.Choices out of the way, for example to !Boot.ChoicesOld.

3   Copy the Choices directory from your backup copy into its place.

4   Shutdown and restart the computer.

 If reverting to an earlier backup of Choices doesn't help, you can also restore the Boot application to its factory default values using the ResetBoot application in the Utilities.Caution directory.

Inside the Boot application

Boot is a collection of files and applications that are used to control the desktop and supplement the operating system. You won't need to know about all of them, just the few essential ones outlined here.

Remember: To view the contents of an application directory such as !Boot, hold down the Shift key when you double-click on the application.

The Resources directory

This contains resources which are checked when the Boot application runs. It contains ancillary resources for the Configure application and the Window Manager (Wimp), and several important resource applications explained below.

Third party software vendors may also provide resource applications that are added here to add new features to the desktop, for example viewers for commercial vector graphics, or codecs to play videos with.

The System application

!System is used to store new system modules which replace or extend parts of RISC OS.

When you add more applications to your computer you may find that additional modules are supplied in the form of a !System application. These must be merged with the one already on the computer using the System setup plug-in; see page 105 for details of how to do this.

The Scrap application

!Scrap is used to store temporary files. Applications often use temporary files during copying, printing and saving; these files are erased when they are no longer needed.

An application called ShowScrap, found in the Utilities directory on your hard disc or network, will open a directory display of the current scrap location when it is run.

The Internet application

!Internet holds extension commands relating to network connectivity, as well as the Internet databases. Even if your computer is not connected to the Internet, the databases are used when offline.

The Fonts application

!Fonts is used to store the fonts needed by the desktop and applications. If you have many fonts there may be more than one !Fonts application, suffixed with numbers.

When you buy additional fonts, or applications that contain new fonts, you will find that the fonts are supplied in a !Fonts application. These must be merged with the one already on the computer using the Fonts setup plug-in; see page 91 for details of how to do this.

The Printer Definitions application

!PrintDefs holds all of the *printer definition files* that the Printer Manager uses (you'll learn when these are used in the chapter *Setting up printers* on page 189). If you delete the PrintDefs application you will not be able to add any new printers that you may wish to print to.

The Theme Definitions application

!ThemeDefs holds descriptions of themes that can be selected with the Theme setup plug-in, described on page 105. If you delete the ThemeDefs application you will only be able to use the default theme held in ROM.

The Unicode application

!Unicode holds encodings and textual names for the very large number of characters in Unicode fonts. If you delete the Unicode application you may experience problems displaying and printing fonts that are not in the default alphabet.

The Library directory

This contains extension commands available on the computer. The `Library` directory is included on the `Run$Path`, one of the *System path variables*, which means the commands can be called upon at any time, from anywhere, without needing to be held in the operating system ROM.

The Choices directory

This contains files and directories which applications create to hold the choices you make during their use, a unique one for each application. The Boot application is no different in that respect, it saves its settings there too.

The Choices.Boot directory

In more detail, this contains:

- The *PreDesktop boot* file, examined in more detail on page 114.

- The `PreDesk` directory, which contains computer configuration information which is to be executed **before** the Desktop starts.

- The *Desktop boot* file used as a supplemental file (see page 115) for commands to be executed **after** the Desktop starts.

- The `Tasks` directory, which contains computer configuration information which is to be executed **after** the Desktop starts. The *Desktop settings* file (see page 116), which records any desktop settings previously saved such as your preferred Filer window positions, resides in the Tasks directory.

- Optionally a PostDesk directory which may contain user Obey files. These are executed **after** the Desktop finishes, when the computer is shutting down.

The remainder of the Boot application

The Utils directory

This contains private utilities for use only by the Boot application.

The Themes directory

This contains private Sprite files for use only by the Boot application.

The RO*xxx*Hook directories

The Boot application can be used by owners of earlier versions of RISC OS, not just the one covered in this Guide. Small differences between versions of the operating system are catered for by having one *hook directory* for each major release that is supported.

When the Boot application is first installed the Choices are absent, which the Boot application detects and uses as a cue to copy a 'blank' set from the relevant hook directory into place.

The hook directory is also where the Configure application is stored, again different versions are used to cater for the configuration changes made over time.

PreDesktop boot

The PreDesktop boot file is used to configure the computer before the desktop environment initialises. It has the following pathname:

```
$.!Boot.Choices.Boot.PreDesktop
```

You can view the file by loading it into Edit (Shift double-click) where you will notice it is divided into sections which have start and end markers. For example:

```
|Start <Company> <Application> <Version> <Section>
|End
```

These markers are used by tools such as the Configure application to automatically find and make edits to the contents of the PreDesktop file. You won't normally need to manually change any of the sections in this file.

Comments

This section summarises how the markers work.

Loading

This section begins loading your chosen theme resources.

Aliases

This section is used for setting system aliases. This part of the file is only of use if you use the command line interface.

Paths

This section of the file is used for defining standard paths and directories. It is only of use if you are programming.

Options

A section for placing other options that may need to be set up.

ResApps

This section registers applications with ResourceFS for display in Resources:$.Apps (the Apps directory on the icon bar). Do not edit this by hand; use the 'Add to Apps' feature of the Boot setup plug-in to add more applications to ResourceFS.

Desktop boot

The Desktop boot file is used to configure the computer once the desktop environment has started. It has the following pathname:

```
$.!Boot.Choices.Boot.Desktop
```

You can view the file by loading it into Edit (Shift double-click) where you will notice it is divided into sections in a similar fashion to the PreDesktop boot file.

Deferred

This section finishes loading your chosen theme resources.

Auto

This section boots applications and checks a selection of system directories. Do not edit this section by hand; use the 'Look at' dialogue in the Boot setup plug-in to boot a different selection of applications.

Resolver

This section is for private use by the Internet application.

Completion

This section is run right at the end of the sequence to finish setting up the desktop.

Desktop settings file

You can use a Desktop settings file to save your current working environment – the desktop – so that when you next switch on the computer you will see the same desktop arrangement again.

The Desktop settings file will remember

- which applications are running on the icon bar
- any changes made to running applications (e.g. default font, window size)
- any network connections.

For instance you could automatically start Edit and Alarm, log onto a network, and then open your 'Letters' directory display each time you switch on. Should you only wish to start (or boot) applications, refer instead to the *Boot setup plug-in* on page 85 which is much simpler to set up than a Desktop settings file.

Use the Task Manager to save the current desktop state, as described in *Saving a Desktop settings file* on page 80. This creates (or overwrites) the file:

```
$.!Boot.Choices.Boot.Tasks.!Boot
```

It is important that anything that you don't want to have in your settings file is quit before saving the state, as otherwise your Desktop settings file will store unwanted instructions. In particular:

- If you want to change the name of your hard disc, do so **before** saving the settings. The name of the disc is referenced in the file and renaming it will cause the computer to ask you where it has gone.

- If you move an application that was running when the settings were saved, the computer will not know where to find it next time, causing an error.

- If there's a removable disc in the disc drive, dismount it first. If you don't, the computer will ask you to insert it every time you switch on!

Inside the Desktop settings file

You can view the file by loading it into Edit (Shift double-click).

This section looks at the typical lines found in a Desktop settings file; the exact lines you see may be different, or not present at all, on your computer.

You don't need to know these details to **use** a settings file, but an understanding may be useful if you decide to **edit** the settings file to your liking.

Note that the following table shows lines wrapped to fit on the printed page. In the actual Desktop settings file all commands appear on **one** line.

Line in Desktop settings file	Action
`WimpSlot -next 640K`	Allocates memory to the next application, usually 640kB.
`ColourTransLoadings &2 &4 &1`	Gives colour balance used by the desktop. Don't change this.
`net:logon :Business Matthew`	Logs user Matthew onto file server 'Business', and prompts for password.
`Filer_OpenDir ADFS::HardDisc4.$` `2 712 712 188 -sn -si`	Displays root directory of HardDisc4. Four numbers define position and size on the screen and are followed by layout switches. Use the command `*Help Filer_OpenDir` to see all the possible switches.
`Filer_Boot` `ADFS::HardDisc4.$.Apps.!SciCalc`	Runs an application's boot file, storing its location and sprite in memory. Adding Filer_Boot lines for files in frequently-used directories speeds up opening these directories the first time, but makes starting up or resetting the computer take longer.

Line in Desktop settings file	Action
`Run ADFS::HardDisc4.$.Apps.!SciCalc`	Starts SciCalc. You can run any application in this way.
`Set Omni$Path` `ADFS::HardDisc4.$.Apps.!Omni.Files.`	Sets up a path variable for OmniClient. Other applications may add their own variables, or you can use `*Set` for options such as those decribed in *Command and application options and other variables* on page 513.

Commenting out lines in a Desktop settings file

If you want to skip one of the commands on start-up, you can comment out the relevant line in the Desktop settings file by typing a | character at the beginning. This is simpler than saving a whole new file.

`| Run ADFS::HardDisc4.$.Apps.!SciCalc`

You can uncomment the line later if you want to run that command once more:

`Run ADFS::HardDisc4.$.Apps.!SciCalc`

Adding lines by hand

Applications written before RISC OS 3 was released cannot automatically be saved using the Desktop settings option in Task Manager. However, you can still add lines to your Desktop settings file by hand to start such applications automatically.

For example, the following line runs the application *!OldApp*.

`Run ADFS::HardDisc4.$.!OldApp`

Deleting the Desktop settings

If you've created a Desktop settings file that you no longer want, simply delete the file.

Other names for the Boot application

When stored on a network file server the Boot application may have a different name. The type of file server determines the name:

● **!ArmBoot** – Windows LAN Manager and AUN Level 4 networks

● **!NFSBoot** – UNIX Network File System

● **!ShareBoot** – Acorn Access

Avoid using the name !Boot directly in any Obey files that you write because this will only work when the Boot application is on the hard disc.

To refer to objects relative to the Obey file use Obey$Dir, and for objects elsewhere in the Boot application use Boot$Dir or BootResources$Dir – these are examples of system variables which are explained in more detail in the appendix *The command line* on page 495.

13 Using discs

This chapter shows you some more desktop options to help you use hard discs and removable media such as USB flash drives, memory cards, or floppy discs.

Fixed and removable discs

Most computers are fitted with a main hard disc, fixed internally to the case, and offer drives or sockets to accept removable discs externally to the case. Which types yours has will be covered in the *Welcome Guide* supplied with your computer.

A hard disc can store large amounts of information for long periods of time; then, when needed, it can retrieve the information quickly so that it can be used again.

Removable discs are typically physically smaller, store less information, and are slower to access than fixed discs. Being removable, they are easily transported and ideal for backing up or transferring information between computers.

Mounting and dismounting discs

When you've displayed a disc's root directory (for both fixed and removable types) the disc is said to be 'mounted'. When you have finished with a disc, you should 'dismount' it. This closes all the files on the disc, ensures any data that was buffered in RAM is written out, removes its directory displays from the screen, and tells the computer to forget about it.

Warning: Do not dismount a disc during a Filer operation on that disc.

Dismounting hard discs

Dismounting a hard disc also parks its heads, so that once you've switched the computer off you can move it safely. The disc remains dismounted until the next time it is accessed, or until the machine is next switched on. It is good practice to dismount the disc before switching the computer off; you can do this automatically by using the **Shutdown** command from Task Manager's icon bar menu. This command logs you off networks, prompts you to save any unsaved files, and dismounts the disc.

Dismounting removable discs

To dismount a disc:

1 Insert the disc into the disc drive (if it's not still in there).

2 Click Menu over the disc drive icon on the icon bar.

3 Choose **Dismount** from the icon bar menu for the disc drive.

Naming discs

All discs can be given names. Names that you recognise and understand are helpful.

Names of removable discs are shown in the title bar of directory displays; but because it is possible to swap discs between drives at any time the drive's icon bar icon only shows the drive numbers (starting from :0).

HardDisc4

The name of a hard disc appears underneath the hard disc icon on the icon bar because it is fixed, and this name also appears in the title bar of directory displays. If a hard disc is not given a name they are numbered (starting from :4) instead.

Each disc may be referred to either by a name, or by the number of the drive on which it is mounted. It is advisable to keep disc names unique, so that the filing system can tell them apart so that if the filing system prompts you to insert a removable disc you know which one to use.

To set or change the name of a disc:

1 Click Menu over the disc icon on the icon bar.

2 Move to the **Name disc/Disc name** box.

3 Type in the name (it must be at least two characters long).

4   Press ↲ (Return) or click a mouse button.

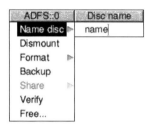

If you have any directory displays open for the disc under its old name, they will be closed when you rename the disc.

Naming restrictions

A disc name must contain at least two, and at most ten, characters. The name must not contain a space or any of the following reserved characters:

$ & % @ \ ^ : . # * " |

Any disc formatted outside RISC OS whose name doesn't meet these restrictions will be adjusted where possible, or a default name given.

Changing the name of a hard disc

If you change the name of a hard disc you may find that certain start-up files no longer operate correctly. This is probably because they refer to the old hard disc name rather than the new one. The files that may need changing are discussed in *The Boot application* on page 111.

Formatting discs

Formatting a disc means setting up a structure on the disc within which data can be stored. You will need to format a disc in the following circumstances:

● To prepare a new, blank disc for use. (If you try to use a disc that has not been formatted, you'll see an error message because the contents of a blank disc are not understood.)

● To erase the entire contents of a disc and bring it to a known, clean state.
    Warning: When a disc is formatted, any data that was previously stored on it is permanently lost.

Formatting a hard disc

Hard discs are supplied ready-formatted, and you should not need to reformat them. In the unlikely event that a hard disc does have to be reformatted, use the HForm application, described on page 467.

Formatting USB flash drives and memory cards

These two types of removable media come in many more capacities than conventional floppy discs, which can be catered for by a menu of common formats. To format a memory card or USB flash drive, use the HForm application, described on page 467.

Formatting a floppy disc

To format a floppy disc:

1   If the disc is not already in the drive, insert it.

2   Move to the **Format** submenu of the icon bar menu for the disc drive.

3   Choose the disc format. You should choose the **ADFS 1600K (F)** or **(F+)** format if you have a standard high-density floppy disc and the **ADFS 800K (E)** or **(E+)** format if you have a double-density floppy disc. This displays the Format dialogue box.

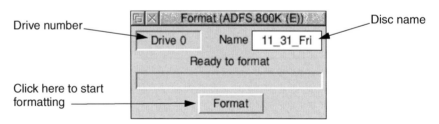

4   Give the floppy disc a unique name by deleting the contents of the Name box and typing in the new disc name. See page 122 for details of file and disc naming conventions.

If you don't give a floppy disc a name, the default name given to the disc is based on the date and time: for example `11_31_Fri`.

5   Click on **Format** to go ahead with the operation or click on the Close icon to abandon the operation.

The disc is first formatted, then verified (checked for errors). During formatting and verification, a coloured bar indicates the operation's progress. You can interrupt the formatting process by clicking on **Pause**.

6   Finish formatting by clicking on **OK** when you see the message `Disc formatted OK`.

If the disc verification process finds errors on the disc, refer to the section *Disc errors during formatting* below for instructions on how to remove them.

RISC OS *floppy disc formats* on page 126 and *Other disc formats* on page 127 describe the available disc formats in more detail.

Disc errors during formatting

Faults that prevent data from being read from or written to a part of the disc are known as *defects*.

The formatting process is designed to deal with any defects found on the floppy disc. Any defects found are displayed during the formatting and verification process.

If a defect is found, click on **Continue**: this marks the area of the disc as defective and ensures that it is not used. If you don't want to continue with the format/verify process, click on the window's Close icon.

This is the defect address

Click on Continue to resume formatting

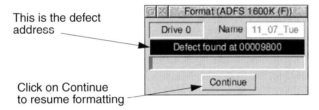

While RISC OS will allow you to use a floppy disc with defects (by 'jumping over' or ignoring those defects) we recommend that, unless you have an immediate need to use the disc, you throw it away at the first opportunity.

When formatting has finished the window shows you how many defects were mapped out (marked as not to be used).

This is the number of defects

Click on OK to finish formatting

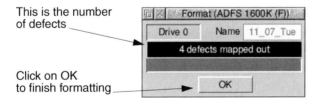

RISC OS floppy disc formats

You choose disc formats from the Floppy disc icon bar menu.

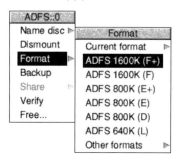

High density

(extra hole)

Double density

Your computer can use both high-density and double-density discs. High-density floppy discs (marketed as 1.44MB IBM type) **must** be used for the formats listed above 1000K and double-density (marketed as 720kB IBM type) **must** be used for the formats listed below 1000K.

There are six different RISC OS formats available:

- **ADFS 1600K (F+)**. This format can store 1.6MB of data.

  This format allows for filenames longer than 10 characters and directories containing more than 77 files and subdirectories. This format was introduced with RISC OS 4, therefore a computer fitted with RISC OS 3.71 or earlier will not be able to read or write this format.

- **ADFS 1600K (F)**. This format can store 1.6MB of data.

  This format uses 10 character filenames. Each directory can contain up to 77 files and subdirectories. It is compatible with RISC OS 3 and later versions.

- **ADFS 800K (E+)**. This format can store 800kB of data.

  This format is the double-density variant of F+, described above.

- **ADFS 800K (E)**. This format can store 800kB of data.

  This format is the double-density variant of F, described above. It is compatible with RISC OS 2 and later versions.

- **ADFS 800K (D)**. The format can store 800kB of data.

  This format is now obsolete and is included for backward compatibility only. It is compatible with RISC iX and the Arthur 1.20 operating system.

- **ADFS 640K (L)**. The format can store approximately 640kB of data.

  This format is now obsolete and is included for backward compatibility only. It is compatible with Arthur 1.20, ADFS on the BBC and Master series computers fitted with 3.5" disc drives. Each directory can contain up to 47 files and subdirectories.

Other disc formats

You can format floppy discs in different formats using the **Format/Other formats** submenu.

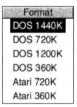

These other disc formats should **only** be used if you are transferring files to or from another computer that doesn't use RISC OS. The DOS formats in particular are so ubiquitous that they can also be used in tranferring files to UNIX or Apple computers, because UNIX and Apple computers can also read DOS discs.

For more information about DOS files and discs, read *Using DOS and Windows discs* on page 140.

Additional formats may appear in this menu through the addition of third party filing systems. There are six extra formats provided by default:

* **DOS 1440K**. This format stores up to 1.44MB of data.

  Discs using this format can be read from and written to by any DOS or Windows computer with a high-density 3.5" disc drive.

* **DOS 720K**. This format stores up to 720kB of data.

  Discs using this format can be read from and written to by any DOS or Windows computer with a double-density 3.5" disc drive.

* **DOS 1200K**. This format stores up to 1.2MB of data.

  Discs using this format can be read from and written to by any DOS or Windows computer with a high-density 5.25" disc drive.

* **DOS 360K**. This format stores up to 360kB of data.

  Discs using this format can be read from and written to by any DOS or Windows computer with a double-density 5.25" disc drive.

* **Atari 720K**. This Atari format stores up to 720kB of data.

  The disc can be read from and written to by any Atari ST computer with a double-sided 3.5" disc drive.

* **Atari 360K**. This Atari format stores up to 360kB of data.

  The disc can be read from and written to by any Atari ST computer with a 3.5" disc drive.

127

Checking a floppy disc's current format

If you want to find out what type of format a floppy disc has, put the floppy disc in the disc drive and go to the **Format/Current format** box. This will tell you the format type and storage capacity of the disc.

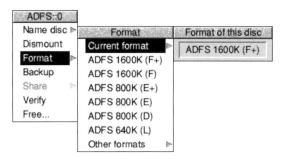

Backing up discs

It's essential that you keep backup copies of your important files, in case they get damaged. You might delete a file by mistake, or you might get a disc error that means some files become unusable.

Backing up hard discs

You can back up a hard disc by copying any valuable data and applications to removable discs. The backup procedure used for hard discs differs from that used for floppy discs.

You should keep backup copies of the following directories:

● !Boot

● Apps

● Printing

● Utilities

You should also back up any data you may have produced and applications that you have installed.

To back up files and directories from your hard disc:

1   Click on your hard disc icon to see the root directory display.

2   Select all of the main directories that you wish to backup. You can only choose directories from a single directory display.

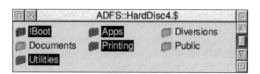

3   Choose the **Count** option from the **Selection** menu.

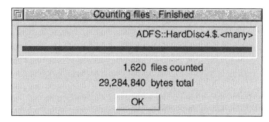

4   Take the figure given by the Count option and divide it by 1,000,000. This will give the **approximate** capacity of disc needed to store the information on. **Warning**: This backup procedure assumes all of the files will fit on a single removable disc.

5   Put the destination disc in the disc drive and click on the drive icon to view the directory display.

6   Select all of the directories you are to backup and drag (copy) them to the removable disc's directory display.

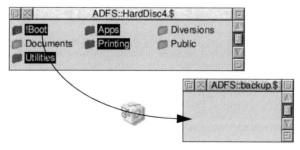

7   Wait while the files are copied.

Fitting more data onto backup discs

To fit more information onto your disc, you can use the file compression application Squash; you'll find more information about this in *Squash* on page 429.

Restoring backed-up data to a hard disc

You can restore your data by inserting the backup disc in the disc drive, clicking on the drive icon and dragging its contents back to the appropriate directory on your hard disc.

Backing up floppy discs

As well as making backups of important files, it is recommended that you make backup copies of applications supplied on discs, and use the backups as your working discs.

You should format the discs that you are using for the backup process and discard any that contain defects, even if they have been mapped out by the formatting process. Do not use discs that have defects.

The backup process copies an entire floppy disc (from the 'source' disc to the 'destination' disc) as a single operation. You can only back up onto discs with the same format as the source disc.

Warning: Backing up a disc deletes the entire previous contents of the destination disc.

Note: The floppy disc drive indicator light will remain on at some stages of the backup process, but don't worry, you can still insert and remove discs as instructed.

To back up a floppy disc:

1   Choose **Backup** from the icon bar menu for the disc drive. If the destination disc is a new, blank disc, format it first (see *Formatting discs* on page 123).

2   When prompted, insert the source disc into the disc drive and click on **OK**. For safety, write-protect the source disc.

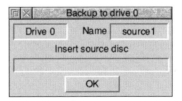

3   Similarly, when prompted, insert the destination disc, and click on **OK**.

4   Repeat steps 2 and 3 as prompted until all of the data has been copied. The destination disc will be given the same name as the source disc.

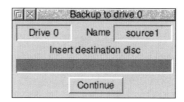

5   When the backup has finished, click on **OK**.

If you're using your computer a lot, it's good practice to back up the files you've been working on at least once a day, and to back up all your files once a week, or once a month. Naming discs with the date of the backup will remind you when the backup was made, without having to check the date of the files on the disc.

Checking for disc defects (verifying)

You can check whether a disc is free from defects by verifying the disc. This checks that all the data on the disc is readable (it does **not** check that the data is correct). This is not something you need to do very often, but is a good idea if, for example, you have made a backup of important data and want to check that it is stored safely.

To verify a disc:

1   If you are verifying a removable disc, insert it in the disc drive.

2   Choose **Verify** from the icon bar menu for the disc drive.

The Verify dialogue box is displayed and the operation starts.

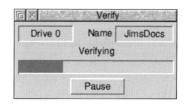

If there are no faults on the disc, the message Disc verified OK appears.

131

Defects on a hard disc

If there is a defect on your hard disc, the position of the error on the disc is displayed during the verification process.

1   Write down the number displayed.

2   Click on **Continue** to carry on with the operation.

3   Repeat this process if any further defects are found.

When the operation ends, you should have a list of the defects found. Turn to *Removing a disc defect* on page 539 and follow the instructions given there.

Defects on a floppy disc

If you find that there are defects on the floppy disc, click on **Continue** to carry on with the verify operation; repeat this process if any further defects are found.

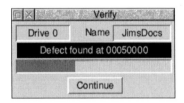

The easiest way to remove the defects is to format the disc again. This allows you to mark the faulty areas of the disc as bad so that they are not used (don't forget to copy any important files off the disc first!).

Checking the amount of free space on a disc

To check how much free space is available on a disc, choose **Free...** from the icon bar menu for the disc drive.

This shows the amount of unused space on the disc, together with the amount of space that has already been used. The total disc size is shown as well. Leaving this window open will keep it updated whenever the space available on the disc changes.

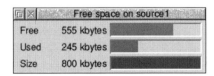

Using several removable discs at once

If the file, directory or application you want is on a removable disc that has been seen by the Filer but is not currently in the disc drive, the Filer asks you to insert the floppy disc. When you do this, the computer finds the required files automatically.

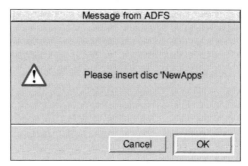

If you decide not to go through with the operation (for example, if the requested disc is not available) click on **Cancel**.

The desktop remembers the names of the last eight discs that have been inserted into the disc drive. If you insert and use a disc that has exactly the same disc name as one already in use, the 'earlier' disc will be forgotten about. You should always try to use unique disc names, and dismount discs before removing them from the disc drive.

Copying between removable discs

When you are copying from one removable disc to another using a single drive (by dragging a group of objects) you may be asked to swap the discs occasionally, which becomes tedious when copying many files and directories. It is probably faster to copy the files from the removable disc to the hard disc or a RAM disc, and then from there to the new removable disc (see *Using a RAM disc* on page 143).

What to do if something goes wrong

Most errors and problems associated with discs are accompanied by self-explanatory messages. Often all you need to do is acknowledge that you have read the error message by clicking in the appropriate box. There are a few cases that are more serious or need a little extra explanation.

Protected disc

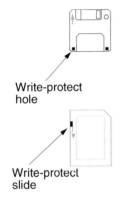

Write-protect
hole

Write-protect
slide

This message indicates that a disc is write-protected, a state which prevents you from accidentally writing to the disc.

On a floppy disc you can remove the write protection by sliding the small tab at one corner of the disc so that the hole is blocked off.

On a memory card you can remove the write protection by sliding a small tab on the left of the card downwards, though not all memory card sockets honour the slide's setting and may permit writing to the disc in either position.

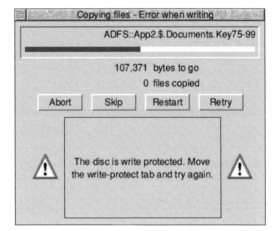

Unreadable disc

The message below indicates that the computer can't read the disc at all, or it may be formatted in a way that cannot be read by the computer. The computer can read discs formatted for DOS and Windows or Atari only, unless you have a third party filing system extension which reads extra formats – ask your supplier.

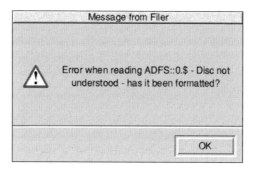

Disc errors during use

If a disc defect error occurs with a removable disc while you are using it (a rare occurrence) you will see a disc error message such as.

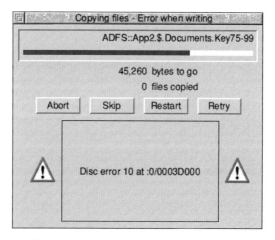

You should copy any files you want to save from the affected disc onto another disc, and then throw the disc away.

If a disc defect error occurs you may be able to remove the defect by having the computer skip over it in future. To do this:

1   Write down the number displayed.

2   Turn to *Removing a disc defect* on page 539 and follow the instructions given there.

14 Other storage devices and filing systems

The previous chapter told you about using fixed and removable discs. This chapter tells you about some other types of storage device, and how to control them using their own filing systems.

You'll find out more about using DOS and Windows discs, optical discs, storage connected via SCSI and SDIO, as well as RAM (an area of computer memory used as a disc).

Types of filing systems

The operating system provides a number of different filing systems, which have been designed to suit the type of storage device on which they are found. Apart from ADFS, the main filing systems are

- CDFS, used witn DVD-ROMs and CD-ROMs
- DOSFS, used with DOS and Windows discs
- NetFS, used with file servers connected via an Econet network (see *Local networks* on page 149)
- NFS and LanManFS, used to communicate with UNIX and Windows computers on a network (see *OmniClient* on page 177)
- RamFS, used with RAM discs
- ResourceFS, used with the read-only resource files held in ROM
- SCSIFS, used with USB connected drives and SCSI discs
- SDFS, used with removable memory cards, such as Secure Digital or MultiMediaCard
- ShareFS, used on an Acorn Access network (see *Local networks* on page 149)
- SparkFS, used to access compressed archives (see *Spark*FS on page 487).

The Filer and desktop give a uniform user interface to all these filing systems, but with each system there are a few special features provided; these are accessed from each device's icon bar menu.

Finding out the filing system type

If you want to find out which filing system you are using, look at the name in the title bar of the directory display. This always starts with the name of the filing system.

Using DVD-ROMs and CD-ROMs

You can read and copy the data saved on a DVD-ROM or CD-ROM disc using a suitable drive and the CD filing system (CDFS).

In general commercially published discs are read-only, so you can't delete files or format the discs. It is possible, with extra software available from third party suppliers, to write to specially coated discs using a DVD or CD rewriter drive. This can be useful as a back up method because optical discs have a long storage lifetime and capacities up to 4.7GB each.

If your computer was supplied with a DVD-ROM or CD-ROM drive already fitted, it will already be configured so that you can use it straight away. If you have fitted a drive yourself, you may need to change the computer's configuration as described in the section *Discs setup plug-in* on page 87 to enable the drive.

Using CDFS

Load the data disc into the DVD-ROM or CD-ROM drive. The precise instructions for doing this will vary according to the make of drive that is fitted. If you are in any doubt, consult the instructions that came with the drive.

To open a directory display for a disc, click on the drive icon on the icon bar. The contents of the disc will be displayed by the Filer:

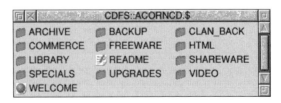

Viewing files on data CDs and DVDs

Data discs must be laid out in ISO 9660 or High Sierra standard format to be recognised, optionally with Joliet or Rock Ridge or Acorn CDFS extensions. These extensions allow some flexibility that the main standards do not. This includes mixed case filenames, and the storing of operating system specific information such as RISC OS file types.

If the file types are not stored then CDFS will try to deduce the file type from the file's name via the MimeMap so that you can load the file by double clicking on it as usual. Filenames will be translated in a manner similar to the list of *File naming limitations* on page 141 for DOS and Windows format discs.

Playing music CDs

You can play ordinary music CDs if the analogue audio cable from the drive is plugged into the computer's sound system analogue input.

Load the audio CD into the CD-ROM drive and click on the drive icon. The disc will be recognised as an audio disc and the icon changes to reflect that.

The CDFS Filer includes a simple CD player application. Menu click on the drive icon then choose **Player...** from the icon bar menu to open the player.

There are buttons, similar to those on a conventional CD player, to

● start playing all of the tracks from start to finish

● jog backward and forward by one track

● pause

● stop

● eject the disc.

A slider allows the volume of playback to be adjusted to suit. It is also possible to set the volume by changing the level that audio is fed into the sound system analogue input. The *Sound setup plug-in* on page 103 has details of how to do this.

It is possible to use the CD player like a jukebox to randomly select tracks on the current disc and play them all until finished. To do this click **Shuffle** followed by the play button to start.

Viewing photo CDs

PhotoCD discs are specially formatted CD-ROMs which contain images (such as photographs). It is possible to have negatives from a camera developed and placed on a PhotoCD disc.

If you own PhotoCD discs, load the CD into the drive and click on the drive icon. The icon will change to show that this is a PhotoCD, and displays the photos as a series of files in a normal Filer window.

Use the ChangeFSI application, described on page 473, to view the photos and convert them to other formats for editing.

Finishing using CDFS

Click Menu on the CD icon on the icon bar, and choose **Dismount** from the menu. Press the Load/Eject button and the CD-ROM will be ejected from the drive.

Some CD-ROM drives have software controlled ejection of discs. Having first dismounted the disc, choose **Eject** from the menu.

Sharing CD-ROM resources

If your computer is connected to a network, you can share your CD-ROM drive with other users on the network (or have access to their CD-ROM drives, if they want you to). There are a couple of ways of going about this. See *Sharing a* CD-ROM on page 152.

Using DOS and Windows discs

Your computer can read and write any removable discs, including floppy discs, that use standard DOS and Windows formats. This makes it easy for you to transfer information between your computer and any computer or device that can use these common formats. For example, the memory card from a digital camera will probably be DOS-formatted.

Working with removable discs

Treat a DOS-formatted removable disc in the same way as you would if it was in a RISC OS format as described in the section *Mounting and dismounting discs* on page 121; insert the disc into the disc drive, then click on the icon for the drive. The Filer will mount the disc and open a directory display.

Transferring files between computers

If you save files from a RISC OS computer to a DOS-formatted disc you can then transfer the files to a DOS or Windows computer (or one that understands DOS-formatted discs too), and vice-versa.

Transfer of text files

You should be able to read RISC OS text files on a DOS or Windows computer. However, there are differences in the 'top-bit-set' characters used to those shown in the tables in the appendix *Character sets* on page 543. In practice this means that the letters and shifted letters on a conventional keyboard (except the £ and € sign) will be readable. Most other characters generated using the Alt key modifier may be displayed as different characters when opened.

The reverse is also true; when moving files created on a DOS or Windows computer to RISC OS some top-bit-set characters will be displayed differently.

DOS and Windows computers finish each line of a text file with a carriage return and a line feed; this makes text appear with an [0d] on the end of each line when viewed in Edit, which only uses line feeds. You can cure this easily by using Edit to replace the carriage returns with nothing: use a wildcarded expression to **Find** Hex [0d] but leave the **Replace with** field empty.

Some word processors use only carriage returns at the end of each line. When these files are imported into Edit the text is shown as one long continuous line. Choose the **Edit/CR↔LF** option in the Edit menu to convert it back into multiple lines again.

File naming limitations

This section shows you how filenames translate between systems.

On a DOS or Windows computer names are typically comprised of an initial part followed by a three letter extension which describes the file's type. For example SHOPPING.TXT might be a shopping list held as a text file. The rules used are:

- Filenames are not case sensitive on either system.

- The longest permitted path name on DOS and Windows is 260 characters. While RISC OS allows for paths up to 1024 characters, this is rarely seen because messages passed in the desktop are limited to 212 characters.

- There are characters on both systems that are illegal to use in filenames on the other. These are automatically mapped between one another. For example a '.' cannot appear in a RISC OS filename but can on a DOS disc, whereas a DOS disc cannot use a '/', therefore the example file cited above would be displayed as SHOPPING/TXT by the Filer.

- The three letter extension will be looked up in the MimeMap database to try to determine the correct RISC OS file type for the file, for example TXT corresponds to Text (&FFF). If the extension is not known the default file type used is DOS (&FE4).

Copying files from RISC OS to a DOS disc

When writing files to the DOS disc the RISC OS file type is kept in reserved bytes in the directory entry alongside the file. Some disc utilities may reset these bytes to zero or fail to copy them when the file is copied, resulting in the file type being lost.

Copying files between two DOS discs on a RISC OS computer

When copying from one DOS disc to another the filenames are converted to RISC OS representation then back again, so overall the filenames are unchanged.

File access

Since there is not a complete mapping between RISC OS file attributes and those provided by DOS, access rights are set as follows:

- A RISC OS file which is locked will be **read-only** under DOS.
- A DOS file which is **read-only** will be locked under RISC OS.

Working with DOS disc partition files

If you have a DOS-formatted disc partition (file type &FC8) the Filer displays it with the DOS disc file icon. Double-click on this icon to display the files it contains. The Filer treats a DOS disc file as a normal directory and allows you access to the DOS files stored within it in a directory display.

Copying and moving DOS disc files

If you want to copy or move your DOS disc file, it will be copied or moved as a single file, not as a series of files and directories.

If you want to copy it as a series of files and directories, double-click on the DOS disc file to open it as a directory, select all of the files from within it, and then copy those instead.

Deleting DOS disc files

If you want to delete your DOS disc file, the **Delete** option on the Filer will delete it as a single file (not as a directory).

You should be very careful not to delete a DOS disc file this way by accident. You could lock it to protect it against accidental deletion – see *Detailed access permissions* on page 55.

Using spare RAM as a disc

RAM

A RAM disc is an area of computer memory that is being used just like a disc drive, which gives it its name. However, the important thing to remember is that objects on the RAM disc are not 'safe' in the way that objects on real discs are safe: they will be lost when the computer is switched off or reset.

The main reason for using a RAM disc is that saving and loading files and applications to or from the RAM disc is much faster than to a removable or fixed disc.

Creating a RAM disc

There are two ways of creating a RAM disc. One method is to use the Discs setup plug-in to create a RAM disc of a given size every time you switch on the computer (see page 87).

Preferred method

The preferred method is to use the Task Manager to create a RAM disc for the current session only (see *Create a* RAM *disc* on page 76). This is because

● it's less wasteful of memory

● configuring too large a RAM disc from !Boot may cause problems on start-up (e.g. if the disc is larger than the total amount of free space available, or if you physically remove some RAM from your computer and forget to alter your boot sequence). See *Configuration held in* CMOS RAM on page 82.

The largest RAM disc allowed is 512MB.

Using a RAM disc

A RAM disc is a convenient way of speeding up some operations, at the cost of using some of the computer's memory. Here are two examples:

Copying between removable discs

When you are copying a group of objects from one removable disc to another, you have to change the disc after each file or directory. An alternative is to allocate as much space as you can to a RAM disc, copy as many files as will fit into RAM, and then copy them from RAM disc to the destination disc. When you've finished, delete the files from RAM, and quit the RAM disc by choosing **Quit** from the icon bar menu.

Keeping frequently-used files in a RAM disc

Another common use of the RAM disc is to hold programs and data files that you use frequently. Keeping them in the RAM disc reduces the time they take to load.

Don't keep files that you are **changing** in the RAM disc: it's too easy to switch off the computer and forget to transfer them to a permanent storage medium.

RAM disc icon bar menu

The RAM disc has its own icon bar menu with options specific to the filing system.

To see how much space is available, click Menu on the RAM icon, and choose **Free...**. This displays the total free and used space.

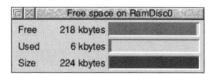

When your computer is connected to an Access network you may wish to share the the contents of your RAM disc with other users. The **Share** menu is used to select how the RAM disc is to be shared; the options available are the same as for *Sharing your hard disc* on page 152.

You can remove the RAM disc from the icon bar by choosing **Quit**. If the RAM disc is not empty you'll be warned that you will lose its contents if you go ahead.

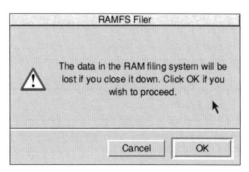

Using read-only resources

ResourceFS is built into the operating system ROM. It is a read-only filing system which contains resources on the computer for use.

Apps

Every time you click on the Apps icon on the icon bar you are using ResourceFS, reflected by its name in the title bar of the Apps directory display. These applications are not really stored in ResourceFS (because it is read-only), but are links to the real applications elsewhere on disc, provided as a useful resource.

You can add or remove applications from the Apps directory display by using the Boot setup plug-in as described on page 85. Those applications that are held in ROM (such as Alarm and Edit) cannot be removed.

There are other resources besides the Apps directory display in ResourceFS. To view these, choose **Open '$'** from the icon bar menu. These resources are mainly in support of installed operating system modules.

Using USB connected drives and SCSI discs

SCSIFS is the filing system which can talk to discs and drives that conform to the *Small Computer System Interface* protocol. This includes a wide variety of storage devices including:

- optical drives used by CDFS
- back up tape streamers
- scanners
- flash memory
- some makes of digital camera
- external hard discs in a caddy

The SCSI protocol is widely used over different types of physical connection:

- One or more special expansion cards may be fitted which *hosts* the SCSI bus, with up to seven SCSI *peripheral devices* attached to each. Use the Discs setup plug-in (see page 87) to configure this type of SCSI host.

- One or more Universal Serial Bus sockets. USB sockets use a much smaller connector than a conventional expansion card because the data is sent serially rather than in parallel, making USB devices smaller and cheaper to manufacture. Storage such as flash memory will often be supplied with the connector moulded into the plastic case, making the disc and drive a single part.

Regardless of how the SCSI device is physically connected, RISC OS presents the discs in the same consistent manner that ADFS does; as either fixed or removable drive icons on the icon bar. The chapter *Using discs* can equally be read with ADFS substituted for SCSIFS throughout.

Using removable memory cards

SDFS is the filing system which can talk to discs and drives that conform to the *Serial Digital Input Output* protocol.

 Secure Digital and MultiMediaCard are examples of flash memory that use the SDIO protocol to store large amounts of information in a physically small card. These cards are often found in portable devices such as digital cameras and mobile phones because they have no moving parts, making them robust against the device being dropped.

When it is not necessary to remove the memory card manufacturers may opt to use an *embedded MultiMediaCard* (eMMC) fixed directly to the computer's circuit board. This means the storage is always available, making it suitable for holding the Boot application for example.

Regardless of the shape or brand of memory card, RISC OS presents the discs in the same consistent manner that ADFS does; as either fixed or removable drive icons on the icon bar. The chapter *Using discs* can equally be read with ADFS substituted for SDFS throughout.

Part 3 – Networking

15   Local networks

$\mathbf{I}$f your computer is connected to a network – maybe it is part of your school or office network – you will be able to communicate with the other computers around you to exchange information. This chapter shows you how to use a network to achieve this.

If your computer isn't connected to a network you don't need to read this chapter.

Networking uses many jargon terms – Econet, Ethernet, AUN, TCP/IP and file server – to name a few. However, as you'll see from this chapter, using a network is actually quite easy.

Types of network

A *local area network* (LAN) joins computers in the same building or on the same site and is said to be a private network, usually administered by the network manager.

A *wide area network* (WAN) joins multiple local area networks together and is spread over a much wider geographical area. The public internet is an example wide area network, and allows you to communicate with other users anywhere in the world.

Topology

Within a LAN it is possible to follow the network from the computer in front of you to its nearest neighbour. This will typically be

- another computer
- a *hub* to connect together several computers in a desk area to a single cable which runs to another room
- a *switch* which is similar to a hub but that also analyses the network messages and sends them only to specific recipients, reducing unnecessary traffic
- a *gateway* which routes messages addressed to computers outside the LAN to the WAN
- a *modem* or similar equipment that provides your connection outside the LAN, for example to the telephone or cable TV network.

In the home environment it's common to find the modem combines a switch in the same box and acts as the gateway also.

Protocols

RISC OS uses several types of networking systems, based on Ethernet and Econet cabling. You can use all these types of network at the same time, if you want:

Econet

Once the standard networking in schools, a central file server holds the data of all the network users. However, by modern standards data transmission rates are fairly low and all stations on the network share the same transmission clock.

You can instead use Econet protocols sent over an Ethernet network. This is part of the *Acorn Universal Network* (AUN) strategy.

Access

An easy-to-install Ethernet network for small to medium-sized installations. Allows simple *peer-to-peer* disc and printer sharing between all RISC OS computers on the local area network without needing a central file server.

In larger installations you can also have a dedicated computer which is always available that acts as a file server **and** a printer server.

TCP/IP

Originally implementing the *Transmission Control Protocol* and *Internet Protocol*, TCP/IP is now a more general term to refer to a family of protocols used over large Ethernet networks. This includes the protocols used to connect to the internet.

Addressing

In order to route messages efficiently between computers they are each assigned a unique address. In Econet this is sometimes called the *station number*.

Some addresses are usually set aside for special purposes by the designers of the protocol, such as a *broadcast* address (to send one message to everybody at once) and *multicast* addresses (to send one message to a group of computers). Broadcast addresses do not pass through gateways because otherwise the LAN would be overwhelmed by millions of unwanted messages from around the world.

Configuring networking

The protocols introduced above correspond to the three icons in the Network setup plug-in described in the chapter *Setting up networking*.

This chapter assumes that the network has been suitably configured already; go to page 167 if this is not the case, then come back to this chapter.

Disc sharing on an Access network

Discs

If you have an icon like this on your icon bar it means you're connected to an Access network; there may be other discs on the network that you can access.

Click on the discs icon to display the available discs.

Discs with a lock on them are *protected* – you can only read and write to files and directories where public access has specifically been given. The ones with a CD-ROM symbol represent CD-ROMs of course, and those with an 'Apps' type symbol inside are read-only.

Double-click on the disc that you want to use. The disc name is displayed under the discs icon on your icon bar. You can now use the shared disc. It is also possible to share your own disc with other users and to print using a shared printer.

Options

Click Menu on a shared disc icon on the icon bar to display the ShareFS menu:

Choose **Save choices** to ensure that your selection will be remembered when your machine is next restarted.

Sharing your hard disc

To share your hard disc with other users press Menu over the hard disc icon on the icon bar; choose **Share unprotected** from the **Share** menu. The disc will be made accessible to the network unprotected (see *Protecting a shared disc* below).

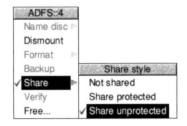

If your disc has the same name as another on the network, you will be asked to change it (first choose **Not shared**, and follow the instructions in the section *Naming discs* on page 122 if you need assistance on how to do this).

Protecting a shared disc

If you want to stop others changing or deleting, or even reading files on the shared disc (which they can otherwise do), choose **Share protected** from the **Share** submenu. If you do this, only files and directories you specifically grant public access to (using the Filer **Access** menu) can be read and written to by others.

Sharing a CD-ROM

Any number of CD-ROMs may be shared in much the same way as hard discs using Access, but because you cannot change the name of a CD-ROM like you can a normal disc, the dialogue is a little different.

You can change the name that the CD-ROM will be shared as using the CDFS icon bar menu:

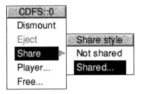 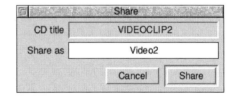

Type in the new name in the **Share as** box and click on **Share** to start sharing it.

Sharing other drives

You may share any filing system or indeed just a single directory with Access, but not all icon bar filers have a **Share** menu included. To share any other filing system, you will need to either enter a * command (press F12, then type the command) or add the command as a part of your Boot file. The syntax of the command is

```
*Share <Pathname> [<Discname>] [-options]
```

For example, to share just the Work directory from a Secure Digital memory card currently in SDFS drive 0 use the command

```
*Share SDFS::0.$.Work MyWork -protected
```

would share the directory `SDFS::0.$.Work` as Access disc 'MyWork'. If you do not specify the share name, it will be shared with the disc or directory name.

Protected mode is an example of an option to the `Share` command, the possible options are:

- **protected** – restricts access based on the Filer's access permissions.
- **readonly** – exports all files and directories as read-only (uses an Apps icon).
- **cdrom** – denotes this shared disc is an optical disc (uses a CD-ROM icon).
- **noicon** – this option is reserved for use by certain applications.
- **auth <key>** – is for internal use with Access+ which is described on page 154.
- **subdir** – is for internal use with the **auth** option.

You may stop sharing by using the command

```
*Unshare <Discname>
```

Sharing across a gateway

The Access protocol discovers which discs and printers are currently available by using periodic broadcast messages, therefore you cannot normally share discs across gateways because they do not forward broadcast messages (as explained in *Addressing* earlier).

Your network manager can set up an Access server to pass messages between subnets of the LAN, or through the `FWAddNet` star command, see *Creating a 'structured' sharing method* on page 155.

Sharing private data

You may wish to share data in such a way that it does not appear automatically in the Discs window, but only becomes available to those who know its name and a password.

To do this, double-click on the !Access+ application icon. Access+ is in the `Utilities.Access` directory on your hard disc or network. The Access+ icon will appear on the righthand side of the icon bar.

If you want to share a disc, or part of a disc, with chosen users, there are two ways in which you can do it:

● Dragging a directory into the Access+ dialogue box.

● Creating a 'structured' sharing method.

Dragging a directory into the Access+ dialogue box

The simplest method is by clicking on the Access+ icon to open a dialogue box:

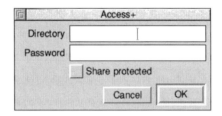

You may drag any directory into this box, from any filing system – it will then automatically fill in the directory pathname for you. You must then type in a password that others must enter if they want to access this directory. This password can be from zero to six characters long.

To share a whole disc, display the root directory of the disc, choose **Select all** and drop the selection into the dialogue box.

You also have the option to share the directory in protected mode.

You can **Show** which resources you are sharing from the Access+ icon bar menu:

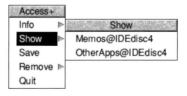

You can save or remove shared directories using this menu, too.

154

Creating a 'structured' sharing method

The structured sharing method allows a small group of computers to be set up without needing a dedicated file server.

Users in the group can log on to their own 'world', which could include private data, common read-only applications and general read-write resources such as !Scrap. These resources are served by one of the computers in the group.

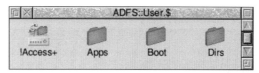

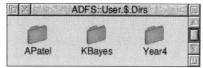

- Apps is a read-only directory for applications.
- Boot contains !Scrap and !ShareBoot (the group's Boot application).
- In the Dirs directory you can create directories for private data for users to log on to.

The network manager can set up this share structure on the server machine as follows:

1   Place the directory containing Access+, Dirs, Apps and Boot at the chosen point on the hard disc, adding it to the applications which are run at startup up using the Boot setup plug-in (refer to page 85 for details of how to do this).

2   Make sure that the Boot and Apps directories, and their contents, have public read access set.

3   Create a text file containing all the user names in the Dirs directory along with the password each will have to use to log on to their 'world'. The following format must be used:

```
U       KBayes      abc123
P       APatel      xyz789
U       Year4       why234
```

U signifies Unprotected and P is Protected. This will share the directory KBayes inside Dirs with a password of abc123. It is an unprotected mount (U) in this case. You may omit the password if you do not require this level of security.

4   Save this file onto the Access+ icon. This text file can subsequently be removed by the network manager and used for reference (if someone forgets the name or password) to ensure security.

Users, when they log on (see below), will see their own directory
(`Year4@Server2`, for example), as well as the Apps directory containing
commonly-used applications available to all users listed.

Note that this use of Access is designed for small groups of users – the computer
serving files to the group will slow down when more than a handful of users are in
the group. A dedicated file server would offer better performance in that scenario.

Accessing private data

To access private data, users 'log on' at their computer, using the Access icon bar
menu to enter their name and password.

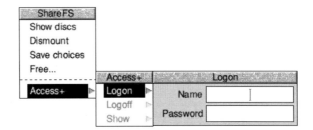

They do not log on to a server machine in the traditional sense, but onto the
network as a whole, as any computers that have data for a particular user will place
their private disc into the window that opens up when the user logs on:

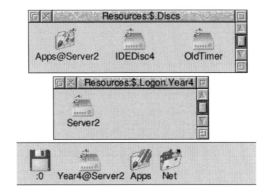

In the illustration above, the user has logged on with a name `Year4`. The private
directory is `Year4@Server2`. The Apps directory available to `Year4` is displayed
in the Discs window, together with two other discs which are being shared
unprotected on the network.

Remote booting with Access

Client computers can be set up to boot from a remote server and load the user's environment as required. Remote booting is most useful when the client computer has no hard disc, or there is a requirement to manage and backup user environments centrally.

This can be set up as follows:

1   Configure the client machine to boot from the ShareFS filing system. This is done by pressing F12 on each client machine and typing:

```
*Configure Boot
*Configure FileSystem Share
```

When switched on, the computer will now search for a file with the name of !ShareBoot in the root of the first-saved mount. The next step is to create such a file.

2   The first-saved mount is the leftmost disc of those displayed on your icon bar when you choose **Save choices** from the ShareFS icon bar menu. To select the disc you want to be the first-saved mount, **Dismount** any shared discs using the ShareFS icon bar menu, then click on the Discs icon to display the available discs. Double-click on the disc you want to be the first-saved mount, followed by any other discs you want to be loaded automatically. Choose **Save choices**, and the discs will be saved in the required order.

3   Now, from the shared disc icon (i.e. not from the machine where the shared disc is located) set up the environment you want for your computer when you first switch it on (files and applications loaded, directory displays open and so on).

4   Go to the Task Manager menu and choose **Desktop settings/Save settings**. Change the name of the boot file to !ShareBoot, then save it in the root directory of the first-saved mount you set up in the previous step.

5   Make sure that the !ShareBoot file you have created has public read access, if the disc is shared protected.

Printing over an Access network

(See also the chapter *Setting up printers*.)

A printer connected to a computer on an Access network can be shared by other users on the network. The computer connected to the printer should have a hard disc with at least 5MB of free space at all times.

To print over an Access network, first go to the computer connected to the printer...

1   Load Printer Manager by double-clicking on the !Printers application icon.

2   Choose **Printer control**... from the Printer Manager icon bar menu.

3   Select the printer to be shared, press Menu and choose the option **Shared.**
(You will see a duplicate of your printer displayed in your Printer control window, with Connection **Remote**. You can ignore this; do **not** set it to **Active**.)

4   Choose **Save choices** from the icon bar menu.
It is useful to set up a Desktop settings file to run Printer Manager when the computer is switched on, so that the printer will be shared again without manual intervention.

Then on any other networked computer wishing to print...

1   Load Printer Manager by double-clicking on the !Printers application icon.

2   Choose **Printer control**... from the Printer Manager icon bar menu, and a list of available printers (Connection **Remote**) will be displayed.

3   Select one of these printers and choose **Active** from the Printer control menu.

4   It will then appear on the icon bar.

5   Choose **Save choices** to remember this printer set up in future.
You can now print using the remote printer.

A greyed-out printer with a question mark through it indicates that the printer is not available. Is it switched on? Is the computer it's connected to switched on?

Printing on a 'server' computer

While a computer is rendering a picture (i.e. processing the display before sending it to the printer) an hourglass appears. At this stage, the computer is very busy, and requests from other machines to read or write to its shared disc will take some time to be met. The time taken to render is generally fairly short, but if a great deal of printing is to be performed it might be preferable to ensure that this computer is not the same one which contains a frequently-used shared disc.

During the time that a 'server' machine is busy, and not communicating with other machines, the hourglass on other machines that are trying to communicate with it will turn red, and start counting down, until communication is re-established.

Re-starting Printer Manager at the server machine will result in any outstanding print jobs being flushed.

Speed of printing

Use the lowest reasonable resolution (dots per inch) to get the desired result, as a client machine will take a long time to render a high-resolution page.

Note that the whole document or image is required before the printer will actually start, which will increase the time before printing is complete – especially if very high resolutions are selected from a relatively less powerful machine. The size of available memory will also affect the speed of printing.

File sharing on an Econet network

An Econet network consists of a number of computers connected together to a dedicated computer called a file server.

Net

This type of network is usually looked after by your network manager. The network manager often allocates each person a user name. This name is used to identify them to the file server.

File server

A *file server* is a computer that holds a central store of computer programs and data. If your network manager allocates you storage space on the file server, you can store data there in your own special user area.

Printer server

A network usually also includes a *printer server*. A printer server is a networked computer that is directly connected to a printer. All users of the network can use the printer.

Other services

You may also be able to use electronic mail (email) – a way of sending electronic messages between network users. Ask your network manager if this facility has been made available to you.

Logging on

Before you can use a file server, you need to log on to it. If there is more than one file server on your network, you will need to choose which one to log on to.

Choose **FS list** from the Net icon bar menu to open a display showing a list of file servers available; there is an icon for each file server. If a file server has more than one storage device available for you to use (for example, an extra hard disc) there is an icon for each device in the window.

If you click on one of the file server icons, the Logon dialogue box appears, with the file server name already filled in. For example:

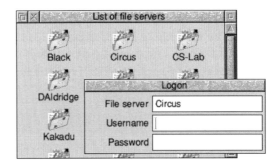

If you're not already logged on, you can also display this dialogue box by clicking on the Net icon on the icon bar. If you are logged on already, clicking on the Net icon will open your 'user directory' – there's more on this later.

To log on to a network file server:

1   Click on the Net icon. This displays the **Logon** window.

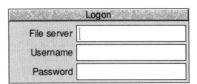

2   Type in the name of the file server (this may already be set up), your user name, and (if needed) your password.

(Press ↵ to move to the next line.)

Your user name is set by the network manager. Your password does not appear on the screen: this is to prevent other users seeing your password.

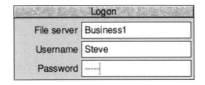

Business1

If you enter your user name and password correctly:

● A directory display for your user directory (the top-level directory in your own network directory) is opened.

● The Net icon on the icon bar changes to show a connection (the text under the icon shows the file server's number or name).

If you get your user name or password wrong, an error message is displayed.

If you do not have a user directory, you are logged onto the root directory of the file server instead (but you'll only have limited access to its contents).

You can, of course, log on to several file servers; a Net icon is displayed on the icon bar for each file server.

You can set up the computer to fill in the file server entry automatically – see *Configuring connection to an Econet network* on page 168.

File server network menu options

FS list

To check which file servers are available, choose **FS list** from the File server menu. A list of file servers is shown in a window. **Full info**, reached via the Display menu in this window, shows the file server net address (a number) as well as its name.

Logon

To log on to a network file server from the File server menu, move to the **Logon** dialogue box.

Open '$'

On a file server you log on to your user directory. This will normally be one or more levels down from the top level (root) directory. The user directory is sometimes referred to as the user root directory (URD). Pathnames to the user root directory begin with &.

In some cases, you may be prevented from looking at any directories other than your own. If you are not sure about your privileges, ask your network manager.

You can open the root directory of the file server by choosing **Open '$'** from the File server menu. If the file server has more than one disc, the disc names are displayed as a submenu; click on the disc whose root you want to display.

Free...

To check how much space is available to you on a file server, choose **Free...** from the File server menu. This displays the free space on the file server. **Free** is the amount of space you have left in your user area. **Used** is the amount of space that has been used (by all users) on the file server. **Size** is the total size of the file server disc.

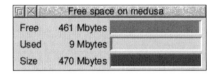

If you find that you are running out of space, ask your network manager for more.

Bye

When you have finished using a file server, log off by choosing **Bye** from the File server menu. Any directory displays for the file server will be closed. Choosing **Shutdown** from the Task Manager icon bar menu does this automatically.

Logging on without displaying a directory

To log on **without** displaying the user directory, hold down Shift and press Return for the last time when logging on; do not release Shift until the file server name or number appears under the Net icon, indicating that you are logged on.

Updating the file server directory display

If a file shown in a file server directory display on your screen is deleted by another user, your display is not updated automatically. If you try to open the deleted file, you will get a 'File not found' error message. The same applies to anything added. You can update the display by choosing **Refresh** from the Filer menu.

Your network 'User' directory

Normally every user has their own directory on a file server in which they can work and save files. Your own network directory usually has the same name as your user name. It is represented on screen by the character &, so if you logged on to a file server on a hard disc called History, the directory display for your directory would have the title `Net::History.&`.

If the file server can't find your user directory, the directory display shows some or all of the files and directories in the root directory of the file server; however, you won't 'own' this directory (unless you are the network manager), and so your access to many of the files and directories it contains may be restricted.

Using files and applications

Applications copied from a network

You can use files and applications on the file server in the same way as you would use them directly from your own computer. They load from the hard disc on the file server into your own machine.

If you copy an application from the network, you need to run the application from your local disc. If you don't do this, and try to load a file produced by the application after logging off the network, you will see the message `Not logged on`. This is because the computer, having 'seen' that the application came from the network, is still trying to find it there.

Note: Take care that you're not breaching any copyright by copying applications.

Using files from other users' directories

When you want to save a file to your file server directory, just drag its icon into your network user directory.

You may sometimes need to use a file that is stored in another user's directory. If the file has Public read access you can look at it, but not save any changes, attempting to save when you do not have the privilege to do so will report an `Insufficient access` error message. However, you can save a copy in your own directory by dragging the **Save as** icon to your own directory display.

To load a file from another user's directory, you need to display the file server's root directory, and then move down the directory structure into the other person's directory. To display the root directory, choose the menu option **Open '$'** (see page 161).

The root directory display may allow access to all the user root directories. Double-click on the directory for the user whose files you want to use. There may be some icons missing from the directory display: these are for files that the owner has locked against all public access. If you try to load an application from someone else's directory, it will generate an error message if the owner has not given public read access to it. There are other reasons why you may get an error message doing this; ask your network manager for advice.

Setting the access permissions to your own files

File ownership

You can look at, change and delete any files in your own user directory, but you cannot change or delete files from someone else's user directory (though you may be able to look at them). Some files and directories may be hidden from you completely, so that you do not even see their icons in the directory display.

By default, other users will have no access to your files. This section gives you a quick overview of access permissions on networks. For a full explanation of access options see *Setting file access permissions* on page 55.

You can set the public access to your files using the **Access** command from the Filer menu.

The Owner access sets what **you** can do with the file; the Public access controls what **other users** can do with the file. You can lock a file against deletion to prevent you accidentally deleting it yourself, but you don't need to set this to prevent other users deleting your file as it is locked to them anyway.

If you allow public write access to your file, other users are able to alter it without your knowledge. If you allow public read access only, they can look at the file but not alter it. Never completely remove the access rights to your files by denying read and write access to yourself as well as to others.

You cannot specify the access rights to a directory, only to the files within it, but you can lock a directory against deletion using **Access**.

Hidden objects

If you lock a directory or allow no public access to a file, and the network manager has enabled the hidden objects option (at the file server) the directory or file becomes a hidden object and is not visible to other users.

Setting your password

The password is a security measure to prevent other users logging on with your identity and gaining access to your protected files.

You should change your password occasionally to help preserve the security of your files. To change your password, use the *Pass command:

1   Press F12 to move to the command line.

2   Type:

        Net:Pass *oldpassword newpassword* ⏎

3   Press the Return key (⏎) again to go back to the desktop.

The first time you set a password you may not have an old password, so use the null string "" in place of *oldpassword*. For example, to set your password for the first time to Hebrides, type

```
Pass "" Hebrides
```

If you later wanted to change this to Shetland, you would type

```
Pass Hebrides Shetland
```

Your password must be at least six and not more than 22 characters long.

Choosing a password

When you are choosing a password, do not select something very obvious that could be guessed by someone else. Do not, for example, use the date of your birthday, the name of a member of your family or a pet, your telephone number, or the registration number of your car.

In some cases, the network manager may prevent you resetting your password, or looking at any directories other than your own. If you are not sure about your privileges, ask your network manager.

Network errors

Network failures

Serious errors, such as damage to the disc of a file server, should be handled by the network manager. The only error you are likely to meet when using the network is failure of the network itself, rather than the filing system. This can happen for a variety of reasons: both 'hard errors', such as the network becoming disconnected, and 'soft errors', such as the network becoming jammed as a result of too many people using it at the same time. Most problems tend to be soft and can be cured by trying the operation again, or by logging on to the file server again.

Common error messages

`Station xxx not listening`	The file server is switched off, or is too overloaded to be able to deal with your request at the moment (try again later).
`No reply from station xxx.xxx`	The file server has received and acknowledged your request, but has subsequently failed to comply with it.
`Network not plugged in`	Your machine is physically disconnected from the network, either at the back of the computer or at the socket box at the other end of the cable.

Printing over an Econet network

If your file server also has a printer attached to it, this printer may be accessed by other users on the network. Use the Printer Manager application to access a printer server in the same way as you would an ordinary printer.

Ask your network manager for details about which printer driver to use and the name of the network printer, then set up the printer according to the instructions given in *Setting up printers* on page 189.

File sharing using other protocols

The TCP/IP protocol suite also lets you communicate with computers using common protocols. For example, if the host computer is running the UNIX Network File System (NFS) then you can display and manipulate files resident on the host computer in a directory display in the same way as you would files on your own computer.

 OmniClient provides a simple, consistent view of network file services to RISC OS users, irrespective of the server type or protocol used. You can read more about how to go about using this application in the chapter *OmniClient*.

If you prefer to, it is even possible to use OmniClient as the filer for Access sharing and Econet file servers.

16   Setting up networking

> **T**his chapter tells you all about changing your computer's network configuration
> by using the Network setup plug-in to enter the settings for your local network
> requirements.
>
> **If your computer isn't connected to a network you don't need to read this
> chapter.**

Introduction

The different network types to which RISC OS can connect are detailed in the
chapter *Local networks* on page 149. You will need to configure the network software
in order to connect to these networks; your supplier or the network manager may
already have done this for you.

Firstly, open the Configuration window by clicking Menu on the Task Manager icon
then choosing **Configure...** from the menu. Click on the Network icon from the
main Configuration window to display the Network setup plug-in:

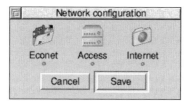

There are three icons, one for each type of network:

●   Econet (connecting to a central Level 4 Fileserver using the Econet protocol)

●   Access (peer-to-peer sharing using the Access protocol)

●   Internet (connectivity using the full TCP/IP protocol)

Configuring connection to an Econet network

If you are going to use Level 4 Fileserver Econet protocols, choose Econet; the Acorn Universal Networking dialogue box will be displayed:

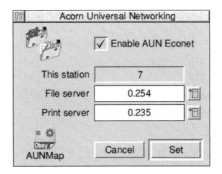

There are two ways Econet can operate:

● With specialised Econet hardware over inexpensive 5 core screened cables. This is 'native' Econet.

● By placing the Econet protocol messages inside ordinary TCP/IP packets which are then sent over whichever medium the TCP/IP network uses. This is 'Acorn Universal Networking' Econet.

Your network manager will have set the station number for your computer; it is not possible to change this yourself because station numbers must be unique on each net.

1   Tick **Enable AUN Econet**. This is not necessary if you are using 'native' Econet.

2   If you will be using Econet and Internet together it is possible to define mappings from Internet style IP addresses (4 numbers separated by full stops) and Econet style net and station addresses (2 numbers separated by full stops).

Double-click the **AUNMap** icon (or drag an existing AUNMap file onto the dialogue box) and enter any mappings between IP addresses and Econet addresses. For details, see the comments inside the AUNMap file itself.

3   Enter names or numbers for your default File server and Print server.

Note: If your network is already up and running, you will be able to choose from the appropriate menu icons instead of typing in names manually.

4   Click on **Set** to confirm the changes and close the dialogue box, or **Cancel** to leave without making any changes.

Configuring connection to an Access network

If you are connecting to a peer-to-peer disc and printer sharing network, choose Access; the Access dialogue box will be displayed:

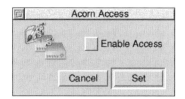

1   Tick **Enable Access** to turn on peer-to-peer sharing

Note: It is possible to use Access without needing to set up a full TCP/IP connection when only sharing with other computers on the local network.

2   Click on **Set** to confirm the changes and close the dialogue box, or **Cancel** to leave without making any changes.

Configuring connection to the Internet

If you are connecting to computers other than through the Access or Econet protocols, or to remote computers on the wider internet, you will need to configure a full TCP/IP network connection.

1   Click on the Internet icon and the Internet configuration dialogue box will be displayed:

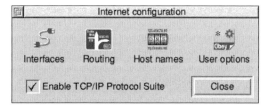

2   Click on **Enable TCP/IP Protocol Suite.**

Setting the network interface

1   Click on the **Interfaces** icon in the Internet configuration window to display the network interface configuration options:

Each line in the interfaces window represents one available interface, its physical location, and the name of the driver which controls it.

Most often this window will show the Ethernet interfaces available as that is by far the most common medium for sending TCP/IP packets. Examples of other types of medium include *asynchronous transfer mode* (ATM), *point-to-point protocol* (PPP) using a modem on the telephone line, and it is even possible to use native Econet.

2   Click on **Configure...** to display the interface configuration options:

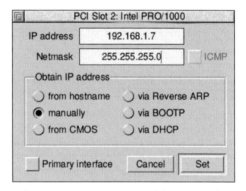

The interface must be given a unique **IP address** for the network. You can obtain the address from any one of a number of sources:

● **from hostname** – this reflects whatever is entered in the Host name field in the Host names dialogue box.

● **manually** – enter the IP address of the interface as 4 numbers separated by full stops. The network manager will need to ensure each computer using this method has a unique address, the network will not work if there is more than one computer on each IP address.

● **from CMOS** – you can use this option for discless booting, where the IP address is read from CMOS locations. The network manager will need to use the SetStation utility to set this up for you.

- **via Reverse ARP** – the Internet module will broadcast an *address resolution protocol* (ARP) message when the computer boots up to convert the interface's hardware address into an IP address. The network manager will need to have configured a server, with a list mapping between the two address types, to respond to this.

- **via BOOTP** – the *bootstrap protocol* also broadcasts a message to a central server in order to find out its IP address assignment. For large networks with many subnets it avoids needing one server per subnet, which would otherwise be needed if Reverse ARP was in use.

- **via DHCP** – the *dynamic host configuration protocol* discovers all of the network settings automatically, and will continue to update them periodically in the background should they change dynamically. Obtain your address using DHCP where possible in preference to any of the other possible sources, because it ensures all computers on the network are similarly configured.

The **Netmask** defines which parts of the IP address are used to match on when deciding whether a message originates from the same subnet as your computer resides, any non-matching address is considered to be from the wider internet.

The BOOTP and DHCP options (only) will complete the Netmask for you.

The Reverse ARP option (only) can complete the Netmask for you by sending out an ICMP *request* message. Select the **ICMP** option to enable this.

For the other options you must specify a Netmask; ask your network manager for the mask to use for the subnet to which you are connected. As a last resort, it can be set to `default` which will leave the computer to decide the Netmask from the IP address based on some simple *classful network* rules.

3   When the **Primary interface** option is enabled it nominates this interface to be used in preference to any other in the event of redundancy.

4   Click on **Set** to confirm the changes and close the dialogue box, or **Cancel** to leave without making any changes.

To view the status of interfaces that have already been configured, click on **Status...** which will open the status window:

```
┌─────────────────────────────────────────────┐
│ ▣        PCI Slot 2: Intel PRO/1000           │
│                                               │
│        IP address │    192.168.1.7    │       │
│                                               │
│          Netmask  │   255.255.255.0   │       │
│                                               │
│  Hardware address │  04:B3:D5:04:F0:04 │      │
│                                               │
│          Gateway  │    192.168.1.1    │       │
│                                               │
│  ┌ Activity at 100Mbps ───────────────────┐   │
│  │           OK ☑        Full duplex ☑     │   │
│  │       Active ☑           Polarity ☑     │   │
│  │                                         │   │
│  │  Transmit frames │        789    │█│    │   │
│  │  Transmit errors │          0    │ │    │   │
│  │                                         │   │
│  │   Receive frames │        959    │█│    │   │
│  │   Receive errors │          0    │ │    │   │
│  └─────────────────────────────────────────┘  │
│                                   ┌─────────┐  │
│                                   │  Close  │  │
│                                   └─────────┘  │
└─────────────────────────────────────────────┘
```

The window will update:

- The link speed.
  Measured in bits per second (bps).

- The link status.
  Ordinarily this will be **OK** and **active** when the network cable is plugged into a working network socket. The duplex and polarity will depend on the equipment at the far end of the network cable.

- The transmit and receive counters.
  Every frame received or sent is counted, and any that are reported with errors by the interface will also be counted, with the ratio of the two counts being shown as a bar graph to the right. Ordinarily there should be no errors and the bar graphs are solid green.

Click **Close** to finish using the status window.

Setting the routing options

1   Click on the **Routing** icon in the Internet configuration window to display the routing options:

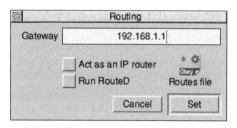

2   If you have a connection to the wider internet via a gateway machine, enter the IP address into the **Gateway** field. For broadband internet connections, this is often the address of the modem.

If you selected DHCP when setting up your primary interface, leave the gateway blank; the correct value will be obtained automatically.

3   If necessary, set the other options in the dialogue box:

● **Act as an IP router** – this lets your machine act as a gateway if you've got more than one network interface.

● **Run RouteD** – on more complex network setups the routes between networks can be distributed centrally so that they are always up to date. Enable this option to run the *route daemon* (RouteD) in the background to continuously check for changes to the known routes. Pressing Menu will allow you to set the RouteD options; consult the network manager for any special options required, otherwise use the `default` setting.

● **Routes file** – this lets you specify more advanced routing information. Double-click on the icon to edit the default file, or drag a custom Routes file onto the icon to replace the default.

4   Click on **Set** to confirm the changes and close the dialogue box, or **Cancel** to leave without making any changes.

Setting the Host name

The host names dialogue box allows more memorable names to be used whenever an IP address is required, for example when setting up the gateway on page 173 you could use the name of the gateway machine rather than numbers.

1   Click on **Host names** to display the eponymous dialogue box:

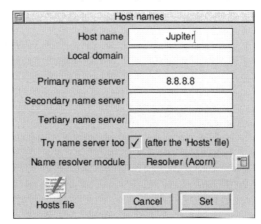

2   Type in a **Host name** of your choosing. Your network manager will be able to tell you if there is a **Local domain** set up, for example it could be the name of the site for a company with several offices.

3   Host names will always be searched for in the Hosts file first. The Hosts file is initially empty. To declare the names of hosts on your network, you can either drag an existing Hosts file onto the **Hosts file** icon in the dialogue box, or double-click the **Hosts file** icon to edit the default version.

4   When no match is found in the Hosts file you can use a *name resolver* to try to turn a name into an IP address. To enable this click on **Try name server too** and select an installed resolver module from the drop down list:

●   Acorn's Resolver module (default)

●   Gnome's Resolve module

●   Adam Goodfellow's InetDB

●   Stewart Brodie's DNSResolve

Finally, enter the IP address of at least one server set up to perform name resolution and designated the **Primary name server**. For broadband internet connections, this is often the address of the modem (and the gateway).

Secondary and tertiary ones can be set should the primary one be unavailable.

5   Click on **Set** to confirm the changes and close the dialogue box, or **Cancel** to leave without making any changes.

Editing the User options script

All of the options set from the Network dialogue boxes are automatically saved in CMOS RAM or in scripts. Do not manually edit any of these scripts as it may prevent the Network setup plug-in from reading them.

When the computer is turned on these automatically generated scripts are run first, then afterwards the **User options** script is run. Experienced users may wish to set up custom configurations using this script.

Double-click the **User options** icon to open the options script in a text editor.

Saving your Network Configuration

Having closed the dialogue boxes in which you made configuration changes, you should now have returned to the top level Network setup plug-in:

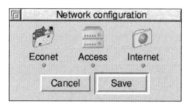

To save your configuration click on **Save** which will change certain CMOS RAM settings and generate scripts inside the Boot application. When it is finished you will be prompted to **Reset now** or **Reset later**; the new configuration will only take effect when you restart the computer, but this can be deferred if necessary.

To discard the configuration changes you made, click on **Cancel**.

17 OmniClient

OmniClient provides a simple, consistent desktop filer for network-based filing systems. It enables you to store and retrieve files on both 'native' RISC OS file servers and file servers hosted on other operating systems, whether they are on the local area network (LAN) or wider internet.

Examples of the server types that you can connect to via OmniClient include:

- Windows LAN Manager (SMB protocol)
- UNIX Network File Server (NFS protocol)
- Acorn Access (Access protocol)
- AUN Level 4 (Econet protocol)
- Supplementary protocols provided by third party client modules

Selecting OmniClient's protocols

Before starting OmniClient for the first time, it is necessary to review which protocol modules it will attempt to load each time it is run.

The protocol module selection is made in the Obey file !Omni.Files.Startup inside the application directory, and OmniClient itself is in the Apps directory on your hard disc or network. Protocol modules can reside in ROM or be held in !Omni.RMStore, though only those in ROM can be used to boot from.

Loading the startup file into Edit will show the current list of enabled and disabled protocol modules near the top. Enabled protocols have their respective variable set to 1, while any set to 0 will not be loaded. For example, to enable the LAN Manager change its selection line to say:

```
SetEval Omni$LanMan 1
```

Save any changes you have made. There are other protocol configuration options also saved in the startup file, which are covered in the section *The Startup file* on page 186.

Starting OmniClient

To start the application, double-click on the !Omni application icon. The application icon appears on the icon bar.

Using OmniClient

Displaying available file servers

Click on the OmniClient icon displayed on the lefthand side of your icon bar, or choose **FS list** from the icon bar menu.

There will be a short delay while OmniClient checks the network for active file servers, then a window will open with those which are available for you to access. The different icons represent different protocol types that the servers use.

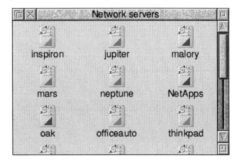

Sorting the file server window

The Filer menu on the file server window gives you the familiar display choices of **Large icons** and **Small icons**, as well as a **Full Info** display which contains more detailed information about each type of server. It also allows you to sort the servers by server name or protocol.

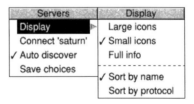

File server discovery

By default OmniClient automatically asks each enabled protocol to search the network for active file servers. To skip this discovery step turn off **Auto discover** in the Servers menu. In future, only mounts that you have saved will appear in the list of available file servers.

The selected display and discovery options can be retained for the next time you run OmniClient by choosing **Save choices** from the Servers menu.

Mounting a file server

A file server can be mounted

- by clicking on a file server icon in the list of file servers
- by choosing a pre-saved file server from the icon bar icon menu
- by filling in a Mount dialogue box from the icon bar Mounts menu (this is for file servers which do not appear on the list of file servers)
- by specifying the file server to be automatically mounted (including the password if required) in the startup file.

Mounting a file server from the file server window

To connect to a particular server, double-click on its icon; either you will be connected directly with the server, and a directory display for the mount will appear, or a Mount dialogue box will be displayed:

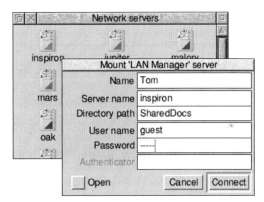

The **Name** field will be shown under the mount's icon on the icon bar, and can be any name of your choosing not already used. The **Server name** will be pre-filled. The optional **Directory path** is needed by some protocols to choose from several *mount points* that are on one server, in this example the SharedDocs directory is just one of several directories shared by Tom. The **User name** and **Password** fields are often not needed on an unsecured local area network; ask the owner of the computer if user level access permission is needed or not.

Mounting a pre-saved file server from the icon bar icon menu

If you have already mounted a file server, or saved the details of a mount in the Mounts file (see the section *The Mounts file* on page 184) then you can go to the **Mounts** submenu to display the (partially) completed dialogue box for that mount. All you will have to enter is the password, if one is expected.

This enables easy access to regularly accessed file servers.

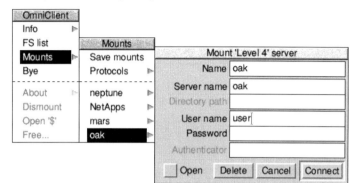

Mounting a file server which is not displayed in the file server window

If you need to mount a file server that is not displayed in the list of file servers, you can go to the **Protocols** submenu and click on one of the available protocols displayed. A dialogue box will then appear (with a default user) enabling you to enter all the necessary details before attempting to mount the file server.

For example:

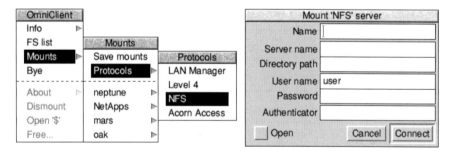

The **Authenticator** field is needed for the UNIX Network File System protocol to specify a second server where the user name and password can be verified. If you don't know the authenticator, enter nobody as the **User name** which will cause NFS to try to log in anonymously with limited access using a UID of 32767 and GID of 9999.

Mounting a file server automatically

You can mount one or more file servers automatically on starting up OmniClient by appending a list of *mount alias names* at the end of the OmniClient startup file. The list of mount names must follow the command *OmniMount, for example:

```
*OmniMount mars neptune
```

A mount alias is simply the name that appears under a mounted server icon on your icon bar and is the same as used for the **Name** field in the Mount dialogue box.

When the OmniClient application is started each called out mount alias is looked for in the mounts file (see the section *The Mounts file* on page 184). If the mount is with a filing system or server that needs no password, or if the password is in the mounts file, the mount will be accessed immediately and an icon will appear on the icon bar. If the mount requires a password, a Mount dialogue box is displayed for you to fill in.

It is also possible to have OmniClient use every mount alias in the mounts files without calling out each one individually using the command:

```
*OmniMount -all
```

After you have mounted a file server

When you have successfully logged on to a file server, an OmniClient icon with the name (i.e. the mount alias) of the new mount will appear on the icon bar. This now behaves like any other drive icon; if you click Select on it a directory display for the root of the mount will be opened with the Filer.

Enable the **Open** option in the Mount dialogue to automatically open the directory display when OmniClient first mounts the server.

Displaying available servers

After you have established a mount, to display the list of available servers you must either choose **FS list** from the OmniClient icon bar icon menu, or click Adjust (not Select) on the OmniClient icon.

Icon bar menu

Info

This gives you information about the OmniClient application, and each of the loaded protocols.

FS list

Displays the network server window, as described on page 178.

Mounts

Opens a submenu where previously saved mounts can be selected and new mounts established, as described on page 179.

Bye

Disconnects from all mounts that OmniClient has currently has open.

About

This gives you a summary of the connection information for the specific mount that you clicked Menu on.

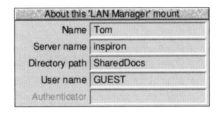

About this 'LAN Manager' mount	
Name	Tom
Server name	inspiron
Directory path	SharedDocs
User name	GUEST
Authenticator	

Dismount

Disconnects the specific mount that you clicked Menu on.

Open '$'

Opens the user root directory for the specific mount that you clicked Menu on.

Free...

This opens a dialogue box that gives you information about the free and used space on the specific mount that you clicked Menu on.

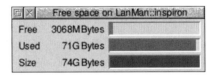

Free space on LanMan::inspiron	
Free	3068MBytes
Used	71GBytes
Size	74GBytes

Printing through an OmniClient protocol

Some protocol modules also provide remote printing facilities for networked printers which may be added through the Printer Manager as described in the section *Manually loading a printer definition file* on page 192.

1   Click Menu over the Printer control window and choose the **Connection...** option. This displays the Connections window.

2   Click on the **File** radio icon.

3   Enter a filename of the following form:
    ```
    OmniPrint#FilingSystem;Server;Printer;
            User;Password;Options;Size:
    ```

4   Save the new printers configuration.

The fields you must fill in are the *FilingSystem*, *Server* and *Printer* names, although the latter two may be the same for some situations. Note that *User*, *Password*, *Options* and *Size* are all optional fields.

The filename **must** end with a colon. Any filename given is ignored – the critical data is contained in the special field between the '#' and ':' symbols.

Examples:

```
OmniPrint#NFS;nixie;lp;fsmith:
OmniPrint#LanMan;xeon;photocopier;guest;guest:
```

For protocols that require the file size prior to the transmission of any data, an optional field *Size* can be included in the special field.

Unusual characters in printer names

Any characters in the special field which are illegal in RISC OS filenames should be encoded as follows:

RISC OS character	Encoded form	
Space	~_	(underscore)
"	~'	(apostrophe)
| (solidus)	~l	(lowercase L)
:	~1	(number one)
;	~!	
, (comma)	~.	
~	~~	

The encoded form will be translated by OmniClient before contacting the network printer.

Quitting OmniClient

To quit OmniClient, click on the Task Manager icon on the icon bar to display the Tasks window, click Menu over the OmniClient entry and choose **Task/Quit**.

Advanced OmniClient configuration

The Mounts file

The mounts file contains the details of any mounts you have specified. The file is saved in the Choices directory as `Omni.Mounts` when you choose **Mounts/Save mounts** from the OmniClient icon bar menu.

Mounts file contents

Each line of the mounts file contains information for one mount. Usually this will be all the information needed to connect a mount with the exception of the user's password, although this can be supplied if you are happy it is not a security problem.

The fields on each line are separated by a comma and white space of any sort other than a new line. The trailing fields on a line may be left off if the null string is to be used. Any line beginning with a '#' character is treated as a comment, and will be lost if the file is next saved from OmniClient's menu.

Below is an example mounts file:

```
# Mount list saved by OmniClient at 16:14:54 on 08 Nov 2014
#
# Protocol, Alias, Flags, Server, Path, User, Pass, Auth
#
LanMan,Tom,L,inspiron,SharedDocs,guest
Net,NetApps,L,NetApps,,Fred,letmein
Net,oak,P,oak,,Fred
Access,mars,HL,mars,,Fred
```

In the previous example the mount called NetApps could be mounted without typing a password (it has the one it needs). Also, note that Access does not require a password or authenticator to gain access to a hard disc or CD-ROM.

A null password can be represented in the mounts file with "" (i.e. two double-quotes without any spaces). This could be used where a guest account has no password, and the user doesn't wish to be prompted for a password to be entered.

Flags in the mounts file

The third column in the mounts file sets the flags field:

Letter	Feature	Meaning
L	Locked	Mounts with this flag present do not get saved into the user mounts file.
P	Preset	Mounts with this flag present do not appear in the mounts list submenu unless they are currently connected.
		Allows extra servers/mounts to be presented in the network servers window – perhaps non-local servers which protocols cannot automatically scan for.
		This flag has a higher priority than Hidden, and mounts file entries that mistakenly have both set will be treated as Preset.
H	Hidden	Mounts with this flag present do not appear in the mounts list submenu, in the 'servers' window, or on the icon bar.
		It is provided to allow for 'system' mounts which are used in a networked boot sequence (e.g. scrap area) but which remain hidden from the user. In conjunction with the Locked flag this permits system level complexity to be hidden by the network manager.
		Note that the Hidden flag will not prevent servers/mounts appearing in the 'servers' window that have been auto-located by a network scan (if this is enabled, see section *File server discovery* on page 178).
O	Open	Mounts with this flag present will **not** automatically be opened when mounted. This is the default feature flag.

Note that Preset and Hidden are mutually exclusive, since the purpose of Preset is to have mounts that cannot be located automatically (for whatever reason) appear in the servers window, and the purpose of Hidden is to stop them appearing.

Using more than one mounts file

If your computer is moved between networks and you wish to use an alternate set of mounts for the current network, it is possible to temporarily load extra mounts into memory in addition to the user mount file from the Choices directory.

Use the *OmniLoadMounts command to do this.

The Startup file

The startup file contains protocol settings to configure OmniClient when run. The file is saved in !Omni.Files.Startup which you may have already edited to enable or disable protocol modules as described on page 177.

Default user names

The Omni$User system variable sets the default user name used in Mount dialogue boxes.

You can also use the system variable Omni$User*FilingSystem* to set the value of the user name on a per filing system basis. If the variable is not set but Omni$User is set then the value of this will be used as the default user name.

For example:

```
Omni$UserNFS fsmith
Omni$User Fred
```

This would fill in the **User name** field with Fred's UNIX name for the Network Filing System, and simply 'Fred' for all other protocols.

Part 4 –
Printing

18 Setting up printers

All printing is handled by the Printer Manager, !Printers. This provides an interface between your printer and the file that is being printed.

Before you start printing, you need to set up the Printer Manager so that it is using the correct printer driver for your printer and communicates correctly with it.

If your printer is already set up correctly you can skip this chapter and find out how to print files by referring to *Printing your files* on page 207.

This chapter tells you how to

- set up and connect your printer
- choose which printer driver to use
- configure the printer driver.

Setting up the printer

Before you can print from your computer, you need three things:

- a suitable printer
- a printer cable, with connectors for the computer and the printer
- an appropriate printer driver

If you are connecting to a network printer, you'll need to make sure that you have the appropriate network connection for your computer. Contact your network manager for more information.

Types of printer supported

Your supplier will advise you on suitable printers for your computer. RISC OS supports most types of popular dot matrix, inkjet, and laser printers. It also supports laser printers using the PostScript standard.

The following printers are among those supported:

Acorn JP150	Apple Imagewriter
ArcFax modem fax machine	Brother HL series
Canon Bubblejet series	Citizen Swift series
ENCAD NovaJet	Epson EX, FX, JX & LX series
Epson MX & LQ series	Epson EPL series
Epson Stylus Colour	Fujitsu printers
HP LaserJet & DeskJet series	IBM Proprinter series
Integrex Colourjet	Linotype 100 and 200 printers
Mannesmann Tally MT series	NEC P series
Olivetti JP series	Panasonic printers
QMS ColourScript	Qume ScripTEN
Ricoh 6000 series	Star DP, LC & XB series
Star Laser Printers	TI OmniLaser printer

Most PostScript colour and monochrome laser printers

Other printers

If your printer is not on this list, check your printer's manual for more information because often your printer can be run in emulation mode. Most dot matrix printers can emulate the Epson FX or LQ printer. Most non-PostScript laser printers can emulate the HP LaserJet or DeskJet printers.

Printer Manager also supports direct-drive printers. These are high performance printers that connect directly to the computer using a specialised expansion card.

Connecting the printer

Universal Serial Bus

Your supplier will be able to advise you on which cables are suitable for connecting to a USB printer; the cable has a different shaped plug at each end so it is only possible to connect it one way round. Once connected the computer will detect the printer and query it to find out which model it is.

Serial and parallel

If your printer can use either of these types of connection, prefer to use the parallel port (it's quicker!). Your supplier will be able to advise you on which cables are suitable – a standard 25 pin male D-Sub to 36 pin Centronics printer cable will usually work for parallel, serial cables have either 9 or 25 pins depending on the printer and always a 9 pin female D-Sub to connect to the computer.

Econet and NFS

If you are connected to a network of computers, you may have access to a network printer or printer server. Consult your network manager for more information.

Direct drive

Direct drive printers connect to their own expansion card inside the computer. Consult the instructions provided with the card on how to proceed with connecting this to the printer.

Loading the Printer Manager

In this section we assume that you have connected your printer to one of the communication ports on your computer or that you're using a printer on a network.

The Printer Manager application, !Printers, provides an interface between the printer and your application software (an editor or word processor, for example). It's used for printing files, and to provide printer support for applications. To do this it uses printer definition files (often called printer drivers) to tell the computer what type of printer you are using.

1   Double-click on the !Printers icon (it's in the Apps icon bar directory).
    After a few seconds the Printer Manager icon appears on the icon bar.

2   Click Menu over the Printers icon on the icon bar and choose **Printer control...** which displays the Printer control panel:

Loading a printer definition file

For a USB connected printer, ensure the printer is switched on. Printer Manager will communicate with the printer and attempt to select the right printer driver, if this succeeds the driver is installed and you can move directly to *Configuring the printer* on page 193.

Unrecognised printers will result in Printer Manager asking how best to proceed:

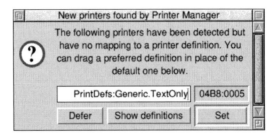

The 8 digits (in this example, 04B8:0005) displayed uniquely identify the make and model of printer you have which may be useful when talking to your supplier.

If you know the name of the printer driver, for example your supplier has recommended which to use, type the name of the printer driver file at the caret then click **Set**.

To browse the other available drivers click **Show definitions** to open the printer definition resources, select a suitable printer driver, then drop it onto the writable icon to replace the default filename. Once done, click **Set** to confirm the selection.

Should you be unsure at this time, click **Defer** to close the window. Printer Manager will ask again next time the printer is plugged in and powered on.

Manually loading a printer definition file

To load a printer definition file:

1 Choose **Install new printer** from the icon bar menu. This opens the printer definition resources.

2 Open the directory that corresponds with the manufacturer of your printer.

3 Double-click on the appropriate printer definition file.

   The definition file will have a similar name to that of your printer. See *Choosing a printer type* below.

   The printer name appears in the control window.

JP-150

4 If you want to have more than one printer loaded, double-click on additional printer definition files.

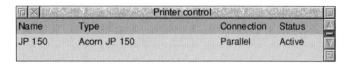

Choosing a printer type

You should choose the printer definition file that is closest to the printer you have. If there isn't a file specific to your printer, you may be able to choose one that's compatible. 9-pin dot matrix printers can usually emulate the Epson FX printer, while 24-pin dot matrix printers can usually emulate the Epson LQ printer; your printer manual should give details.

Non-PostScript laser printers can often emulate the HP LaserJet, or have a compatibility mode that emulates the HP LaserJet (or DeskJet); again, your printer manual should give details.

Configuring the printer

After you have loaded your printer driver, you must choose the correct printer configuration to give the results you want.

To display the configuration window, either double-click on the printer driver in the printer control window, or click Menu on the printer entry and choose **Configure**.

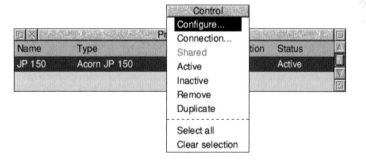

If you want to change the configuration of a printer that is already on the icon bar, click on the printer icon on the bar while holding down Shift.

There are three classes of printers:

● PostScript compatible printers (type PS)

● LaserJet and DeskJet compatible printers (type LJ)

● Dot matrix and Inkjet printers (type DP)

The following subsections describe how to configure each type of printer.

Configuring dot matrix and inkjet printers

 Dot matrix and inkjet-type printers use the Bit image printer configuration window:

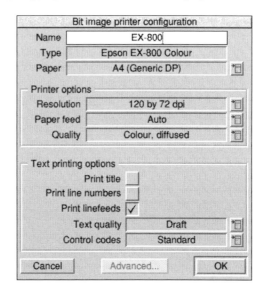

Choosing the printer name and paper type

The **Name** box gives the name that will appear beneath the printer icon on the icon bar. You can change this, if you wish, or leave it blank (in which case, the name is set to the connection type, e.g. Parallel).

The **Paper** box gives the paper size to be used by the printer. This is usually **A4 (Generic DP)**. If you want to change the paper size, click on the menu icon; this displays the **Paper sizes** menu. Choose the alternative paper size you wish to use. The correct paper sizes are marked **Generic DP**. You can also generate other page sizes using the **Edit paper sizes...** option from the icon bar menu (see page 204).

Printer options

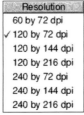

To display the printer **Resolution** menu, click on the menu icon. Increasing the resolution usually gives a better quality image, but printing usually takes longer. Note that some high resolutions (e.g. 720dpi on an Epson Stylus colour printer) are only useful on special paper; see the manual supplied with your printer.

To display the **Paper feed** menu, click on the menu icon. This menu lets you choose between Auto, Manual and Roll paper feed. Choose **Auto** if your printer has a sheet feeder or uses fanfold paper. Choose **Manual** if you have to insert each page by hand while printing is under way; you are prompted to insert paper at the end of each page. Choose **Roll** if your printer is using a paper roll.

194

The **Quality** menu lets you choose the type of printout quality. Click on the menu icon to display the menu.

- **Mono** prints black and white output only. It does not halftone fonts or sprites; it only halftones Draw files. This is the fastest print mode.

- **Grey** prints pictures in shades of grey. It halftones all types of files. You should always choose this option, unless speed of printing is more important than print quality, in which case choose **Mono** instead.

- **Colour** prints in colour on colour printers. Only use the lower quality modes (32k or 256 colours) if you're short of memory. You'll get the best results using the 16 million colour options.

- **halftoned (fine)** prints in 3×3 pixel halftones for grey scales and colour.

- **halftoned** prints in 6×6 pixel halftones. (Large) halftones give better quality than fine halftones.

- **diffused** usually gives the best quality results, especially for grey scale pictures (try halftone, as well, though). However it takes longer to print than the halftone options.

Text printing options

These options control the way text is printed from an editor (such as Edit).

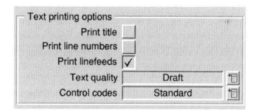

Print title puts the filename, time, date, and page number at the top of each page.

Print line numbers puts line numbers at the beginning of each line.

Print linefeeds sends a linefeed to the printer (as well as a carriage return) at the end of each line. If you find that your printer is producing a blank line after each line of text, you should turn this option **off**. If your printer is printing everything on one line, then you should turn this option **on**.

The **Text quality** menu controls the quality of the output print. Text quality can be either **No highlights, Draft** or **NLQ** (near letter quality). NLQ looks better but takes longer to print. (NLQ also uses more ink so the printer consumables run out quicker).

195

The **Control codes** menu alters the way in which text files are printed. This should normally be set to **Standard**. **Display** causes all control codes and top-bit-set characters to be printed in hexadecimal notation. **Ignore** causes all control codes and top-bit-set characters to be ignored.

When you have finished configuring your printer, click on **OK**. If you want to exit without saving your changes, click on **Cancel**.

Configuring LaserJet and DeskJet printers

LaserJet is the collective name given to all laser printers that can emulate the HP LaserJet printer.

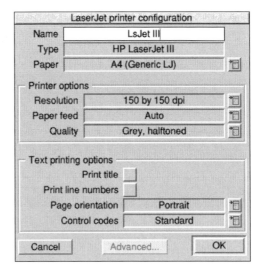

Choosing the printer name and paper type

The **Name** box gives the name that will appear beneath the printer icon on the icon bar. You can change this, if you wish, or leave it blank.

The **Paper** box gives the paper size to be used by the printer. This is usually A4 (Generic LJ) in Europe; if you are using a DeskJet explicitly change this to A4 (Generic DeskJet). If you want to change the paper size, click on the menu icon; this displays the **Paper sizes** menu. Choose the alternative paper size you wish to use. The paper sizes marked **Generic LJ** are usually best for LaserJet type printers; paper sizes marked **Generic DeskJet** are usually best for DeskJet type printers (including the Acorn JP150). It is also possible to generate other page sizes using the **Edit paper sizes...** option from the icon bar menu; see page 204 for more details.

Printer options

To display the printer **Resolution** menu, click on the menu icon. Increasing the resolution usually gives a better quality image, but printing usually takes longer. Most modern LaserJets (and LaserJet copies and clones) can use 300×300dpi. Some early models (LaserJet and LaserJet II) do not contain enough memory to print full page graphics at full resolution; in this case use 150×150dpi or purchase more memory.

To display the **Paper feed** menu, click on the menu icon. The menu lets you choose between Auto and Manual paper feed. Choose **Auto** if your printer has a sheet feeder or uses fanfold paper. Choose **Manual** if you have to insert each page by hand during printing.

The **Quality** menu lets you choose the type of printout quality. Click on the menu icon to display the menu.

- **Mono** prints black and white output only. It does not halftone fonts or sprites; it only halftones Draw files.

- **Grey** prints pictures in shades of grey. It halftones all types of files. Unless speed of printing is more important than print quality, choose this in preference to **Mono**.

- **Colour** prints in colour on colour printers. Only use the lower quality modes (32k or 256 colours) if you're short of memory. You'll get the best results using the 16 million colour options.

- **halftoned (fine)** prints in 3×3 pixel halftones for grey scales and colour.

- **halftoned** prints in 6×6 pixel halftones. (Large) halftones give better quality than fine halftones.

- **diffused** usually gives the best quality results, especially for grey scale pictures (try halftone, as well, though). However it takes longer to print than the halftone options.

Text printing options

The text printing options control the way text is printed from an editor (e.g. Edit).

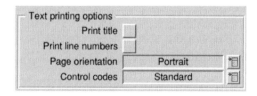

Print title puts the filename, time, date, and page number at the top of each page.

Print line numbers gives each page line numbers.

The **Page orientation** menu gives you a choice between portrait or landscape orientation text. Portrait prints along the shorter side of the paper while landscape prints along the longer side.

The **Control codes** menu alters the way in which text files are printed. This should normally be set to **Standard**. **Display** causes all control codes and top-bit-set characters to be printed in hexadecimal notation. **Ignore** causes all control codes and top-bit-set characters to be ignored.

When you have finished configuring your printer, click on **OK** then save the setup as described on page 203. If you want to exit without saving your changes, click on **Cancel**.

Configuring PostScript printers

PostScript is the name given to all laser printers that are PostScript-compatible.

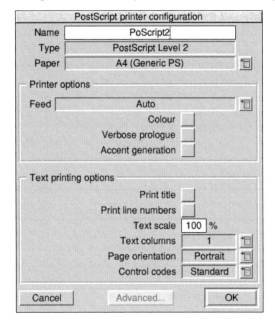

Choosing the printer name and paper type

The **Name** box gives the name that will appear beneath the printer icon on the icon bar. You can change this if you wish, or leave it blank.

The **Paper** box gives the paper size to be used by the printer. This is usually A4 (Generic PS). If you want to change the paper size, click on the menu icon; this displays the **Paper sizes** menu. Choose the alternative paper size you wish to use.

The paper sizes marked **Generic PS** are usually best for PostScript type printers. It is also possible to generate other page sizes using the **Edit paper sizes...** option from the icon bar menu; see page 204 for more details.

Printer options

To display the **Paper feed** menu, click on the menu icon. Normally the **Paper feed** option should be set to **Auto**. If you are feeding paper or envelopes through the manual feed choose **Manual**.

Choose **Colour** if you are printing in colour on a colour PostScript device.

Choose **Verbose prologue** if you wish to declare all of the PostScript printer fonts. This option gives you the same prologue as that used by the RISC OS 2.00 printer drivers; it is included for backward compatibility only. Do not choose this option unless your application requires it.

The **Accent generation** option will automatically generate accented characters even if they are not supported by your printer. Unless you need to print unusual accented characters such as w or y circumflex (used in Welsh) leave Accent generation off, as it slows printing and does not work with printers with small internal memory.

Text printing options

The text printing options allow you to control the way text is printed from an editor (such as Edit).

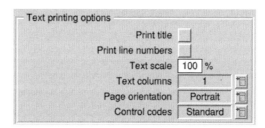

Print title puts the filename, time, date, and page number at the top of each page.

Print line numbers gives each page line numbers.

You can adjust the size of the printed type by giving a **Text scale** factor. PostScript printers have a wide range of available sizes, so you can scale the text from 20% to 200%. 100% gives standard sizes, 200% gives twice the size, and 50% gives half the size (twice as many characters per inch). Invalid sizes reset the text size to 100%.

To display the **Text columns** menu, click on the menu icon. Text columns specifies the number of columns of text to be printed on each sheet of paper. The Printer Manager defaults to one column for portrait printing and two for landscape printing.

To display the **Page orientation** menu, click on the menu icon. Page orientation allows choice of portrait or landscape orientation text. Portrait prints along the shorter side of the paper while landscape prints along the longer side.

Note: If you change this setting, the **Text scale** and **Text columns** values are reset to default values suitable for the current orientation.

The **Control codes** menu alters the way in which text files are printed. This should normally be set to **Standard**. **Display** causes all control codes and top-bit-set characters to be printed in hexadecimal notation. **Ignore** causes all control codes and top-bit-set characters to be ignored.

When you have finished configuring your printer, click on **OK** then save the setup as described on page 203. If you want to exit without saving your changes, click on **Cancel**.

Configuring the printer connection

Once you have loaded the printer driver, you need to set it up so that it can communicate with the printer.

Click Menu over the Printer control window. (If you are on an Access network and wish to share the printer connected to your machine, choose **Shared**.)

Choose **Connection...** to display the Connections window.

If you want to change the printer connection of a printer that is already set up on the icon bar, Shift-Adjust-click on the printer's icon.

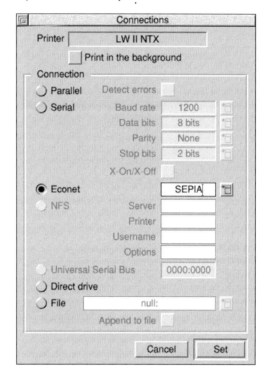

Printer connection options

The printer driver can send printed output to the printer using one of the connection methods described in *Connecting the printer* on page 190, or it can save printer output to a file for printing later.

Some of the options may be 'greyed out' so that you cannot choose them if that interface isn't present or is disabled on your computer.

Print in background allows you to choose whether you want to define the printer and printing speed as a high or low priority task. If the box is ticked printing can be slower, although you can continue to use the computer while the printing takes place. If this option is not ticked, printing can be quicker, although you will usually have to wait for printing to finish before you can use the computer again. This option only works with applications that send their files to the print queue; some applications bypass the queue.

Parallel allows you to connect a printer to the parallel port.

Serial allows you to connect a printer to the serial port. You can set the Baud rate, Data bits, Parity, Stop bits and XON/XOFF. To alter the values, click on the menu icon and choose a new value. Consult your printer manual for the correct values.

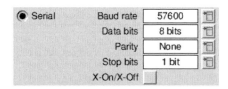

Econet allows you to connect to a Econet network printer. To use a different printer, click on the menu icon. Alternatively you can type in the name or station number of the printer to use.

NFS allows you to connect to printers available on UNIX Network File Server networks. For an explanation of how to fill in the NFS fields, ask your network manager. Alternatively, you may find it more convenient to use OmniClient to print using NFS, which is described in more detail in the section *Printing through an OmniClient protocol* on page 182.

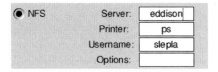

Universal Serial Bus allows you to select a USB printer. The 8 digits displayed uniquely identify the make and model of printer you have.

Direct drive allows you to connect a direct drive printer to the computer.

File allows you to send printer output to a file. Type the name of the file into the File field (using the complete pathname). Alternatively click on the menu icon and drag the **Save as** box to the desired directory display; your output will now be directed to this file.

Append to file works in conjunction with the **File** option. It adds printer output to the end of the file. Using this you can print several small files and produce a single file of the printed result. You must have Printer Manager loaded during printing, otherwise printing will over overwrite the file, rather than append to it.

Activating the printer

The Printer control menu allows you to make a printer **Inactive**, so that it can't be used and is not displayed on the icon bar. However, its settings are saved so you can used it later by simply choosing **Active**.

You can remove a printer from the Printer control window permanently by choosing **Remove** followed by **Save choices** from the icon bar menu.

Using more than one printer

If you have dragged more than one printer to the Printer control window you can activate them all. A printer icon is displayed on the icon bar for each active printer. This facility can be useful if you have a printer connected directly to your computer, and you also have access to another printer connected via a network.

Although you can have many printers activated on the icon bar, only one of these printers is highlighted; all of the others are greyed out. When you click on the Print option in an application, the file to be printed is sent to the highlighted printer.

You can choose to print using a different printer by clicking on that printer's icon on the icon bar. This highlights the new printer driver and greys out the old one.

You can also print using any of the printer drivers (highlighted or not) by dragging files directly onto the desired printer's icon.

Using one printer with more than one configuration

When several similar configurations for one printer are needed, for example to output to different paper trays, the Printer control menu can be used to **Duplicate** the current printer. You can then make any changes to the configuration for the duplicate, and activate and deactivate each variant as described above.

203

Editing paper sizes

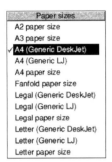

Paper sizes
A2 paper size
A3 paper size
✓ A4 (Generic DeskJet)
A4 (Generic LJ)
A4 paper size
Fanfold paper size
Legal (Generic DeskJet)
Legal (Generic LJ)
Legal paper size
Letter (Generic DeskJet)
Letter (Generic LJ)
Letter paper size

You can, if you wish, set up new page sizes for your printer. From the icon bar menu, display the **Edit paper sizes...** dialogue box. If you use one of the standard paper sizes you need not read this section.

From this dialogue box you can select your paper size by clicking on the menu icon and choosing a paper size. These are:

A2	594×420mm
A3	420×297mm
A4	297×210mm (the default option)
Fanfold	279×203mm
Legal	355.6×215.9mm
Letter	279.4×215.9mm

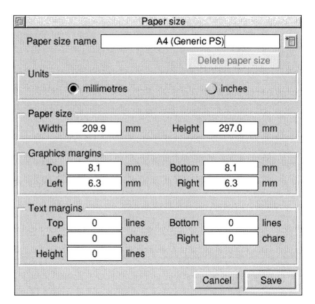

These are the generic types of page size. Additional sizes that fine-tune these dimensions are also given for the various printer types: DP for dot matrix printers, PS for PostScript printers and LJ for LaserJet and DeskJet for DeskJet printers. These additional sizes define the Graphics and Text margins for the printers.

204

Defining your own paper dimensions

Once you have selected your basic paper size you can fine-tune it to your own requirements. Change the name in **Paper size name** and change the **Height** and **Width** if you are using a special sized paper. Finally you can change the margins within which text and graphics will be printed. Click on the **Save** box to save the new paper dimensions for future use.

PostScript printers, and some other printers, need to know which tray to take paper from. This information is derived from the Paper size name. The name should therefore be in the form *paper size (name)*, where the paper size is the size of the paper in the paper tray. For example, Letter (memo-letter) will use paper in the Letter tray.

Note: Don't use the plain paper sizes directly (A3 paper size for example); they are only given to define the basic paper size. Always use a paper size defined for a particular printer – A4 (Generic DeskJet), for example.

If you wish you can delete a paper size by selecting it and then clicking on **Delete paper size.** You can only delete sizes that you have created or altered.

Graphics margins

The graphics margins must reflect the true printable area of the page (look this up in your printer manual). The margins ensure that graphics are printed properly and they are also used by applications (such as Draw). The margins correspond to those of a portrait page; landscape page values are worked out automatically. The graphics margins exist to tell the printer where to print on a piece of paper. The margins cannot be used to move the printed result around on the page.

Text margins

Text margins are measured as relative to the printable area of the page (defined by the graphics margins). The **Left** and **Right** margins are measured in characters and the **Top** and **Bottom** margins measured in lines. The **Height** is the total number of lines on a page, including the text margins. If you want to move the position of the text output on the page, alter the text margin settings.

PostScript and HP LaserJet compatible printers

For these printers, the total number of lines per page and characters per line are determined automatically.

The printer is configured to use 10 characters per inch and 6 lines per inch in portrait orientation and 14 characters per inch and 8.5 lines per inch in landscape orientation.

A LaserJet II cannot match these defaults exactly and uses its internal font at 10 characters per inch and 6 lines per inch in portrait orientation and 16.66 characters per inch and 8 lines per inch in landscape orientation instead.

PostScript printers determine the font size from the **Text scale** and **Text columns** values in the **Configure** dialogue box.

Changing the page length on dot matrix printers

If you require an unusual page length you should set it by altering the Text margins **Height** box, as well as the Graphics margins. For example, if you are printing labels, you may have six rows of labels on a sheet of A4 paper. Set the Text height to be something like 11 lines so that the printer will form feed to the start of the next label correctly. This is because the Text height is used to tell the printer how long the paper is for both text and graphics printing.

Saving your choices

You should save any changes you make to the settings for your printer or page sizes, otherwise you will have to go through the setting-up procedure again, next time you start the Printer Manager. To do this, choose **Save choices** from the printer icon bar menu.

Once you have saved your settings to disc, the Printer Manager automatically loads your printer driver and page sizes each time you start it.

Creating your own Printer definition file

Advanced users can create a *Printer definition file* that is specifically tailored for a particular printer. PrintEdit allows you to create a new printer driver (see page 215).

19   Printing your files

All printing is handled by the Printer Manager, !Printers. The Printer Manager looks after the job of sending the file you want printed to the printer and making sure that it is printed correctly.

This chapter assumes that you have already set up the printer driver configuration (or it has been set up for you) and that your computer is connected to the printer, either directly or via a network.

If you need more information, or you wish to configure some of the more advanced features of the Printer Manager, turn to *Setting up printers* on page 189.

Starting Printer Manager

Printer Manager is in the Apps icon bar directory display. To start Printer Manager, double-click on the !Printers application icon. After a few seconds the Printer Manager icon appears on the icon bar.

If you see more than one printer icon on the icon bar you will be able to print on more than one printer (or print in different ways on the same printer).

Printing a file

There are three ways you can print a file:

Drag the file you want printed to the printer icon

To print a Draw file, Paint file or other application file, drag the file (from a directory display or **Save as** box) onto the printer driver icon. If the application is not already running, it will be loaded before the file is printed (as long as the Filer has 'seen' the application).

For example, if you want to print a Draw file, Draw will be loaded onto the icon bar. However, Text files are printed directly (without loading Edit). While a file is being printed, **Printing** appears beneath the Printer Manager icon.

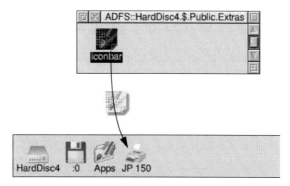

Choose the Print option from the application's menu

You can also print Paint and Draw files (and those of many other applications) by selecting **Print** from the appropriate menu:

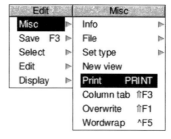

The **Print** option sometimes offers additional size or layout options; for example in the Paint application:

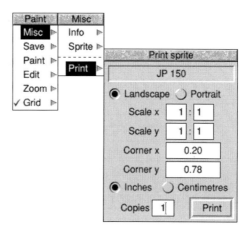

Press the Print Screen key on the keyboard

Alternatively you can press Print Screen on the keyboard. This will often lead to the same print dialogue box as through the application's menu.

Stopping a print job

You can stop a print job by pressing Menu over the Printer queue window and choosing **Delete entry** (see page 211).

You can also stop a print job at any time by pressing Escape, although the above method is preferable. After pressing Escape you should reset your printer (see your printer's manual for details on how to do this); this allows the printer to be ready for printing again. This may not work with text print jobs.

Things you can't print

You cannot print directories and applications; if you try to do so you will see an error message.

If you try and print a file and RISC OS cannot find the application associated with the file, a dialogue box asks if the file should be printed as plain or fancy text.

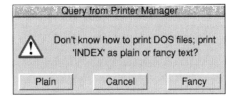

If you see a message like this, you should click on **Cancel** and try to find the application that the file requires to print properly. For an application to be known to RISC OS it must have been displayed in a directory display.

If you don't have the application, try printing it using the **Plain** option. The **Fancy** option is most often used to print files created using the 1st Word Plus word processor application.

Using more than one printer

If you see more than one printer icon on the icon bar you will be able to print on more than one printer (or print in different ways on the same printer). For example, you might have a printer connected directly to your computer and another printer connected via a network.

Although you can have many printers on the icon bar, only one of these can be selected at a time; all of the others are greyed out. When you choose the **Print** option in an application or press the Print Screen key, the file to be printed is sent to the selected printer.

To print using a different printer, click on that printer's icon on the icon bar. This selects the chosen printer and greys out all others. You can also print using any of the printers (selected or not) by dragging files onto the desired printer's icon.

Using the same printer with different options

You can also set up several printer icons that print to the same printer but use different print options. For instance, ones set up with different print resolutions and quality. If you need more information, turn to *Setting up printers* on page 189.

Print queue control

Printing several files

You can print several files one after another by dragging their icons onto the printer icon on the icon bar. You can select multiple files to be printed and then drag their icons onto the printer icon together. The files waiting to be printed are placed in the printer queue. You don't have to wait until one has finished printing before sending the next.

The print queue

Files to be printed wait in a print queue until the printer is ready for them. This way you can carry on with your work at the same time as the printer is printing.

To control the print queue, choose **Queue control** from the Printer Manager icon bar menu. This displays a list of files to be printed in the **Printer queue** window. You can also display this window by clicking Adjust on the printer icon on the icon bar.

The Queue menu

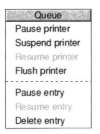

Clicking Menu over the Printer queue window displays the **Queue** menu from which you control the printer.

Pause printer stops sending your file to the printer. The rest of the unprinted part of the currently printing file is not printed until you click on **Resume printer**.

Suspend printer prints the file currently being printed and then stops the printer. No further files are printed until you click on **Resume printer**. The printer queue is frozen in its current state.

Flush printer removes all files currently in the queue.

Pause entry stops the current entry from printing until you click on **Resume entry**.

Delete entry removes an entry from the queue completely**.**

If you click Menu over one of the other entries in the printer queue (an entry not currently printing) you can choose the additional **Suspend entry** option. **Suspend entry** stops the printer from printing a file in the print queue. The print queue 'jumps over' the suspended file. The file can be put back in the queue to be printed by clicking on **Resume entry**.

These controls only effect your personal printer queue; they have no effect on other users using a shared network printer.

Text printing and graphics printing

Your computer uses two modes of printing: text printing and graphics printing.

Text printing

Text printing sends only characters to the printer, such as text from the application Edit. These characters are printed using the standard font built into the printer, which makes text printing very fast. Check your printer's manual to see if it offers a text printing facility or not.

There are two types of text printing – P*lain* and F*ancy*. The way in which a file is printed depends upon its type:

● Command and Obey files are always printed as plain text.

● Text files are always printed as fancy text (where you can also embed 1st Word Plus control codes in the text).

Graphics printing

Graphics printing sends a complete image to the printer, effectively making the printed output the same as that seen on the screen. The applications Paint and Draw use graphics printing. If you print a JPEG file (photo-realistic image) by dragging its file icon to the Printer Manager, that also uses graphics printing.

This section refers only to dot matrix, inkjet and HP LaserJet type printers; PostScript printers handle graphics printing in a different way.

You can speed up graphics printing in the following ways:

- Print in monochrome instead of grey scale. You only need grey scale if you are printing fonts, or printing sprites in shades of grey or in colour.

- Maximise the free memory in your computer by quitting all the applications you are not currently using and any RAM disc you may have.

- Configure a fairly large font cache – at least 256kB. You can change the font cache temporarily using the Task Manager. See page 74 for information.

Printing other file types

- PostScript files (with the file type PoScript) are sent to the PostScript printer for interpretation.

- Other files check with their respective application to see how they are printed.

Saving your choices

You should save any changes you make to the settings for your printer, otherwise you will have to go through the setting-up procedure again, next time you start the Printer Manager. To do this, click on the **Save choices** option on the printer icon bar menu.

212

Using PostScript printers

You don't need to read this section unless you are printing to a PostScript printer.

Dot matrix, LaserJet and inkjet printers use RISC OS fonts for both displaying text on screen and for graphics printing. PostScript printers, however, use RISC OS fonts for displaying text on screen and use PostScript fonts for printing. These PostScript fonts can be both built into the printer and downloaded by (sent from) the computer.

Whenever you send a file to the printer, the Printer Manager

- converts any fonts needed to their equivalent in PostScript (if they are not already resident in the printer)
- sends these fonts to the printer
- sends the file to be printed
- erases the fonts it has sent.

The Printer Manager uses the printer's built-in PostScript fonts when they are available, speeding up printing text files considerably.

Speeding up printing

There are other (more advanced) ways of speeding up printing. These options are handled by the FontPrint application. They are *downloading* and *mapping*:

Downloading

If you constantly use fonts that are not resident inside the PostScript printer, you may find that your files print faster if you pre-send (download permanently) the fonts when you first start using the Printer Manager. Permanently downloaded fonts stay inside the printer, ready for use, until the printer is reset or switched off.

Mapping

Instead of fonts being downloaded to the printer they can instead be mapped to a corresponding PostScript font. Mapping is the technique by which a RISC OS font is used by the computer, but the equivalent PostScript font is used by the printer. For example, the font Homerton Medium is always mapped to the PostScript font Helvetica. This way the built-in PostScript fonts are used whenever possible.

For information on how to download and map fonts, refer to the chapter *FontPrint* on page 227.

Hints and tips

Attempting to print to non-existent printers

If you attempt to print to a printer which is not connected to your computer, the computer can freeze, waiting for the printer to be connected. Try using the System monitor (see page 77) or pressing Escape to stop the print job. If that fails, you may need to restart your computer.

Blank pages on dot matrix printers

If you find that a dot matrix printer with fan-fold paper is printing alternate blank pages, try turning off the printer's form feed if it is switchable, or reduce the number of lines printed per page on the **Edit paper sizes...** dialogue box.

Printing BASIC listings

To print a listing of a BASIC program, drag the program file from a directory display to your printer icon. This will print it as text even if the program itself is tokenised.

Printing Maestro music files

To print a Maestro music file, you have first to load it into Maestro and choose Print, rather than just drag it from a directory display to your printer icon.

20 PrintEdit

This chapter provides an introduction to PrintEdit, an application which enables experienced users to edit existing printer definition files and experts to create them from scratch. It's unlikely that you'll need the information in this chapter, but it's provided for reference.

Printer definition files are used by the Printer Manager application. They define how the operating system translates the characters in the document into signals that can be used by the printer to print the document.

Creating new printer definition files

Creating printer definition files is technically very complex and requires a deep understanding of how printers work. This chapter gives you only a very brief introduction and you should not expect to be able to design your own printer definition files using the information provided here alone. The chapter *Printer definition files* in the RISC OS *Programmer's Reference Manual* contains the detailed information you will need for creating printer definition files.

Modifying existing printer definition files

Occasionally, step-by-step instructions might be issued by your printer supplier that tell you how to modify an existing printer definition file to change its use slightly.

The instructions list the exact operations you need to perform in each PrintEdit window. You will not need a full understanding of the features of PrintEdit.

The overview of PrintEdit in this chapter should give you enough information to enable you to use the application to alter one of the existing printer definition files.

Before you can use PrintEdit you should

● have the user guide and technical manual for your printer, or

● have some step-by-step instructions from an expert.

Most people use PrintEdit to alter one of the existing printer definition file configurations, rather than make up a completely new one. So we shall use the printer definition file for the Epson FX-85 as an example.

Starting PrintEdit

PrintEdit is in the Printing directory on your hard disc or network. To start the application, double-click on the !PrintEdit application icon. The application icon appears on the icon bar.

To load an existing printer definition file:

1   With Printer Manager loaded, choose **Install new printer** from the icon bar menu.

2   Open the printer directory that corresponds to the printer you wish to modify.

3   Select the printer definition file you require and drag it over the PrintEdit icon on the icon bar.

    Note: You can also load non-PostScript printer definition files by double-clicking on them.

The PrintEdit window

The appearance of the PrintEdit window when the Epson FX-85 definition file is loaded is as follows:

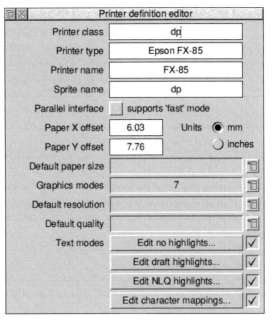

The **Printer class** represents a type of printer; it determines which processing type Printers uses for the printer. Use **dp** for dot matrix and other bit-image printers and **lj** for HP LaserJet compatibles. This application cannot be used for defining printer definition files for PostScript printers.

Printer type is the full name of the printer. If you are creating an alternative version of a standard printer definition file, alter this name.

Printer name is the name you want to appear underneath the printer icon on the icon bar. The name can be up to 10 characters long. If you are creating an alternative version of a standard printer definition file, alter this name.

Sprite name is the sprite to be used as the printer icon on the icon bar. These can again be **dp** for dot matrix and other bit-image printers and **lj** for HP LaserJet compatibles. You can also define your own sprites for this icon.

If your printer's parallel port supports the fast parallel handshaking protocol then choose this option for its **Parallel Interface**. Check in the printer technical manual for information; if you're not sure, don't use this option.

The paper offsets represent the top (Y) and left (X) sections of the paper on which the printer cannot physically print. Together the paper offsets define the logical (0,0) origin on the paper. Offsets only affect graphics printing.

The **Paper X offset** is the small section at the lefthand edge on which the head cannot print, although why this is so is not always obvious.

The **Paper Y offset** is the amount of cut sheet paper which has already gone past the print head before it can print anything; this differs for different printer models.

Default paper size defines the standard paper type used by the printer.

Graphics modes displays how many graphics modes have been defined for this printer.

Default resolution defines the resolution that will be picked when you first install the printer.

Default quality defines the print quality that will be picked when you first install the printer.

Text modes defines the type of text modes your printer can use. Find this information out from your printer manual.

- **Edit no highlights** defines the simplest print options of plain text only.
- **Edit draft highlights** includes all the standard highlights such as bold, italic, superscript and subscript in draft mode.
- **Edit NLQ highlights** is the same as Edit draft highlights but for the NLQ (Near Letter Quality) mode.

Graphics mode

- **Edit character mappings** allows a character from the Latin1 character set to be converted to the same character in the printer's character set.

The differing text mode titles (**Edit portrait mode** and **Edit landscape mode** rather than 'Edit no highlights', 'Edit draft highlights' and 'Edit NLQ highlights') are set up by PrintEdit when the **Printer class** is **lj**. The information is still stored in exactly the same way as for **dp** class.

For the rest of this chapter you should have your printer manual ready so that you can look up the information required by PrintEdit. It may also help to have the Help application active, as this will give you quick summaries about the function of each field in the dialogue boxes.

Graphics mode

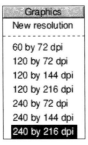

Display the Graphics modes dialogue box by clicking on the right arrow by the **Graphics modes** entry. Choose an existing resolution to edit or **New resolution** if you want to start afresh. In most cases it is probably easier to edit an existing file and tailor it to your needs. Here is the Graphics mode window for the Epson FX-85 at a resolution of 240×216dpi.

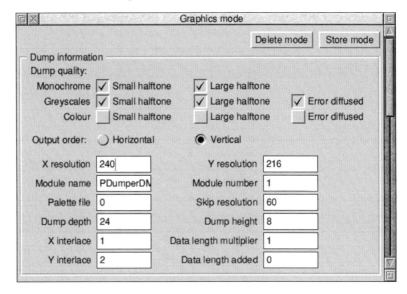

Dump information

The first part of the window gives the **Dump information** – the information the printer uses to print correctly.

The **Dump quality** boxes should normally all be ticked, as the software supports these features on all printers. However, don't tick the colour options unless you have a colour printer.

Output order defines how the image is printed. Most printers use **Vertical**. Some, like the Integrex Colourjet 132, use **Horizontal**. Note that when **Horizontal order** has been selected many of the other **Dump information** and **Dump strings** settings either become irrelevant, or must be set to certain values.

X (horizontal) and **Y resolution** (vertical) define the graphics resolution in dots per inch. These should be given in your printer manual, but may be in different units. The printer manual will usually quote resolutions before vertical interlacing has been applied (see later), so in this case the manual would quote 240×72dpi, rather than 240×216dpi (since 216/3 = 72). The manual is also likely to give dots per line rather than dots per inch for the horizontal resolution; for example, 960 dots per line on 8 inch paper is 120dpi horizontal resolution. The vertical resolution is often omitted altogether, in which case it is likely to be 72dpi for 9-pin printers, 180dpi for 24-pin printers doing 24-pin graphics, 60dpi for Epson 24-pin printers doing emulated 8-pin graphics, and 72dpi for IBM 24-pin printers doing emulated 8-pin graphics.

Module name and **Module number** define the dumper files used by the printer. These are currently four dumper files, although more can be defined if needed.

PDumperCX:	Module number 11 (Canon Extended Mode compatible printers)
PDumperCX2:	Module number 14 (same as PDumperCX, except for a different margin escape code)
PDumperDM:	Module number 1 (dot matrix and other bit-image printers)
PDumperE2:	Module number 6 (ESC/P2 compatible printers, such as the Epson Stylus Colour printer)
PDumperIW:	Module number 3 (Apple Imagewriter II compatible printers)
PDumperLJ:	Module number 2 (HP LaserJet compatible printers)

Palette file defines the Palette file – this is currently set to zero or one.

Skip resolution defines the leading zero skip resolution of the dump. This is always 60 for Epson printers and 120 for IBM printers.

Dump depth is the depth of one group of interlace passes.

Dump height is the number of rows of pixels in each vertical pass. This is the same as the number of pins on the print head; a 24-pin printer would print 24 dots.

X interlace defines the number of horizontal interlace passes.

Y interlace defines the number of vertical interlace passes.

Data length multiplier and **Data length added**. For Epson printers, you specify a line of graphics by saying '<27><42><0><number of columns>'. For IBM printers, you need '<27>|g<number of columns times 6 (or 3) plus 1><graphics mode>'. So, for Epson printers, the Data length multiplier is 1 and Data length added is 0. For IBM printers, Data length multiplier is either 6 or 3, and Data length added is 1.

Additional Dump information for Printer Class lj

Copies should be selected if the printer supports this option.

Compression should be selected if the printer supports this option.

The Output order choices do not apply for this class of printer.

Dump strings

The second part of the window gives the Dump strings (use the scroll bar to see this).

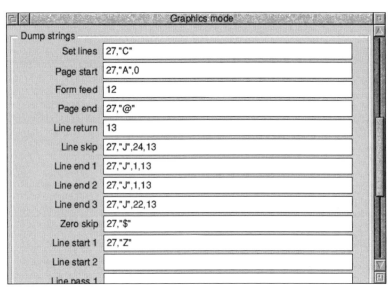

These are codes sent to the printer that tell it to perform certain actions.

Set lines is the string set to define the number of lines per page.

Page start is the string sent at the start of a page.

Form feed is the form feed character. The string sent to the printer to tell it to form feed the paper after each page has been printed.

Page end is the string sent at the end of each page.

Line return moves the print head to the beginning of the line. Usually this will be a carriage return.

Line skip moves the print head to the beginning of the next line. It is used for skipping entirely blank lines.

Line end 1 to **Line end 3** are the strings sent at the end of each vertical interlace pass. There can be up to three passes.

Zero skip is issued to skip leading zeros on graphics data lines, hence optimising out the white section at the left hand edge of the paper.

Line start 1 is the string sent at the beginning of a graphics line. For Epson printers, **Line start 2** is not needed. For IBM printers, **Line start 2** must be '<graphics mode>', while **Line start 1** is '<27>|g'.

Line pass is the string sent for each pass of a colour graphics dump. There can be up to four passes.

Text modes

Almost all printers can use the first two text modes and many also support an NLQ (Near Letter Quality) mode.

Choose which text modes your printer will use by clicking on the tick next to each Text mode button. Changing to a tick allows you to select that mode.

Display the text mode window by clicking on the appropriate text mode button. Here are the Text draft highlights settings for the Epson FX-85.

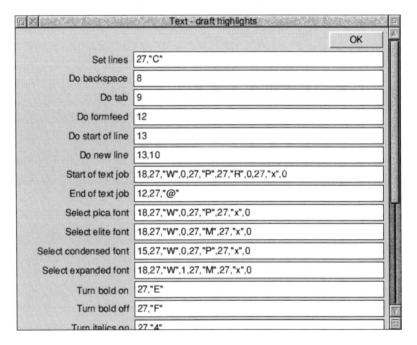

	Text - draft highlights
	OK
Set lines	27,"C"
Do backspace	8
Do tab	9
Do formfeed	12
Do start of line	13
Do new line	13,10
Start of text job	18,27,"W",0,27,"P",27,"R",0,27,"x",0
End of text job	12,27,"@"
Select pica font	18,27,"W",0,27,"P",27,"x",0
Select elite font	18,27,"W",0,27,"M",27,"x",0
Select condensed font	15,27,"W",0,27,"P",27,"x",0
Select expanded font	18,27,"W",1,27,"M",27,"x",0
Turn bold on	27,"E"
Turn bold off	27,"F"
Turn italics on	27,"4"

Edit no highlights

The no highlights mode is a very simple mode without any special effects, so most of this window is blank.

Set lines sets the number of lines per page.

Do backspace moves the print head back one space.

Do tab moves the print head to the next tab.

Do formfeed starts a new page.

Do start of line moves the print head to the start of the line.

Do new line moves the print head to the beginning of the next line.

Start of text job is the string that denotes the start of a text print.

End of text job is the string sent at the end of a text print.

Edit draft highlights

The draft highlights mode uses the same basic definitions as the no highlights mode, but expands this to include pica, elite, condensed, expanded, bold, italics, light, superscript, subscript and underline printing.

Select pica font sets pica font (10cpi).

Select elite font sets elite font (12cpi).

Select condensed font sets condensed font (17cpi).

Select expanded font sets expanded font (6cpi).

Turn bold on sets bold text on.

Turn bold off sets bold text off.

Turn italics on sets italic text on.

Turn italics off sets italic text off.

Turn light on sets light text on.

Turn light off sets light text off.

Turn superscript on sets superscript text on.

Turn superscript off sets superscript text off.

Turn subscript on sets subscript text on.

Turn subscript off sets subscript text off.

Turn underline on sets underline text on.

Turn underline off sets underline text off.

Edit NLQ highlights

The NLQ highlights mode uses the same basic definitions as the draft highlights mode, but alters these to enable the printer's NLQ operation.

Edit character mappings

Edit character mappings allows a character from the Latin1 character set to be converted to the same character in the printer's character set. Although all the standard characters normally map directly onto the corresponding printer characters, the top-bit-set characters normally need mapping where they differ from the printer's character set table.

Mapping is done from the Edit character mappings window. Here is part of the Epson FX-85's character mappings.

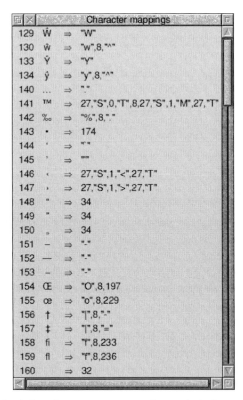

The number down the left column represents the Latin1 character in decimal; next to it is the character itself in the desktop font. To the right of the arrow are the commands sent to the printer that reproduce the same character.

Modifying an existing mapping

To alter an existing mapping:

1 Press Menu over the character to display the **Mappings** menu.

2 Choose **Mappings/Modify** to display the Modify mapping dialogue box.

3 If you want to modify the printer commands, type the printer commands that produce the character in the **Maps to** box.

4   Press Return to modify the mapping list.

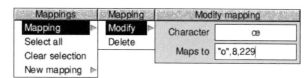

Entering a new character mapping

To enter a mapping:

1   Press Menu to display the **Mappings** menu.

2   Go to the **New mapping** dialogue box and type in the Latin I character to map in the **Character** box. You can type the character by using the Chars application or by using its decimal character code as described in *Typing special characters* on page 14.

3   Type the printer commands that produce the same character in the **Maps to** box.

4   Press Return to add the mapping to the list.

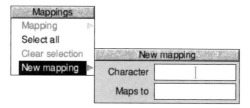

Saving and quitting

When you have finished making changes to your the printer definition file, save the modified file by clicking Menu over the main Printer definition editor window and choosing **Save**.

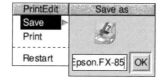

If you want to discard any changes you have made and start again click on **Restart**.

To finish using the application, choose **Quit** from the icon bar:

21   FontPrint

This application allows you to download fonts to a PostScript printer or to map RISC OS fonts to PostScript fonts on a PostScript printer. Once downloaded, the fonts stay in the printer until you reset or switch off the printer.

If you don't print to a PostScript printer you don't need to use this application.

RISC OS fonts are used both for displaying text on screen and for printing on dot matrix, LaserJet and InkJet printers. PostScript printers use PostScript fonts that are stored in the printer for printing.

When you print to a PostScript printer, the Printer Manager has to make sure that for each RISC OS font used there is an equivalent or suitable PostScript font available in the printer.

FontPrint is a tool for configuring this aspect of PostScript printing. It allows you to tell the Printer Manager which PostScript fonts are present in the printer and how your RISC OS fonts correspond to those in the printer.

It is important to understand that even if you don't use this application, RISC OS and the Printer Manager will always try to print your documents correctly. Any fonts that are not available in the printer will be downloaded within the print job as required.

Starting FontPrint

Before running FontPrint you must have the Printer Manager application loaded onto the icon bar. The Printer Manager must also be active and configured with the correct printer driver for your PostScript printer.

To start the application:

1   Click on the hard disc icon to view the directory display.

2   Double-click on the Printing directory icon to display the contents of the Printing directory.

Printing

3   Double-click on the !FontPrint application to start the application. The application icon appears on the icon bar.

4   To start using the application, click on the FontPrint icon on the icon bar.

The Printer Manager makes RISC OS fonts available to the printer in one of two ways: *mapping* and *downloading*.

Mapping

The first, preferred, way of making fonts available to a printer is to map the RISC OS font to a PostScript font that is already resident in the printer's ROM. The Printer Manager instructs the printer to substitute fonts; for example, whenever the print job uses Corpus, the printer substitutes Courier. This technique is particularly useful for the standard RISC OS font families Corpus, NewHall, Selwyn, Sidney, Trinity and Homerton because they are visually close copies of the standard PostScript font families Courier, New Century Schoolbook, ZapfDingbats, Symbol, Times and Helvetica.

The standard set of RISC OS fonts are mapped to PostScript fonts (except for System and Sassoon, which are downloaded 'on the fly' each time you use them). You can map additional RISC OS fonts you have purchased to the same, or other PostScript fonts. This gives the most efficient way of printing with your fonts, but may give results that differ slightly from those on-screen due to slight variations in the design of the fonts.

Mapping a RISC OS font to a PostScript font

To map an RISC OS font to a PostScript font:

1   Load FontPrint and display the FontPrint window.

The window displays lines consisting of the RISC OS font name on the left and the equivalent PostScript font name on the right.

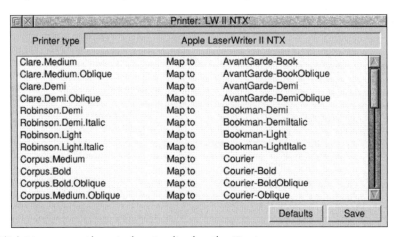

2   Click Menu over the window to display the **Fonts** menu.

3 If the RISC OS fonts you wish to map are not already shown, select the fonts that you wish to map to PostScript fonts from the **Add font** submenu. They will be added to the FontPrint window at the end of the list.

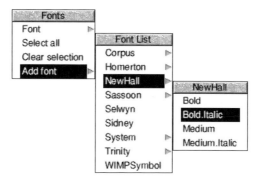

4 Choose each font in turn and map it to the corresponding PostScript font using the **Font/Map to** submenu, which lists the fonts available on the printer.

5 When you have finished mapping the fonts, click on **Save**. This saves the font mapping with Printer Manager's choices which will now use this information to map fonts in your documents to those in your printer. Each time the Printer Manager is started this font mapping information is sent to the printer.

Mapping to a non-standard PostScript font

If you want to map to an additional PostScript font resident in the printer (you may have an additional font cartridge for the printer), but which is not in the standard list of fonts in the printer driver, you can add the PostScript name in the field at the end of the **Map to** submenu. Repeat this for each font you want to add.

Choosing the encoding type

If you are mapping fonts, you can also choose **Font/Encoding**. The *encoding type* determines the character set used by the PostScript printer. Most fonts will use the Adobe standard encoding; this is the default encoding.

Downloading

The second way of making a RISC OS font available to a PostScript printer is to download the font into the printer. The Printer Manager converts the RISC OS font into the PostScript language and sends this to the printer. The print job may then use the font as if it were stored in the printer. The disadvantage of downloading is that fonts take a long time to send to the printer and occupy a lot of the printer's memory.

229

Downloading fonts permanently

Downloading normally happens automatically during the print job, and fonts downloaded in this way are erased from the printer's memory at the end of the job.

If you constantly use fonts that are not resident inside the PostScript printer, you may find that your files print faster if you download the fonts permanently when you first start using the Printer Manager. Permanently downloaded fonts stay inside the printer, ready for use, until the printer is reset or switched off.

To prepare fonts for downloading:

1   Click Select on the FontPrint icon to display the FontPrint window.

2   Click Menu over the window to display the **Fonts** menu.

3   Select the RISC OS fonts that you wish to download by choosing the fonts from the **Add font** submenu. They will be added to the FontPrint window at the end of the list.

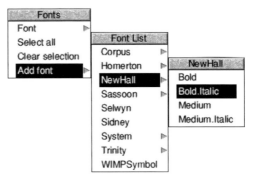

4   When you have selected the fonts you wish to download, click on the **Save** box. This saves the font mapping with Printer Manager's choices.

5   The PostScript font password box is displayed. You should now type in the password for your printer.

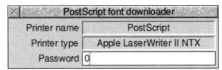

Unless the password has been changed, the printer will have the password '0' (the number zero).

The fonts are only downloaded if you type in the correct password. If you enter the wrong password, FontPrint still attempts to download the fonts but the download fails and the printer may issue an error message.

When you clicked on the **Save** box you stored the information about which fonts you wanted downloaded. The Printer Manager downloads your chosen fonts to the printer whenever the Printer Manager is started. The password box will be displayed each time you start using the Printer Manager.

Clicking on the **Default** button automatically loads the default PostScript Mappings. Any Mappings or Downloading that you have previously set up are lost.

Saving FontPrint settings

To save any changes you've made permanently, so that font mappings will be used every time you switch on, you need to choose **Save choices** from the Printers icon bar menu.

Downloading fonts to a network printer server

Since a network printer is a shared resource, excessive use of permanent font downloading can inconvenience other users. To avoid this, it is suggested that only one machine on the network should be responsible for permanently downloading fonts.

Other machines may then map to the downloaded fonts as if they were ROM fonts within the printer. This is possible because you can identify the PostScript name under which the downloaded font is stored. The downloaded name is the RISC OS font name prefixed by the letters 'DL_'. For example, if one machine has downloaded the RISC OS font called "Futura.Bold", it will be stored in the printer as the PostScript font "DL_Futura.Bold". Other machines wanting to print this font can use FontPrint to map "Futura.Bold" to "DL_Futura.Bold". Be careful to preserve the capitalisation of the font name. If the printer is switched off and on, the font will be lost. In this case, exit and re-start Printers on the machine responsible for downloading and the fonts will be downloaded again.

Bitmap fonts

You cannot download bitmap fonts to a PostScript printer. However, you can map them to one of the printer's resident fonts.

Advanced information

To avoid the overhead of downloading every font you use, the printer driver uses the fonts built into the PostScript device whenever possible. To do this, the printer driver has a list describing which PostScript fonts are visually similar to which RISC OS fonts.

This list is set up automatically when you initialise a new printer, and you can subsequently change it using FontPrint.

Although a PostScript font might look very similar to a particular RISC OS font, the various glyphs can occupy different character codes, with the result that characters are jumbled when the font is printed.

A mechanism called 'remapping' is used to reorder the PostScript font so that the characters occupy the expected positions. The remapping is performed according to a textual description known as an 'encoding'.

Mapping symbol fonts

A symbol font's mapping depends on the availability of an appropriate encoding file. The encoding tells the system which PostScript glyph to render for each ASCII character code.

The encoding file should be given the name `Encoding` and placed in the same directory as the font's Outlines and IntMetrics files. If you need an encoding file for a third party font, contact your vendor.

An encoding file should contain exactly 256 lines of the form

`/glyphname`

where a glyph called *glyphname* is known to exist in the printer font.
Non-existent glyphs should be entered as `/.notdef`.

If a particular glyph name is the Nth entry in the encoding file, then that glyph will be rendered for character code N.

For details about how to construct your own encoding files refer to the RISC OS *Programmer's Reference Manual*.

Part 5 –
RISC OS applications

22 RISC OS applications

This chapter introduces the suite of applications provided with your RISC OS computer which are covered in this part, Part 6 – RISC OS *diversions* and Part 7 – RISC OS *utilities*. Many more are available from your supplier.

This chapter tells you where to look for the applications supplied with your computer. The next two chapters describe how to choose and work with colours and fonts.

Four main applications are provided. These are comprehensive programs that show off the power and versatility of RISC OS.

- **Edit** – a fully featured text editor (also suitable for editing program listings).
- **Draw** – a sophisticated drawing program capable of producing full colour drawings.
- **Paint** – a painting and sprite editing program.
- **Printers** – a manager allowing you to print your work on a number of different types of printer (see Part 4 – *Printing*).

Where to look for applications

Your computer comes supplied with many useful applications. They're stored in the following locations:

- the computer's internal memory (ROM), which you can access from the Apps icon on the icon bar
- different directories on the hard disc or network

Start by familiarising yourself with the locations of the different applications:

1 Click on the Apps directory on the icon bar to see the main applications.

2 Click on the hard disc (or network) icon and explore the various applications directories there.

The icon bar Apps directory

Apps

Click on the Apps icon on the icon bar and you'll see a directory display containing some of the more important applications. The three most generally-used applications (Edit, Draw and Paint) are among those shown here.

Changing the contents of the icon bar Apps directory

You can't remove or delete any of the applications displayed here by default, but you can add applications from the hard disc, using the Boot setup plug-in of Configure. This saves you having to search the directories on your hard disc to load an application that you use frequently – you can see it with a single click on the Apps icon on the icon bar.

For more information turn to *Boot setup plug-in* on page 85.

Applications stored on hard disc

Click on the hard disc (or network) icon on the icon bar and you'll see many directories containing the other applications.

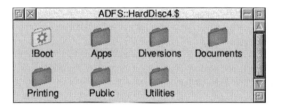

Each of the applications provided with RISC OS 5 has a separate chapter in this Guide. The main applications are covered in this part, followed by *Part 6 – RISC OS diversions*, and lastly *Part 7 – RISC OS utilities*. Those concerned with printing were dealt with earlier in *Part 4 – Printing*.

Note: Double-click on a directory to open its display, as normal. However, if you double-click on !Boot you'll actually start the Configure application (see page 81).

Starting applications

This is introduced in section *Starting an application* on page 29. To recap, there are three ways of starting an application:

● Double-clicking on an application icon.

  Clicking or double-clicking on the name next to an icon in a directory display has the same effect as clicking or double-clicking on the icon itself.

● Double-clicking on an associated file.

● Dragging an application icon onto the icon bar.

If an application has been 'seen' by the Filer, or is in the Apps icon bar directory, then double-clicking on a file whose type is associated with that application will start it. For example, double clicking on a text file would start Edit.

If an application won't load, there may not be enough memory. Depending on how much memory your computer has, you will need to quit one or more of the applications that are already loaded into its memory. Move the pointer over an icon on the icon bar and press Menu; choose **Quit** to remove the application from the computer's memory. Now try loading the application you want to use. If there still isn't enough space, quit another application you don't need.

Loading any file into Edit

You can load any file (not just text files) into the Edit application. Just hold down Shift and double-click on the file icon. Alternatively, you can drag the file icon onto the Edit icon on the icon bar. However, the result may not be quite what you're expecting! For example, if you load a DrawFile into Edit, you won't see a drawing, you'll see a text file containing all the information used by the Draw application to display a drawing on the screen.

This can be useful – you can often fine-tune something you're doing in an application by loading a file into Edit and 'tweaking' it by hand, but this is really for advanced users.

Transferring data between applications

The techniques used for loading and saving applications are also used to transfer data between applications. When you want to do this, call up the first application's **Save as** dialogue box, and instead of dragging the file's icon to a directory display, drag it to an open window of the second application (or onto the application's icon on the icon bar). You can use this, for example, to

- load a Paint file into Draw
- load a text file into Draw
- load most types of file into Edit.

If the direct transfer fails (perhaps through lack of memory), some applications will attempt to use a temporary disc file for the transfer.

Not all applications can transfer data by this method, as data types are not always compatible. You can't, for example, drag a Draw file into Paint.

Setting application options in Boot files

Some of the applications accessible from the Apps icon bar directory can have their current state saved in a Desktop settings file. This state includes any options that you've set and the size and position of the application windows on screen.

Refer to the section *Desktop settings file* on page 116 for details of where the state is saved.

Adding more applications to a hard disc

Adding applications to the hard disc is quite easy. Usually you only need to copy an application to a directory on the hard disc to install it.

Some applications require you to add system modules or fonts to the computer. These are normally supplied as !System and !Fonts files. To add these to the hard disc, merge them using Configure (see page 84).

Do **not** copy a !System or !Fonts directly onto your hard disc; there should only be one copy in use at any one time, managed by the System setup plug-in and Fonts setup plug-in respectively within Configure.

23   Using colour in applications

Many of the applications you can run on your computer (such as Draw and Paint) make use of colour. This chapter uses Draw as an example.

Note: There are actually two ways of choosing colour in Paint, depending on the screen mode. In modes up to 256 colours, you'll choose colours from a standard Paint Colours window (see *Paint* on page 353). In 4096-colour modes and higher, you'll use the methods described in this chapter.

Colour models

First, here's a short explanation of the three different ways in which colour can be defined or specified; they are the three *colour models*:

- RGB (Red, Green, Blue) – uses the principle of **emitted** colour.
- CMYK (Cyan, Magenta, Yellow, Key) – uses the principle of **reflected** colour.
- HSV (Hue, Saturation, Value) – uses the principle of **reflected** colour.

RGB

This colour model is the one used by colour monitors. They mix beams of red, green and blue light in different proportions to display colours. With the green beam switched on and the other two switched off, you see the colour green. Mixing red, green and blue together at full intensity produces white.

CMYK

This model works like an artist mixing colours on a palette. You see green on an artist's palette because the pigment being used absorbs every colour of the spectrum **except** for green, which it reflects back to your eye. Unlike the RGB model, if you mix all the colours on a palette together you get a muddy brown!

This model is used in four-colour process printing. Printers discovered that they can print any colour from a combination of cyan, magenta, yellow and black dots. They use white, too, but this is the paper colour, where no coloured ink is applied.

The black colour (Key) in CMYK is used to reinforce dark colours and grey shades that may otherwise appear muddy when printed.

HSV

The HSV colour model uses the principle of reflected colour too.

Hue is the basic look of the colour – a particular tint of red or green for example.

Saturation is the strength of the colour compared with the amount of white added. A green hue at full saturation (100%) is a very deep green, while a low saturation green has lots of white added, and is a very pale pastel green.

Value is the brightness of the colour compared with the amount of added black. 100% is the brightest (no added black), while 0% is all black.

Using colour in Draw

The Draw application uses colour extensively. You can choose different colours for the graphic objects and for text. All the colour options are in the **Style** menu. Graphics can be given a **Line colour** and a **Fill colour**, while text can be shown in any **Text colour** blended against a chosen **Background** colour. Moving the pointer to the right over one of these menu items displays the RGB colour dialogue box:

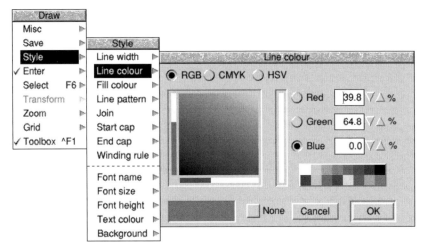

The **RGB**, **CMYK** and **HSV** option buttons allow you to toggle between the three different colour models.

Which colour model?

Each of the colour models has its own colour selection dialogue box. Which is the best one to use? Well, that depends on the colour you want to end up with, and whether you're already familiar with a particular model. Each model has its pros and cons.

Using the RGB colour model

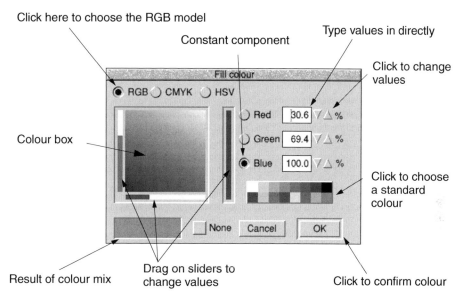

Click here to choose the RGB model

Constant component

Type values in directly

Click to change values

Colour box

Result of colour mix

Drag on sliders to change values

Click to choose a standard colour

Click to confirm colour

There are six ways of choosing a colour in the RGB model. You can use one or a combination of two or more to choose the colour you want. The easiest ways are:

● Click anywhere in the colour box. You can also drag continuously around it.

● Drag the bars in the sliders. As you move the slider the colour you have chosen is shown in the box at the bottom left of the window. At the same time the numeric values change to show you the percentages of the colours chosen.

The other four ways apply to all the colour model dialogue boxes – see *Specifying a colour accurately* on page 244.

Click on **OK** to apply your chosen colour to the selected tool or graphic object. **Cancel** ignores any colour changes you've just made.

Using the CMYK colour model

The colours in CMYK are added together. The amount of each colour can range from 0% (no colour) to 100% (full colour).

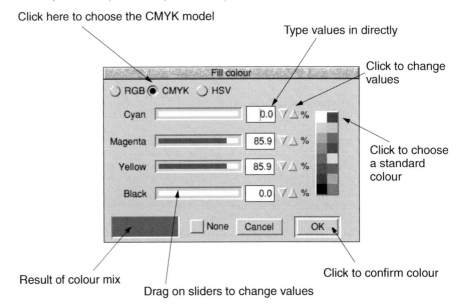

Click here to choose the CMYK model

Type values in directly

Click to change values

Click to choose a standard colour

Result of colour mix

Drag on sliders to change values

Click to confirm colour

There are five ways of choosing a colour in the CMYK model. The first is the easiest:

Drag the bars in the sliders. As you move the slider the colour you have chosen is shown in the box at the bottom left of the window. At the same time the numeric values change to show you the percentages of the colours chosen.

The other four ways apply to all the colour model dialogue boxes – see *Specifying a colour accurately* on page 244.

Click on **OK** to apply your chosen colour to the selected tool or graphic object. **Cancel** ignores any colour changes you've just made.

Using the HSV colour model

Click on the **HSV** button to display the HSV colour dialogue box.

The HSV colour model is useful for trying out different shades of the same colour – pick a colour then add black to it to make it darker, or add white to it to make it lighter (more of a pastel shade).

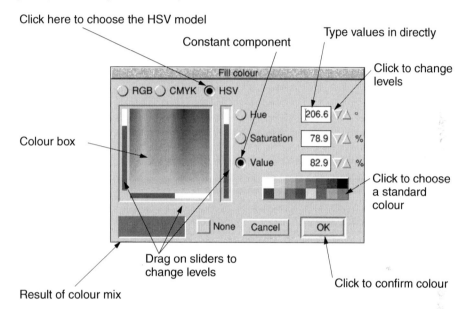

Click here to choose the HSV model

Constant component

Type values in directly

Click to change levels

Colour box

Click to choose a standard colour

Drag on sliders to change levels

Click to confirm colour

Result of colour mix

1   Choose the Hue you want by clicking on a colour in the colour box. The Hue will appear in the trial box at the bottom lefthand corner of the window, and as a number (in degrees) in the Hue writable icon.

2   Click on the **Hue** option button to make the hue constant while you change the Saturation and Value.

3   Drag the bottom slider to add white (to make the colour lighter) or to subtract white (to make it stronger).

4   When you have the right Saturation, drag on the lefthand slider to change the Value – to make the colour darker, if you want to.

Click on **OK** to apply your chosen colour to the selected tool or graphic object. **Cancel** ignores any colour changes you've just made.

Specifying a colour accurately

You can use the writable fields or up/down arrows in any of the three colour model dialogue boxes to specify a colour very accurately:

- If you know the percentages of the colour you want then it is easiest to type it into the writable fields directly. Use the Tab key to move between fields.

- You can fine-tune the currently selected colour by clicking on the up/down arrows. This changes the value in the appropriate writable field by 1%. Clicking with Shift held down changes the value by 0.1%.

- Click on one of the sixteen standard colours. This gives you access to the standard desktop colours directly.

- Click on **None**. The selected text or graphic will be transparent. This is especially useful in sprites (see page 373). This button may be greyed out if not applicable.

Colour and the desktop

Although the Colour picker allows you to select from 16 million possible colours, the number of colours that can actually be displayed depends on current desktop display mode (see page 62).

The screen and colour selection box only show an approximation of what you've chosen; in a 16-colour display mode the representation will not be very accurate. The colour shown in the Colour picker can be different to that displayed in an application.

Colour information is stored within the application and is not lost when you change modes.

You can still choose colours when the desktop is in a greyscale mode – it is probably best to specify the colours by numerical value in this case, as otherwise you will have no idea from the appearance of the desktop what sort of colour you have chosen. If you particularly want to select a shade of grey in your application, use the CMYK model and set all colours except for Black at 0%.

24 Using fonts in applications

RISC OS uses fonts in all its windows and directory displays. This chapter shows you how to choose, use, control and print with fonts.

Strictly speaking, a **font** is a set of characters with the same typeface, weight, style and size. An example is Homerton Bold Oblique 18pt:

- **Typeface** is the name (e.g. Homerton) given to a whole font family and describes all fonts with the same general appearance.
- **Weight** indicates the thickness of the characters (e.g. Bold).
- **Style** is the variation of the basic typeface (e.g. Oblique).
- **Size** is measured in points (see page 246).

RISC OS fonts

Your computer is supplied with a set of fonts permanently built-in. You can choose the font used by the Desktop (see *Merge the new !System as described in Merging updates using Configure on page* 84. on page 105) and use different fonts in some application windows that allow it (e.g. Draw). Here are the fonts supplied:

This font is called System

This font is called Corpus

This font is called Homerton

This font is called Newhall

This font is called Sassoon

✳□▢▲ ✳□■▼ □▲ ✗☎●●★❄ ✳★●▮■ (Selwyn font)

Τηισ φοντ ισ χαλλεδ Σιδνεψ (Sidney font)

This font is called System Fixed

This font is called System Medium

This font is called Trinity

Most RISC OS fonts are conversions of standard typefaces. The table overleaf tells you more about this.

Most fonts can be used in any size and have italic and bold variants; some of them use proportional spacing, so that a narrow letter such as 'l' takes up less horizontal space than a wide letter, such as 'M'. Other fonts are 'monospaced' (or fixed pitch).

RISC OS font	Equivalent	Description
Corpus	Courier	Fixed pitch
Homerton	Helvetica	Proportional
Newhall	New Century SchoolBook	Proportional
Sassoon		Proportional
Selwyn	Zapf Dingbats	Includes arrows, stars, ticks and crosses
Sidney	Symbol	Includes greek and mathematical symbols
System (fixed)		'Old style' fixed pitch
System (Medium)		'Old style' proportional
Trinity	Times Roman	Proportional
WimpSymbol		Used by the desktop; don't use this in applications

Serif and sans serif fonts

A serif font (like Trinity) has strokes at the edges of the letters which allow your eye to follow on from one letter to another. Sans serif fonts (like Homerton) don't have these. Sans serif fonts can make the page look tidier; they're often used for headings and other places where large font sizes are used.

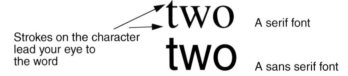

Strokes on the character lead your eye to the word

two — A serif font

two — A sans serif font

Font size

Most applications let you select the size of the font you want to use. Font size is measured in points (a point being 1/72 of an inch) and is the distance between the highest ascender and lowest descender of characters in the font:

Font size
=18pt

Here's some example text

Some applications also allow you to set the font height separately. If you want characters with different height and width values, set the size first and then the height. RISC OS fonts can be sized to any height or width allowed by the application:

This is homerton 7pt

This is homerton 10pt

This is homerton 12pt

This is homerton 18pt

Outline font painting

Fonts are controlled by a part of the operating system called the Font Manager. Initially, the Font Manager just holds the outlines of fonts in memory.

When you choose to use a particular font, the computer calculates the *bitmap* font needed to display that font at the desired size. A bitmap tells the computer exactly which pixels to paint on the screen to render a given character at a given size.

Outline fonts are converted into bitmap fonts in this way because the computer can send these to the screen much faster, but a bitmap font takes up more space than the outline that describes it.

Adding more fonts

You can purchase additional RISC OS outline fonts for your system from third party suppliers (installing these is outlined in the *Fonts setup plug-in* on page 91). You can also use many of the PostScript Type 1 fonts available (see page 463).

Choosing and using fonts in applications

Two applications (Edit and Draw) are supplied that use fonts, but they use them in different ways:

- Edit can display text on the screen in any RISC OS font. However, it can only print out in the font that is standard on your printer.

- Draw can both display and print fonts of varying size and typeface.

Most applications you'll buy that can make use of fonts (e.g. desktop publishing packages, word processors or drawing tools) will behave like Draw.

Using fonts in Edit

You can use the **Display/Font/Font List** menu to change the font used to display text on the screen.

Using fonts in Draw

To use different fonts in Draw:

1   Select the Text tool.

2   Click Menu over the Draw window.

3   Choose a font from the **Style/Font name/Font List** menu by clicking Adjust.

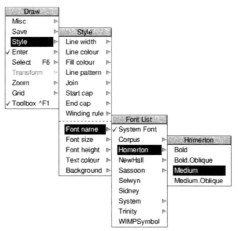

4   Choose a font size from the **Style/Font size/Size** menu.

Now, when you type in text, it will appear in your chosen font. See *Defining a path object's style* on page 325 for more details. You can also choose the background and text colours which will be used.

Using Chars to preview a typeface

You can use the Chars application to see what a particular typeface looks like before you decide to use it. You can also use Chars to enter special characters into an application window or dialogue box. See *Chars* on page 403.

For other ways of entering special characters, see *Character sets* on page 543.

How the Font Manager works

The Font Manager uses various techniques to optimise font quality (on-screen or printed) whilst ensuring that your computer's performance doesn't suffer:

● anti-aliasing

● hinting

● font caching

Anti-aliasing

If the outline of a character passes partially through a pixel (a pixel is the smallest building block available on the monitor screen), a non-anti-aliasing font can only paint the whole pixel or none of it. The result is a jagged edge to the character.

Anti-aliasing relies on an optical trick: the jagged edges are smoothed out by the addition of extra pixels in intermediate colours. You can see how this is done by first typing some text in an **Edit** window using a fairly small size (12 or 14 point) and choosing **Display/Font/Trinity/Medium** to display the text in an anti-aliased font. Then use CloseUp (described on page 409) to have a closer look at the text.

Sub-pixel anti-aliasing

This controls a refinement of anti-aliasing in which four separate versions of each character are stored in the font cache. This can have a beneficial effect on the quality of characters at small sizes. However it is heavy on computing power (see *Controlling anti-aliasing* on page 250) and may result in unacceptably slow screen updates. This parameter is relevant only to the screen; it does not affect printing.

Hinting

This is another technique used by the Font Manager to improve the appearance of fonts. It applies both to the screen and to printers. The outline of the character being displayed (or printed) is subtly altered in ways that depend on the resolution of the image being produced. It is used on-screen if anti-aliasing is disabled.

Hinting is particularly effective when fonts are scaled, and when half-tones are not available (as on most printers). You can't control hinting, as you can anti-aliasing; it's used automatically if you disable anti-aliasing.

Font caching

To save time converting font outlines to bitmaps, as many bitmaps as possible are kept in an area of memory called the *font cache*. If the font cache is not large enough to hold the bitmaps of all the current fonts, any extra fonts are loaded as necessary.

The computer attempts to retain in memory the fonts which are in greatest demand, but this requires some sophisticated guesswork. Since this is not always totally successful (the computer cannot read your mind!) there is sometimes a delay as the font is loaded from the filing system and displayed on the screen.

Matching font performance to your needs

 The Font Manager is set up to provide a reasonable blend of screen quality and performance for the majority of users. There is inevitably a trade-off between speed and font appearance. RISC OS provides two ways of tailoring font performance to your needs and preferences. You can

- change the way anti-aliasing is done (or switch it off altogether)
- change the size of the font cache.

Controlling anti-aliasing

You can use the Fonts setup plug-in of Configure (see page 91) to place an upper limit on the size of anti-aliased fonts; fonts in larger sizes are printed without anti-aliasing. Larger fonts benefit less from anti-aliasing, and since a computed anti-aliased bitmap font occupies a lot more memory than a non-anti-aliased bitmap, for most purposes it is not worth displaying large fonts with anti-aliasing. This parameter is relevant only to the screen display.

Note: If you use sub-pixel anti-aliasing, you should increase your font cache by four times to store the extra font shapes needed. If you don't, your computer may slow down considerably.

Changing the minimum size of the font cache

If you're using a lot of different fonts, increasing the minimum size of the cache means that the text is drawn more quickly. You can set it permanently (see *Fonts setup plug-in* on page 91) or for the current session only (see *System memory allocation* on page 76).

The best size for the font cache depends on several factors: how much memory your computer has, whether you have a hard disc, and the number of fonts you're using.

If the cached bitmaps value is set high, and you're using a few large fonts – for headlines, perhaps – they may take up all the font cache, flushing out smaller fonts. The smaller characters will then have to be cached again when needed. This effect can slow down printing and the display.

This parameter is relevant for the printer, especially if you are printing documents with a lot of text. Its ideal value depends on the screen mode, printer type and the printer resolution. If you are printing at a high resolution, you may want to increase the font cache.

Note: Do **not** set a font cache of less than 32kB. Sub-pixel anti-aliasing (see page 249) requires more font cache. For example, Homerton.Medium as a desktop font needs a font cache of 32kB. With sub-pixel anti-aliasing turned on, it needs 128kB. If you see an hourglass on the screen as the desktop is redrawn you may need to increase the font cache size.

Printing with fonts

When printing, there are conflicting requirements for memory. The Font Manager needs memory to cache fonts, and the printer driver needs memory to build up a page image to send to the printer. As both of these affect printing speed, you will have to experiment to find the optimum. Typically, more memory given to the font cache (or maximum font cache option) results in quicker printing.

The maximum size of cached bitmaps affects whether fonts are cached when printing. If this value is smaller than your typical body text size, there may be a very long pause at the start of each printed page, as all the characters on the page are rendered from the outline form.

The RISC OS Printer Manager program sits between an application and the printer, and oversees the printing process. Printers, printing and printer drivers are explained fully in *Printing your files* on page 207 and *Setting up printers* on page 189.

PostScript printers

PostScript printers have their own set of fonts stored internally. When you print to a PostScript printer, most RISC OS fonts are mapped to these internal PostScript fonts. RISC OS fonts that cannot be mapped to PostScript fonts (e.g. Sassoon) are sent to the printer by the Printer Manager as they are needed.

For more information about using fonts with PostScript printers, refer to *FontPrint* on page 227.

Converting PostScript fonts to outline fonts

It is possible to convert standard PostScript Type 1 fonts to RISC OS outline fonts using the T1ToFont application (see *T1ToFont* on page 463).

Changing the desktop font

You can change the font displayed in directory displays, menus and so on (see page 105). It's best to choose one of the fonts stored in the computer's ROM (e.g. Homerton or Trinity) as the screen will redraw more quickly.

Troubleshooting

If every screen redraw causes intensive disc and hourglass activity, then the font cache may be too small to hold the range of fonts you are trying to use. In these circumstances, try the following:

- Increase the size of the font cache using the **Task Manager/Task display** window. The addition of even small amounts of cache can often improve things dramatically.

- Reduce the maximum size for anti-aliasing. This will enable the font cache to be used more economically with a large number of fonts. You should not normally reduce the maximum anti-aliasing size below 12pt.

- Reduce the maximum size of cached bitmaps value. This should reduce disc activity, but the action of redrawing the screen will become much slower.

- Use a smaller selection of fonts and font sizes in your document.

25   Edit

Edit is a text editor which you can use to create and edit plain text, and to generate simple text documents and command scripts.

Edit is also a BASIC program editor. It converts BASIC programs into text format for editing, and then converts them back again when they are saved.

Although Edit does have some sophisticated features for handling text, it has not been designed as a word processor; word processors offer facilities for pagination and page layout control as well as paragraph styles and printable fonts.

Starting Edit

Edit is in the Apps icon bar directory display. To start Edit, double-click on the !Edit application icon. The application icon appears on the icon bar.

Displaying a text file

To display an **existing text file**, just double-click on it, or drag the file's icon to the Edit icon on the bar.

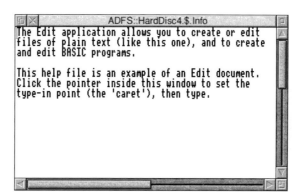

Displaying other file types

To display **any other file type**, drag the file icon to the Edit icon on the bar, or hold down Shift and double-click on it. BASIC files are displayed as text.

Creating a new document

Click on the Edit icon on the icon bar to open an empty document.

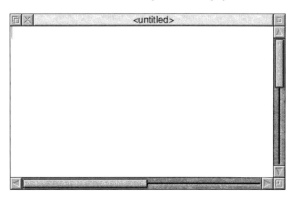

Creating other file types

You can open new windows for other specific types of file: Text, BASIC, Obey and Command files. To do this, choose **Create** from the Edit icon bar menu and specify the file type you want. Alternatively you can type in a file type of your own choice at the bottom of the Create menu.

Typing in text

When you first open a new Edit window, a red I-shaped bar – the *caret* – appears at the top left of the window. This is where text appears when you start typing. You can open more than one Edit window (see *Other features of Edit* on page 270) but only one (the current window) has the caret in it. This window is said to have the *input focus*, and is also identified by its cream rather than grey title bar. You can only type in the window which has the input focus.

If you type in some text without pressing ↵ (Return) at all, the window scrolls sideways (if your Edit window is smaller than your screen). You can break your text into lines by pressing ↵. Alternatively, click on the Toggle size icon to extend the window to the full size and avoid having to scroll sideways.

As you type, notice that Edit fills the current line and then carries on to the next line, often breaking words in the middle. By default, it doesn't automatically enter formatting characters such as newline, as these might create problems in scripts and programs, and in transferring text into other editors. *Formatting text* on page 265 tells you how to set wordwrap and other formatting options if you want them.

Editing text

Here are some basic techniques for entering and deleting text:

To	Do this	Notes
Insert new text in an Edit window	Click Select to position the caret. You can now insert text by typing.	
Overwrite existing text	Press Menu and choose **Misc/Overwrite**.	Normally, when you type, new characters are **inserted** at the caret.
Delete characters to the left of the caret	Position the caret after the character and press Backspace.	Hold the key down to delete more characters.
Delete characters to the right of the caret	Position the caret before the character and press the Delete key.	Hold the key down to delete more characters.

There are quicker ways of deleting a lot of text – see *page* 256.

The clipboard

Edit supports the use of the *global clipboard*, an imaginary off screen area for temporarily holding blocks of text for later retrieval. The clipboard allows you to transfer objects held on there to other applications that support it, for example copying a table produced in Edit to be inserted into an email.

The process usually involves two steps: an initial copy (or cut) operation, followed by a paste operation.

Cut removes the selection from the document and stores it on the clipboard.

Copy makes a copy of the selection and stores it on the clipboard. The selection in the document remains in place.

Paste pastes the current contents of the clipboard into a document at the position of the caret, or replaces the current selection in a document.

The clipboard holds a single item, so if you copy (or cut) a second block there it will cause the previous contents to be forgotten.

Selecting text

You can edit more than one character at a time by defining a block of text you want to edit, then cutting, copying or pasting the whole block. A block of text can be one or two characters, a word, a line, a paragraph or the whole document:

To	Do this	Notes
Select a word	Double-click on the word.	
Select a line	Triple-click on the line.	
Select an area of text	Click Select at the start, then Adjust at the end of the block.	Another way is to drag Select across the block.
Extend a selected block	Click Adjust at the new start or end.	
Select the entire text	Choose **Select/Select all**.	You can also press Ctrl-A.
Cancel a selection	Choose **Select/Clear**.	You can also press Ctrl-Z.

Block editing operations

First select a block of text as described in the previous section.

To	Do this	Notes
Copy a selection to the clipboard	Choose **Select/Copy**.	You can also press Ctrl-C.
Cut a selection to the clipboard	Choose **Select/Cut**.	You can also press Ctrl-X, or Delete or Backspace.
Paste a selection from the clipboard	Place the caret where you want the selection to appear and choose **Select/Paste**.	You can also press Ctrl-V or Insert.

To	Do this	Notes
Delete a selection without affecting the clipboard contents	Choose **Select/Delete**.	You can also press Ctrl-K.
Swap upper and lowercase characters in a selection	Choose **Select/Swap case**.	You can also press Ctrl-S.

Undoing changes

If you make a mistake or have second thoughts about an edit, choose **Edit/Undo** (or press F8) to step back through your most recent changes. The number of changes you can reverse in this way varies according to the complexity of the operations involved.

Edit/Redo (or the F9 key) allows you to remake changes you reversed with **Undo**.

Finding and replacing text

Edit has a very sophisticated find and replace function, to enable you to find words or characters in a document and replace them by others if you wish.

To find a particular word or character (the 'target string') position the caret at the start of the file before choosing **Find**. The target string may be any combination of words, numbers, letters, spaces or other non-printing characters.

Searching for a string

1   Choose **Edit/Find:**

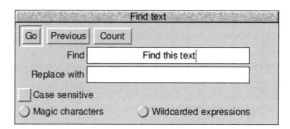

2   Type in the string you wish to find. If you've already tried to find the string once and want to search for it again, click on **Previous**.

3   Click on **Go**. If the string is not located, the message Not found is displayed. Otherwise, the Text found dialogue box appears.

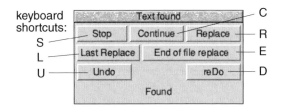

The buttons in this dialogue box allow you to do the following things:

To	Do this
Replace one string by another	Choose **Edit/Find** as above. Type in the string to be found, then press ↵ once. Type in the string to replace it and click on **Go**: To replace just this string, click on **Last Replace**.
Replace the found string and move to the next instance	Click on **Replace**.
Replace all instances of the found string	Click on **End of file replace**.
Undo the last replace	Click on **Undo**. Click on **reDo** to replace it again
Resume searching for the next instance of the string	Click on **Continue**.
Quit **Find**	Click on **Stop**.

Other useful facilities

To	Do this
Delete more than one instance of a string	Find the string and replace it with nothing (leave the **Replace** box blank).
Count the number of instances of a string	Choose **Edit/Find** then click on **Count**.

Making searches case sensitive

By default, **Find text** makes no distinction between upper and lower case: it will find for example HELLO, hello, or HeLLo. If you click on **Case sensitive**, however, it will find only those instances which match exactly in case.

Using magic characters

You can also use find and replace special, or 'magic' characters. Click on **Magic characters** (or press F5) in the **Find** dialogue box and a list of them will be displayed in the lower half of the dialogue box:

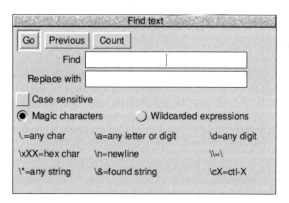

Magic characters start with a \ character, and you type them into the **Find** and **Replace with** boxes exactly as shown:

To	Type in	Notes
Match any character at all, including spaces and non-alphabetic characters	\.	
Match any single alphabetic or numeric character	\a	So t\ap matches tip, tap, and top, but not trap.
Match any digit (0 to 9)	\d	
Match characters by their ASCII number, expressed in hexadecimal	\x*XX*	Thus \x61 matches lower-case a. This is principally useful for finding characters that are not in the normal printable range.
Match the newline character	\n	To the computer, this is a character just like any other.
Search for a string actually containing the backslash character \ while using magic characters	\\	To search for the strings cat\a or cot\a, type c\at\\a.
Match any string (including a string consisting of no characters at all)	*	This is most useful in the middle of a search string. For example, jo*n matches jon, john, and johaan.
Represent the found string in the **Replace with** box	\&	This is particularly useful when you've used magic characters in the Find string. For example, if you've searched for t\ap, and you want to add an s to the end of all the strings found, \&s in the **Replace with** box will replace tip, tap and top by tips, taps and tops.
Match control code Ctrl-X, where X is any character	\c*X*	Thus \cI matches the tab character, and is equivalent to a \x09 search.

Using wildcarded expressions

There is also a facility for specifying wildcarded expressions in search strings. Click on **Wildcarded expressions** (or press F6) in the **Find** dialogue box to display the ones you can use:

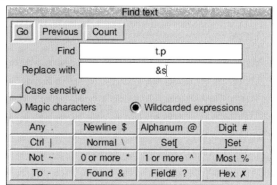

Click on the wildcard character you wish to enter and it is copied into the text box at the caret.

To	Click on	Notes
Match any single character	Any .	
Match linefeeds	Newline $	
Match any alphanumeric character (A to Z, a to z, 0 to 9, and _)	Alphanum @	
Match 0 to 9	Digit #	
Match a control character	Ctrl |	For example, to search for Ctrl-Z, type in | z.
Match the character following it even if it is a special character	Normal \	# would be searched for as \ #.
Match any one of the characters between the brackets	Set[	This is always case sensitive.

To	Click on	Notes
Match any character (in the ASCII character set) between two given characters (e.g. `a - z`)	To -	
Not match character	Not ~	~C matches any character apart from C. This can also be applied to sets.
Match zero or more occurrences of a character or a set of characters	0 or more *	T*O matches T, TO,TOO, TOOO etc.
Match one or more occurrences of a character or a set of characters	1 or more ^	T^O matches TO, TOO, TOOO etc.
% is the same as ^, except when used as the final element of a search string	Most %	In this case the longest sequence of matching characters is found.
Match the found string	Found &	This is useful with wildcard characters in the Find string. For example, if you've searched for `t.p`, and want to add an `s` to the end of all the strings found, `&s` in the **Replace with** string will replace `tip`, `tap` and `top` by `tips`, `taps` and `tops`.

To	Click on	Notes
Match the nth ambiguous part of the search pattern, where n is a digit from 0 to 9	Field# ?	Ambiguous parts are those which could not be exactly specified in the search string; e.g. in the search string `%#fred*$` there are two ambiguous parts, `%#` and `*$` – which are `?0` and `?1` respectively. Ambiguous parts are numbered from left to right. (Only to be used in the **Replace with** string).
Match the character whose ASCII number is nn, where nn is a two-digit hex number	Hex ✗	✗61 matches lower-case a. This is principally useful for finding characters that are not in the normal printable range.

The full power of the wildcard facility can be illustrated by a few examples:

- To count how many lower case letters appear in a piece of text:
  Find: **[a-z]**
  and click on **Count**.

- To count how many words are in a piece of text:
  Find: **%@**
  and click on **Count**.

- To surround all words in a piece of text by brackets:
  Find: **%@**
  Replace with: **(&)**
  and click on **Go**, then on **End of File Replace** in the Found dialogue box.

- To change all occurrences of strings like `#include "h.foo"` into `#include "foo.h"`:
  Find: **\#include "h\.%@"**
  Replace with: **#include "?0.h"**
  and click on **Go**, then on **End of File Replace** in the Found dialogue box.

- To remove all ASCII characters, other than those between space and ~, and the newline character, from a file:

Find: `~[ -\~$]`

Replace with: (*nothing*)

and click on **Go**, then on **End of File Replace** in the Found dialogue box (i.e. find all characters outside the set from the space character to the ~ character, and newline, and replace them with nothing). In fact this could be written without the \, since ~ would not make sense in this context if it had its special meaning of **Not**:

Find: `~[ -~$]`

Reading in text from another file

If you want to add all the text from another file into the current file:

1 Position the caret at the point where the inserted text is to appear.

2 Open the directory display for the source file, and drag its icon into the destination text window.

The entire contents of the source file is then copied into the destination file, starting at the caret position. The caret appears at the end of the text you have inserted.

There are two ways of reading in **part** of one file into another:

- Highlight the text you want to save out from the source file, then choose **Edit/Copy** or press Ctrl-C. Move the pointer over the destination document and click to position the caret, then choose **Edit/Paste** or press Ctrl-V.

- Position the caret in the destination file. Highlight the text you want to save out from the source file, then drag the **Edit/Save selection/Save as** icon into the destination file.

Formatting text

Formatting describes how the text in Edit is arranged on the page.

Before you can use these features, click in the Edit window to get the input focus (the title bar will turn yellow).

To	Do this	Notes
Set a margin	Choose **Display/Margin**. Type in a value and press ↲.	You can have one lefthand margin set at a time in Edit. The margin is set in pixels.
Set the line spacing	Choose **Display/Line spacing**. Type in a value and press ↲.	Line spacing is set in pixels, and can be a positive or negative value.
Reformat all lines in a paragraph to a given length	Place the cursor anywhere in the paragraph, choose **Edit/Format text**, type in a value for width and press ↲.	Useful for tidying up after editing. Width is measured in characters per line: this value is also used by the **Wordwrap** option.
Make your text fit the size of the window	Choose **Display/Window wrap**.	Revert to default by choosing the option again.
Prevent words being split over lines as you type	Choose **Misc/Wordwrap**.	A newline character is inserted at the end of a line and the next whole word is wrapped onto the next line. Line length is set in the **Edit/Format text** option.
Convert linefeeds to carriage returns (and vice-versa)	Choose **Edit/CR↔LF**. Choose again to undo.	Carriage returns appear as [0D] in the text.

Indenting text

You can indent a selected block of text in Edit. The indent is defined in character spaces. You can indent using just spaces, or add a text prefix to the beginning of each line of a block.

To indent a selected block of text, choose **Edit/Select/Indent**:

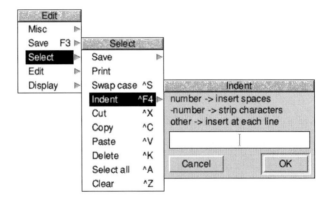

You can then type in one of three different types of indent:

● **A positive number** gives you an indent of the specified width.

● **A negative number**: –5, for example, deletes the specified number of spaces or characters from the beginning of the block line – use this to cancel an indent.

● You can also type in text: **IGNORE**, or **Note**, for example. This will then appear at the beginning of every line in the selected block. You can remove this text by indenting with a suitable negative number:

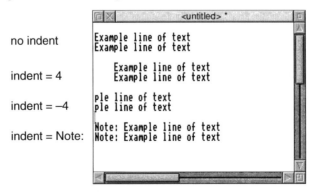

Using tabs

Tabs in Edit are designed to work with fixed-pitch fonts, such as the System font. If you use tabs in Edit with proportionally-spaced fonts (such as Trinity, for example), tables will not line up properly.

Laying out tables with irregular columns

Lay out the first line of a table (the headings, for example) using spaces between each column. On the next line, press Tab and the cursor will jump to each column in turn:

column headings

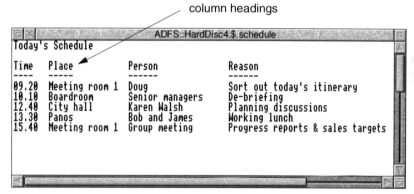

Laying out tables with regular columns

Pressing Tab with **Misc/Column tabs** switched on sets tabs every eight spaces.

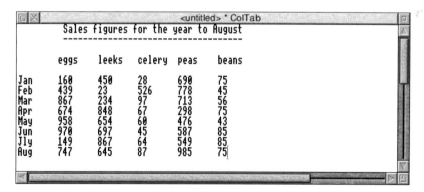

Converting tab characters to column tabs

You may have text, imported from another application, which has tab characters (appearing as [09]) embedded in it. These can be expanded into Edit regular column tabs (eight spaces for each tab character) by choosing **Edit/Expand tabs.**

The text will be reformatted so that each tab character is replaced by eight spaces.

Changing the display font

You can display text files using any available desktop font:

To	Do this	Notes
Change the screen font displayed by Edit	Choose from the **Display/Font** submenus.	Tabs and columns will not look right in proportional fonts.
Change the screen font size	Choose the size in points from the **Display/Font size** menu.	You can specify a different size in the bottom of the **Font size** menu.
Change the screen font height	Choose **Display/Font height** then the size you want (in points).	The current width will not be changed (use **Display/Font size**).
Change the text colour	Choose a colour from the **Display/Foreground** submenu.	
Change the background colour	Choose a colour from the **Display/Background** submenu.	
Invert text and background colours	Choose **Display/Invert**.	Choosing this option again toggles back.

Note: Font information is not saved with the text file, so does not print. You can only have one style of text at a time in each Edit document.

Saving text files

The **Save** menu allows you to save a complete file; you can also save part of a file.

To	Do this	Notes
Save a new file	Press Menu over the text file and drag the **Save/Save as** icon to the destination directory (changing the default name TextFile if necessary).	You can also press F3 to display the **Save as** box.
Save a file that's already been saved	Press F3 followed by ↵ (Return).	
Save part of a text file	Select the text you want to save. Press Menu, drag and drop the **Selection/Save /Save as** icon.	You can use this method to export text to another text file, or another application (e.g. Draw – see page 340).

Printing text files

There are several ways of printing a text file; to use them, you first need to load the Printers application (refer to *Printing your files* on page 207).

To	Do this	Notes
Print an open text file	Choose **Misc/Print**.	You can also press the Print Screen key, or drag the **Save/Save as** icon onto the printer's icon bar icon.
Print a selection	Choose **Select/Print**.	You can also drag the **Select/Save as** icon onto the printer's icon bar icon.
Print a text file not currently open	Drag the file's icon to the printer's icon bar icon.	

Note: Text files are always printed out using the printer's default font. This overrides any screen font (chosen from the **Edit/Display/Font** menu).

Other features of Edit

This section describes some features of Edit that you won't need to use very often.

To	Do this	Notes
Extend an Edit window so it's wider than the current screen mode	Enter the line length (in terms of System font characters) in the **Display/Work area/Width** box.	The units of measurement are System font characters, even if you are using a different display font. The maximum size is 480 System font characters. Not available when **Window wrap** is on.
Send the caret to a specific line of text	Choose **Edit/Goto**. Goto text line current line 8 current char 265 Go to line 43 OK	'Line' means the string of characters between two presses of ⏎. If you have not formatted your text, a line in this sense may run over more than one display line.
See information about Edit	Display the **Misc/Info** box.	You can also choose **Info** from Edit's icon bar menu.
See information about the current file	Display the **Misc/File** information box. About this file Modified? NO Type Text (fff) ADFS::HardDisc4.$.Info Size 265 Date 11:58:58 22-Jul-1991	This tells you the file type, whether it's been modified, the size in characters and creation (or modification) date.
Change a file's type	Enter the new type in the **Misc/Set type** box.	See also *Creating other file types* on page 254.
Open another window on the same file	Choose **Misc/New view**.	Changes you make in one window will be reflected in any others.

Writing and editing BASIC programs

Edit allows you to write BASIC programs, converting the Text files produced in Edit to tokenised BASIC files. A tokenised file is one where BASIC keywords are replaced by seldom-used ASCII characters, to make the program smaller and faster in execution.

Writing a new program

To write a new program, choose **Create/BASIC** from Edit's icon bar menu. You can type your program directly into an Edit window. There is no need to include line numbers, as Edit will insert them for you when you save the file. Press ↵ at the end of the last line of the program.

Editing an existing program

To use Edit for working on an existing BASIC program, simply drag the program's icon from its directory onto the Edit icon on the icon bar, or Shift double-click on its icon.

Line numbers

By default, line numbers will be stripped when a BASIC file is loaded. To turn this option on or off, choose **Strip line numbers** from the Edit icon bar menu. If a reference to a line is found, an error box will appear.

Line numbers are added when a BASIC file is saved. Use **Line number increment** from the Edit icon bar menu to set the number increment between successive lines in the program.

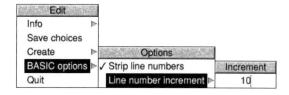

Converting to a tokenised file

A tokenised file saves space: top-bit-set characters and control characters (non-printing characters) are used to stand for the BASIC keywords. So, for example, the Hex character E3 stands for the keyword FOR.

Converting a text file to a tokenised file is usually quite straightforward. If there are no line numbers, by default Edit will start at 10 and increment by 10. If line numbers are supplied, these are used as a basis for any lines without line numbers.

Warnings

If there are line numbers, Edit will **not** sort them into ascending sequence and the resulting BASIC program may behave strangely.

If your code is incomplete, Edit will warn you about the following problems:

● Line number reference too large.

● Mismatched quotes.

● Mismatched brackets.

In all cases Edit will also quote the offending line number. After you have clicked on **OK**, the tokenising continues.

Attempts to tokenise a crunched program (e.g. one with the spaces removed) will generally result in a non-functioning program.

Printing a BASIC program

If you have Edit running, you can print a BASIC program on paper by dragging its icon onto a printer driver icon. Edit will perform the conversion to allow the program to be printed.

Quitting Edit

Choose **Quit** from the Edit icon bar menu to stop Edit and remove it from the computer's memory. A dialogue box may be displayed, warning you if there are any current files you have not saved.

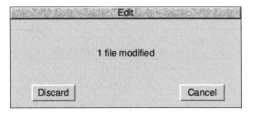

Saving Edit application preferences

You may wish to change some aspects of the way new Edit windows appear. For example, a new window normally opens using black text on a white background, but you may prefer to have blue text on a red background.

You can set features of this type by setting up Edit just as you wish to use it, then choosing **Save choices** from the icon bar menu. Next time you start Edit and open a new window your choices will be used as the defaults.

272

Keystroke equivalents

On occasions, it can be quicker when you are working in Edit to use the keyboard instead of the mouse, especially once you are familiar with Edit through its menus.

When editing

To	Press
Move caret one character left, right, up or down	←, →,↑, ↓
Move caret one word left or right	Shift-←, Shift-→
Move caret one windowful up or down	Shift-↑, Shift-↓
Move caret to start of file	Ctrl-↑
Move caret to end of file	Ctrl-↓
Move caret to start or end of line	Ctrl-←, Ctrl-→
Scroll file one line without moving caret	Ctrl Shift-↑, Ctrl Shift-↓
Cut selection, or delete character to left of caret if none	Backspace
Cut selection, or delete character to right of caret if none	Delete
Place caret at top of document	Home
Place caret at end of document	End
Delete word at current caret position	Shift-End
Delete line at caret	Ctrl-End
Scroll up or down one window	Page Up, Page Down

Keystroke equivalents in the Misc menu

To	Press
Print the file.	Print
Toggle overwrite mode on or off.	Shift-F1
Toggle column tabs on or off.	Shift-F3
Toggle word wrap on or off.	Ctrl-F5

Keystroke equivalents in the Select menu

To	Press
Swap case of text under the selection	Ctrl-S
Indent selection	Ctrl-F4
Cut selection to clipboard	Ctrl-X, Delete
Copy selection to clipboard	Ctrl-C
Paste from clipboard, replacing any selection	Ctrl-V, Insert
Delete selection without affecting the clipboard	Ctrl-K
Select all	Ctrl-A
Clear selection	Ctrl-Z, Escape, Shift-F6

Keystroke equivalents in the Edit menu

To	Press
Display **Find** dialogue box.	F4
Display **Goto** dialogue box.	F5
Undo last action.	F8
Redo last action.	F9
Format text block.	Ctrl-F6
Toggle between CR and LF versions of the file.	Ctrl-F8
Expand tabs.	Ctrl-Shift-F1

Keystroke equivalents in the Find menu

Note: these keystroke definitions only come into play once the **Find** dialogue box has been displayed (e.g. by typing F4).

To	Press
Move caret between the find and replace text in the Find box.	↑, ↓
This starts the search and displays the **Text found** dialogue box if the text string is found.	F1
Use previous find and replace strings.	F2
Count occurrences of find string.	F3
Toggle case sensitive switch.	F4
Toggle magic characters switch.	F5
Toggle wildcard expressions switch.	F6

Keystroke File options

To	Press
Open a dialogue box enabling you to load an existing text file into a new window.	F2
Open a dialogue box enabling you to insert an existing text file at the caret position. If any text is selected, it will be replaced with the loaded file.	Shift-F2
Save the file in the current window. This is a shortcut to the normal **Save as** dialogue box.	F3

26   Draw

Draw is a powerful and sophisticated drawing package; you can use it to draw and edit diagrams and pictures made up from various kinds of graphical objects.

Draw uses coordinates to describe the position of objects on the page in a technique often referred to as *vector graphics*. These have an advantage over pixel-based graphics in that to transform the picture requires only moving the coordinates around; rotating the image, for example, causes no loss of clarity.

You'll probably find that the easiest way of learning Draw is to read through *Basic ideas* (on the next page) and then work through the *Draw tutorial* which follows, before reading the more detailed sections.

Starting Draw

Draw is in the Apps icon bar directory display. To start Draw:

1   Double-click on the !Draw icon, to install it on the icon bar.

2   Click on the Draw icon bar icon to open a new Draw window.

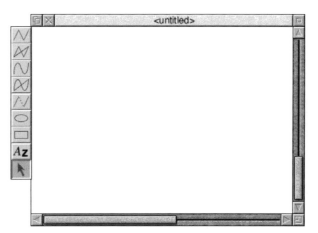

Alternatively, edit an existing drawing by dragging its file icon to the Draw icon on the icon bar, or by double-clicking on it.

Basic ideas

The Draw window

The Draw window looks similar to other application windows when you first load it, except that down its lefthand side there is a strip of icons called *the toolbox*. The toolbox allows you to draw or select objects without having to use menus.

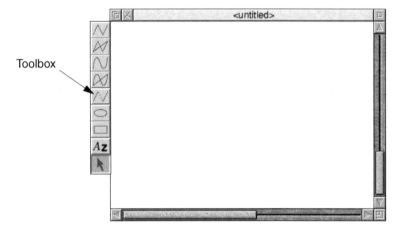

Toolbox

Draw objects

A Draw diagram is built up from objects of a number of different types. Draw stores information about each object, which means you can subsequently change individual objects without affecting the other objects.

The basic object types are:

- **Paths,** consisting of a sequence of line segments. Each line segment can be straight or curved. A path can be closed to form a polygon or curved object, or left open. The path is the basic element of a drawing.

- **Rectangles and ellipses**, which are also made from path objects. This means that you can edit them.

- **Text lines**, in a range of fonts, sizes, and colours.

- **Text areas**, consisting of several lines of text. Text areas can be used for simple desktop publishing, and for annotating drawings.

- **Sprites**, which are graphic shapes made up of an array of coloured pixels. You can create sprites using Paint (see chapter on page 353) and then load them into Draw.

- **JPEG** files – compressed photographic images – such as those in the `Documents.UserGuide.Pictures` directory.

You can combine objects together as a group which you can then (usually) manipulate like any other object. Draw records the objects that were used to build a group, so that it may subsequently be 'ungrouped' into its constituents. Groups can also be used as components of other groups.

Each object has a style consisting of a number of *attributes*. Attributes are used to define the colours of an object, line widths, text fonts and sizes, and so on. The exact range of attributes depends on the type of object.

Draw modes

You can use Draw in three operating modes:

- **Enter mode** – used to create new Draw objects (like lines and squares).
- **Select mode** – used to change object attributes (like line colour) and to move and alter objects.
- **Path edit mode** – used to reshape an object by altering its paths and segments.

Don't worry about these names too much – when you're actually using Draw you'll change between the modes without thinking about it!

The mouse pointer changes according to which mode you are using: in Enter mode it is shown as a star, and in Select and Path edit mode as an arrow.

Tools and shortcuts

To make it easier to construct a diagram, Draw has a number of tools and shortcuts:

- The **Toolbox** is attached to the lefthand edge of each Draw window. You can use this to draw and edit shapes, without having to use menus.
- You can display a **Grid** to help you align objects in a diagram. Various different sizes and shapes of grid are available.
- **Keyboard shortcuts** duplicate the effect of the more frequent Draw actions. These are listed at the end of this chapter on page 350, and also appear alongside the corresponding menu entries on the screen.
- You can use **New view** to display more than one view of a diagram; different views can have different grid and zoom factor settings. Changes made to the drawing in one view affect the other view as well.

The drawing area

When you start a drawing, the Draw window displayed on your screen only shows part of your actual drawing area. The drawing area is usually the size of an A4 sheet of paper, but you can make it as small as A5 or as large as A0, depending on the size of the drawing you want to create. You can also decide whether the drawing area is a landscape rectangle (where the horizontal side is longer) or a portrait rectangle (where the vertical side is longer). You can use the scroll bars on the Draw window to move around the drawing area.

This drawing area is Landscape A4

The Draw window shows
part of the whole drawing area

Draw tutorial

This tutorial section introduces Draw by helping you create the picture below.

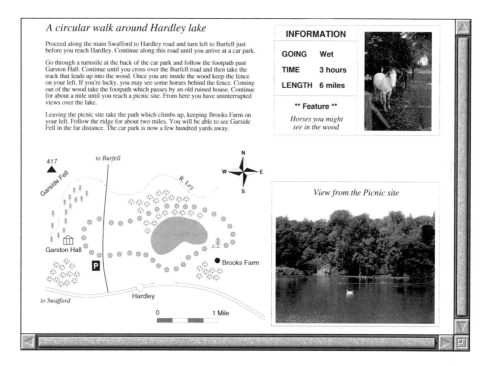

A circular walk around Hardley lake

Proceed along the main Swafford to Hardley road and turn left to Burfell just
before you reach Hardley. Continue along this road until you arrive at a car park.

Go through a turnstile at the back of the car park and follow the footpath past
Garston Hall. Continue until you cross over the Burfell road and then take the
track that leads up into the wood. Once you are inside the wood keep the fence
on your left. If you're lucky, you may see some horses behind the fence. Coming
out of the wood take the footpath which passes by an old ruined house. Continue
for about a mile until you reach a picnic site. From here you have uninterrupted
views over the lake.

Leaving the picnic site take the path which climbs up, keeping Brooks Farm on
your left. Follow the ridge for about two miles. You will be able to see Garside
Fell in the far distance. The car park is now a few hundred yards away.

INFORMATION

GOING   Wet

TIME   3 hours

LENGTH   6 miles

** Feature **

*Horses you might
see in the wood*

View from the Picnic site

The drawing above shows a six mile walk through the countryside, and is divided
into four parts:

- A map showing the route of the walk and how to get to the starting point.

- A written description of the walk.

- A photographic view of part of the walk.

- An information box describing how many miles long the walk is, how long it
  takes to complete, the going (wet) and any points of interest.

The following pages will take you step-by-step through the process of creating the
above drawing, showing you how to draw a map compass, lake, roads, road scale,
woods and rivers. You'll also learn how to drag text files (created by Edit) and
sprites (created by Paint) into a Draw window.

Undoing your mistakes

If you do something by mistake while you're working through this tutorial, try pressing F8. This is a keyboard shortcut for the **Misc/Undo** option, and should undo your last operation. If you decide that you didn't want to undo something after all, just press F9 (**Redo**).

Selecting Draw objects

Before you start on the map, it's worth spending a short time practising how to select objects. This is important: before you can do anything to a Draw object – move it, for instance, or change its colour – you need to select it.

A Draw picture will typically contain lots of objects overlapping each other, and often one object will be completely behind another. Selecting just the object you want to alter needs a bit of skill.

1   Open the `Documents.UserGuide.DrawTutor` directory and double-click on the file called `Sign`. Once this file is loaded it looks like this:

This drawing consists of three objects:

- the outside circle – this is at the front (i.e. on top) of the three objects
- the triangle
- the exclamation mark – at the back of the stack of three objects

 2   Choose the Select tool from the toolbox (if it's not already highlighted). The toolbox is the strip of icons down the lefthand side of the Draw window – click on the arrow at the bottom of the toolbox and it will be highlighted.

3   Click on the circle to select it. A dotted box (known as a bounding box) will appear around it, indicating that it is selected:

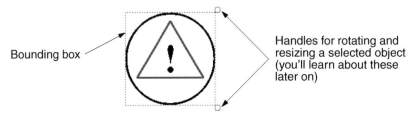

Bounding box

Handles for rotating and resizing a selected object (you'll learn about these later on)

Selecting 'buried' objects

When an object's bounding box extends beyond others, it's easy to select: as long as you click on that part of the object, it will be selected. When an object is in front of others (as the circle is), again you'll have no problem: click anywhere within it to select it.

However, it can be difficult to select an object that's 'underneath' other objects. You can often see many objects apparently occupying the same physical place, but in fact they're 'stacked' on top of one another.

For instance, clicking on the triangle will in fact select the circle, because the circle is in front of the triangle. To select the triangle, you need to **double-click** on it.

If you double-click many times, you'll 'tunnel down' through the objects that are stacked on top of each other, selecting each one in turn.

Changing the 'stacking order' of overlapping objects

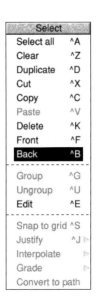

The exclamation mark is behind the triangle, so you **could** select it by double-clicking and tunnelling down through the stack of objects to reach it. However, another way of getting to a buried object is to send the objects covering it to the back of the stack:

1   Select the circle, press Menu and choose **Select/Back** (or press Ctrl-B).

2   Select the triangle (by double-clicking) press Menu and choose **Select/Back.**

3   Select the exclamation mark by single-clicking on it.

Now the exclamation mark is always at the front; you don't need to double-click repeatedly each time you want to select it.

You can change the stacking order of objects using this method (e.g. you could bring the circle to the front of the stack by selecting it and choosing **Select/Front**).

Moving selected objects

Once you've selected an object, you can drag it anywhere within the Draw window. For example:

1   Select the exclamation mark and move the pointer inside the bounding box.

2   Now hold down Select and drag the exclamation mark outside the circle (don't click on the 'handles', these stretch and rotate the object):

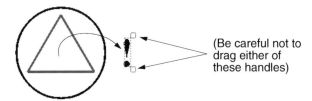

(Be careful not to drag either of these handles)

Having practised selecting objects, there is nothing else you need to do with this file, so you can close it by clicking on its Close icon. If during your experimenting, you have changed the file at all, you'll see a message warning you of this; click on **Discard** to tell the computer you don't want to save your changes.

Start the drawing: create the map symbols

Six different symbols are used on the map; two types of tree, a picnic site, a mountain, an historic building and a parking site symbol:

The first part of this tutorial takes you through creating these symbols.

Set the size of the drawing area

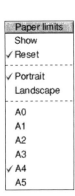

The first step in creating the map is to click on the Draw icon on the icon bar (if you don't have Draw loaded on the icon bar see page 277). This displays an empty Draw window. You should now check that the drawing area is A4, landscape:

1   Move your pointer into the Draw window and press Menu.

2   Make sure both **Landscape** and **A4** are ticked in the **Misc/Paper limits** menu.

Make the Draw window larger

The Draw window that is displayed is quite small. Increase the size of this window:

1   Make sure that the zoom is 1:1 (press Menu and check the **Zoom** option).

2   Drag the window to the top left of your screen.

3 Drag the Adjust size icon down and to the right so the window is larger, and looks nearly square.

Switch on Draw's grid

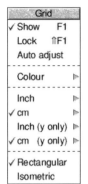

To superimpose a grid within the window:

1 Press Menu on the Draw window.

2 Choose **Grid/Show** by clicking with Adjust.

3 Choose **Grid/Lock** (this time click Select and the menu will disappear):

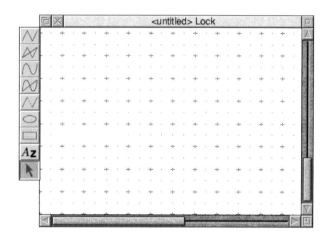

The easiest way to create most of the map symbols is to draw them large and then shrink them down to the size you want. When you have finished creating all the map symbols your Draw window will look something like this:

Toolbox

Create the hall symbol

There are five steps involved in creating the hall symbol:

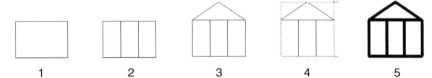

1 2 3 4 5

 1 Choose the Rectangle tool from the toolbox, then move the pointer over one of the grid markers near the top lefthand corner and click. This marks one corner of the rectangle. Move the pointer down two grid units and right three grid units and click again. The rectangle will be displayed, locked to the grid.

 2 Now choose the Straight line tool. Create two vertical lines within the rectangle. (To draw a single line, click once at the start point of the line, move the pointer, then double-click at the end point of the line.)

3 Now draw a two-segment line for the roof: Move to the top left of the rectangle and click once. Move right one and a half grid units and up one grid unit and click again. Finally move to the top right of the rectangle and double-click.

4 Next, to make the rectangle and all the lines in the symbol into one object, you have to select them all and then group them:

Choose the Select tool at the bottom of the toolbox. Select all the objects in the hall symbol (by dragging a *select box* around them), press Menu and choose **Select/Group**:

Select	
Select all	^A
Clear	^Z
Duplicate	^D
Cut	^X
Copy	^C
Paste	^V
Delete	^K
Front	^F
Back	^B
Group	^G
Ungroup	^U
Edit	^E
Snap to grid ^S	
Justify	^J
Interpolate	
Grade	
Convert to path	

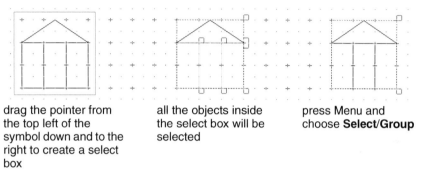

drag the pointer from the top left of the symbol down and to the right to create a select box

all the objects inside the select box will be selected

press Menu and choose **Select/Group**

If you now click outside the new bounding box, it will disappear. To select the symbol again just click on it.

5 Finally, thicken the lines in the symbol to make it stand out more: Select the hall symbol, press Menu and choose **4** from the **Style/Line width** menu. All the lines in the symbol will be redrawn 4 points wide (a point is $1/72$ inch).

Create the conifer tree symbol

1   Choose the Straight line tool in the toolbox.

2   Move to the right of the hall symbol and draw a vertical line four grid units high (notice that the lines you draw now are very thick).

3   Move to the left of the line and create a two-line segment to act as the top two branches of the tree (do this in the same way you created the roof of the hall symbol).

4   Now move down and create two more sets of branches.

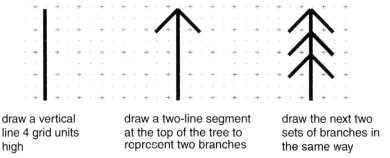

| draw a vertical line 4 grid units high | draw a two-line segment at the top of the tree to represent two branches | draw the next two sets of branches in the same way |

5   When you've finished the tree choose the Select tool, drag a select box around the tree and group it into one object.

Create the picnic site symbol

The picnic site symbol is much easier to create than it looks:

1   Select the tree symbol you have just created, press Menu and choose **Select/Duplicate**. A copy of the tree will appear slightly below and to the right of the original. Drag this copy several grid markers to the right of the original tree.

2   Choose the Straight line tool and add three lines to the copy of the tree to make up the remainder of the picnic site symbol.

3   Once again make the symbol into a single object by grouping it.

Create the mountain symbol

The mountain symbol is just a solid triangle and is very simple to create.

1   Choose the Joined line tool.

This tool allows you to create straight lines with the added feature that, when you double-click to end your path, an extra line is drawn to join the last point to the first point.

2 Move to the right of the picnic site symbol and draw a triangle as shown below. (The third line is drawn automatically when you double-click on the last point.)

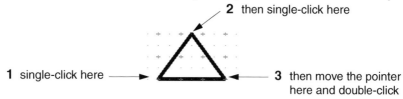

2 then single-click here

1 single-click here

3 then move the pointer here and double-click

3 Now colour the inside of the triangle black: Choose the Select tool and Select the triangle, press Menu and go into the **Style/Fill colour** box. Click on the black patch near the bottom right of the Fill colour box and click on **OK**:

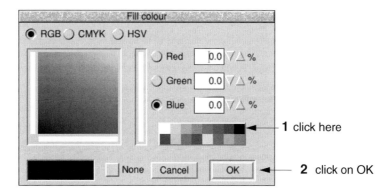

1 click here

2 click on OK

How style options work

Before you draw your next symbol it is important that you understand how the Style menu works. Every time you choose a style, e.g. Fill colour, it stays in force until you change it again, **and** it affects other tools. So if you set Fill colour to black, any subsequent rectangles, lines and curves you draw will also be filled in black. To avoid drawing an object in the wrong style, each time you choose a new tool check that you have the correct fill colour, line width etc. **before** you draw the new object.

Create the deciduous tree symbol

The deciduous tree symbol requires a little more time and 'artistry' to create. Draw this symbol below the other symbols. All your symbols will then be in full view without the need to scroll.

1 Choose the Straight line tool. Move the pointer near to the bottom right of the window and draw a small vertical line.

2 Turn off the **Grid/Show** and **Grid/Lock** options (it's very difficult to draw curves with the grid switched on).

3 Choose the Curved line tool.

4 Choose **None** in the **Style/Fill colour** box, then click on **OK**. This will ensure that whatever you draw next will **not** be filled in.

5 Move the pointer to the top of the small vertical line and click. Now move very slightly down and to the left.

You'll notice that there is a small blue square over the point where you first clicked Select, and as you move the pointer a small orange square will also appear. The blue squares are simply to show you where you clicked Select as you build up a curve. The orange squares are *control points*; they help to show you how the curve is being generated (there's more on this in *Editing curves* on page 331). Both types of square will disappear when you finish your curve. For the time being, just build up your curve clicking Select at roughly the points shown below:

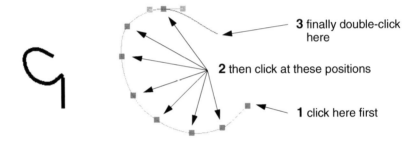

3 finally double-click here

2 then click at these positions

1 click here first

When you come to the end of the curve double-click (and leave your pointer where it is). Don't worry if your curve isn't exactly the same as the one above.

6 Now you can create the other two curves in the same way. By starting the next curve where you finished the previous one you will create a smoother, more continuous effect to the outline of the tree.

If you are dissatisfied with your curves you can either delete them and start again, or edit them. You can delete a curve (or any object) by selecting it and choosing **Select/Delete**. If you want to learn how to edit curves see page 331.

7 Finally, make the symbol into a single object by grouping it.

Create the parking symbol

There are five steps involved in creating the car parking symbol:

1 Turn on the **Grid/Show** option (but leave the **Grid/Lock** option off). Then choose the Rectangle tool and set the **Style/Line width** to **Thin**.

2 Now move to the left of the deciduous tree symbol. Click and drag the pointer to make a small rectangle, about half a grid unit wide, and almost one grid unit tall.

3   Choose the Select tool and select the rectangle. Then press Menu and go into the **Style/Fill colour** box. Click on the black patch near the bottom right of the box and click on **OK**.

draw the rectangle...   ...then fill it in black

4   Choose the Text tool. Position the pointer near the rectangle you've just drawn and click. A caret will appear. Type the letter P.

5   Use the Select tool to select the P. Now go into the **Style/Font size** box and click Adjust on **14pt**. The size of the P will increase to 14 points. Now move to the **Font name** submenu and choose **Homerton/Bold**. The P will be changed into the new font.

6   While the P is still selected go into the **Style/Text colour** box and change the colour of the P to a light grey. Then drag the P so that it is centred inside the rectangle. Now go back into the **Text colour** box and change the colour of the P to white.

drag the P into the centre of the rectangle...   ...then change the text colour of the P to white

Note: Never leave text colour set to white, or you won't see anything next time you type in any text. Always change it to black again. To do this, choose the Text tool, then click Menu and set the **Style/Text colour** to black (don't forget to click on **OK**).

7   Finally, choose the Select tool and group the rectangle and the P to make a parking symbol.

Scale the map symbols

Now reduce the size of the first five symbols to the correct size for the map:

1   Begin by selecting the hall and mountain symbols (by clicking Adjust on each symbol). Press Menu and copy them using **Select/Duplicate**.

2   Now drag the two selected copies down towards the bottom lefthand corner. Notice that both selected objects move as you drag one of them. Deselect them, drag each one separately into the bottom lefthand corner, then select them both again.

3   Press Menu and move to the **Transform/Magnify** box. Use the Backspace key to delete any value already in the box, then type in 0.2 and press ↵ (Return). The two symbols will be reduced in size.

4   Select and copy the picnic site symbol, reduce the copy of the symbol to 0.15, and move it near the two already reduced.

5   Select and copy the two tree symbols, reduce the copies of these symbols to 0.1, and move them near the three already reduced.

6   Now move the parking sign symbol to the right of the five reduced symbols.

7   Finally, select all five original, large symbols and press Delete. All that you should now see are the six symbols at the bottom left of the window:

Save your work for the first time

Now is a good time to save the work you've done so far. To do this:

1   Make sure that you have a directory display visible.

2   Press Menu over the Draw window, go into the **Save/File/Save as** box, delete the word DrawFile and type in a new filename, for example Map1.

3   Drag the **Save as** icon to your directory display.

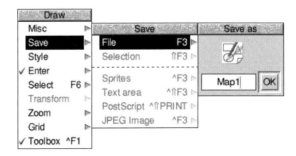

Drawing the map compass

The next task before actually drawing the map is to construct the map compass.

Draw the first compass quadrant

The compass is made up of four quadrants, but you only need to create one.

1. Turn on **Grid/Lock** (**Grid/Show** should still be on).

2. Choose the Joined line tool. Change the **Style/Fill colour** to white. Then move to the middle of the Draw window and click on one of the small grid markers. Now move up 1.5 units and right 0.5 units and click again. Finally move down two grid units and double-click to create a closed triangle:

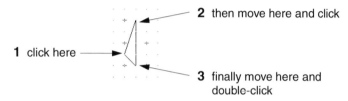

3. Move to the top of the triangle you've just created and click. Now draw a second triangle:

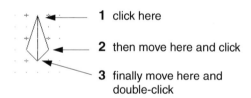

4. Choose the Select tool and select the first triangle (the lefthand one) and fill it in black using the **Style/Fill colour** box:

5. Finally, group the two triangles into a single object.

Create the other quadrants of the compass

The next step is to make three copies of this quadrant and rotate them to form the four quadrants of the compass.

1   With the quadrant selected, duplicate it three times (instead of using the menu, just select the quadrant and then press Ctrl-D three times). As each quadrant is copied it will be drawn in front of the previous one:

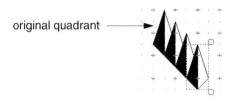

original quadrant

2   The last quadrant copied will still be highlighted. Press Menu and type 90 into the **Transform/Rotate** box, then press ↵ (Return). The quadrant will be rotated anticlockwise around its centre by 90°. Then highlight the quadrant above this one and rotate it by 180°. Rotate the other quadrant by 270°:

original quadrant

rotate by 270°   rotate by 180°

rotate by 90°

Fit the quadrants together

The four quadrants overlap each other at the moment and will be difficult to join accurately:

1   First, drag the three copied quadrants so that they form a fragmented star.

2   Then drag them so that their tips all meet the bottom tip of the original quadrant:

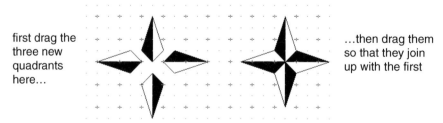

first drag the three new quadrants here...

...then drag them so that they join up with the first

3   Finally, group the four quadrants into a single object.

Add the text

The next step is to add the text indicating north, south, east and west.

1   Choose the Text tool from the toolbox. Press Menu and choose
     Style/Font size/20. From now on the size of any text you type into the drawing
     area will be drawn at 20pt. (The font should still be set to **Homerton/Bold**.)

2   Position the pointer just above the top of the first quadrant and click. A caret
     will appear. Type **N**.

3   Move the pointer and click where you want to put the E. Type in the **E** then
     move the pointer again and add the **S** and **W**.

4   Press Menu and switch off **Grid/Show** and **Grid/Lock**.

5   Now choose the Select tool and drag the letters into the correct positions:

1 add N, E, S and W

2 turn the Grid off and
position letters accurately

Scale and move the compass

When you finish drawing the compass drag a select box around it and group it.
Then press Menu and **Transform/Magnify** the compass by 0.5. Finally drag it to
the top right corner of the Draw window:

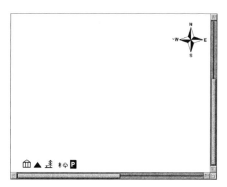

Save your work as you go along

Now is a good time to save your drawing. The easiest way to do this is to use a shortcut – press the F3 button at the top left of the keyboard. This displays the **Save as** box. You've already saved your work in a file called `Map1`, so just click on **OK** and the work you've done since you last saved your file will be saved.

Note: It's a good idea to save your work every 10 minutes or so.

Drawing the map

The next stage is to draw the map itself. When you have finished the map your Draw window will look something like this:

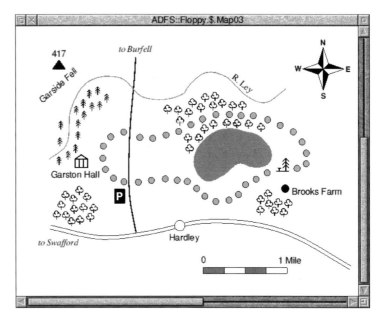

The sequence in which you'll build up the various parts of the map is:

1   Main road to Swafford

2   Road to Burfell and river

3   Hardley Lake, Garston Hall and picnic site

4   Path and Brooks Farm

5   Mountain and parking area

6   Conifers and deciduous trees

7   Map scale

8   Map text.

Draw the main road to Swafford

 Choose the Curved line tool and set the **Style/Fill colour** to **None**. Move the pointer above the Hall symbol and create the following curve (don't forget to double-click at the end of the curve):

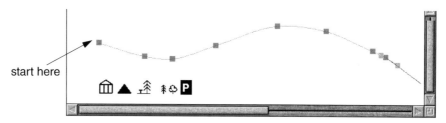

start here

Once you've created the curve, copy it and drag the copy so that it is just below the original curve. The second curve should be parallel to the first curve to give the appearance of a road. Select both lines (**hint**: drag a select box that passes through both lines) and group them.

Note: If you accidentally select one of the symbols immediately beneath the two lines, you can deselect it by clicking Adjust on it.

 To add the circle to the road, first choose the Ellipse tool. Then turn **Grid/Show** and **Grid/lock** on, click on any grid marker, and move the pointer in any direction until a small circle is displayed. Click again to finish the circle. Then turn the Grid off again. Select the circle and magnify it by 0.5. Then go into the **Style/Fill colour** box and fill the circle with white. Now drag the circle so that it sits on the road as shown below:

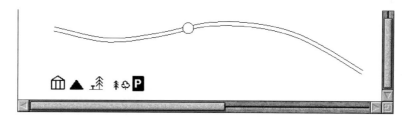

Draw the road to Burfell and the river

 The road to Burfell can be drawn as one thick line. Choose the Curved line tool and set the **Style/Fill colour** to **None**. Set the **Style/Line width** to **1**. Move the pointer to the upper line in the main road and draw a road going upwards almost to the top of the window (see the picture overleaf).

The river can be drawn using a thinner line. Set the **Style/Line width** to **0.5**, then go into the **Style/Line colour** box and choose light blue (the patch at the bottom right of the box). Now move to the left of the window and draw the river.

Construct Hardley Lake, Garston Hall and the picnic site

 Choose the Joined curve tool. Now draw the outline of the lake. (Remember that the Joined curve tool will join your last point and starting point when you double-click. Notice also that the line is drawn in blue, because you selected a blue line colour to draw the river.) Select the lake and fill it with light blue.

Drag the Hall symbol near the bottom left of the river, and then drag the picnic site symbol to the right of the lake. Your Draw window should now look like this:

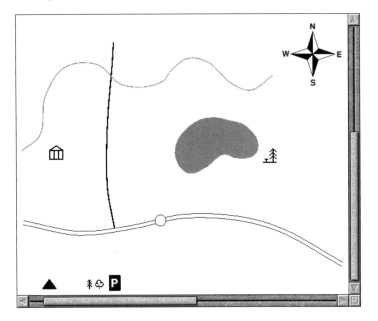

Draw the path and Brooks Farm

The path is made up of a number of filled circles. Select and copy the circle on the main road, then magnify the copied circle by 0 . 5. Go into **Style/Fill colour** and change the colour of the new circle to light grey.

Now drag the new circle to the right of the Hall symbol. Then repeatedly copy the circle and drag the copies to form the entire path (see the picture overleaf). If you drag the wrong object, don't forget you can press F8 to undo a mistake!

Make one more copy of the circle and drag it below the picnic site symbol (this will become the symbol for Brooks farm) then click Adjust on each circle in the path and group them all. (If you accidentally click Adjust on an object you don't want to group, click Adjust on the same symbol to deselect it and continue.)

Finally, magnify the circle below the picnic site by 1.2 and fill it with dark grey.

Now is a good time to save your work again.

Draw the mountain and parking area

Drag the mountain symbol near the top lefthand corner of the Draw window.

Drag the parking symbol below and to the left of where the road to Burfell first passes through the path.

Your map should now look something like this:

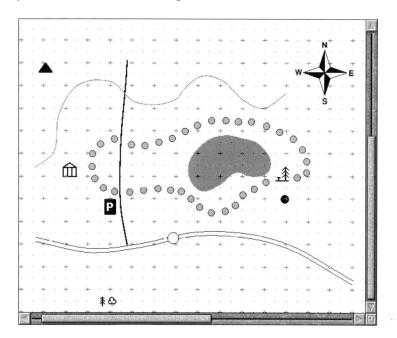

Draw the conifers and deciduous trees

Creating the conifer wood is very simple. Drag the conifer symbol near to the Hall symbol and copy and drag it until you have created a wooded area similar to the one on page 301.

Creating the deciduous woods is just the same. Drag and copy the symbol to each of the three deciduous woods shown on page 301.

Draw the map scale

1 Begin by switching on **Grid/Show** and **Grid/lock**.

2 Choose the Rectangle tool and set the **Line width** to **0.25**, the **Line colour** to black and the **Fill colour** to white.

3 Move below the circle on the main road and draw a rectangle one grid unit long and half a grid unit high.

4 Draw three more rectangles, joined together.

5 Select the first and third rectangle and fill them in dark grey:

6 Turn **Grid/Lock** and **Grid/Show** off, select the four rectangles and group them. While the grouped rectangle is still selected, click on the handle at the bottom right and drag it up so that the rectangle becomes thinner:

drag this handle up to make the rectangle thinner

7 Choose the Text tool. Set the **Font name** to **Homerton/Medium** and the **Font size** to **12**.

8 Type in 0 at one end of the scale, and 1 mile at the other.

0   1 Mile

9 Finally group the scale and text.

Add the map text

1 Type in the following text at the positions shown on the map on page 301:

```
Garston Hall    to Burfell    R. Ley      Garside Fell
Hardley         to Swafford   417         Brooks Farm
```

2 The text you have just typed in should still be in Homerton Medium 12pt. To make the text stand out, change to Swafford and to Burfell to **Trinity/Medium.Italic**. Then change R. Ley to **Trinity/Medium**.

3 Use the rotate handle to rotate R. Ley so that it is parallel to the direction of the river:

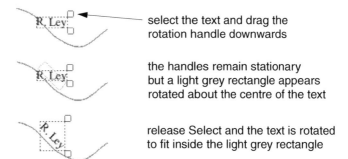

select the text and drag the rotation handle downwards

the handles remain stationary but a light grey rectangle appears rotated about the centre of the text

release Select and the text is rotated to fit inside the light grey rectangle

4 Rotate the text Garside Fell in the same way. Your map should now look like this:

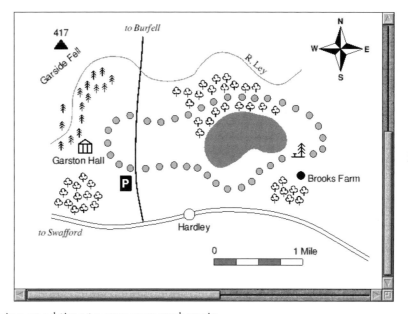

Now is a good time to save your work again.

Adding a written description of the walk

Now to add a written description of the walk immediately above your map...

Add the title

Drag the scroll bar on the righthand side of the Draw window up as far as you can, then choose the Text tool. Set the font to Trinity Medium.Italic at 20pt.

Click at the top left of the window and type in:

```
A circular walk around Hardley lake
```

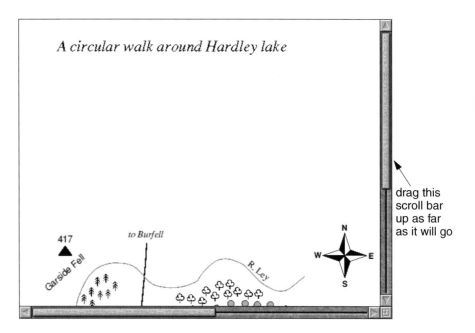

drag this scroll bar up as far as it will go

Import a text file into your drawing

You can include the contents of a text file into a **text area** in a Draw file. A text area is a special object which accepts text from another file. A text file called `MapText` has been included in the `Documents.UserGuide.DrawTutor` directory which contains a description of the walk around Hardley lake. The first few lines of this file contain commands which specify the font, paragraph spacing and so on.

For a full description of text areas, and the special commands that you can include in a text editor to describe how to format the text, see *Text areas* on page 340.

1 Choose the Select tool.

2 Open the `Documents.UserGuide.DrawTutor` directory and you'll find a text file called `MapText`. Drag this file onto your Draw window. When you release Select some text will be displayed:

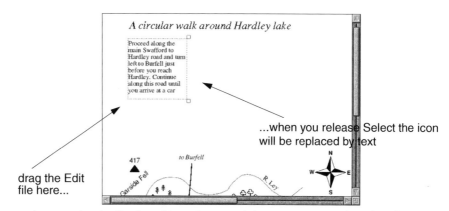

drag the Edit file here...

...when you release Select the icon will be replaced by text

The text that is displayed is only part of the text contained in the file. To display the entire contents of the file:

3 Select the text area and drag it beneath the title.

4 Drag the bottom handle down and to the right so that all the text in the file is displayed:

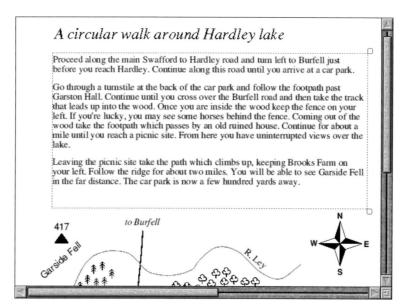

Importing a picture

Now to import a photograph of the lake, which has been scanned into a sprite file:

1   Begin by dragging the scroll bars on of the Draw window as far down and right as you can, then go into the `Documents.UserGuide.DrawTutor` directory and drag the sprite file called `LakeView` onto the Draw window.

2   Select the sprite and magnify it by 0.7. The sprite will now be re-drawn slightly smaller. Drag it to the position shown below:

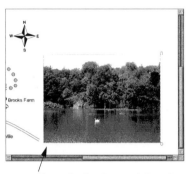

drag sprite file here   magnify sprite by 0.7 and drag here

3   Now choose the Rectangle tool (set the **Style/Fill colour** to **None**) and draw a rectangle around the sprite.

4   Choose the Text tool and type in `View from the Picnic site` at 16pt:

Information box

The final part of the map is the Information box.

Draw the box outlines

1   Begin by dragging the scroll bar on the bottom of the Draw window as far right as you can, and the scroll bar on the right of the window as far up as you can. Then switch on the Grid and Grid lock.

2   Choose the Rectangle tool and draw a rectangle near the top righthand corner of the window 11 grid units wide and 7 grid units deep.

3　Choose the Straight line tool and draw a vertical line dividing the box in two. Now draw a horizontal line one grid unit down from the top of the box, and a second horizontal line four and a half grid units down. The left side of the box is now divided into three smaller boxes:

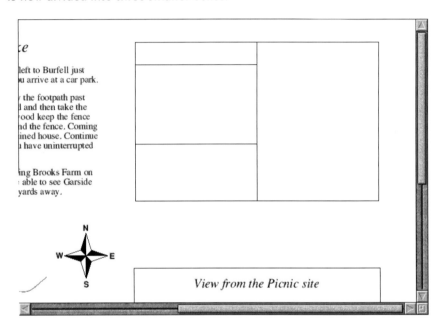

Add text to the box

1　Choose the Text tool and change the font to Homerton Bold 14pt.

2　Click on the grid marker two grid units down from the top of the box and half a grid unit in from the left of the box. Type in the word GOING. Click down one grid unit and type in TIME, then click another grid unit down and type in LENGTH. Now click to the right of GOING and type in Wet, and then type in 3 hours and 6 miles one grid unit down and two grid units down from Wet.

3　Turn the Grid and Grid lock off. Then type ** Feature ** in the centre of the bottom box.

4　Click in the centre of the top box and change the font size to 16pt. Type INFORMATION.

5   Finally click below the word 'Feature', change the Font name to Trinity
Medium.Italic and the Text size to 14pt, and type in `Horses you might`
then press ⏎ (Return) and type `see in the wood`. Now choose the Select
tool and drag the two lines you have just typed in to centre them inside the
box:

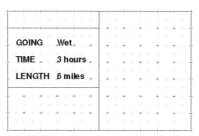

type this text in using the grid   ...then remove the grid and type in
to line up the two columns of text...   the remaining text

Import a picture of some horses

Scroll the Draw window down. Then drag the sprite file called `Horse` from the
`Documents.UserGuide.DrawTutor` directory to a spot just above the word
'Farm' in 'Brooks Farm'. To start with, the horse is displayed far too large, so select
and magnify it by 0.4. Now scroll back up and drag it so that it's centred inside the
righthand side of the box:

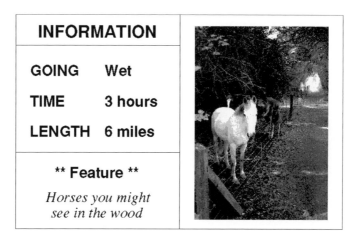

The final map

Your map is now finished. If you want to display the entire map in your Draw
window, press Menu and set the zoom factor to 1:2 in the **Zoom/Magnifier** box.

The entire map will then be displayed (at half its original size) in the Draw window:

A circular walk around Hardley lake

Proceed along the main Swafford to Hardley road and turn left to Burfell just before you reach Hardley. Continue along this road until you arrive at a car park.

Go through a turnstile at the back of the car park and follow the footpath past Garston Hall. Continue until you cross over the Burfell road and then take the track that leads up into the wood. Once you are inside the wood keep the fence on your left. If you're lucky, you may see some horses behind the fence. Coming out of the wood take the footpath which passes by an old ruined house. Continue for about a mile until you reach a picnic site. From here you have uninterrupted views over the lake.

Leaving the picnic site take the path which climbs up, keeping Brooks Farm on your left. Follow the ridge for about two miles. You will be able to see Garside Fell in the far distance. The car park is now a few hundred yards away.

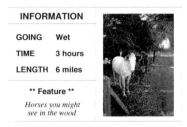

INFORMATION	
GOING	Wet
TIME	3 hours
LENGTH	6 miles

** Feature **

Horses you might see in the wood

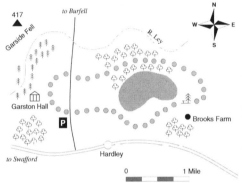

View from the Picnic site

Save your map if you want to, and compare it with the file `Map` in the `Documents.UserGuide.DrawTutor` directory.

If you have a printer connected you can print your finished map by pressing the Print Screen key on your keyboard; it may take a while to print due to the size of the picture files included. If it doesn't quite fit on your printer's paper, try grouping all the objects in the file and magnifying them (e.g. by 0.9). For more details about printing Draw files see page 338.

Draw reference section

In this section, each of the Draw functions, including those you used in the tutorial, are explained in depth. Don't worry if you don't understand every last word; the real way to learn Draw is by using it.

Undoing and redoing operations

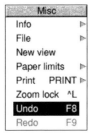

As you create a drawing, you'll often decide that you want to undo the last operation you performed. It's easy to retrace your steps and correct any errors you make:

To	Do this	Notes
Undo the last change you made to your drawing	Choose **Misc/Undo**.	You can also press F8; this is the keyboard shortcut you'll probably find most useful.
Redo an operation, if you decide that you didn't need to undo it after all	Choose **Misc/Redo**.	Keyboard shortcut: F9. You can Undo and Redo all the steps you performed since you last saved the file (providing the Undo buffer is sufficiently large – see page 352).

Using the Grid to place objects accurately

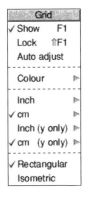

You can superimpose a rectangular or isometric grid on a drawing. This is useful for lining up objects and for checking their relative sizes. The grid is made up of 'major points' (marked by crosses) and 'minor points' (marked by dots).

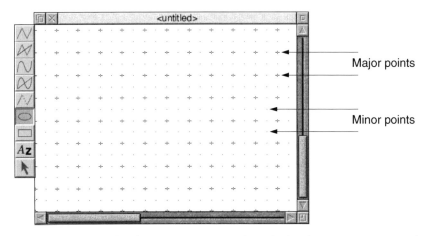

You can use the grid either just as a general guide for drawing, or you can lock objects to it, so that they always align with points in the grid (the exception is if you rotate an object). When you are creating objects with grid lock turned on, you will see them attach to the nearest grid point to the pointer position.

To	Do this	Notes
Switch the grid display on or off	Choose **Grid/Show**.	
Switch the grid lock on or off	Choose **Grid/Lock**.	Causes new objects to align with the grid as you create them. **Show** need not be on in order to use **Lock**.
Allow the grid spacing to change automatically	Choose **Grid/Auto adjust**.*	Draw inserts or removes minor points as you zoom in and out. Objects only lock to displayed points.
Change the colour of the grid points	Choose from the **Grid/Colour** submenu.	

To	Do this	Notes
Define the grid spacing	Choose a spacing from the **Grid/Inch** or **Grid/cm** submenu.	First number gives major point spacing. Second number gives number of subdivisions. You can define your own values at the bottom of the submenu.
		Just clicking on **Inch** or **cm** uses existing submenu settings.
Set Y grid spacings to be different from X spacings	Enter the Y spacings in the **Grid/Inch (y only)** or **Grid/cm (y only)** submenu.	X spacings are still taken from the **Inch** or **cm** submenus.
Use a rectangular grid pattern	Choose **Grid/Rectangular**.	
Use an isometric grid pattern	Choose **Grid/Isometric**.	
Make existing objects snap to the grid	Choose **Select/Snap to grid**.	The baseline of the text snaps to the grid. For grouped objects, the top left of the bounding box snaps to the grid.
Snap all an object's control points to the grid	Go into Path edit mode and choose **Edit/Snap to grid**.	Path edit mode is described on page 330.

In the "Do this" column, under "Define the grid spacing" a submenu is shown:

Inch spacing
✓ 1 × 4
  1 × 16
  1 × 5
  1 × 10
Spacing ▷
Subdivision ▷

* If you turn Auto adjust off and specify a very close spacing, the grid may take some time to draw.

Zooming in and out of your drawing

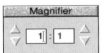

You can alter the apparent size of your drawing. For example, you might want to look at something close-up to position it accurately, or you might 'zoom out' to see your whole drawing at once. This doesn't alter the actual size of your draw objects.

To	Do this	Notes
Zoom in and see your drawing at a higher magnification	Increase the ratio in the **Zoom/Magnifier** box, e.g. from 1:1 to 2:1, or from 1:2 to 1:1.*	You can also press Ctrl-W to zoom in by one magnification factor.
Zoom out to see more of your drawing	Decrease the ratio in the **Zoom/Magnifier** box, e.g. from 2:1 to 1:1, or from 1:1 to 1:2.	You can also press Ctrl-Q to zoom out by one magnification factor, or Shift-double-click Adjust.
Zoom in on a particular area of your drawing	Shift-Adjust-drag a box around the area.	
Return to the previous zoom factor	Press Ctrl-R.	
Go back to original size (1:1)	Press Ctrl-0.	
Lock the zoom factor	Choose **Misc/Zoom lock**.	Keyboard shortcuts are locked to 1:1, 1:2, 1:4, or 1:8. For example, each time you press Ctrl-Q, you halve the zoom factor. When you press Ctrl-W, it's doubled.

* You can't have a number greater than 8 in the Magnifier box.

If you scale up an object in Draw and then highly magnify the view, the object may disappear. To retrieve the object, undo these operations. Reduce the object's scaling so that it doesn't disappear again.

Displaying two views of the same file

Choose **Misc/New view** to create a new view of the drawing you are editing, in a separate window. Edits you make in one view of a drawing show up in the other views as well. You can change the zoom on each view independently, use different grids in the separate views, scroll each one independently, and so on. To get rid of a view, close the window containing it.

Creating objects (Enter mode)

This section describes each tool in the toolbox. When you're in the process of creating any object (except text) you'll see a 'skeleton' version of it on the screen.

Hints

You can cancel most operations part-way through by pressing Escape or choosing **Enter/Abandon**.

You can get a count of the total number of objects present from **Misc/File**.

You can choose tools from the toolbox on the lefthand side of the Draw window, or by using the **Enter** submenu.

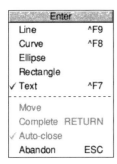

To	Do this	Notes
Draw an open-ended path made up of straight and/or curved line segments	Choose the appropriate line tool. Click to place end points for each segment. Double-click to complete the path (or press ↵, unless there are only two points).	You can change tools part-way through constructing a path. You can also choose **Enter/Line** or **Enter/Curve**.
Draw a closed path made up of straight and/or curved line segments	Choose the appropriate Joined line tool. Click to place end points for each segment. Double-click (or press ↵) to complete the path.	You can change tools part-way through constructing a path. You can also switch **Enter/Auto-close** on and use **Enter/Line** or **Enter/Curve**. If Auto-close is off, choose **Enter/Complete** or press ↵ to close the path.

313

To	Do this	Notes
Create a multi-path object	Use the Move tool.	See page 315. You can also use **Enter/Move**.
Draw an ellipse or circle	Choose the Ellipse tool. Click once to define the centre. Move pointer and click again to draw the ellipse.	You can also choose **Enter/Ellipse**. Turn **Grid/Lock** on (page 310) to help draw a circle.
Draw a rectangle or square	Choose the Rectangle tool. Click once to define a corner. Click again on the opposite corner.	You can also choose **Enter/Rectangle**. Turn **Grid/Lock** on to help draw a square.
Enter a line of text	Choose the Text tool. Click where you want the line to start then type in your text.	You can also choose **Enter/Text**. If using anti-aliased fonts, you may need to increase the size of the font cache.
Select an object so you can edit it	Choose the Select tool and click on the object.	See page 316 and page 330 for more on editing objects.
Switch the toolbox on and off	Press Menu and choose **Toolbox**.	You can use the menu options described above to choose and use Draw's tools without using the toolbox. You can also use keyboard shortcuts (see page 350).

Drawing multi-path objects with the Move tool

 You can use the Move tool to create a single object made up of apparently unconnected paths. This is useful for creating objects that have transparent holes in them. You can only use the Move tool with the four line segment tools.

Creating a multi-path object

To create one object made up from multiple paths:

1   Choose one of the four line segment tools.

2   Construct the first path by clicking on the end points of each segment (don't double-click at the end of the path).

 3   Click on the Move tool – the move icon will **not** be highlighted.
    This lets you move to the start of another segment without drawing a line.

4   Construct the next path.

5   Repeat steps 1 to 4 until you've created all the paths and double-click to finish.

You'll now have a single object, made up of many paths. You can't 'ungroup' such an object. You can edit it, though (see page 330).

Creating a hole in a filled object

Here's an example of how to create a filled rectangle with a transparent hole in it:

1   Choose a fill colour from the **Style/Fill colour** dialogue box.

2   Choose **Style/Winding rule/Even-odd** (don't worry about this for now – it's explained on page 327).

 3   Draw a rectangle using the Straight line tool (don't double-click to complete the shape; just click once to place the last point on top of the first).

 4   Click on the Move tool (the move icon will **not** be highlighted).

5   Draw a smaller rectangle inside the first.

When you double-click, you'll be able to see through the hole:

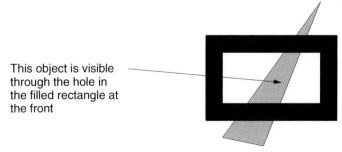

This object is visible
through the hole in
the filled rectangle at
the front

Note: You can't start or end a path with a Move.

Manipulating objects (Select mode)

This section tells you how to select and deselect objects, and how to manipulate a selection.

Selecting and deselecting objects

 Choose the Select tool (at the bottom of the toolbox) to enter Select mode. In Select mode, you can make changes to existing objects. To return to Enter mode and draw another object, choose one of the other tools.

When you select an object, you'll see its bounding box, with handles at two of its corners (not all objects have these – see page 319).

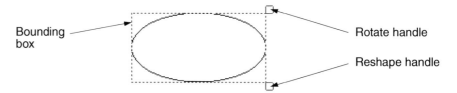

To	Do this	Notes
Select an object	Click on the object.	
Select a group of objects	Drag a select box around (or through) all the objects.	You can also click Adjust on each object in turn.
Select all objects in the drawing	Choose **Select/Select all.**	You can also press Ctrl-A.
Select **only** objects that lie wholly within a select box	Shift-drag a select box.	Normally, a select box selects everything it touches.
Select an object obscured by another	Double-click over the object.	If the object is one or more 'layers' deep, keep double-clicking to 'tunnel through' to it.
Deselect an object	Click Adjust on the object.	
Deselect all currently-selected objects	Click Select on an empty part of the drawing.	You can also choose **Select/Clear** or press Ctrl-Z.

The clipboard

Draw supports the use of the *global clipboard*, an imaginary off screen area for temporarily holding objects for later retrieval. The clipboard allows you to transfer objects held on there to other applications that support it, for example copying a diagram produced in Draw into a spreadsheet.

The process usually involves two steps: an initial copy (or cut) operation, followed by a paste operation.

To	Do this	Notes
Cut a selection	Choose **Select/Cut** or press Ctrl-X.	You can alternatively press Delete.
Copy a selection	Choose **Select/Copy**. or press Ctrl-C.	The selection is copied to the clipboard, but remains unchanged in the drawing.
Paste a selection	Choose **Select/Paste** or press Ctrl-V.	You can alternatively press Insert. Anything pasted from the clipboard will replace the current selection.

The clipboard holds a single item, so if you copy (or cut) a second object there it will cause the previous contents to be forgotten.

To make a duplicate of a selection locally within a drawing, while leaving the global clipboard unchanged, choose **Select/Duplicate** or press Ctrl-D. The new copy will be pasted into your drawing, slightly below and to the right of the original.

To delete a selection, while leaving the global clipboard unchanged, choose **Select/Delete** or press Ctrl-K.

Grouping and ungrouping objects

To	Do this	Shortcut
Group a selection	Choose **Select/Group**.	Ctrl-G
Ungroup a selection	Choose **Select/Ungroup**.	Ctrl-U

Moving objects to the front or back of a stack

To	Do this	Shortcut
Bring an object to the front of a stack	Choose **Select/Front**.	Ctrl-F
Hide an object behind one or more other objects	Choose **Select/Back**.	Ctrl-B

Aligning objects (justification)

Justify
Left
Centre
Right
Top
Middle
Bottom

You can align objects, both vertically and horizontally.

Note: You need to group any objects before you can align them.

To	Do this
Align a selection horizontally	**Group** the objects, then choose **Left**, **Centre** or **Right** from the **Select/Justify** menu.
Align a selection vertically	**Group** the objects, then choose **Top**, **Middle** or **Bottom** from the **Select/Justify** menu.

In the following example three objects have been grouped and then justified left, centre and right:

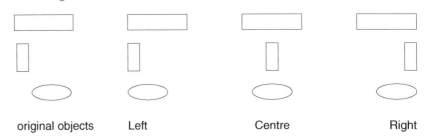

| original objects | Left | Centre | Right |

Moving, rotating and scaling objects

There are different ways of rotating and scaling objects, depending on how accurate you want the operation to be.

To	Do this	Notes
Move a selection	Drag it to the new position and release Select.	If you move a selection when **Grid/Lock** is on, it moves in jumps of the grid spacing (see page 310).
Copy a selection to another drawing or application	Drag it outside of the current diagram window, and drop it onto either another diagram or another RISC OS application.	The receiving application must be able to load the type of object being dragged – be it Draw, Sprite, or JPEG files.
Rotate a selection*	Drag the Rotate handle (at the top righthand corner of a bounding box).	The selection rotates about its centre.
Rotate a selection by a specified angle	Type the angle into the **Transform/Rotate/Angle** box. Angle 90	
Resize a selection	Drag the Resize handle (at the bottom righthand corner of a bounding box).	Linewidths are **not** scaled when you use this method. To preserve the aspect ratio of the object, use the method below.

319

To	Do this	Notes
Resize (scale) an object accurately	Type the scale factor into the **Transform/Magnify** box. Magnify 2.5	You can also choose to scale an object in the horizontal or vertical plane only: Choose **Transform/Scale X** or **Scale Y**.
Scale the line width of an object	Type the scale factor into the **Transform/Line scale** box. Line scaling 2	When you scale an object using this method, its linewidth **is** scaled. You can also define the linewidth of an object along with its other style attributes – see page 325. You can't scale lines of width **Thin**.

* You can't rotate Text in System font, Text areas or imported JPEG files (they have no Rotate handle).

Creating special effects in Draw (interpolation and grading)

Using interpolation and grading you can perform the following operations on two **grouped** objects:

- Change one object into the other object by inserting similar objects between them – cartoon animators call this 'in-betweening', 'tweening' or 'morphing'.

- Create intricate patterns using the two objects.

Changing one object into another object (morphing or tweening)

To change one object into a different object:

 1 Draw two objects using the Joined line tool (see *Restrictions* on page 324).

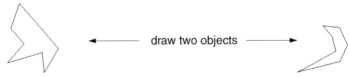

draw two objects

2 Group the two objects together.

 3 Type the number of gradations into the **Select/Interpolate** or **Select/Grade** box (8 is the default value) and press ↵.

A new set of objects will be drawn. Each new object is a partial transformation between the first object and the second object:

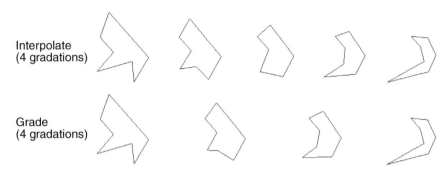

Interpolate
(4 gradations)

Grade
(4 gradations)

Interpolation produces a number of new paths, each consisting of two objects. You cannot ungroup these paths. This means that when you interpolate two objects you'll lose the original objects (**Duplicate** them elsewhere in the Draw window **before** you interpolate them, or use **Undo** to start again if you want).

Grading produces new objects which are not grouped as paths:

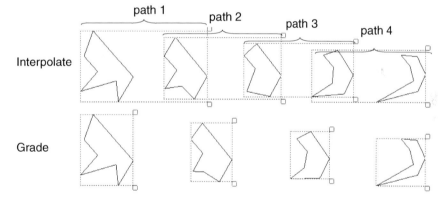

path 1   path 2   path 3   path 4

Interpolate

Grade

Creating intricate patterns

You can create interesting patterns if one object is inside (or on top of) the other:

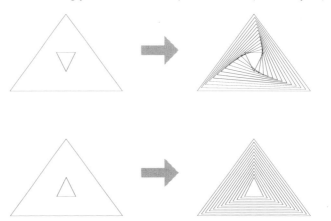

You can interpolate between curved shapes to produce very intricate patterns:

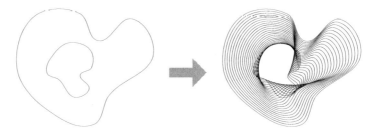

The difference between interpolation and grading is most evident when both shapes are closed and filled:

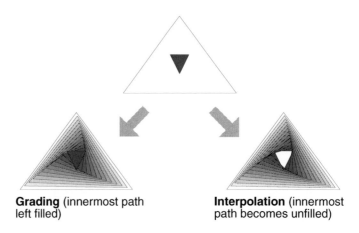

Grading (innermost path left filled)

Interpolation (innermost path becomes unfilled)

Properties used by interpolation and grading

The properties used by interpolation and grading are

- line colour
- fill colour
- line width
- triangle start/end cap height
- triangle start/end cap width

Restrictions

A pair of path objects for interpolation or grading must have certain properties in common. For most practical purposes, this means they should be more or less the same shape (though they need not be the same size): two V-shapes, two rectangles, and so on. Specifically, the requirements are that

- for each line or curve in one, there must be a line or curve in the other
- for each move in one, there must be a move in the other
- for each close in one, there must be a close in the other
- objects must be drawn starting at the same end point
- objects must be drawn in the same direction (clockwise or anticlockwise)
- objects must be single-paths; they cannot be grouped objects.

Defining a path object's style

Each object has a style consisting of a set of attributes (such as fill colour, line colour, line width and so on). Using the various **Style** menu options, you can

● set the style to be applied to every new object you create in Enter mode

Any new object you create is given the style attributes currently defined in the Style menu. We suggest that you set up the style attributes **before** you actually draw an object. This can save you accidentally 'losing' objects because they're the same colour as the background.

● alter the style of existing objects when in Select mode.

Here's how to define an object's style:

To	Do this	Notes
Define the width of line used to draw an object	Choose a width (in points) from the **Style/Line width** submenu, or define your own at the bottom of the submenu.	'Thin' means 'the narrowest width possible'. This produces different widths on different output devices. It's more sensible to use 0.25pt, especially if you'll be printing on a typesetter.
Create path objects with coloured outlines	Choose a colour from the **Style/Line colour** window.	There's lots of help on using the colour picker window in *Using colour in applications* on page 239.
Fill path objects with a given colour	Choose a colour from the **Style/Fill colour** window.	You can fill open objects, as well as closed ones. Complex objects will be filled according to which winding rule you've set – see page 327.
Make a path object transparent	Choose **None** from the **Style/Fill colour** window.	

To	Do this	Notes
Draw a dashed or dotted path object	Choose from the **Style/Line pattern** submenu. 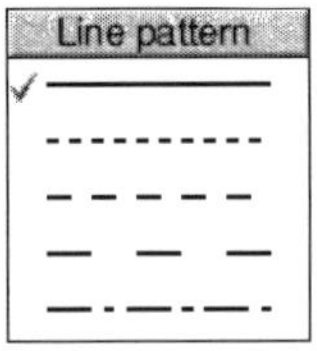	You can modify dashed and dotted lines using the **Start cap** and **End cap** options; the cap settings apply to each segment in the line.
Define how lines* are joined together	Choose a join type from the **Style/Join** submenu.  Mitred Rounded Bevelled	
Define how lines† start and end	Choose an end type from the **Style/Start cap** and **End cap** submenus.  Butt Round Square	This only applies to open paths; though you can use Start caps on a closed path with a dashed line style. Notice how the round and square caps extend the original line (shown here in white) by one line thickness.
Add arrows to line ends	This is an extension of the **Start** and **End cap** submenus.	See *Adding arrows to line ends* on page 327.

* This is only effective for thick lines
† This is only significant for thick lines

Adding arrows to line ends

Triangle caps are useful for creating arrows on the ends of line segments. You can set the height and width of a triangle cap independently. They are defined as multiples of the line width, as follows:

Triangle height   = Cap height × Line width
Triangle width   = 2 × Cap width × Line width

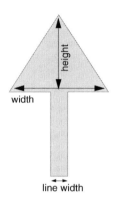

For example, to set an arrowhead of width 16pt and height 16pt on a line of width 4pt, you'll need to choose:

Style/Start cap/Triangle/Width/×2
Style/Start cap/Triangle/Height/×4.

Note: The arrow is added to the line segment, extending the segment by the height of the arrow.

Note: With a dashed or dotted path object, the cap settings apply to each segment in the line. For a single arrow at the end of a dashed or dotted path object, create a second short solid path with triangle caps and move this on top of the longer path.

Filling objects with colour – the winding rule

Style/Winding rule allows you to specify which of two methods is used to fill different regions of an object with colour. It only affects objects for which a fill colour has been set. It's not commonly used, but you'll need to understand it if you're creating objects with transparent holes in (see page 315).

An object can be a single path (e.g. an ellipse), a collection of line segments, or a single line segment that crosses over itself any number of times.

Non-zero winding rule

This rule fills regions on the basis of whether they were drawn in a clockwise or anti-clockwise direction.

Note each region's direction as you draw it, clockwise or anti-clockwise, and give this direction a number: +1 for one direction and −1 for the other.

To see if a region is to be filled, construct an imaginary line from inside the region to outside the object. Keep a total of the direction values for each line it crosses. If the total is non-zero, the region will be filled (see the diagram overleaf).

In the following example, three rectangles were drawn clockwise and one rectangle was drawn anti-clockwise. The clockwise rectangles were assigned a value of +1, and the anti-clockwise rectangles were assigned a value of −1:

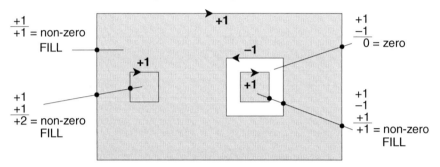

Even-odd winding rule

This rule fills regions if they are enclosed by an even number of other regions.

To determine whether a region inside an object is to be filled, imagine a line passing from inside the region to outside the object. Count the number of lines it crosses. If the number is odd, the area will be filled.

The following example shows this rule applied to a single path object made up of four regions (created using the Move tool – see page 315):

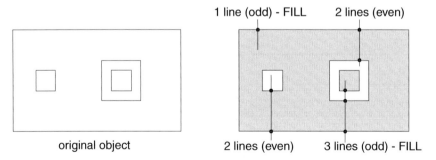

Defining text style

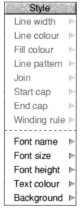

Style
Line width ▷
Line colour ▷
Fill colour ▷
Line pattern ▷
Join ▷
Start cap ▷
End cap ▷
Winding rule ▷
- - - - - - - - - -
Font name ▷
Font size ▷
Font height ▷
Text colour ▷
Background ▷

You can change the style attributes of text lines using the Style menu. If you select a text line first, that line will have the style applied to it. All subsequent text lines will also have that style applied to them.

To	Do this	Notes
Set the font name	Choose from the **Style/Font name** submenu.	See *Using fonts in applications* on page 245 for more details about using fonts.
Set the font size	Choose from the **Style/Font size** submenu.	You can supply a different font size (in points) at the bottom of the submenu.
Change the font height, but not its width	Choose from the **Style/Font height** submenu.	
Define the colour of the text	Specify a colour using the **Style/Text colour** window.	
Set the colours used to anti-alias fonts on a coloured background	Specify a colour using the **Style/Background** window.	See below for more details on this.

Superimposing text on a coloured background

Style/Background sets the intermediate colours used around the edges of anti-aliased fonts. You don't usually need to worry about this, but it's useful if you're creating text on top of a coloured object:

1   Set the **Text colour** of your text.

2   Select the object on which your text is superimposed and note down its colour from the **Style/Fill colour** window.

3   Set the **Style/Background** colour of the text to be the same as that you noted down in step 2.

The anti-aliasing pixels will be in a range of shades between the **Text colour** and the **Background** colour. **Background** applies to both text objects and text areas.

If the text is superimposed on top of a non uniform colour object such as a JPEG photograph, then select **None** as the **Background** colour to anti-alias the text to the background of whatever is underneath the text rather than a uniform colour.

Note: This effect won't be visible if the text size is larger than the value set for anti-aliasing in Configure (see page 91).

Editing Draw objects (Path edit mode)

All objects you construct using Draw's tools are made up of paths. In turn, paths consist of straight and curved line segments. Each segment in a path has end points and (if it is a curve) control points.

You change an object in two ways:

- resize it or transform it in Select mode (see page 316)
- change its basic shape (edit it) by going into Path edit mode and moving individual end points and control points

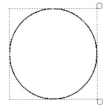 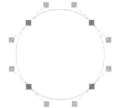 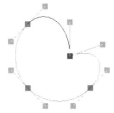

Select mode:	Path edit mode:	circle has been edited:
reshape and rotate	control points (yellow)	control and end points
handles visible	and end points (blue) visible	have been moved

Note: You can't edit Text areas, JPEGs or sprites in Draw. See pages 337 to 340.

Entering and leaving Path edit mode

You can only edit a single-path object in Path edit mode (so you'll need to ungroup any objects first).

To	Do this	Notes
Go into Path edit mode from Enter mode	Choose any path tool and click Adjust on the object you want to edit.	
Go into Path edit mode from Select mode	Select an object then choose **Select/Edit**.	You can also press Ctrl-E once the object is selected.
Edit an object (move a control point or end point)	Drag the point with Adjust.	There's more on editing below.
Leave Path edit mode	Click Select on a blank area of the drawing.	

Editing curves

Curved segments in a path object are defined by two end points and two control points. When drawing or editing a path, the control points are shown connected to the end points by straight lines.

The shape of a curve is determined by the control points as follows:

- The direction of the curve at the end point lies along the line connecting the end point to the control point (i.e. this line is a tangent to the curve).

- The degree to which the curve moves away from this straight line depends on the distance of the control point from the end point: the nearer together they are, the sooner the curve turns away.

By moving the control points, you can produce many different shapes of curve. Some examples are shown below. In each case the thick line shows the path itself, and the control points (shown here as black squares, although they're yellow in the drawing) are joined to the corresponding end points (shown here as open squares) by thin lines.

If you hold down Shift while you drag a control point, the corresponding control point in the next curve is also moved to keep the angle of join constant.

Editing text lines

When typing in text, you can only delete text and type new text in if you are still on the same line. As soon as you press ↵ (Return) or click somewhere else in the drawing, the line is 'frozen'.

To	Do this	Notes
Edit a 'frozen' text line	Select the text line and choose **Select/Edit** to display the Text box. ┌─────────────┐ │ Text │ ├─────────────┤ │ Here's some text│ └─────────────┘	You can also press Ctrl-E after selecting the object.
Convert each letter in a text line into an editable path object	Select the text line and choose **Select/Convert to path**[*].	All the letters are grouped initially; to edit them individually, **Ungroup** them. There's an example below.

* You can't convert back to a text line, nor can you convert text in System font.

Editing text as a path object

Once you've converted a text line to a path, it can be treated like any other path object (for example, you can use **Style** options that apply to objects other than text – see page 325).

For example, the following text was converted into a path, then ungrouped into individual letters, and each letter given a black line colour and a different fill colour (the second row of text was also given a much thicker line width):

Shaded text

Shaded text

Note: You can only convert outline fonts to a path.

Editing objects using the Path edit submenu

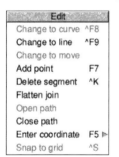

You can also change a path object's shape using menu options. This method gives you much greater control:

1   Enter Path edit mode (see page 330).

  If the path you want to edit is under another object's path, double-click Adjust to tunnel through to the next deeper path.

2   Select a segment by clicking Adjust on an end point or a control point.

  The line segment and end point will be highlighted (if you select the first end point of the path, there is no highlighting).

3   Click Menu to show the Edit menu.

Now you can edit the highlighted segment and end point:

To	Do this	Notes
Change a straight line segment into a curve	Choose **Edit/Change to curve**.	Works if the selected segment is a line, or if you've selected a point inserted using a Move.
Change a curved segment into a straight line	Choose **Edit/Change to line**.	Works on a curved line segment or a Move.

To	Do this	Notes
Break a path at the highlighted segment (by replacing the segment with a Move operation)	Choose **Edit/Change to move**.	You can't change a segment to a move if it's at an end of the path, or if it's already preceded or followed by a move. See page 336.
Insert an extra point into the highlighted segment	Choose **Edit/Add point**.	In effect, this adds an extra segment to the object, of the same type as the selected segment.
Delete the highlighted segment	Choose **Edit/Delete segment**.	
Straighten the join between two segments	Choose **Edit/Flatten join**.	This joins the **control** points by a straight line. See page 335.
Change a closed path into an open path, or vice versa	Choose **Edit/Open path** or **Edit/Close path**.	This 'disconnects' or joins the first and last points in the path.
Specify an end point's position accurately	Choose **Edit/Enter coordinate** and type the position into the **New coordinates** box.	X and Y are offsets from the bottom lefthand corner of the drawing. You can specify them in inches or centimetres.

	New coordinates	
x	3.355556	◯ Centimetres
y	10.200000	◉ Inches
	Cancel	OK

To	Do this	Notes
Make all the end points in an object snap to their nearest major grid points	Choose **Edit/Snap to grid**.	

How 'Flatten join' works

This flattens the join between two adjacent segments (unless both segments are straight lines). The curve is adjusted so that the tangent is continuous at the selected end point. For example:

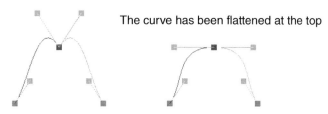

The curve has been flattened at the top

How 'Change to move' works

If the path containing the line was closed, extra lines will be inserted to close each of the two sections of the path:

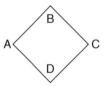

1. Here's a diamond shape, drawn starting at A.

2. Clicking Adjust at C selects segment B-C.

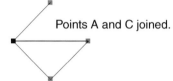

3. Choosing **Change to move**. replaces side B-C by a Move.

Points A and C joined.

Final shape looks like this:

Importing (loading) files into Draw

You can import five types of file into Draw:

- Existing Draw files and other files that use Draw's own file format
- Sprite files (see page 337)
- Text files, used to create text area objects (see page 340)
- Photo-quality images (JPEG files – see page 347)
- DXF files (see page 346)

To	Do this	Notes
Load any of the above file types into an open Draw window	Drag the file's icon over the Draw window.	If you drag a Draw file into an open Draw window, the default settings of the dragged file are used.
Load any of the above file types into a new Draw window	Drag the file's icon over the Draw icon on the icon bar.	

When you drag a file into a Draw window, it is added to any objects already in the window. The file is loaded so that its bottom lefthand corner lies at the mouse position at the instant the mouse button is released.

When you load a file by dragging it to the icon bar, the file appears in a new Draw window, aligned to the bottom lefthand corner of the diagram.

Draw's ubiquity on all versions of RISC OS means that many third party applications will have options to export their content in Draw file format, from spreadsheet pie charts to entire web pages, and import diagrams also. The Draw file format is described in the RISC OS *Programmer's Reference Manual* allowing them to be created from your own programs too relatively easily.

Loading a sprite into Draw

If you drag a sprite file containing many sprites into Draw, only the first sprite will be loaded. A more convenient method of loading a single sprite is to:

1 Load the sprite file into Paint.

2 Open a sprite window for the sprite you want to load into Draw.

3 Make sure the sprite has a palette (click Menu and switch **Edit/Palette** on).

4 Drag the icon in the **Save/Sprite/Save as** box into a Draw window.

This method also ensures that Draw displays the sprite in the correct colours.

Exporting (saving) files from Draw

You can save objects from a Draw file in their own native file format. This means, for example, that if a Draw file has an imported sprite, you can save that out as a sprite again.

Note: You need to be in Select mode to save anything other than the whole Draw file (see page 316).

To	Do this	Notes
Save the whole file as a Draw file	Use the **Save/File/Save as** box as normal.	
Save a selection of Draw objects as a Draw file	Use the **Save/Selection/Save as** box.	

To	Do this	Notes
Save the currently-selected sprite	Use the **Save/Sprites/Save as** box.	You can only save a single sprite at a time (not a group or selection).
Save a selected text area object	Use the **Save/Text area/Save as** box.	
Save the whole drawing as Encapsulated PostScript	Use the **Save/PostScript/Save as** box.	You can use this to import the drawing into another application that accepts Encapsulated PostScript[*]. You must load Printers and a PS printer definition file for this option to be available.
Save a selected image as a JPEG file	Use the **Save/JPEG Image/Save as** box.	See JPEGs (*photo-quality images*) on page 347.

[*] You should not use Encapsulated PostScript files for printing as they do not contain page size information.

Note: The DrawFile format includes a 'Type 11' object which records details about the page size and orientation of the file. Some old applications may fail to load Draw files containing this object. To overcome this problem, load the Draw file into Draw, choose **Select all** and save the selection; this saves a Draw file without a type 11 object.

Printing Draw files

To print a Draw file:

1   Make sure you have a printer connected and set up (see *Printing your files* on page 207 and *Setting up printers* on page 189).

2   Make sure that your drawing will fit on the paper on which you are going to
    print (switch on **Misc/Paper limits/Show** then set the page size and
    orientation to match that of your printer).

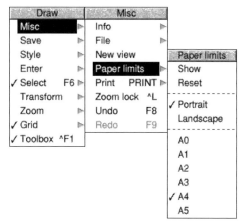

3   Choose **Misc/Print** (or press the Print Screen key)

4   Set the number of copies in the dialogue box and click on **Print**.

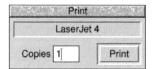

Only objects within the inner limits of the grey border in the Draw file will be
printed. The outer limits of the grey border correspond to the limits of the page. If
no printer driver is loaded, the limits default to A4.

Misc/Paper limits/Reset sets the paper limits to the printer driver defaults.

Printing part of a diagram

You can also select **part** of the diagram to be printed at a time. This enables you to
print a drawing on more than one sheet, so that you can make up a poster, for
example, from several standard-size sheets 'tiled' together:

1   Choose **Paper limits/Show**.

2   Hold down Ctrl and use one of these methods to define the printed area:

    ●   click to mark the bottom lefthand corner of the printed area

    ●   click Adjust to mark the top righthand corner

    ●   drag a bounding box around the area you want to print; it will be scaled to
        fill the page when it is printed

3   Choose **Misc/Print**, or press the Print Screen key.

Text areas

A text area is a special sort of object that allows you to perform simple 'desktop publishing'. A text area consists of a piece of text divided into one or more rectangular regions called **text columns**. Draw breaks up the text into lines which are just wide enough to fit into the columns, splitting it (principally) at spaces.

You can create a text area by using Edit (for example) to prepare a file containing the text, annotated with special commands (described below). When you load the text file into Draw, the text is formatted into columns. The number of columns is given by an annotation. You can move the text columns and change their size in Select mode. As you do this, Draw will reformat the text between the columns.

Text areas only use anti-aliased fonts: you cannot create a text area in the System font. If you try to use the System font you will find that it is automatically converted into the Trinity font. See *Default text area header* on page 346. If you want to create a text area in System font, use the outline font version of the System font: choose **Style/Font name/System/Fixed**.

Creating and editing text areas

To create a text area from a text file, drag the file into a Draw window. The columns in the text area are initially set up to standard sizes. If you drag the text file over the top of a selected text area, the old text in the area is replaced with the contents of the new file. Use this method for altering the text in a text area.

Text area selection works in two slightly different ways, depending on how many text columns there are in the text area:

Single text columns

When there is a single text column in the text area, selection works in the same way as any other object. You can move the text area, scale it, change its style, and so on, as described above.

Multiple text columns

When there is more than one text column, selection is a two-stage process. When you first click (or click Adjust, in multiple object selection) over the text area, the entire area is selected. You can move the area, but it cannot be scaled. Double-click (or double-click Adjust) to select a column of the text area. You can move and scale individual columns. Their new position and size need not lie within the original text area.

When you change the size of a text column, the text is reformatted to fit the new size of the column.

To select more than one column of a text area, select the first as described above, and select further ones by first clicking Adjust and then double-clicking Select over the column.

You can't rotate text areas and text columns (they don't have rotate handles).

Some select mode actions cannot be applied to text columns. If there are any text columns selected when you perform the operation, they are deselected first. An example of this is object deletion: you can delete a text area as a whole, but not a text column from within it.

An example

Try typing the following text into Edit and loading it into Draw as a text file:

```
\! 1
\AD
\D2
\F0 Trinity.Medium 24
\L24
\0
This is an example of a text area containing two columns.
The text was prepared in Edit, and then saved directly
into Draw. The columns were then stretched to the right
size, using select mode, and the rectangles added.
```

creates the following text area:

This is an example of a text area containing two columns. The text was prepared in Edit, and then saved directly into

Draw. The columns were then stretched to the right size, using select mode, and the rectangles added.

The appearance of a text area is determined from commands which are included in the text used to create it. Each command starts with a backslash (\) character. The full list of sequences is given below, but the following is a brief description of the commands used in the example.

- \! 1 tells Draw that this is a text area.
- \AD causes the text to be justified to left and right in its columns.
- \D2 indicates the number of columns to be displayed.
- \F0 Trinity.Medium 24 specifies font 0 as Trinity.Medium, 24pt.
- \L24 sets the line spacing to 24pt.
- \0 selects font 0 for the following text.

Text area commands

The following is a complete list of text area commands. Some commands must be terminated with either a newline or a slash (/) character. Others do not need a terminator (for example, where the command has a fixed number of characters) but may optionally end with a slash character. For clarity, it is often useful to include it. Note especially that **all commands are case sensitive**: this is unusual in RISC OS and applications written for it.

In the following descriptions

- items in italics (for example *code*) indicate a parameter you must supply;
- items in square brackets are optional (for example [/] indicates an optional slash character);
- commands and parameters must normally be separated by spaces (though there does not have to be a space between the command and the first parameter);
- ↵ means a single newline character, and ↵/ means newline or /.

Here's the full list of annotations:

Command	Effect
\! *version* ↵/	This is a special line which must appear at the start of any file which is to be used for a text area. *version* must be 1. However, it forms part of a default header which is inserted at the start of the text; this is described below.
\A *code* [/]	Set alignment. *code* may be L (left aligned), R (right aligned), C (centred) or D (double, i.e. justified to both margins). An alignment setting forces a line break. The default setting is left aligned.

Command	Effect
\B *red green blue* ↵/	Set the background colour to the given red/green/blue intensity, or the best available approximation. Each intensity is in the range 0 to 255; values outside this range will be limited to it (i.e. a value set higher than 255 will be realised as 255; a value set to less than 0 will be realised as 0). Background colour is used in the same way as for text objects; you should set it to be the same as the area of the drawing that the text area is to appear in front of (the text area itself is effectively transparent). The default is the background style attribute of the text area object, normally white (equivalent to \B 255 255 255). To set the background to 'None' use \B -1 -1 -1.
\C *red green blue* ↵/	Set the text colour to the given red/green/blue intensity, or the best available approximation. Each intensity is in the range 0 to 255; values outside this range will be limited to it. The default is the text colour style attribute of the text area object, normally black (equivalent to \C 0 0 0). To set the colour to 'None' use \C -1 -1 -1.
\D *columns* ↵/	Indicates that the text area is to contain the indicated number of columns. This must appear before any printing text. The default is 1.
\F *font-number name size |width|* ↵/	Defines a font reference. `font-number` is either one or two digits. The font number is used subsequently to set the font. `name` is a font name such as Trinity.Medium. `size` and `width` are the height and width of the font in points. If `width` is omitted, the size is used for both height and width. There are no defaults.
font-number |/|	Indicates that the text from the point at which the command appears is to appear in the specified font. If the font is not available when the text is being drawn, the effect is undefined. Draw will attempt to check that the font number and the corresponding definition are reasonable. There is no default.

Command	Effect
\L *line-spacing* ↵/	Sets the line spacing (the distance from the base of the characters in one line to the base of the characters in the next) to the given value, measured in points. Line spacing changes take effect from the end of the output line in which the command appears. The default is 10pt.
\M *left-margin* *right-margin* ↵	Sets the left and right margins to the given values, measured in points. If the total size of the margins is greater than the width of the column, no text is displayed. Margin settings apply from the end of the output line in which the command appears. The default is 1pt at each side.
\P *paragraph-spacing* ↵	Sets the extra space inserted between paragraphs to the given value, measured in points. Paragraph spacing changes take effect from the end of the output paragraph in which they appear. The default is 10pt.
\U *position thickness* ↵	Switches on underlining, at the given position relative to the base of the characters. `position` is limited to the range −128 to 127, and `thickness` to the range 0 to 255. Both values are measured in units of 1/256 of the current font size. Underlining may be turned off by specifying a thickness of 0.
\U. [/]	An alternative way of turning underlining off.
\V[-] *vertical-move* [/]	Moves the following text by the given amount, measured in points, relative to the current character position. This is intended for superscripts and subscripts; use positive values for superscripts, negative values for subscripts.
\-	Inserts a soft hyphen. This tells Draw that it may split the word at this point if necessary, inserting a hyphen character in the output. If the word is not split at the soft hyphen, it has no printing effect.
\↵	Forces a line break.
\\	Inserts a backslash character.
\;*text* ↵	Treated as a comment. Characters up to and including the next newline are ignored.

Rules for displaying text areas

Line splitting

Draw displays text in text areas by splitting it into lines and columns. When deciding where to split the text, Draw tries to split it at the space or soft hyphen that gives the most characters that will fit in the column. If this is not possible, the text is split at the character that gives the longest line that just fits in the column.

Special characters and paragraph formatting

Certain characters have special interpretations:

- All control characters are ignored, except tabs, which are treated as spaces.
- Newline characters appearing before any printing text insert a paragraph spacing.
- A single newline character in the body of the text is treated as a space, unless it is preceded or followed by a space, in which case it is ignored.
- A sequence of n newline characters in the body of the text inserts n–1 paragraph spacings.

For columns other than the first, paragraph spacings at the head of the column are ignored. Lines which protrude vertically beyond the limits of the column are not displayed; however, all commands occurring in them are interpreted. This can occur if the line spacing is significantly smaller than the font height. You should take care (by using the \M command) to ensure that lines do not protrude beyond the limits of the column horizontally, since the text may not be displayed correctly in this case. The only circumstances in which this is likely to happen are when an italic font is used and the margin setting does not allow for it.

Font usage

When a text area is being constructed from a text file, or being loaded as part of a Draw file, checks are made on the fonts contained in it. If a font is not available, a warning message is displayed. Text that should be in this font will appear in the most recently-used font.

Exporting text from a text area

You can re-export text used to construct a text area back into a text file, by choosing **Save/Text area**. This can be useful for altering text areas in a Draw file, when the original text file used to create them is no longer available.

Default text area header

If the text does not start with a version number line (\! 1), Draw will insert the following standard header:

```
\! 1
\F 0 Trinity.Medium 12
\F 1 Corpus.Medium 12
\0
\AD
\L12
```

This defines two font references, sets the text to be displayed in font 0 (Trinity Medium) justified to both left and right margins, with a line spacing of 12pt. If you subsequently export the text, the standard header will be exported as well.

DXF files

Draw can read files in DXF (data interchange) format. This is a file format used by other graphics programs such as AutoSketch. Draw cannot save files in DXF format.

When you load a DXF file into Draw by dragging it into a window or onto the Draw icon, a dialogue box appears, in which you can specify

- whether coordinates and sizes in the file are to be interpreted as being in inches or centimetres;

- a scaling unit to be applied to all coordinates and sizes;

- the name of the font in which text is to be plotted. If the name you give is blank, or is not the name of an outline font known to Draw, the text will be plotted in the System font.

To load the file, click on **OK**. If you click on **Abandon**, the file is not loaded.

The following restrictions apply to DXF files loaded into Draw:

- The following DXF object types are not implemented: SHAPE, ATTDEF, ATTRIB, 3DLINE, 3DFACE, DIMENSION.

- Line types are ignored: all lines are created as solid.

- Layers are not implemented.

- Text justification may be approximate in outline fonts.

- Straight line objects are drawn in a single width and colour.

- Colours are guessed from a set of standard values. Unknown colours are converted to black.

- Text may not be rotated or oblique. The text style table is not used. There is no backwards or upside-down plotting.

- A single font is used for all the text in the file.

- There is no curve fitting.

- Block INSERTs do not use column and row values, attribute entries, rotation, or z scaling.

JPEGs (photo-quality images)

Draw can read files in JPEG format. JPEG stands for **J**oint **P**hotographic **E**xperts **G**roup, and is a standard format for compressing photographic images (see the samples in the `Documents.UserGuide.Pictures` directory, for example).

Unlike Paint, if you load a JPEG into Draw, all the original file information is kept. This means, amongst other things, that you can save an imported image back out of Draw as a JPEG file again. It also means that if you change from one screen mode to another with more colours, you'll see an imported JPEG file at a higher quality.

When you display a DrawFile containing a JPEG object, the graphics system requires some workspace for processing the JPEG data. You can see this on your Tasks display as the dynamic area 'JPEG workspace', and its required size depends on the height in pixels of your JPEG image.

If there is insufficient free memory to allocate this workspace, Draw displays a JPEG image as a light grey rectangle containing the message 'Not enough memory available to plot JPEG'.

JPEG objects were added to the DrawFile standard in RISC OS 3.60 yet some third-party applications may not interpret that object correctly, either displaying a blank box where the JPEG image should be or reporting an error.

If this is a problem, use Paint or ChangeFSI to convert your JPEG images into sprites, and replace the JPEG images in your Draw file with these sprites. This can produce a picture with the same appearance, but using far more space on disc and in your computer's memory to store.

Working with multiple Draw files

You can work on several Draw files at the same time; simply click on the Draw icon on the icon bar to start up another Draw window.

It's easy to copy objects between Draw windows. Select the object you want to copy, move the pointer to the destination Draw window and choose **Select/Copy**. The selected object is copied into the new window. Alternatively you can use the **Save** and **Save Selection** menu options to drag Draw icons into new Draw windows.

If you are working with multiple Draw windows, only one window can be 'active' at a time. So, if you select an object in one window and then select an object in another window, you will nullify the selection in the first window. Additionally clicking on the Draw icon to create a new diagram nullifies any current selection.

Saving Draw application preferences

You may wish to change some aspects of the way new Draw windows appear. For example, a new window normally opens with the Joined line tool selected, but you may prefer to have the Select tool ready to use each time you start Draw.

To change the application preferences, open the **Choices...** dialogue box from Draw's icon bar menu.

You can modify the **New diagram settings** to reflect how a new Draw window should appear. Click on the pop-up menu icons to show menu lists to set

- the **Mode selection** which will be active from the toolbox (**hint**: the mode can always be changed later from the toolbox, if it is showing)

- the **Paper limits**, its size, and orientation

- the **Grid** appearance, colour, style, and spacing.

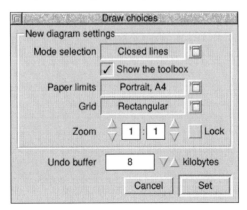

The default zoom magnification and setting of the zoom lock can also be set. These act as described in *Zooming in and out of your drawing* on page 312.

The amount of memory reserved to implement the **Undo buffer** across all Draw windows can also be changed from this dialogue. A larger value will give a longer history of operations at the expense of more memory.

Click on **Set** to make the changes, or **Cancel** to close the window. Use Adjust click to keep the choices window open.

Keyboard shortcuts

Many Draw operations can be carried out from the keyboard instead of the menus and mouse; when you are familiar with the application, you may find this more convenient.

In Enter mode

To	Use this keystroke
Save a file (calls up the normal **Save as** box)	F3
Save a selection	Shift-F3
Save a sprite or JPEG Image	Ctrl-F3
Save a text area	Ctrl-Shift-F3
Save as Encapsulated PostScript (this option is only available if a PostScript printer driver is loaded)	Ctrl-Shift-Print
Load a named file (calls up a dialogue box into which you can type the name of the file you want to load)	F2
Insert a named file (calls up a dialogue box into which you can type the name of the file to insert into the Draw file you are working on)	Shift-F2
Close a window	Ctrl-F2
Print a file	Print
Toggle between show and hide grid	F1
Toggle grid lock on and off	Shift-F1
Switch the toolbox on or off	Ctrl-F1
Zoom out	Ctrl-Q
Zoom in	Ctrl-W
Zoom to 1:1	Ctrl-0
Go back to the previous zoom	Ctrl-R
Toggle **Zoom lock** on and off	Ctrl-L
Undo an action	F8
Redo an action	F9
Enter **Select** mode	F6
Move the pointer one pixel	←, ↓, →, ↑

In Select mode

To	Use this keystroke
Cut a selection to the clipboard	Ctrl-X or Delete
Copy a selection to the clipboard	Ctrl-C
Paste from the clipboard, replacing any current selection	Ctrl-V or Insert
Delete a selection without affecting the clipboard	Ctrl-K
Duplicate a selection	Ctrl-D
Select all	Ctrl-A
Clear selection	Ctrl-Z
Bring a selection to the front	Ctrl-F or Ctrl-F4
Send a selection to the back	Ctrl-B or Ctrl-Shift-F4
Group a selection	Ctrl-G or F4
Ungroup a selection	Ctrl-U or Shift-F4
Snap a selection to grid	Ctrl-S or Shift-F5
Enter Path edit mode	Ctrl-E or Ctrl-F6
Justify a selection	Ctrl-J or Ctrl-F5

In Path edit mode

To	Use this keystroke
Change a line to a curve	Ctrl-F8
Change a curve to a line	Ctrl-F9
Add a point	F7 or Ctrl-C
Delete a segment	Ctrl-K, or Delete, or Shift-F8
Enter a coordinate	F5
Finish a path edit	Return
Snap to the grid	Shift-F5 or Ctrl-S

351

For tool selection

To	Use this keystroke
Enter text	Ctrl-F7 or Tab
Enter a closed line	Ctrl-F9
Enter a closed curve	Ctrl-F8
Complete a path	Return
Abandon an operation	Escape

27   Paint

Paint is a pixel-based picture editor; you can use it to 'paint' coloured images by applying colours to an area with a variety of brushes and painting tools.

You'll probably find that the easiest way of learning Paint is to read through *Basic ideas* (on the next page) and then work through the *Paint tutorial* which follows, before reading the *Paint reference section* starting on page 367.

Starting Paint

Paint is in the Apps icon bar directory display. To start Paint and create a new sprite:

1   Double-click on the !Paint icon to install it on the icon bar.

2   Click on the Paint icon bar icon to display the Create new sprite window.

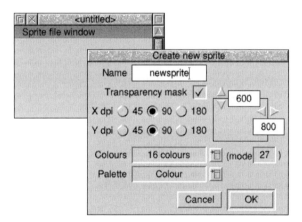

3   Fill in the details for your new sprite and click on **OK** (it's probably best to follow the tutorial starting on page 355 if you don't already know how to do this).

Alternatively, edit an existing sprite file by dragging its file icon to the Paint icon on the icon bar, or by double-clicking on it.

Basic ideas

 The pictures produced by Paint are called *sprites*.

A sprite is a graphic shape made up of an arrangement of pixels (the smallest unit the screen uses in its current mode). Sprites are stored in *sprite files*, which can contain more than one sprite. Sprites and sprite files use a standard format, so you can freely export images produced by Paint to other RISC OS applications (such as Draw) that recognise sprites. You can also use Paint to edit sprites produced by other RISC OS applications, and to import and edit JPEG files.

The important difference between Paint and Draw is that, unlike Draw, Paint knows nothing about 'objects' such as rectangles and circles; all it knows is the colour of each pixel in a sprite. Although you can paint regular shapes, you cannot then select them in order to delete, move or resize them.

When you export (save) a sprite from Paint into Draw, this remains true: regular shapes forming part of the sprite cannot be edited like Draw objects. The whole sprite becomes a single object in your Draw diagram; you can move or resize it, but not otherwise edit it.

Choosing colours in Paint

Paint can create and edit pictures in any RISC OS screen mode: 16 million colours, 64 or 32 or 4 thousand colours, 256 colours, 16 colours, 4 greys and black and white. There are two different ways of choosing colours in a sprite:

- Sprites created in up to 256 colours use a Colours window arranged as a set of coloured squares, each with a colour number, to choose from (the following tutorial uses this method – see page 357).

- Greater than 256 colours make use of the Colours window described in *Using colour in applications* on page 239.

Creating sprite files compatible with earlier versions of RISC OS

If you want to create sprite files that are compatible with earlier versions of RISC OS, make sure you choose a sprite type that has an equivalent old-type mode number. See page 387 for more information.

Paint tutorial

This tutorial section shows you how to use Paint to produce a small, simple picture, made up of two flowers in diagonal corners. In fact you'll only need to paint one flower, you can then copy it and re-colour it:

you'll paint this
flower first...

...then copy it and
change its colour

You can then use the Pinboard application to repeat this picture all over your screen producing a 'wallpaper' type background:

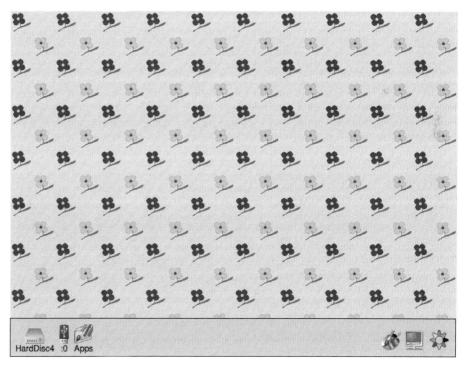

The tutorial is not designed to show you how to use all the Paint tools – in fact it only uses a few – but to give you a general idea of how the application works.

All of Paint's tools are described in detail in the *Paint reference section* on page 367.

Create a new sprite

1   Click on the Paint icon on the icon bar.

This displays the **Create new sprite** and **Sprite file** windows.

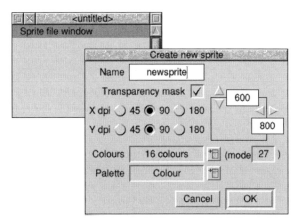

2   Delete the existing name `newsprite` (using the Backspace key) and type in the name for your sprite: `flowers`.

3   Make sure the **Transparency mask** box is ticked.

4   Change both the width and the height of the sprite to be 80.

5   Change the number of colours to 16.

6   Choose **Colour palette**.

7   Click on **OK** and your new (blank) sprite is created.

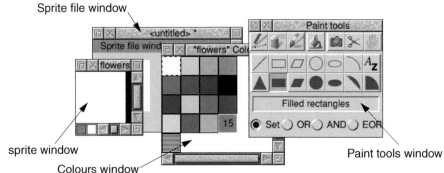

Sprite file window

sprite window

Colours window

Paint tools window

You should now have four Paint windows on your screen:

- the Sprite file window – shows all the sprites in that sprite file
- the sprite window – where you can make changes to the sprite using Paint
- the Paint tools window – contains the tools you can use for painting
- the Colours window – contains the colours you can paint with

Drag the tools window and the colours window to the right of your screen, and drag the Sprite file window to the bottom left of your screen. Leave the sprite window in the middle of the screen.

Zoom in

The sprite you've just created is very small. To help you see what you're doing, click Menu on the sprite window and change the **Zoom** factor to 8:1 (see page 376 for more on zooming):

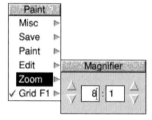

The blank sprite will now fill most of your screen, and at this magnification a grid is superimposed over the painting area. Each square in the grid represents one pixel.

Create the first flower petal

1 Choose the **Use sprite as brush** tool from the Paint tools window (click on it).

   The bottom of the tools window will expand to display an area where you can define the type of paint brush you want to use and its size. The default brush type is a circle.

2 Reduce the brush size by changing the **X scale** and **Y scale** boxes to **1:2**, and then click on **OK**.

3 The first flower will be dark blue: Click on the dark blue colour in the Colours window.

   That colour will be highlighted and overlaid with the number 8 (to signify that this is colour 8 out of a palette of 16 colours).

4 Move the pointer into the sprite window. You'll notice that the pointer is now attached to the centre of a circle. Move the pointer to the approximate position shown below and click. A solid, dark blue circle will appear:

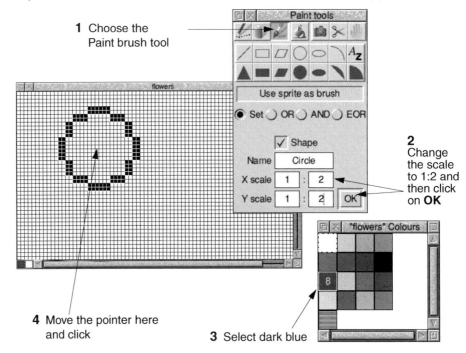

1 Choose the Paint brush tool

2 Change the scale to 1:2 and then click on **OK**

4 Move the pointer here and click

3 Select dark blue

Note: If you accidentally remove either the colours window or the tools window from your screen you can restore them by pressing Menu over the sprite window, and choosing **Paint/Show colours** or **Paint/Show tools**.

Save your sprite for the first time

Now is a good time to save your sprite:

1 Click Menu over the Sprite file window (**not** the sprite window).

2 Change the name in the **Paint/Save/Save as** dialogue box to Flower.

The name of the sprite file appears in the Title bar of the sprite file window.

Note: You should save your work frequently as you proceed. You can then return to the last step if you go wrong. This is an especially good idea with Paint, since with some of the tools you can easily make mistakes. Unlike Draw, you can't undo your work in Paint.

Paint the next three petals

Move the pointer to the centres of the three other circles shown below and click. Don't worry if your circles are in slightly different positions:

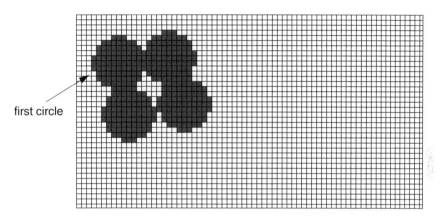

first circle

Tip: If you've put a circle in the wrong position don't despair, change the colour to white then paint over the incorrect circle. You can then change the colour back to blue and redo the circle.

Save your work again

Once you're satisfied with your four petals, save your work again before you go on: Just click Menu over the Sprite file window (not the sprite window) and choose **Save**. You don't need to supply a name this time.

Create the middle of the flower

You need a smaller brush to paint the middle of the flower:

1   Change the **X scale** and **Y scale** boxes in the Paint tools window to **1:4**.

2   Select yellow (colour 9) from the Colours window.

3   Paint a small circle in the centre of your four petals:

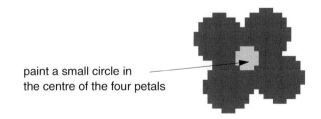

paint a small circle in
the centre of the four petals

Touch up the centre of the flower

If you find that there are one or two white pixels still in the centre of the flower, you can turn them into dark blue pixels:

1 Choose the **Set/Clear pixels** tool from the tools window (the icon for this looks like the tip of a pencil).

2 Choose dark blue as your current colour.

3 Click Select over any white pixels inside your flower.

Save your work again at this point.

Paint the stem

The final step in creating the flower is to paint in a green stem:

1 Choose light green (colour 10) from the Colours window.

2 Choose the **Set/Clear pixels** tool from the tools window (you may already be using this tool if you did any touching up).

3 Paint the pixels beneath the flower to look like a stem (click on each pixel in turn).

   If you click over one pixel, only that pixel will be coloured. If you drag the pointer while holding down Select button, each pixel it moves over will be coloured:

Tip: If you make any mistakes, click Adjust to change the incorrect green pixels back into white ones.

This is another good point to save your work before going on.

Create the second flower

The second flower goes in the bottom right corner of the sprite. However, you don't have to paint a new flower; you can copy the one you've just made:

1 Go into the Zoom dialogue box and slightly reduce the magnification factor, then click on the Toggle size icon (in the top right corner of the sprite window) to display the entire sprite.

2 Choose the **Copy block** tool and make sure the **Local** option is switched on at the bottom of the tools window.

3 Position the pointer at the top left corner of the flower.

4 Hold down Select, drag the mouse to the bottom right corner of the flower and release Select. A rectangle will show the block of pixels that you have copied.

5 Move the pointer to the bottom right corner of the sprite window and click.

position pointer here...   ...then drag to here

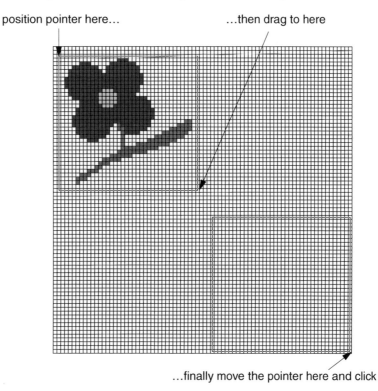

...finally move the pointer here and click

The rectangle will be replaced by a copy of the flower.

Modify the second flower

There are two changes you can make to the second flower to make it clearly different from the first one; change the colour of its petals and centre, and trace around the petals.

Change the colour of the flower

1   Choose the **Replace colour** tool.

2   Choose red (colour 11) from the Colours window.

3   Move the pointer over any part of the yellow centre of the flower and click. The centre will become red.

4   Choose yellow (colour 9) from the colours window.

5   Move over any part of the blue petals and click. All the blue pixels that touch each other will be instantly changed to yellow pixels.

Trace around the petals

The final change to make to the second flower is to trace around the edge of the petals to give it more impact:

1   Choose orange (colour 14) from the colours window.

2   Choose the **Set/clear pixels** tool.

3   Carefully trace around the outermost yellow pixels of the flower replacing them with orange:

start tracing here…   …and continue around the entire flower

You can click on each pixel individually, or drag the pointer round the edge of the petals in one go.

Change the background colour

The white background will be too stark when you use the flowers to cover your entire screen, so:

1   Choose the **Replace colour** tool, and switch the **Global** option on (at the bottom of the Tools window).

2   Choose cream (colour 12) from the Colours window.

3   Move to any white pixel in the sprite and click.
    The entire background of the sprite will be changed to cream.

Your sprite is now finished, so save it and then close the file.

Turn the sprite into a backdrop

You're now ready to wallpaper your screen with your flower sprite.

1   Click Menu over the desktop background; the Pinboard menu will appear.

2   Choose **Configure...** from this menu.

3   Drag your sprite file (called `Flower`) from its directory and drop it on the **Custom image** box.

4   Make sure that **Tiled** is selected then click **Set**.

5   Your whole screen will now be tiled with the flower sprite:

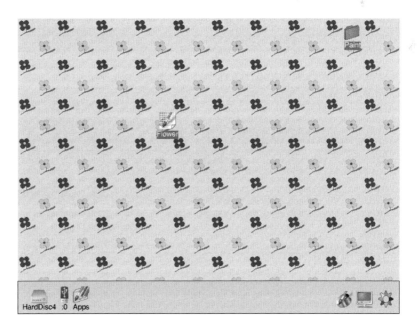

You've finished this part of the tutorial. Take a breather. The next two sections (before the *Paint reference section* on page 367) show you some advanced tricks you can use.

Painting with a sprite

This section, and the next, show you how to create some special effects in Paint. Here's how to use a whole sprite as a brush tool, to produce interesting patterns:

1 Open the sprite file called `Flower`.

2 Now click on Paint's icon bar icon and create a sprite, 400 pixels by 300.

3 In the tools window, choose the **Use sprite as brush** tool.

4 Delete the default name `Circle`, and type in the name of a sprite (in this case – `flower`).

(The sprite file containing the sprite you want to use as a brush must be open.)

5 If **Shape** is switched on, switch it off.

6 Click on **OK**.

7 You can now paint using the sprite as a paintbrush. Clicking once paints a single sprite, and dragging the brush produces a snakelike effect of sprites:

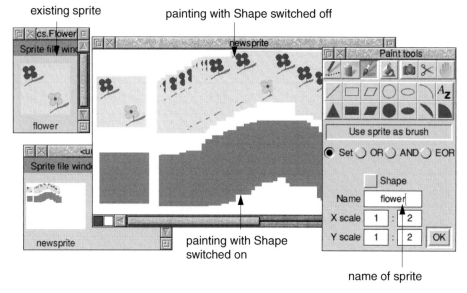

existing sprite

painting with Shape switched off

painting with Shape switched on

name of sprite

Painting with the mask of a sprite

This section tells you how to use a special colour (a mask) to make parts of a sprite transparent:

1   Make sure the sprite file `Flower` is open.

2   Click Menu over the Sprite file window and copy your flower sprite – give it the name `flower2`:

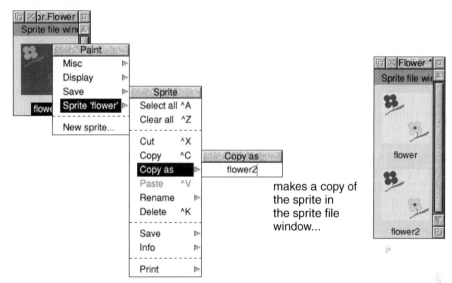

makes a copy of
the sprite in
the sprite file
window...

3   Open `flower2`, choose **Edit/Adjust size** from the main menu, and change the width of the sprite to 40 pixels.

This will chop off the right half of the sprite leaving only the flower in the top left half of the sprite.

4   Now, if it's not already ticked, choose **Edit/Mask** from the main menu to create a mask colour.

5   Choose the **Replace colour** tool and click on the **Global** button.

6   Choose the transparent colour (colour T) at the very bottom left of the Colours window – you might need to extend the Colours window down a bit to see it.

7   Click on the background of the sprite to fill it with the transparent colour.

8   Close the sprite by clicking on the Close icon.

9   Click on Paint's icon bar icon and create a new sprite (don't forget to click on **OK**).

10 In the tools window, select the **Use sprite as brush** tool.

11 Delete the default name and type in the name of the sprite you just created – `flower2`.

12 If **Shape** is switched on, switch it off and click on **OK**.

13 You can now paint individual flowers, which will have a transparent background colour:

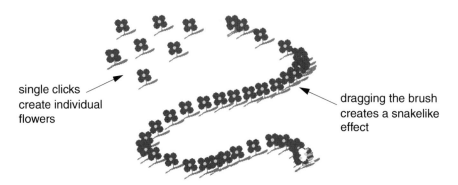

single clicks
create individual
flowers

dragging the brush
creates a snakelike
effect

You have now completed the Paint tutorial. Save the files you've just created, if you want, or just quit Paint.

The rest of the chapter is a reference section describing the basic elements of Paint, the tools in detail, and how to customise Paint so that it always starts up the way you prefer it.

Paint reference section

This section tells you in detail how to use Paint, and outlines the terms, concepts and basic techniques for creating and editing sprites. For a brief introduction to Paint and sprites, see *Basic ideas* on page 354.

Paint has several windows with specialised functions:

- **Create new sprite** window – Use this to set up a new sprite.

- **Sprite file window** – Think of this as a sort of Paint 'directory'; it can contain more than one sprite (see page 369).

- **Sprite** window – This is like any other application window (e.g. a Draw window): It contains the current file (in this case, a sprite) you're editing.

- **Colours** window – You use this in conjunction with the tools window to change the colour of pixels in a sprite.

- **Paint tools** window – This contains the different tools you use to edit a sprite's pixels.

Creating a new sprite

To create a new sprite:

1 Click on the Paint icon on the icon bar.

2 Define the sprite's attributes in the Create new sprite window:

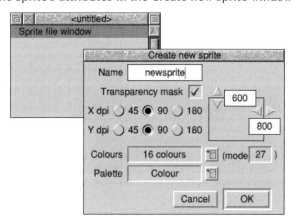

The table overleaf tells you what all the options in this dialogue box mean.

To	Do this	Notes
Name a new sprite	Fill in the **Name** box.	Sprite names can be up to 12 characters long.
Allow a sprite to use transparent pixels, as well as coloured ones	Switch the **Transparency mask** option on.	This defines an extra 'colour' in the Colours window.
Define the size of the sprite in pixels	Fill in the width and height boxes.	The default is the size of the current display. You can also click on the resize arrows adjacent to the boxes.
Change the pixel size	Choose from **45**, **90** and **180** dots per inch (dpi).	Larger dpi settings give smaller pixels.
Set the number of colours in the sprite	Choose from the pop-up menu **2**, **4**, **16**, **256**, **4k**, **32k**, **64k**, or **16M.**	Usually the same as in the current display mode.
Define whether the sprite uses a palette	Choose from the pop-up menu **Colour** for a user-definable colour palette, **Greyscale**[*] for uniform grey shades, or **None** for the default palette for the chosen number of colours.	Sprites with more than 256 colours have no palette. 256 colour sprites may also be created with 64 or 16 (fixed) colours for backward compatibility with earlier versions of RISC OS. Colour sprites with a palette have white as colour 0; greyscale sprites have black as colour 0.

[*] Greyscale palettes may not display correctly on earlier operating systems.

Note: You can normally ignore the **mode** box. If there's a number shown here, the sprite is created as an old format sprite. If it's blank, the sprite created is a new format sprite.

Handling sprite files

It's easy to become confused over the difference between sprites and sprite files. This section shows you how to create and manipulate sprites and sprite files.

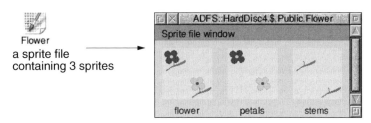

Flower
a sprite file
containing 3 sprites

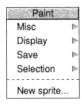

If you prefer, you can keep just one sprite in each sprite file. However, you can store many sprites in a sprite file:

To	Do this	Notes
Open a Sprite file window	Double-click on a sprite file icon, or drag its icon onto Paint's icon bar icon.	Shows all sprites in the sprite file at actual size if possible.
Save a sprite file (and all the sprites it contains)	Click Menu over the Sprite file window and drag the **Save/Save as** icon to a directory display*.	You can save it under a different name, if you want.
Create a new sprite in a Sprite file window	Click Menu over the Sprite file window and fill in the **New sprite...** box.	You can also double-click on a blank part of the sprite file window.
Change the Sprite file window display	Click Menu and choose one of the **Display** options.	This is rather like changing directory displays.
See information about Paint or the sprite file	Click Menu and display the **Misc/Info** or **Misc/File** box.	**File** gives you the sprite file's name, number of sprites and size in bytes.
See how the sprite would look if used as an icon	Choose **Display/Using desktop colours**.	This option is ignored if the sprite has its own palette.

* If you drop the **Save/Save as** icon onto another Sprite file window instead, any existing sprites in that window with the same name will be replaced.

Manipulating sprites within a sprite file

Sprite	
Select all	^A
Clear all	^Z
Cut	^X
Copy	^C
Copy as	▶
Paste	^V
Rename	▶
Delete	^K
Save	▶
Info	▶
Print	▶

You can perform various operations on the sprites in a Sprite file window:

To	Do this	Notes
Open a sprite for editing	Double-click on its picture in the Sprite file window.	See page 377 and page 381 for more on editing sprites. You can also open other views of the same sprite (rather like the **New view** option in Draw) at different zoom settings.
Select all sprites within a sprite file	Choose **Sprite/Select all** or press Ctrl-A.	You can also hold Select and drag a rectangle around multiple sprites to select them.
Deselect all currently-selected sprites	Click Select in the Sprite file window in a space where there is no sprite.	You can also choose **Sprite/Clear all** or press Ctrl-Z.
Cut the selected sprite(s) to the global clipboard	Choose **Sprite/Cut** or press Ctrl-X.	
Copy the selected sprite(s) to the global clipboard	Choose **Sprite/Copy**. or press Ctrl-C.	
Copy a sprite within a sprite file	Click Menu over the sprite's picture in the sprite file and type a new name in the **Sprite/Copy as** box.	You can also enter a new name in the **Sprite/Save as** box and drag the icon onto the Sprite file window.
Paste sprite(s) from the global clipboard into the sprite file	Choose **Sprite/Paste** or press Ctrl-V.	
Rename a sprite	Use the **Sprite/Rename** box from the sprite file window menu.	You can also press Alt and click Select on the name, as you can in the Filer.

To	Do this	Notes
Delete a sprite from a sprite file	Click Menu over the sprite's picture in the sprite file window and choose **Sprite/Delete**, or press Ctrl-K.	Don't delete the last sprite from a sprite file, or you won't be able to save the sprite file.
Save a sprite from a sprite file	Click Menu over the sprite's picture in the sprite file window and drag the **Sprite/Save/Save as** icon.	You can also drag the sprite from the sprite file window and drop it where it should be saved.

Adding an existing sprite to a sprite file

There are four ways of adding an existing sprite to a different sprite file:

- Drag a sprite file icon and drop it onto the destination Sprite file window.

  If the source sprite file contains many sprites, they're all added to the destination Sprite file window. Sprites with the same name will be overwritten.

- Drag a sprite from another Sprite file window, or application, and drop it onto the destination Sprite file window.

  Dragging a sprite from a Draw window to Paint is an example of adding a sprite to a sprite file from another application using drag and drop. This also works in the other direction to easily add a sprite to a Draw drawing from Paint.

- Click Menu over a sprite's picture in the source Sprite file window and drag the **Sprite 'name'/Save/Save as** icon onto the destination Sprite file window.

- Click Menu over an open Sprite file window and drag the **Sprite/Save/Save as** icon onto the destination Sprite file window.

Handling JPEG images

You can also use Paint to edit JPEG images. To load a JPEG file into Paint, drag the JPEG file icon onto Paint's icon bar icon.

The image will be converted into a sprite in the current screen mode. This means that it will be given the same number of colours as the current mode, so make sure you change to the correct mode before you load the image.

If you drag a JPEG file onto Paint's icon bar icon, a Sprite file window, a sprite window and a colours window will all open, ready for you to edit the image. There are some JPEG files in the Documents.UserGuide.Pictures directory to try this out with.

Notes:

- Paint may automatically perform some dithering when you load a JPEG file. You can often get a better quality sprite by using ChangeFSI to process the JPEG file and saving the resulting sprite into Paint.

- Once you've loaded a JPEG file into paint, you cannot use Paint to change it back into a JPEG file. You can use ChangeFSI to do this, though – see *Output options* on page 478.

Choosing and using colours

You use the Colours window to choose the colour that you are painting with. There is a separate Colours window for each sprite. To open the Colours window (if it's not already displayed) click Menu on the sprite window and choose **Paint/Show colours**.

There are in fact two different Colours windows (see *Using colour in applications* on page 239 for details on the second of these two windows):

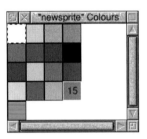

Colours window for modes up to 256 colours (this one's for 16 colours)

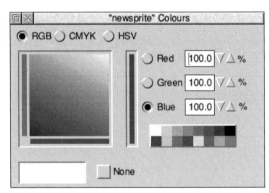

Colours window for greater than 256-colour modes

Choosing a colour

To choose a colour, click on it in the Colours window.

For sprites with up to 256 colours, the *foreground* colour (and its number) is highlighted in the colours window with a solid outline, while the current *background* colour is has a dashed outline. Clicking Adjust on a colour changes the background colour.

The colours shown are the shades that can be displayed in the current screen mode. These may be an approximation to the actual palette of the sprite (see *Mixing new colours using a palette* on page 374).

Finding out the colour of an individual pixel

Another way to choose a colour is to point at a pixel in the sprite window, click Menu and choose **Paint/Select colour**. You can use this method to find out exactly which colour has been used to paint the pixel.

It is also possible to pick the colour without opening the Paint menu at all: to do this, Shift-Select-click on a pixel will set the foreground colour, or Shift-Adjust-click for the background colour.

Making the Colours window smaller

You can make the Colours window smaller by clicking Menu over the sprite window and choosing **Paint/Small colours**. This toggles the size of the sprite colours window; the colours window must be open. The small colours window takes less screen space than the large one. This is particularly valuable in 256-colour modes.

Reviewing the current colour without the Colours window

The currently selected colour is shown in the colour swatch at the bottom lefthand corner of the sprite window.

Using a transparent mask

If a sprite with up to 256 colours has a mask, an extra, special colour is shown in the bottom lefthand corner of the sprite Colours window as a shaded square.

mask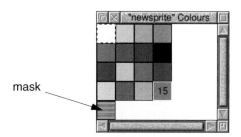

For sprites with a mask and more than 256 colours, you will be able to select it by choosing **None** in the bottom of the Colours window.

Adding a mask

If a sprite doesn't have a mask, you can add one by clicking Menu over the sprite window and choosing **Edit/Mask**.

For more information about using masks, see page 365.

Applying colours using logical operators

There are four different ways in which you can apply colour to a sprite, using the **Set**, **OR**, **AND** and **EOR** buttons in the tools window (the tools themselves are described starting on page 377).

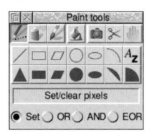

Set causes the colour itself to be painted into the sprite. The remaining three styles cause the indicated logical operation to be applied between the colour number of the pixel on the screen and that selected in the Colours window.

For example, if you choose **EOR**, spraying with colour 11 (binary 1011) onto an area that is currently colour 12 (binary 1100) will produce pixels in colour 7 (binary 0111). For a description of logical operations, see the BBC BASIC *Reference Manual*.

- **OR** sets more pixels towards the higher numbered colours in the palette.

- **AND** sets more pixels towards the lower numbered colours in the palette.

- **EOR** maintains a wider variety of colours than **OR** or **AND**.

You can set a sprite's palette to a custom one by dropping a palette file onto the sprite window – see page 375 for more on saving palette files.

The most interesting effects are achieved when spraying over a range of existing colours, or drawing overlapping filled shapes. Experiment for yourself!

Mixing new colours using a palette

Sprites which use 256 colours or less only have a limited range of colours to choose from. In such cases, if a sprite has a palette, you can use it to mix new colours.

Giving a sprite a palette

If a sprite doesn't have its own palette, and you want to give it one, click Menu over the sprite window and choose **Edit/Palette**. Sprites which don't have their own palettes use the default desktop palette for a given mode (unless **Display/Use desktop colours** is off, in which case the old BBC and Master series colours are used).

By default, when you create a new sprite, it is given a palette.

Redefining colours (editing a palette)

This method works for all sprites with up to 16 colours, and with 256-colour sprites with true-colour palettes.

1   Click on the colour in the Colours window that you want to change.

2   Click Menu over the sprite window and display the **Paint/Edit palette/Edit colour** box.

3   Mix a new colour and click on **OK** to redefine the Colours window.

Using colour in applications on page 239 tells you how to mix colours. The colour displayed is the best approximation available in the current screen mode to the shade you select. The exact colour is recorded by Paint; it is displayed more accurately if you change to a mode with more colours.

Saving a palette

To save a sprite's palette:

1   Click Menu over the sprite window and display the **Save/Palette** box:

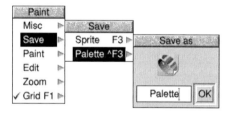

2   Drag the **Save as** icon to a directory display.

If you want to use the same palette in another sprite, drag this palette file onto the new sprite window. This modifies the palette used by the sprite.

Creating an extended colour fill (ECF)

Note: ECFs are only really provided for backwards compatibility. We don't recommend that you use them.

To create an ECF, click Menu over the sprite window and choose **Paint/Select ECF**. This leads to a dialogue box which you can use to extract the bottom lefthand pixels of a named sprite as an ECF pattern. ECFs are patterns that you can use in place of a colour, and are added to the sprite palette, below the plain colours.

You can't define an ECF for sprites with more than 256 colours. You can define up to four ECFs for each sprite.

Zooming in and out (scaling a sprite window)

To scale the size of a sprite window to make it easier to edit, press Menu over the sprite window and set a zoom factor in the **Zoom/Magnifier** dialogue box:

The magnification only changes the size at which the sprite is displayed in the window; the actual definition, height and width are not affected. The magnification is expressed as a ratio; for example 2:1 means twice normal size, 3:4 means three-quarters of normal size, and so on. You can change the ratio either by clicking on the up and down arrows, or by typing in a new value at the caret.

If your mouse has a scroll wheel, the magnification can also be changed by pressing the Ctrl key and scrolling the wheel while the pointer is over the sprite.

Using a grid

You can use a grid to see the boundaries between individual pixels in a sprite:

To	Do this
Toggle the grid on or off	Press Menu over the sprite window and choose **Grid**, or press F1.
Change the grid's display colour	Press Menu over the sprite window and choose a colour from the **Grid** submenu.

The grid is automatically displayed when the magnification is at 4:1 or higher and the menu is toggled to on.

Using Paint's tools

You choose tools from the Paint tools window to edit a sprite.

If, when you open a sprite for editing, the tools window doesn't appear on the screen, you can display it by clicking Menu on the sprite window and choosing **Paint/Show tools**.

The top section of the window shows the tools. The currently-selected tool is highlighted and its name shown below the icons.

Below this are buttons used to define how colour will be applied to the image. When certain tools are selected, an extension may appear at the bottom of the tools window for setting extra parameters.

Choosing tools

To use a tool to edit a sprite:

1 Click on the tool in the Paint tools window.

2 If you want, set or change any parameters, such as the size of the spray or brush to be used.

3 Choose a colour from the Colours window.

4 Move the mouse to the sprite window, and apply the tool as described below.

For operations such as drawing lines and rectangles, you can click Adjust instead of Select. This moves the point you just set to the current position.

While some operations are in progress, a skeleton line or area is shown.

You can cancel any of the sequences of operations described below by clicking again on the current tool in the Paint tools window.

To	Choose this tool	Notes
Paint a pixel	Set/clear pixels	Click Adjust to clear a pixel to the background colour. Drag the pointer to paint many pixels.
Spray pixels in an area around the pointer position	Spray can	Set the spray **Density** and **Radius** at the bottom of the tools window. Spray with Adjust to clear pixels to the background colour.
Paint another sprite into the current one	Use sprite as brush	See *Using a sprite as a brush* on page 380.
Replace one colour with another (flood fill)	Replace colour	**Local** changes all touching pixels of the same colour. **Global** changes all similarly-coloured pixels in the sprite.
Copy a rectangular block from one part of a sprite to another	Copy block (switch **Local** on)	Drag a select box around the block to be copied. Click to position the copied block.
Save (export) a rectangular block of a sprite	Copy block (switch **Export** on)	Drag a select box around the block to be copied. Drag the **Save as** icon to a directory or sprite file.
Move a rectangular block from one part of a sprite to another	Move block (switch **Local** on)	Works in the same way as Copy block (Local), but area left behind is filled with colour 0, or transparent if a mask is present.
Save (export) a rectangular block of a sprite	Move block (switch **Export** on)	Works in the same way as Copy block (Export).

To	Choose this tool	Notes
Move the entire sprite within the sprite window	Move whole sprite	Drag the pointer to the new position in sprite window. With the **Wrap** option enabled any parts of image which move outside window appear on the opposite side, without wrapping they are lost.
Paint a solid line of pixels	Lines	Click at each end of the line.
Paint a solid triangle	Filled triangles	Click on each corner of the triangle.
Paint an outline or solid rectangle	Rectangle outlines Filled rectangles	Click on opposite corners of the rectangle.
Paint an outline or solid parallelogram	Parallelogram outlines Filled parallelograms	Click on three corners of the parallelogram.
Paint an outline or solid circle	Circle outlines Filled circles	Click at the centre, then on the circumference.
Paint an outline or solid ellipse	Ellipse outlines Filled ellipses	Click at the centre. Second click defines the width.
Paint an arc or solid circular segment	Circle outline sections Filled circle segments	Click to define the centre of a circle, then click at each end of the arc.

379

To	Choose this tool	Notes
Paint a solid circular sector	Filled circle sectors	Click to define the centre of a circle, then click at each end of the arc.
Paint a text line onto a sprite	Insert text	Enter the text, character sizes (pixels) and spacing (pixels) in the tools window. Click to define centre of text line. Only System font is available.

Using a sprite as a brush

 Here's a bit more on using a sprite as a brush (there are a couple of examples of using this tool in the *Paint tutorial*, on page 364):

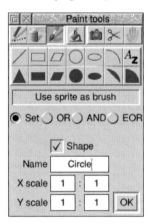

To	Do this	Notes
Use one of the default brush shapes	Type one of the default names into the **Name** box and click on **OK**.	You can use square, triangle, circle or brush.
Use one of your own sprites as a brush	Open the Sprite file window and type the sprite's name in the **Name** box and click on **OK**.	

To	Do this	Notes
Use just the outline of the source sprite	Switch **Shape** on and click on **OK**.	Pixels in brush sprite which are not transparent are set to the current colour.
Paint with the full coloured sprite image	Switch **Shape** off and click on **OK**.	
Use the source sprite at a different size	Set the **X scale** and **Y scale** multipliers and click on **OK**.	This is useful for using the same source sprite at different sizes.

Changing a sprite's size, shape and orientation

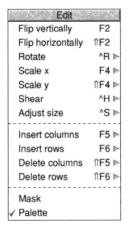

You can perform many operations on a sprite using Paint's Edit menu (click Menu over a sprite window and choose from the **Paint/Edit** submenu):

To	Use this option or submenu	Notes
Invert a sprite vertically about its centre	**Flip vertically**, or press F2	
Invert a sprite horizontally about its centre	**Flip horizontally**, or press Shift-F2	
Rotate a sprite about its centre	**Rotate**	Type the angle in the Rotation box, or press Ctrl-R. The sprite size changes if you rotate for angles other than multiples of 90 degrees (unless the sprite has an even aspect ratio and pixel height/width).

381

To	Use this option or submenu	Notes
Scale the sprite horizontally or vertically	**Scale x** or **Scale y** Factor 1	Type the scale factor in the Factor box. Negative scale factors are not allowed.
Slant the sprite horizontally	**Shear** Factor 1	Type the shear factor in the Shear box, or press Ctrl-H. The top row of pixels is moved right. The rows below are moved proportionally. The factor is the tangent of the angle you want to shear by. A factor of 1 slants the sprite 45°.
Add or delete rows or columns from the sprite	**Adjust size** Adjust size Width 80 △ ▽ Height 80 △ ▽ Edge adjustment 0 0 ◁ ▷ Sprite ◁ ▷ 0 0 Cancel Adjust	Use the arrows in the Sprite size box, or fill in the **Width** and **Height** boxes, then click **Adjust**. Rows or columns added to enlarge the sprite are added to the top/right by default. To make the adjustment to a specific edge use the **Edge adjustment** boxes instead of the Width/Height boxes.
Add or delete columns at the pointer position	**Insert columns** **Insert rows** **Delete columns** **Delete rows** How many? 1	Inserted rows or columns are filled with colour 0. Columns are deleted to the right of the pixel over which you clicked Menu. Rows are deleted upwards. See below for more information.

More on adding and deleting rows and columns

Enter the number of rows or columns in the **How many?** box and click Select or press ↵.

Alternatively, without passing over a menu, move the pointer over the sprite window to change the size of the highlighted area that appears and click when the **How many?** box shows the right number. Doing it this way can be tricky; increasing the zoom scale can help to make this operation more controllable.

Taking screen snapshots

You can use Paint to save part of the screen as a sprite file (this is how the pictures of menus, windows and so on were produced in this Guide).

Start snapshot by choosing **Snapshot...** from the icon bar menu. This displays the snapshot dialogue box:

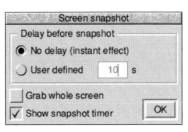

To	Do this	Notes
Take a snapshot of the whole screen	Tick the **Grab whole screen** box and click on **OK**	Drag the resulting **Save as** icon to a directory display.
Take a snapshot of part of the screen	Switch **Grab whole screen off** and click on **OK**. Then drag a select box (using the camera pointer that appears) round the area you want to snapshot.	Drag the resulting **Save as** icon to a directory display.
Set a delay before the snapshot is taken	Switch on **User defined** in the Delay before snapshot area and enter the delay in seconds. Then take the snapshot as above.	This allows you to take shots of transient items (like menus): while the timer is counting down, you can position menus etc. in the snapshot area you defined.

Printing a sprite

Before you can print a sprite, you must have the Printer Manager loaded (see *Part 4 – Printing*). There are two ways you can print a sprite:

● Click Menu over the sprite's picture in the Sprite file window and display the **Sprite/Print/Print sprite** dialogue box.

● Click Menu over the sprite window and display the **Misc/Print/Print sprite** dialogue box.

The dialogue box is the same in both cases. The exact contents of the dialogue box depend on the printer driver in use, but it typically allows you to choose the orientation (**Portrait** or **Landscape**) scaling, and position on the paper.

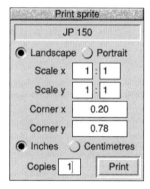

Scale allows you to change the proportions of the printed image. Setting both x and y to 1:2 will produce a half-sized image.

Corner defines where on the printed page the image will be printed. The default settings define the edge of the printable page for your printer. Changing these settings will move the printing position of the image.

Saving Paint application preferences

You may want to change some aspects of the way new Paint windows appear when you first open them. For example, a new window normally opens with Zoom magnification set to 1:1, but you may prefer to have the Zoom option set to 2:1.

To change the application preferences, open the **Choices...** dialogue box from Paint's icon bar menu.

You can modify the **Sprite file window** appearance to show extra details of each sprite, and whether to **Use desktop colours** to show the sprites in the Sprite file window or not (in which case the old BBC and Master series colours are used).

The remainder of the choices relate to the **Sprite window** used to edit sprites.

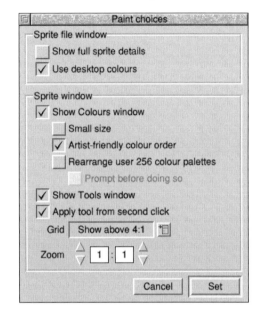

When a sprite is opened, you can choose to **Show Colours window** at the same time, and also to **Show Tools window**. The default **Grid** colour and appearance can be set via the pop-up menu, along with your preferred **Zoom** settings.

There are further refinements possible to the Colours window:

● To choose to open it at **Small size**.

● To show 256 colour palettes in *artist-friendly* order, where similar colours and shades are grouped together in the Colours window.

● To automatically rearrange user-defined 256 colour palettes to be in artist-friendly order.
  Note: Rather than showing the colours in artist-friendly order, this option changes the sprite data instead. Once saved the data will always be in artist-friendly order, which makes the sprite larger and slower to plot. For this reason Paint can display a **Prompt before doing so** to confirm that rearranging the data is safe.

For keyboard shortcuts (see page 388) to be accepted the Sprite window must have the input focus which requires clicking in the window. However, if a tool is currently selected this would paint into the sprite. Enable **Apply tool from second click** to take your first click to gain the input focus, and subsequent clicks for painting.

Click on **Set** to make the changes, or **Cancel** to close the window. Use Adjust click to keep the choices window open.

386

Types of sprite that can be created by Paint

This table gives the various types of sprite which can be created by Paint, and whether they are backward compatible with earlier versions of the operating system – they have a mode number.

You can select these combinations using the **Create new sprite** window. See page 367 for more information.

Number of colours	Dots per inch (dpi)	Equivalent old-type screen mode number
Two	90×90	25
	45×45	no equivalent
	90×45	0
	Other combinations	no equivalent
Four	90×90	26
	45×45	1
	90×45	8
	Other combinations	no equivalent
Sixteen	90×90	27
	45×45	9
	90×45	12
	Other combinations	no equivalent
256	90×90	28
	45×45	13
	90×45	15
	Other combinations	no equivalent
4k	All combinations	no equivalent
32k	All combinations	no equivalent
64k	All combinations	no equivalent
16M	All combinations	no equivalent

You can find out the earliest version of RISC OS able to display a sprite that you created by opening the **Info** window for the sprite and looking at the **Compatibility** statement.

Keyboard shortcuts

Many Paint operations can be carried out from the keyboard instead of the menus and mouse; when you are familiar with the application, you may find this more convenient.

In the Sprite file window

To	Use this keystroke
Select all	Ctrl-A
Clear selection	Ctrl-Z
Cut a selection to the clipboard	Ctrl-X
Copy a selection to the clipboard	Ctrl-C
Paste from the clipboard, replacing any current selection	Ctrl-V
Delete a selection without affecting the clipboard	Ctrl-K
Move on to rename the next sprite (having started a rename by Alt clicking on the sprite's name)	Tab
Move on to rename the previous sprite	Shift-Tab

In the Sprite window

To	Use this keystroke
Save the sprite (calls up the normal **Save as** box)	F3
Save the sprite's palette	Ctrl-F3
Flip the sprite vertically	F2
Flip the sprite horizontally	Ctrl-F2
Open the rotate sprite box	Ctrl-R
Open the scale in X direction box	F4
Open the scale in Y direction box	Ctrl-F4
Open the shear sprite box	Ctrl-H
Open the adjust sprite size box	Ctrl-S
Open the insert columns box	F5
Open the insert rows box	F6
Open the delete columns box	Ctrl-F5

To	Use this keystroke
Open the delete rows box	Ctrl-F6
Show the sprite's Colours window	Ctrl-Shift-F1
Show the Tools window	Ctrl-F1
Zoom out	Ctrl-Q
Zoom in	Ctrl-W
Print the sprite	Print
Toggle the grid on or off	F1

28 Alarm

Alarm is a sophisticated alarm clock.

You can use Alarm to

- display an analogue or digital clock on the icon bar
- set the computer's date and time

- set up alarms that can go off at a specified time in the future
- set up applications so that they are automatically started at a particular time
- set up urgent and repeating alarms
- store alarms automatically and remember them even when you switch off the computer.

Starting Alarm

Alarm is in the Apps icon bar directory display. To start the application, double-click on the !Alarm application icon. The clock icon appears on the right hand side of the icon bar showing the time.

Setting the time and date

You can set the computer's time and date either manually or, if it is connected to the internet, automatically from an internet time server.

In either case can you make use of the *Time and date setup plug-in* described on page 107 in the chapter *Changing the computer's configuration*. Alternatively, you can open the same setup dialogue from the **Set clock...** icon bar menu item.

Setting an alarm

To define an alarm, click on Alarm's time display on the icon bar to open the Set alarm dialogue.

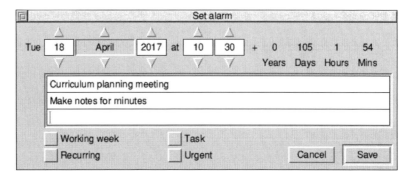

To set an alarm:

1   Choose the date and time of the alarm by clicking on the adjuster arrows above and below the date and time boxes. It is also possible to type the required date and time as numbers directly into the boxes.

2   In the message box, type up to 3 lines of text that you want to display when the alarm goes off.

3   Click on **Save** to define the alarm.

When an alarm is set, the border of Alarm's time display on the icon bar changes colour from blue to red.

The following options are also on the Set alarm window:

Working week

This limits the alarm settings for any recurring alarms to be within the specified working week; the working week is defined in the Alarm Choices window, and is Monday to Friday by default. This option only takes effect if the Recurring alarm option is also selected.

If you have set an alarm that falls outside the working week it will always go off on the last working day before the appointment. This is to prevent you missing an appointment that is scheduled outside the working week.

Any changes to the working week affect all Alarms, including those already set and saved.

Task

Instead of merely giving you a message when an alarm goes off, Alarm can carry out a task. A task can be anything you can do on the Desktop or command line: running a program or loading an application, for example. Click on the **Task** option and enter the command you want carried out in the message boxes.

You can also set up a Task alarm by dragging a file onto the Set alarm window. If you drag an application onto the window, for example, that application will run at the time set for the alarm. If you drag a text file, the text will be displayed in an Edit application window; you might use this option to display, at the start of the day, a list of things you have to do.

Urgent

You can mark an alarm as urgent by clicking on the **Urgent** box. It will then sound an audible alarm when it goes off, even if you have selected the **Silent** option from the setup dialogue box menu (see *Configuring the Alarm choices* on page 397).

Recurring

You can set an alarm to go off more than once by switching on the **Recurring** option. Doing this displays some further options:

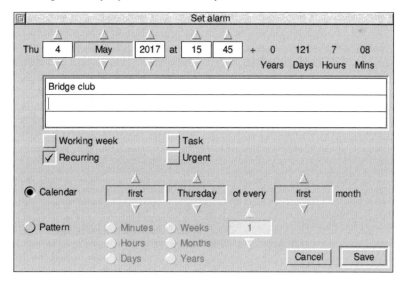

Use the radio buttons and arrow icons to specify whether you want the alarm to recur by calendar definition (as in the example above), or by a pattern definition (as in the example below):

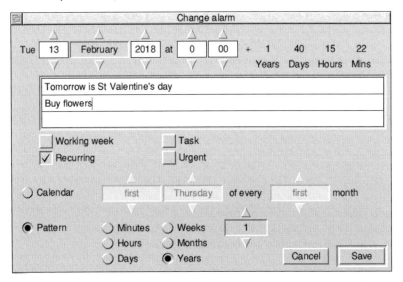

To limit the current alarm to the working week, turn the **Working week** option on. To limit all your alarms to the working week by default, choose the **Recurring alarms fit into a working week** option in the Alarm choices dialogue.

You can define more than one alarm by simply repeating the Set alarm procedure.

Saving alarms

When alarms are not being automatically saved, open the list of alarms by clicking **Alarms...** on the icon bar menu. The title bar of this window shows the name of the alarms file with an asterisk appended if updates have not yet been saved.

To complete the setting of any new or changed alarms, click Menu over the list of alarms, slide from **Save as alarms** to the Save as box, then click **OK**.

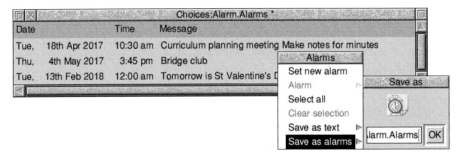

When an alarm goes off

When the alarm time is reached, a window similar to the one below appears on the screen. Click **Accept** to dismiss the window.

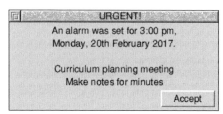

If Alarm is not running when an alarm is due to go off, the alarm will be triggered next time Alarm is started. If the alarm is a recurring alarm, you will receive a message for the first occurrence due for the period when Alarm was not running, but not for subsequent ones.

Browsing through your alarms

Choosing **Alarms...** from the icon bar menu displays the alarm browser. The browser lists the alarms you have set.

Clicking Menu over the browser window displays the menu options available for setting, changing, copying, deleting and saving alarms.

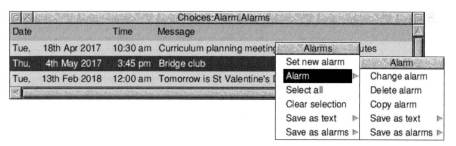

The Alarms browser menu

Set new alarm

Choosing this option displays the Set alarm dialogue box.

Alarm

This option is only available when an alarm is selected. Select an alarm by clicking on an alarm line in the browser.

This option displays a submenu which allows you to perform the following operations:

- **Change alarm**. This displays the Change alarm dialogue box. Use this in the same way as the Set alarm dialogue box. You can also display the Change alarm box by double-clicking over the appropriate line in the browser.
- **Delete alarm**. Use this option to delete an alarm.
- **Copy alarm**. Use this option to copy an alarm so that it is duplicated in the alarm browser. You can then use the Change alarm option to modify the copied alarm.
- **Save as text**. This option saves the alarm text (as seen in the browser) as a text file. Drag the **Save as** text file icon to an appropriate directory.
- **Save as alarm**. This option saves your alarms in an alarm file. You can use the Save as box to drag the file elsewhere, in which case its use is described below in Alarm files.

Select all

Selects all alarms in the browser.

Clear selection

Deselects all selected alarms in the browser.

Save as text

This option saves the selected alarm text (as seen in the browser) as a text file. Drag the **Save as** text file icon to an appropriate directory.

You can load this text file into Edit to display a list of all your currently set Alarms, or, if you have Printer Manager running, drag the icon straight onto the Printer Manager icon to print the list on paper.

Save as alarms

This option saves the selected alarms as an alarm file. Drag the **Save as** alarms file icon to an appropriate directory, or click on **OK** to save in the default file in the Choices directory. Alarm files can be read back into Alarm at a later date.

Note: If you save the Alarms file into the $.Public directory on your hard disc, it will be updated even if the disc is locked.

Configuring the Alarm choices

The setup dialogue box allows you to configure

- how alarms are acted upon
- how the alarm database is used
- the alarm display format.

If your computer is locked (password protected) you won't be able to change any Alarm choices until it is unlocked.

To change the Alarm setup options:

1   Click Menu over the Alarm icon on the icon bar.

2   Choose **Choices...**

3   Change the options to suit your needs.

4   Click **Set** to save the options.

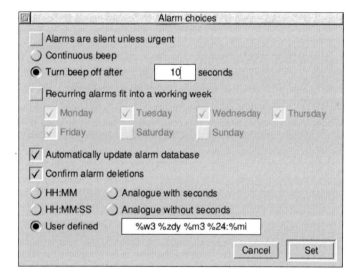

Alarms are silent unless urgent

When this is selected, only urgent alarms sound an audible beep at alarm time. When it is not selected, all alarms sound an audible beep.

Recurring alarms fit into a working week

When this is selected, any subsequent recurring alarms you set, or alarms that you defer, will skip those days you have not selected. An alarm repeating monthly or annually will go off on the working day before its due date.

Continuous beep

Click on this box if you want an audible alarm to sound continuously until you cancel the alarm.

Turn beep off after

The figure you type into the box is the number of seconds that the computer's beep will sound when there is an alarm.

Automatically update the alarm database

This option lets Alarm automatically update the alarm database file whenever you set or change an alarm. If you choose this option then each time Alarm starts it automatically remembers any alarms that have been stored. (If your hard disc is locked, you'll see an error box.)

Confirm alarm deletions

When this option is selected, you are prompted for confirmation each time an existing alarm is deleted.

Display format

This section allows you to choose how you wish the alarm clock to be displayed on the icon bar. The formats available are:

- analogue (with and without a second hand)
- digital (with and without seconds displayed) – called HH:MM and HH:MM:SS
- your own format.

Typing in your own formats:

For example, try typing in these formats in the **User defined** box.

```
%z12:%mi:%se %pm %zdy/%zmn/%zyr
```

or

```
%we %zdy%st %m3 Week %wk
```

For information on how to set up your own formats, see *Time and date display formats* on page 400. The format and other features you select for Alarm will be saved in the Choices directory (see *Inside the Boot application* on page 112 to read where this is).

Alarm files

Alarm files contain information about the current alarms. If you double-click on an Alarms file and Alarm is not running, then Alarm is started and the data file is read and treated as the main alarm file. If you double-click on an alarms file and Alarm is currently running, the contents of the alarms file is added to the existing list of alarms, if there are any.

Quitting Alarm

To close down Alarm, choose **Quit** from the icon bar menu. Alarm will warn you if you have any alarms that have not been saved.

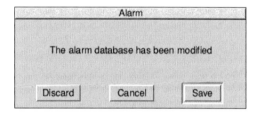

Time and date display formats

Use the choices window to change the date and time format by choosing the **User defined** option and specifying a string made up of variables as listed below.

Name	Value	Example
%se	seconds	59
%mi	minutes	05
%12	hours in 12 hour format	07
%24	hours in 24 hour format	23
%am or %pm	'AM' or 'PM'	pm
%we	weekday, in full	Thursday
%w3	weekday, in three characters	Thu
%wn	weekday, as a number	5
%dy	day of the month	01
%st	'st', 'nd', 'rd' or 'th' suffix	st
%mo	month name, in full	September
%m3	month name, in three characters	Sep
%mn	month as a number	09
%ce	century	19
%yr	year within century	87
%wk	week of the year, Mon to Sun	52
%dn	day of the year	364
%tz	local time zone	BST
%%	insert a %	
~IN	alternating '.' and ':' once per second	
~AH	analogue clock, hours hand	
~AM	analogue clock, minutes hand	
~AS	analogue clock, seconds hand	

Numbers are generated as a fixed-width with leading zeros. To remove leading zeros, prefix the code with 'z' (e.g. %mn might show 05, %zmn gives a result of 5).

Your own text may be included along with system variables whose current value is displayed; for example:

```
%we the %dy%st %m3 %yr          (Sunday the 22nd Jan 95)
```

In particular, when Alarm is running it maintains the amount of free memory in the system variable Alarm$Free; for example:

```
%24:%mi, <Alarm$Free> spare     (14:55, 127 Mbytes spare)
```

29 Help

The Help application is a program that displays information about applications whilst they are working, and about the desktop generally. When you first use an application, you may find it useful to have Help running.

Starting Help

Help is in the Apps icon bar directory. To start the application, double-click on the !Help icon. The Help icon appears on the icon bar. It will always appear in the same place next to the Task Manager even if other applications are loaded beforehand:

Seeing what help is available

Just move the pointer over the part of the desktop that you want help about, and concise help text will appear beside the pointer. Whenever you can't remember what an icon means or what an option does, use Help.

As you move the mouse to a different part of the desktop or application, the help information changes. You can get help with windows, icons, menu options and dialogue boxes.

For example here is the help you get when you are drawing a path in a Draw window:

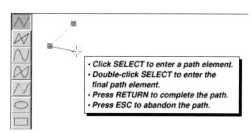

- *Click SELECT to enter a path element.*
- *Double-click SELECT to enter the final path element.*
- *Press RETURN to complete the path.*
- *Press ESC to abandon the path.*

Controlling Help

Once you have reminded yourself of the help text, you may wish to stop any more help being shown should it become distracting. Click Select on the Help icon on the icon bar to temporarily suspend the interactive help; the icon will become faded. Click Select again to resume the interactive help.

The current status of Help is shown in its icon bar menu, clicking on **Suspend** when it is ticked will resume the help text and unfade the Help icon bar icon.

To close down Help altogether, choose **Quit**.

You can alter the font used to display help messages, the delay before they appear, and even hide common messages by configuring the Help application as described in the section *Help setup plug-in* in the chapter *Changing the computer's configuration* on page 93.

30   Chars

C hars is an application that enables you to use text characters that are available on your computer but that cannot be typed in easily using the keyboard. It's also useful for previewing available outline fonts.

Starting Chars

Chars is in the Apps icon bar directory. To start the application, double-click on the !Chars application icon. The application window appears on the desktop.

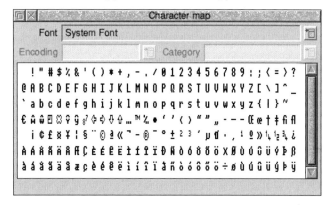

The Chars window shows the entire character set of the font. At the top of the window is the name of the font. Underneath that, the current *encoding* and current *category* of displayed characters is shown for fonts that support it.

Moving the mouse pointer over a character displays information about it in the area at the bottom of the window, such as the character's name and the key combination needed to enter it.

You can use Chars to insert a character into any document, window or menu. For example you can insert characters into an Edit window, in a 'menu item' (such as the **New directory** box or file **Rename** boxes), or in any application that uses text, such as a word processor.

Inserting a character

There are two ways of using Chars to insert characters. The method you use depends whether you want to insert the character into an application window or a menu dialogue box.

Inserting characters into application windows

To insert a character into a window, such as a word processor, click on the character. It will appear at the caret position in the window you are currently typing in (the window with the light-coloured title bar).

Inserting characters into menus

You can also insert a character by positioning the pointer over the character you wish to use, then pressing Shift. Use this method if you want to use a character from Chars as part of a filename (by entering it into a **Save as** dialogue box) or as part of any other menu box. Clicking on the character in the normal way would make the **Save as** box disappear.

Using fonts

When you first run Chars, the font that appears is the System font. If you want to use a different font, click on the pop-up menu at the top of the window next to the **Font** name field. This displays a menu list of all the currently available fonts. Choose the one you want to use, and the characters for that font will appear in the Chars window.

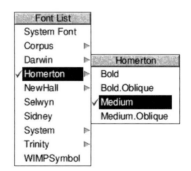

You will also need to select the corresponding font in the application you are using to ensure that the character you select in Chars matches the one that appears. For example, suppose the caret is in the middle of a text line displayed in the font Trinity Medium. Even if you display the Selwyn font in your Chars window, any characters you select from Chars will appear in the corresponding Trinity Medium form, rather than in Selwyn.

Using an outline desktop font

When you use Chars to insert characters into menus, as suggested on page 404, make sure that the font selected matches your desktop font. If you don't, you may find that the character you choose is not the same as the one entered in the menu box.

Alphabets and encodings

Outline fonts in RISC OS can be displayed in a range of *encodings*. Encodings determine the order of characters within the font and the range of characters available. To see the list of encodings available for a font, click on the pop-up menu next to the **Encoding** name field.

Selecting the **Default** encoding means that no special encoding information is applied to the font. This is useful for symbol fonts, like Selwyn and Sidney, which do not display traditional alphanumeric characters. The **UTF-8** encoding is a special setting that enables thousands of characters to be displayed. All other encodings, such as Latin1, are limited to fewer than 256 characters.

In addition to fonts having encodings, the desktop also uses its own encoding, known as the *system alphabet*. The font encoding and system alphabet should match in order to guarantee that a character selected in Chars will be reproduced correctly when inserted elsewhere.

For example, if your system alphabet is UTF-8, then you should use fonts in the UTF-8 encoding. If the system alphabet is Latin1, then you should use the Latin1 encoding for standard fonts, or the Default encoding for symbol fonts. Characters that cannot be inserted are displayed in light grey rather than black, and clicking on them or pressing Shift has no effect.

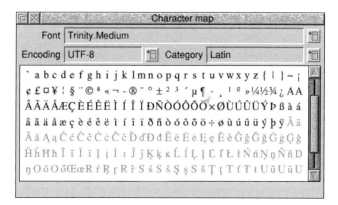

You can find out more about alphabets and how to set them in the appendix *Character sets* on page 543.

Using font categories

The UTF-8 encoding is unique in that it allows thousands of characters to be displayed (provided they are defined within the font). Finding the right character in very large fonts can be cumbersome, so Chars allows you to limit the display to a smaller *category* of characters. A category can be based on language such as Greek or Hebrew, or type such as Maths or Currency.

To see the list of available categories, select a font in the UTF-8 encoding, then click on the pop-up menu icon next to the **Category** name field.

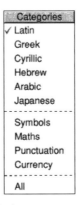

Choose **All** to show all the defined characters in a font.

Keyboard entry

Alt key-numeric keypad combinations

The characters entered using Chars can also be entered using Alt+numeric keypad combinations. To enter a character using the numeric keypad, hold down the Alt key, type the number on the numeric keypad, then release Alt. The numbers map to letters in whatever system alphabet is active.

Chars displays the keypad combination for the character under the mouse pointer in the information bar.

For example, in the Latin1 alphabet, Alt-169 will enter the © character.

Inserting spaces

Be careful when using Chars to insert spaces. Undefined characters in a font are represented by white spaces in the Chars window, so inserting what looks like a space may cause unpredictable results in other applications.

To be sure of only inserting the correct space character, make sure that the information bar shows Character &20 (in alphabets such as Latin1) or U+0020 SPACE (in the UTF-8 alphabet).

The no-break space

Sometimes called a *hard space*, this character is used

● to suppress word wrapping at the end of a line in a word processor or similar

● to insert a space where otherwise Character &20 would not be permissible.

Make sure that the information bar shows Character &A0 (in alphabets such as Latin1) or U+00A0 NO-BREAK SPACE (in the UTF-8 alphabet). The keyboard layout on page 14 shows that pressing Alt-Space also produces a no-break space.

Spaces in file names

Spaces are not permitted in file and disc names because a space is also used as a separator in * commands. It can be useful to include spaces though, to make the name more readable: compare 'holidaychecklist' with 'holiday check list'.

In the desktop, where such a name is expected in a writable icon, the Window Manager will automatically translate soft spaces into hard spaces. This helps users that don't know about Alt-Space to easily achieve the result they want.

Icon bar menu

Info

This gives you information about the application.

Help...

Opens a short description of how to use Chars based on this Guide.

Choices...

Opens a dialogue allowing settings for Chars to be changed.

Quit

Quit ends the Chars application, removing the Chars icon from the icon bar.

Choices

From here you can set whether to open the Chars window automatically when the application is run, and whether to use the System font or your current desktop outline font as the default.

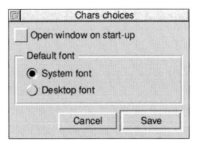

When finished, click **Save** to use them for any future sessions. Click **Cancel** to close the dialogue without making any changes.

31   CloseUp

CloseUp acts like a magnifying glass. It displays a magnifying window on the screen which allows you examine portions of the desktop in greater detail.

Starting CloseUp

CloseUp is in the Apps directory on your hard disc or network. To start the application, double-click on the !CloseUp application icon. The application icon appears on the icon bar.

Click on the CloseUp icon on the icon bar icon to start the magnifier. You will see the magnifier on the screen. The CloseUp window simply shows a magnified portion of the desktop that is currently under the pointer. Move the pointer to see another area of the screen.

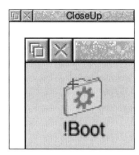

CloseUp options

Click Menu on the CloseUp icon bar icon to display the following options:

Info

This gives some information about the software.

Zoom

This allows you to choose the enlargement ratio that will be displayed in the magnifier window. For example, a setting of 4:1 will make the picture in the magnifier window four times the size of the original.

Key-cursor

This option lets you move the pointer around the screen using the cursor keys as well as the mouse. Anything under the pointer is shown magnified in the CloseUp window. This only operates if none of the windows on the desktop currently uses the cursor; for example, you can't have an active Edit window.

Follow caret

If this option is ticked, and there is an application that uses a caret on the screen, for example Edit, the area around the caret is magnified. The magnified area follows the caret position as you type so that the letters you type in are shown magnified.

If the option is not ticked, the magnifying window will show the area that is around the pointer position.

Quit

This will remove the program from the icon bar and the CloseUp box from the desktop if it is being displayed.

Maestro

Maestro enables you to transcribe music in standard musical notation and play it through the computer's own sound system or to externally connected instruments; it also provides some simple editing facilities. This chapter assumes that you are familiar with the basic ideas of musical notation.

Starting Maestro

Maestro is in the Apps directory on your hard disc or network. To start the application:

1 Double-click on the !Maestro icon. The application icon appears on the icon bar.

2 Click on this icon to display the Maestro window:

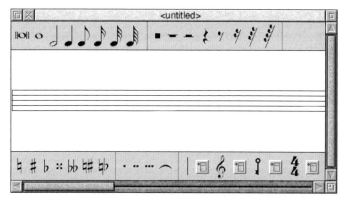

Note that only one copy of Maestro can be run at a time – attempting to load more copies will result in an error message being displayed.

Playing a tune

The best way to get started with Maestro is to load one of the tunes stored on the hard disc (or network). To do this, double-click on one of the Music File icons in the `Documents.Music.Maestro` directory, or drag it onto the Maestro icon on the icon bar.

If you load the file Fanfare, the window that appears looks like this:

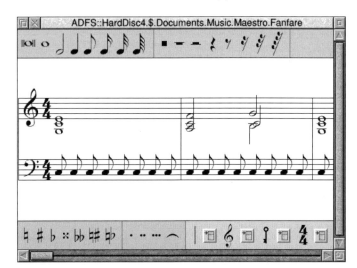

To play the tune, press Menu to open the main Maestro menu. Choose **Play** to start the music. The score will scroll in time with the music playing and so, during playback, you will not be able to manually adjust the horizontal scroll bar.

To stop playback, click on **Play** again in the main Maestro menu. You can now use the horizontal scroll bar as usual to return to the beginning of the score.

Editing the score

The Maestro window is divided into three horizontal panels, with the staves positioned in the centre. Scrolling affects only the central panel. Above and below the stave are toolbars containing icons for notes, rests, clefs and other symbols.

Before setting up your own score, try out the following editing procedures on one of the tunes supplied on the disc.

Adding and deleting notes and rests

To add a note or rest, select the value you want by clicking on its icon in the window above the score. The selected item will appear highlighted with a frame around it, and when you move the pointer on to the score window, a 'ghost' copy appears, which moves around as you move the pointer. When the item is in the position you want, click Select. To get rid of the ghost copy without adding a note or rest to the score and without selecting an alternative object, press Menu, move the pointer off the menu and press Select.

You can place notes anywhere. Above and below each stave they will create their own ledger-lines. In the case of notes with stems, the stem trails behind the moving ghost note: if the pointer is moved downwards, the stem will be above the note; if upwards, the stem will be below the note.

Rests operate in a similar manner to notes, except that the range of positions is more restricted.

To delete a note or rest, select the icon for the same type of object, and position the ghost copy exactly over the item you wish to remove (it doesn't matter whether the stem goes the same way or not). When it is in the right place, the floating copy will appear to blot out the original item. Click Select and the item will be deleted.

Adding dots, accidentals, bars and ties

Select a lengthening dot in exactly the same way as a note or rest. Move the pointer over the note you wish to lengthen and click Select. To delete a dotted note, you do not have to delete the dot separately: delete the note and the dot will disappear too.

Select and place accidentals and ties in the same way: like notes and rests, they will appear only in valid positions. The tie character is of a fixed length, but when placed between notes of the same pitch, a single note will sound, with a duration equal to the two notes added together.

Barlines are inserted across all the staves in the score. Maestro allows you to insert both single and double barlines. To select the barline type, click Select on the pop-up menu next to the Barline icon in the toolbar.

Adding clefs and key and time signatures

You can select and place clefs like other item, though they will appear only at the beginning of a bar. Clicking Select on the pop-up menu next to the Clef icon allows you to choose the clef type.

Clicking Select on the pop-up menu next to the Key Signature icon opens a menu with a list of key signatures. Both major and minor keys are available. Once a key signature has been selected from this menu, you can add it to the score in the same way as other objects.

Clicking Select next to the Time Signature icon opens a small box enabling you to choose a time signature. Use the up and down icons to cycle through the available options, then click **Set** to choose the time signature. Once added to the score, the new time signature will appear on all staves.

The Maestro menu

As in any application, clicking Menu on the Maestro window will display the top-level menu.

Aside from the **Play** menu item already described on page 411, this menu gives access to the **File**, **Edit** and **Score** submenus.

The File menu

Info gives you some information about the file you are working on.

The **Save** procedure is exactly the same as for other applications such as Edit or Draw. Save a score by dragging the Maestro icon into the directory window where you want to save it, or by typing in the full pathname and clicking on **OK**.

Print... allows you to print your score.

The Edit menu

Goto enables you to jump to a numbered bar.

Clear all removes the current score from the stave but leaves the Maestro window on the screen.

The Score menu

Staves...

Choose **Staves...** to open a dialogue box where you can control the number of staves used in the score.

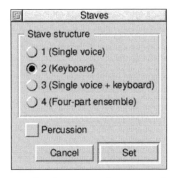

Music Files contain 1 to 4 standard staves, plus an optional percussion stave. The available voices will be distributed across each stave once the selection is made.

Clicking on **Cancel** removes the dialogue box with no changes made; clicking **Set** will set the number of staves.

414

Instruments...

Choose **Instruments...** to open a dialogue box which assigns the voices used during score playback.

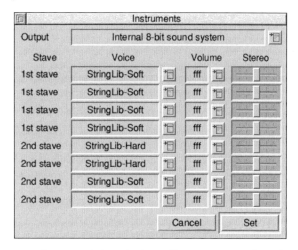

The pop-up menu at the top of the window allows you to select the audio **Output** device. By default, this is the computer's internal sound system, but if you have a *Musical Instrument Digital Interface* (MIDI) device attached then you can opt to play the score through an external instrument instead.

A Maestro score has eight separate voice channels distributed roughly equally across the active staves. By clicking on the pop-up menu icon next to each of the fields in the **Voice** column, you can choose a voice from the list of those installed on your system to attach to each channel. If you have chosen to use a MIDI device for audio output, then you can instead select a MIDI channel here.

The **Volume** column allows you to set the volume for each voice channel, and the **Stereo** column enables the channel's stereo position to be controlled.

Click on **Set** to make the changes, or **Cancel** to close the window.

Volume

This item enables you to set the overall volume of the score, on a scale from *pianississimo* (ppp) to *fortississimo* (fff).

Tempo

This item allows you to set the tempo for the score, on a scale from *largissimo* to *prestissimo*.

Setting up your own score

The preceding description of the Maestro menu options gives you the information you need to set up your own score. However, for the sake of clarity, the following section sets out the steps to take in their most convenient order (though they can all be changed at any time). The menu options are shown in bold type.

1 Choose the **Staves** you want.

2 Choose your **Instruments...**, and their volume and position.

3 Select your **Key signature**, and place it on the score.

4 Select your **Time Signature**, and place it on the score.

5 Choose the **Volume** and **Tempo** you want.

You are now ready to start placing notes on the staves.

Some tips

If you copy a piece of music from a written score it will occasionally need some minor modifications to play correctly.

Staccato

To achieve the effect of staccato, shorten the note value and make up the difference with a rest.

Grace notes and trills

These are not implemented as such, but the effect can be achieved by entering notes of the appropriate small duration, and deducting their value either from the note they would normally be attached to (for an appoggiatura) or from the preceding note (for an acciaccatura). Somewhat effective trills can be produced using an elaborated form of the same method.

Rests in earlier versions of Maestro

Versions of Maestro prior to 2.13 did not allow placing rests on any line other than the centre, making it hard to score multi-part staves. Files created with Maestro after version 2.13 will be loaded without error by older versions, but if the file is re-saved in the older application then the position data for the rests will be lost.

Maestro's use of memory

Maestro cannot extend its memory slot once it has started up. Initially it takes at least 256kB, to allow for the editing of long transcriptions. However, if the Next slot in the Task Manager is set to more than 256kB, Maestro will use it all up to a limit of 640kB. Since this may be more than you need, you can use the Task Manager (described in *Managing the desktop* on page 73) to reduce Next to 256kB, before loading Maestro.

33 SciCalc

SciCalc is a scientific calculator providing a range of scientific functions in addition to simple arithmetic ones.

Starting SciCalc

SciCalc is in the Apps directory on your hard disc or network. To start the application, double-click on the !SciCalc application icon.

SciCalc's icon will appear on the icon bar and, dependent on the saved configuration, will open in either scientific or simplified view:

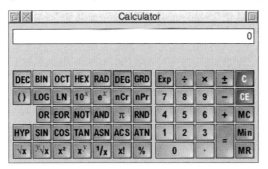

You can toggle between these two types of view by clicking on the Toggle size icon, or by pressing Ctrl-S when the window has the input focus, or via the **View** item in the main menu. Many of the advanced functions described in this chapter are only available in the scientific view.

Entering numbers

There are two ways of entering numbers into the calculator. You can move the pointer over the required key and then click, or you can use the keyboard directly. Clicking in the numeric display gives SciCalc the input focus, indicating that numbers and selected operators may be entered from the keyboard.

If you use the numeric keypad, make sure that the Num Lock key is on. The keys in the numeric keypad are also equivalent to those on the calculator keypad.

Arithmetic functions

These operate exactly like an ordinary calculator: when you enter a number it appears in the calculator's display. When you first load SciCalc it is set for normal **decimal** arithmetic (base 10). This is shown in the scientific view by the DEC button being pressed inwards.

Rules of precedence

SciCalc treats the calculation you enter as a formula and does not perform the calculation until you click on the Equals button. SciCalc performs the calculation according to the precedence of operators (from highest to lowest): Multiply, Divide, Add and Subtract.

Multiplication takes place before addition so:

$$2 + 6 \times 5 = 32 \qquad (\text{not } 40)$$

You can change the order of calculation by using brackets:

$$(2 + 6) \times 5 = 40$$

Simple multiplication

To multiply 2 by 5 and view the result, enter the following in this order:

$$2 \times 5 =$$

The result will appear in the display.

To calculate the area of a circle of radius 7 units, enter the following:

$$\pi \times 7 \times 7 =$$

The result appears in the display. Immediately below the result display is a summary of the most recent calculation:

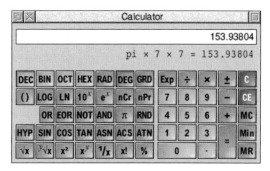

420

Changing the sign

The ± key switches the sign of the number in the display.

Calculating percentages

To increase x by y percent, enter:

    x + y % =

To decrease x by y percent, type – instead of +.

To calculate x% of y, enter:

    x % × y =

Clearing the last entry

Press CE to clear the current display. For example, pressing the following:

    2 + 6 × 3 CE 5 =

calculates

    2 + 6 × 5 =

and thus gives the result 32.

Clearing all calculations and errors

Press C to clear all input so far, or to dismiss an error message.

Memory functions

SciCalc has a single memory. To store the displayed value into the memory, press Min. To recall the contents of the memory, press MR. To clear the memory, press MC.

Advanced functions

Calculating roots

To calculate the **square root** of x, press √x.

To obtain the yth root of x, press y√x, followed by y. For example, to calculate the fourth root of 52, click on the following keys:

    52 y√x 4 =

which will display the result 2.685349614.

Calculating squares and powers

To calculate the **square** of x, click on x^2, so the circle area calculation introduced on page 420 can also be done thus:

$$\pi \times 7 \ x^2 =$$

To raise x to a power other than 2, click on x^y followed by the power you want to take. For example, to raise 52 to the power 4, click on the following keys:

$$52 \ x^y \ 4 \ =$$

which will display the result 7311616.

To raise 10 to the nth power, enter n then press 10^x. To raise e to the nth power, enter n then press e^x.

Calculating reciprocals and factorials

For the **reciprocal** of x, enter x then click the $1/x$ key.

For x **factorial**, enter x then click the x! key.

Calculating logarithms

To obtain the **logarithm** (base 10) of x, enter x then press LOG.

For the **natural logarithm** (base e), enter x then press LN.

Using brackets

To obtain a bracket, press ( ). The same key produces a left or right bracket, whichever is appropriate in the context. For example, to calculate $(2 + 3) \times 5$, press

$$( ) \ 2 + 3 \ ( ) \ \times 5 \ =$$

Only one level of brackets is available.

Calculating exponents

To express x in exponent form, press Exp followed by y, the exponent. For example:

$$50 \ \text{Exp} \ 4 \ =$$

displays the result 500000.

Combinations and permutations

To find the number of **combinations** of r items from a set of n items, enter:

```
n nCr r =
```

To calculate **permutations**, where the order of n should be considered, enter:

```
n nPr r =
```

Trigonometric functions

Among the more advanced functions available in SciCalc are the standard
trigonometric functions:

SIN	sine
COS	cosine
TAN	tangent
ASN	arcsine (sine^{-1})
ACS	arccosine (cosine^{-1})
ATN	arctangent (tangent^{-1})

To obtain hyperbolic trigonometric functions, press Hyp before pressing the
function button.

Changing the number base and angle unit

When first started, SciCalc works in the number base set by its choices, by default
this is decimal. Clicking DEC, BIN, OCT or HEX changes the base to Decimal (base
10), Binary (base 2), Octal (base 8) or Hexadecimal (base 16) respectively, and the
layout of the keys changes appropriately for the selected base. For example, in
base 16 a number entered into SciCalc looks like this:

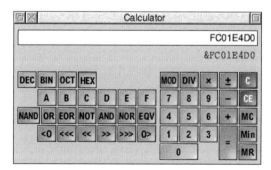

Changing base provides a handy way of converting a number between bases. Once
you have a number in the display, clicking on a different base key converts the
value to that base. Note that when changing from a decimal to non-decimal base
the value will be rounded to the nearest integer, as are values recalled from the
memory into a non-decimal base.

When in decimal mode, for the trigonometric functions you can calculate in units of degrees, radians or gradians by clicking RAD, DEG or GRD, but angles are not converted on a change of unit. A right angle is 90°, 100 grad and $\pi/2$ radians.

Logic functions in the non-decimal bases

In the non-decimal bases the scientific functions are replaced by:

MOD	integer modulus (remainder)
DIV	integer division
NAND	logical NOT AND
OR	logical inclusive OR
EOR	logical exclusive OR
NOT	logical inverse
AND	logical conjoin
NOR	logical NOT OR
EQV	logical equivalence (NOT EOR)

Bitwise functions in non-decimal bases

In the non-decimal bases, numbers may be bitwise rotated and shifted using:

<O	bitwise rotation to the left
>O	bitwise rotation to the right
<<<	logical shift left
>>>	logical shift right
<<	arithmetic shift left
>>	arithmetic shift right

In each case enter the number, press the function followed by the number of bits. You may wish to switch base to enter the number of bits more conveniently.

Keyboard shortcuts

Calculator functions and their keyboard equivalents

Calculator	Keyboard	Function
0…9	0…9	numbers
+, −, ×, ÷	+, −, *, /	standard operators
=	Return, Enter	same as =
±	#	change sign on number or exponent
Exp	E	allows entry of exponent
.	.	decimal point
()	(,)	brackets (one level only)
%	%	percentage
x!	!	factorial
x^Y	^	x raised to the power y
C	Escape, Delete	clear calculation
CE	Backspace	clear last entry
A…F	A…F	hexadecimal base digits
	Ctrl-S	toggle between simple and scientific views
	Ctrl-C	copy displayed number to the clipboard
	Ctrl-Shift-C	copy calculation summary to the clipboard

Icon bar menu

Info

This gives you information about the application.

Help…

Opens a short description of how to use SciCalc, based on this Guide.

Choices…

Opens a dialogue to alter SciCalc's settings, described in *Choices* on page 426.

Quit

Quit ends the SciCalc application, removing the SciCalc icon from the icon bar.

Choices

To open the Choices dialogue box, where you can vary the initial view and other settings, select **Choices...** from the icon bar menu.

When finished, click **Save** to use these settings now and also for any future sessions. Click **Cancel** to close the dialogue without making any changes.

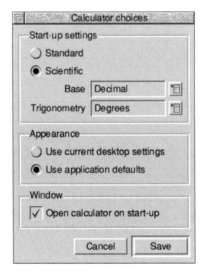

Start-up settings controls which view type, base and trigonometric settings are applied when the application is run.

Appearance controls which graphical style SciCalc uses – one that matches the current desktop theme, or the application's own default set.

Window sets whether or not to open the SciCalc window automatically when first run. When this option is on, you can set where on the desktop to open by first positioning the window then choosing **View/Remember position** from the main menu.

Technical notes

Numeric range

Mode		Numeric range
Decimal	Real values	−9.9E99 to 9.9E99 entry
		−9.9E307 to 9.9E307 displayable
Binary	32bit signed	10000000000000000000000000000000 to
		11111111111111111111111111111111
Octal	32bit signed	20000000000 to 17777777777
Hexadecimal	32bit signed	80000000 to 7FFFFFFF

Accuracy

SciCalc's accuracy is limited to that of BASIC VI – 64-bit floating point.

Mode	Accuracy	Number of digits displayed
Binary	Absolute	32
Octal	Absolute	10 - 11
Hexadecimal	Absolute	8
Decimal	64 bit FP	10 or 10 + 2 digit exponent

Note: Real number underflow is not trapped.

Trigonometric results

Strictly, zero and infinite results are displayed as very small and very large values.

Operator precedence

Operators are evaluated in the following order of precedence (highest shown first):

1   unary operators

2   $y\sqrt{x}$

3   x^Y

4   nCr, nPr

5   *, /, DIV, MOD

6   +, −

7   <O, O>, <<, >>, <<<, >>>

8   AND, NAND

9   OR, EOR, NOR, EQV

34   Squash

Squash is a simple application that compresses files and directories. Compression means that they take up less space, enabling more files to be fitted onto a disc or to be sent more quickly over a network.

Starting Squash

Squash is in the Apps directory on your hard disc or network. To start the application, double-click on the !Squash application icon. The Squash icon appears on the icon bar.

Compressing a file

1   Drag the file that you wish to compress onto the Squash icon on the icon bar. This displays the Squash **Save as** box.

2   Drag the icon from the **Save as** box to the directory display in which you want to save the compressed file. If you want to save it with a different filename, first change the name in the Save box.

If you want to replace the original file with the compressed version of the file, just click on **OK** instead. The compressed file uses the squashed file icon.

Decompressing a file

1   Drag the squashed file that you wish to decompress onto the Squash icon on the icon bar. This displays the Squash **Save as** box.

2   Drag the icon from the **Save as** box to the directory display in which you want to save the decompressed file. If you want to save it with a different filename, first change the name in the Save box.

If you want to replace the compressed file with the original file, just double-click on the squashed file and it is replaced by the uncompressed file.

Compressing a directory or application

1   Drag the directory or application onto the Squash icon on the icon bar. This displays the **Save as** box with two options, **Squash** and **Unsquash**.

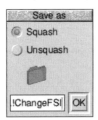

2   Click on **Squash** to compress the entire contents of the directory or application.

3   Drag the icon from the **Save as** box to the directory display in which you want to save the compressed directory or application.

If you want to replace the original directory or application with the compressed version, just click on the **OK** button instead.

The directory or application's icon are not replaced by the squash icon when their contents are squashed.

Note: You can't use compressed applications; you must decompress them first.

Decompressing a directory or application

1   Drag the squashed directory or application onto the Squash icon on the icon bar. This displays the Squash **Save as** box with two options, **Squash** and **Unsquash**.

2   Clicking on **Unsquash** will decompress the entire contents of the directory or application.

3   Drag the icon from the **Save as** box to the directory display in which you want to save the decompressed directory or application.

To replace the compressed directory or application with the decompressed version, just click on the **OK** button.

Icon bar menu

Info

This gives you information about the application.

Save box

When the Save box is ticked (normally) each compression (or decompression) prompts you with a **Save as** box. If you are converting a large number of files, you can use this option to turn off the Save box. Turning off the Save box allows all files and directories to overwrite the original versions during the conversion process.

Squash apps

If you choose this option, then when you drag a directory onto the Squash icon that contains any applications within it (or any subdirectories), these are also squashed.

This option is not selected by default; Squash does not compress applications it finds inside directories, they are copied instead.

Applications that are dragged to the Squash icon alone will always be squashed.

Quit

Quit ends the Squash application, removing the Squash icon from the icon bar.

Checking your archive

As with any archival mechanism, you should check that you can correctly compress and decompress back to the original size any information which is valuable or difficult to replace. Make a copy of the file before you compress it.

Exceptions

Occasionally Squash decides not to compress a file. This is usually because either the file is already compressed in some way that would make squashing it uneconomic or because the file is so small that squashing it would make no difference to the amount of disc space used.

Part 6 –
RISC OS diversions

35   Blocks

Blocks is game of spatial awareness where you must try to line up various shaped blocks to complete lines which score points. If you're not quick enough then the blocks will accumulate until they pile up to the top at which point the game is over.

Starting Blocks

Blocks is in the Diversions directory on your hard disc or network. To start the application:

1 Double-click on the !Blocks icon. The application icon appears on the icon bar.

2 Click on this icon to display the Blocks window and start playing:

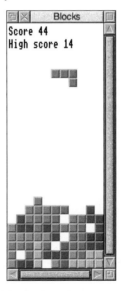

One point is awarded for each block placed. Any completed rows are removed, and the incomplete rows above shunt downwards accordingly. The game is over when the pile of disorganised blocks forming incomplete rows has filled the play area right to the top.

The colours of the blocks correspond to their arrangement, so with practice you will become familiar with the colours and how that shape might be useful to you.

Keys

While the Blocks window is selected the following keys are active, clicking away to another window in the desktop pauses the game temporarily.

Key	Action
1	Nudge block left
2	Rotate block a quarter turn
3	Nudge block right
Space	Drop block

Pressing the Space bar causes the currently falling block to immediately drop into place.

Blocks menus

New game

To start a new game, press Menu when you are over the Blocks window and choose **New game**.

New keys

If the keys listed above are inconvenient they can be altered by moving the pointer to the right and picking four new keys. They can be any letter or number key or the Space bar or Return.

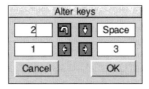

Click OK to use the keys shown, or Cancel to restore the former key choices.

Auto

The computer can be left to play Blocks on its own. Choose the Auto option to enable this, and see what high score it can achieve.

Quit

Quit ends the Blocks application, removing the Blocks icon from the icon bar.

36   Flasher

Flasher makes it easy to locate the caret when you are working on lots of documents at the same time in the desktop.

Starting Flasher

Flasher is in the Diversions directory on your hard disc or network. To start the application, double-click on the !Flasher application icon. The Flasher icon appears on the icon bar.

The caret is the place at which new characters typed on the keyboard will be inserted into the text, and is usually shown as a slim vertical red bar.

To locate the caret with Flasher running, click Select on its icon bar icon.

Icon bar menu

Info

This gives you information about the application.

Flash

When Flash is ticked the caret will flash between visible and invisible. Studies have shown this catches the eye, making the small caret even easier to see.

Scroll

When finding the caret Flasher will ask the application to scroll the text window to centre the caret in the text window. Not all applications respond to such a request.

Find

Choosing this option is equivalent to clicking Select on the Flasher icon bar icon. If the caret is not anywhere on screen, this menu item will be greyed out and attempts to find it will make a beep sound instead.

Quit

Quit ends the Flasher application, removing the Flasher icon from the icon bar.

37   Hopper

Hopper is a classic two dimensional arcade game, sometimes known by its alternative name Frogger. The objective is to direct frogs to the safety of their lair by crossing a busy road and navigating a river full of hazards.

Starting Hopper

Hopper is in the Diversions directory on your hard disc or network. To start the application, double-click on the !Hopper application icon.

The game runs in numbered screen mode 13 and will report an error if this is not available, the chapter *Old-type screen modes* on page 533 describes the properties of mode 13.

To rescue a frog move him from the starting point at the bottom of the screen, across the busy road, avoiding the rapids, to the safety of his lair. When all five lairs are occupied with frogs, the level is complete and the screen will clear ready for the next level.

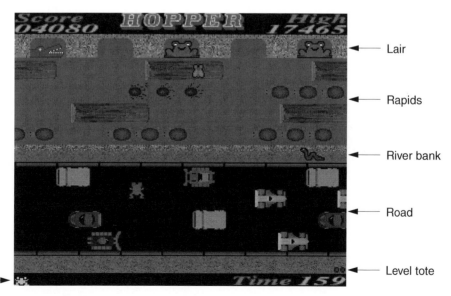

The current level number is shown by the number of dots in the level tote in the corner of the screen.

There are several ways that the frog might meet an untimely death:

● The timer counts down to zero before the frog has made it to the lair.

● Being run over on the road.

● Being bitten by the poisonous snake (level 2 onwards).

● Falling into the rapids.

● Being swallowed by the crocodile waiting in a lair (level 2 onwards).

Points are accumulated for moving northwards on the level, with a bonus for each frog which makes it to the lair. Additionally, sometimes a fly will be resting on a log in the rapids, which also gains a tasty bonus. The current score can be seen in the top left of the screen as it goes up, along with the current high scorer's target to beat in the top right of the screen.

Each successive level is increasingly difficult, with

● more traffic, faster speed limit, and fewer crossing slots

● more hazards, such as the snake and crocodile

● fewer passing logs in the rapids on which to transit

● turtles which dive under water in the rapids.

Keys

Clicking on the Hopper icon will display a repeating series of introductory screens showing the credits, high score table, and a reminder of the in game keys. Press the Space bar to start the game.

During the game the following keys are active.

Key	Action
Z	Hop left
X	Hop right
'	Hop forwards
/	Hop backwards
Escape	Quit the game and return to the desktop
F9/F10	Pause/resume the game
F1/F2	Enable/disable the sound effects
F5/F6	Enable/disable the background music

If your computer has a joystick attached, it is also possible to make the frog hop using a joystick instead of the keyboard.

Icon bar menu

Info

This gives you information about the application.

Choices...

Choosing this option will open a dialogue allowing settings for Hopper to be changed.

Quit

Quit ends the Hopper application, removing the Hopper icon from the icon bar.

Choices

The choices dialogue has four sections that can be configured. Select the radio icon for the name of the section whose options you wish to alter.

When finished, click **Set** to use these settings for the current session, or click **Save** to use them now and also in any future sessions. Click **Cancel** to close the dialogue without making any changes.

Control keys

If you would prefer to use keys other than those listed on page 440 to move the frog, for example because they are uncomfortably positioned, use this section to change them.

Click **Change** then press each movement key on the keyboard when prompted.

Miscellaneous

This section has two options available. Saving the high score table on exit will mean you can build up a list of most skilled players over several days even if the computer is turned off in between games. Use the **Reset** button to wipe the high scores at the end of a tournament.

The auto-repeat option will make the control keys repeat when held down so that multiple hops are produced from just one key press.

Sound and music

This section adjusts the relative volumes of the sound effects and background music within the game.

It is also possible to temporarily enable and disable the sound effects and background music within the game using the keys listed on page 440.

Advanced

Ordinarily the settings in the advanced section can be left at their default values.

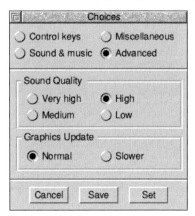

Reducing the sound quality reduces the number of calculations the computer must do, which saves power. However, only on a slow computer will this make any noticeable difference.

The graphics update option also reduces the number of calculations the computer must do, but may also reduce flickering which can be tiring when using the computer for extended periods of time.

38   Madness

Madness will very quickly drive you to the brink of insanity. It silently shuffles the windows around the screen while you try in vain to use the computer.

Starting Madness

Madness is in the Diversions directory on your hard disc or network. To start the application, double-click on the !Madness application icon.

You will immediately notice that any open windows on the screen will start to randomly move around, even the ones you are trying to use. It's very maddening!

Quitting Madness

Look carefully in the bottom left hand corner of the screen, you will notice a small window entitled Madness. Madness never moves its own window, so it will always be positioned there.

If it is obscured by the icon bar toggle the icon bar position with Shift-F12, then click on the Close icon, as described in the section *Manipulating windows* on page 45.

39   MemNow

MemNow provides a live display of how much free memory is available in your computer. This is useful to see when there are many applications running and a lot of memory is in use.

Starting MemNow

MemNow is in the Diversions directory on your hard disc or network. To start the application, double-click on the !MemNow application icon. MemNow will appear on the icon bar and display the amount of free memory, expressed in kilobytes, and keep the value up to date as you use the computer.

When memory is low the background of the MemNow icon bar display will flash to catch your attention. See the section *Managing memory* on page 79 for ideas of how to free unused memory.

Compact display

When there are many applications running you may have a lot of icons already on the icon bar, and would like to see the free memory without the space that MemNow takes up.

A compact way to achieve this if you also have Alarm running is to let Alarm show the free memory beside the time. You can achieve this by adding `Alarm$Free` to the user defined display format, as described in the section *Time and date display formats* on page 400.

40   Meteors

Meteors is a game set in space where the aim is to knock out all the meteors without colliding with them. Little meteors, being harder to hit, score more than big ones.

Starting Meteors

Meteors is in the Diversions directory on your hard disc or network. To start the application, double-click on the !Meteors application icon.

The game will start immediately with 3 rocket ships; the one currently in play, plus two spares.

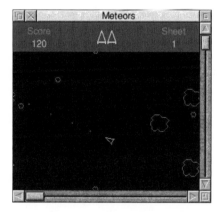

As meteors of varying size tumble through space it is your job to avoid them, or to score points by destroying them.

Firing at a meteor will cause it to break up into several smaller pieces, a collision with a meteor of any size is fatal and costs one spare rocket ship. When all the spares have been used the game is over.

Points are accumulated in the status bar at the top of the window, which also shows the number of spare rocket ships and the current sheet number.

Keys

While the Meteors window is selected the following keys are active, clicking away to another window in the desktop pauses the game temporarily.

Key	Action
Z	Rotate rocket left
X	Rotate rocket right
Shift	Accelerate forward
Return	Fire
Escape	Toggle full screen/windowed view
P	Toggle pause/resume
N	New sheet with even more, faster, meteors

If a collision looks inevitable you can hyperspace to another location by pressing the Space bar. Note, however, that there is a random chance that this manoeuvre will destroy your rocket.

41   MineHunt

MineHunt is a game of luck and lateral thinking. The objective is to safely uncover all mines hidden behind a grid of squares. At the start of the game you will have no idea where the mines are, so you will have to use deduction to locate them all.

Starting MineHunt

MineHunt is in the Diversions directory on your hard disc or network. To start the application, double-click on the !MineHunt icon.

To start the game, click on the MineHunt icon on the icon bar. The main window will open.

The counter in the top left of the window shows the number of hidden mines. The counter in the top right shows your playing time in seconds. Clicking on these counters changes the colour of the text.

Playing MineHunt

To start a new game, select **New game** from the main menu, or click on the central player icon in the top centre of the board. To uncover a square, click Select over it. The timer will begin to count from your first click.

If the square you uncovered contained a mine, then the game is over, and MineHunt will reveal the locations of all the mines. The mine with a red background is the one you just uncovered, the mines with green backgrounds are the ones you correctly marked, and all the others are ones you hadn't found yet.

If the square you uncovered did not contain a mine, then MineHunt will turn it into number indicating how many of the adjacent squares contain mines. If any of these adjacent squares are blank, then MineHunt will uncover all of those squares too.

Keep going until you have uncovered all the squares and hit none of the mines. Once this happens, you have won!

Marking squares

To mark a square that you know contains a mine, click Adjust over it. The square will then be marked with a red flag, and the mine counter in the top left of the window will reduce by one.

Flagged squares cannot be uncovered by clicking Select, and so are safe.

If you click Adjust again on the same square, the flag will turn into a question mark. This can be used to indicate that a mine might be present, but that you're not sure. These squares are not safe – clicking Select will uncover them.

Clicking Adjust a third time will clear the question mark and return the square to normal.

High scores

If you have achieved one of the five lowest times for the level you are on, then you will be asked to type your name for the high score table. You can look at the high score table any time by choosing **High scores/Show** from the main menu. You can also clear the tables by choosing **High scores/Reset**.

Clearing squares faster

If a square has the correct number of neighbouring squares marked as mines, you can quickly clear around it by either clicking Select whilst holding down the Shift key, or clicking Adjust.

This has the same effect as if you had clicked on all the other uncovered neighbours individually. If any of the neighbours are incorrectly marked, then clearing around will cause you to uncover a mine and the game will be over.

Choosing a level

There are five predefined levels.

Name	Size of board	Number of mines	Squares which are mined
Beginner	8×8	10	15.6%
Better	16×8	20	15.6%
Intermediate	16×16	40	15.6%
Good	24×16	60	15.6%
Expert	30×16	99	20.6%

In addition, you can set up a custom level using the **Level/Custom** dialogue box.

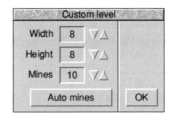

The maximum size of the game area is 64×64, but MineHunt will not let you go any bigger than the current screen mode will allow. If you click on the **Auto mines** button, MineHunt will choose a suitable number of mines for you.

Click **OK** to create the new level with your custom sizes.

Choices

The main menu allows to control a number of the game features.

Question marks

Turns question mark availability on or off.

Safe corners

This option ensures that when you start a new game, the corner squares are always free from mines.

Sound

You can click on this to control whether sound effects are played, or use the submenu to control the volume.

Icon bar menu

Info

This gives you information about the application.

Save choices

This option will save any changes you have made to the MineHunt options so that you can use these options as your default options next time you run MineHunt.

Quit

Quit ends the MineHunt application, removing the icon from the icon bar.

42   Patience

Patience is probably one of the best-known solo card games, sometimes known by its alternative name Solitaire.

Starting Patience

Patience is in the Diversions directory on your hard disc or network. To start the application, double-click on the !Patience application.

To start the game, click on the Patience icon on the icon bar. The Patience window appears on the screen:

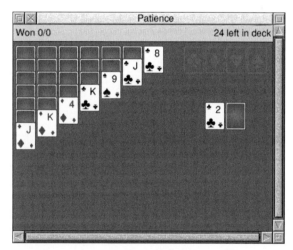

There are seven columns of cards, with the bottom card in each column turned up. The columns range in length from seven cards (on the left) to one (on the right). The rest of the pack is in a face-down 'pile' on the righthand side of the screen. At the top right-hand corner of the game area there are four card outlines, each marked with the symbol for one of the suits. The area across the top of the window shows the number of games won, and the number of face-down cards in the pile.

The rules

The object of the game is to place all four suits on top of their symbols in ascending order, starting with the ace and finishing with the king. To do this, you must reveal all the hidden cards by going through the pack and building chains of cards. Here are the basic rules:

- The chains you build downwards from each column must be in descending order (king, queen, jack, ten, nine, eight, seven, and so on) and must alternate between red and black suits (ten of hearts, nine of spades, eight of diamonds, seven of spades, for example). If you try to place a card incorrectly, the computer will refuse to move the card.

- When you move the top card from one column to another, the next hidden card is automatically turned up. You can move all or part of a chain to another column.

- There are only seven columns allowed in the game. If you have used up all the cards in one column you can only start a new column with a king (unless you have changed the default choices).

- Once you have placed a card on one of the suit symbols, in ascending order, at the top righthand corner of the screen it cannot be taken off again.

Playing Patience

To play the game, proceed as follows:

1   Look at the cards which are revealed at the bottom of each column. If a card can be moved, use the mouse pointer to drag it to the correct place. When you release the button, the card will be in its new place and the next card turned up in the column where it came from. Continue this procedure until you have no more cards that can be moved.

2   Click on the pile of cards on the right, to reveal the next card (by default, every third card in the pile is turned over). If you can use it, drag the card to the appropriate column. You may now be able to move one or more cards from one column to another. If you can't, click on the pile of cards again. If you can't use a card, continue clicking on the pack until one is revealed that you can use. When you use a card from the pack, the card beneath it is again revealed.

3   As soon as an ace is revealed, drag it to its place at the top righthand corner of the screen (alternatively, clicking Adjust on a card that can be added to one of these stacks automatically moves it to the correct stack). You can then start building (in ascending order from ace to king) as the cards that follow come up.

4 Continue going through the pack and moving cards. The number of cards left in the pack will continue to be indicated in the area above the board. An empty space indicates that you have gone through the pack once; click on it to go round again.

5 If you can't go any further and want to see where the hidden cards were, click Menu and choose **Resign**. If there are any cards left in the pack, you can see what they are by clicking on the pack; this will display each card in turn.

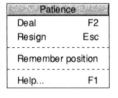

If you want to start a new game, choose **Deal** from the menu. If you do not wish to continue playing Patience, choose **Quit** from the icon bar menu.

In addition to starting a new game and quitting Patience, the menu has two other options. Selecting **Remember position** stores the screen position of the game window such that it will re-open in the same place the next time you run Patience. Selecting **Help...** opens a short description of how to play Patience based on this Guide.

Choices

To open the Choices dialogue box, where you can vary the game rules and other settings, select **Choices...** from the icon bar menu.

When finished, click **Save** to use these settings now and also for any future sessions. Click **Cancel** to close the dialogue without making any changes.

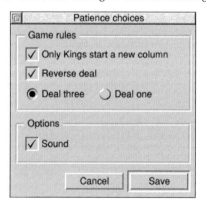

Game rules

The default game rule is that *Only Kings start a new column*. Turning this option off makes the game very much easier; you can now move any card into an empty column instead of being constrained to having to start with a king.

Reverse deal refers to the process by which cards are turned over from the pack. The default is that when a group of three cards is turned over, their order is reversed as they are moved. This means that if you run through the pack twice, you will see two-thirds of the cards. Switching this option off means that the cards are not reversed, so you will only see one-third of the cards, making the game much harder.

Deal three or *Deal one* refers to the number of cards dealt from the deck on to the pile with each click. Choosing the first option makes the game harder.

Options

The Sound option determines whether Patience beeps to indicate an illegal move.

43   Puzzle

Puzzle is a simple move-the-tiles game. The objective of the game is to move the tiles so that they are all in ascending order left-to-right and top-to-bottom.

Starting Puzzle

Puzzle is in the Diversions directory on your hard disc or network. To start the application, double-click on the !Puzzle application icon. The Puzzle window appears on the display.

The puzzle comprises fifteen number tiles and one space in a four-by-four grid. The objective of the puzzle is to move the tiles into numerical order in four lines from the top left to the bottom right. Rearrange the tiles by clicking on any of the number tiles next to the space to move it into the gap.

Here is what the completed puzzle looks like:

If you want to learn some tricks how to solve the game you should look at the Help file supplied with the application.

Puzzle menu

New board

To display a new board, press Menu when you are over the Puzzle window and choose **New board**.

You can make the board more difficult to solve by adding more tiles, to a maximum of 25×25. Move the pointer to the right and use the arrows to increase the size, then click **New board** on the button on the board size window to start playing.

Display...

Choosing this option will open the display options window, allowing you to change various visual aspects of the display. Including

● the font size and style

● the colours used for the numbers

● the tile colour scheme.

For example, to make all the tiles the same colour change the (A) and (B) colours to be equal.

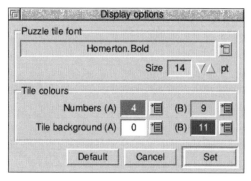

Clicking **Set** will redraw the display with the new options set. To make these settings permanent for when you next run the application, click **Save choices** on the icon bar menu.

Use the **Default** button to restore the factory default settings.

The **Cancel** button closes the window without making any changes to the current display options.

Part 7 –
RISC OS utilities

44   T1ToFont

T1ToFont is a program that converts fonts from Adobe Type 1 format to the RISC OS outline font format. Once you've converted fonts, you can use them in your documents just like any other Acorn outline font.

Note: This application is for advanced users **only**. Most people will never need to use it. Some complex fonts (and fonts not conforming exactly to Adobe Type 1 format) may not convert successfully.

This application should only be used to convert public domain fonts. While it is possible to convert proprietary fonts, it would, most probably, be a breach of copyright to do so without the consent of the copyright holder.

Converting a font

Before you can use the converter you need to have your source font comprising the Type 1 file and an AFM file available. The Type 1 file (often called the PFB file) should be given the file type PoScript (&FF5) and the AFM file (described on page 465) given the file type Text.

1   Load T1ToFont from the Utilities directory on your hard disc or network.

2   Click on the icon bar icon to display the Font converter window.

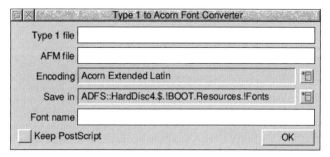

3   Drag the Type 1 PFB file icon from its directory display onto the **Type 1 file** field in the converter window.

4   Drag the AFM file from its directory display onto the **AFM file** field in the converter window.

5   After a few seconds the name of the RISC OS font to be generated is displayed in the **Font name** field. You can change this name if required.

6   Use the **Save in** field to select a font directory to save the resulting font in. However you should not normally change this from the default path which is

`$.!Boot.Resources.!Fonts`

within the Boot application. Click on the menu icon to display the alternatives.

7   Select the **Encoding** you need for the font, **Acorn Extended Latin** is nearly always used. Click on the menu icon to display the alternatives.

8   Click on the **Keep PostScript** option button if you want to keep the Type 1 font and the AFM files with the Outline font. This is useful if you are printing to a PostScript printer as the printer will then use the PostScript font directly.

9   Start the conversion by clicking on **OK**.

When the conversion is finished (the hourglass reverts back to a pointer) the font is now stored in the computer as a RISC OS font.

You should now try to display the font using Chars (see page 403). If the font displays correctly the conversion was successful. If the font does not display properly then it cannot be used with RISC OS and should be deleted from the font directory it was saved in.

Other information

The **Save in** menu selects a font directory to save the resulting font in. The menu is constructed from the contents of the Font$Path system variable, so !Font directories can be added to the menu by installing them on Font$Path (you can do this by double-clicking them).

Encoding

The **Encoding** type for most fonts will almost always be **Acorn Extended Latin**.

Some fonts have their own special encoding information. If you have one of these fonts you should choose the Encoding type, **As specified in Type 1 file**.

If you don't have an AFM file you can convert the font by leaving the AFM field blank. The resulting font will lack kerning (font spacing) information, so always use the AFM file if you have one.

Selwyn, Sussex and Sidney are encodings for special symbol fonts. The encoding file is automatically stored within the font's directory.

Font types

Fonts must conform strictly to the Type 1 font definitions. Many Public Domain fonts do not obey the structure rules laid down by Adobe and consequently they may not convert properly. Type 3 fonts cannot be converted.

Printing to a PostScript printer

If you print to a Postscript printer, the printer uses the original PostScript font (for downloading) if it is available. If it is not available, it converts and downloads the RISC OS outline font. To keep the original PostScript font available, select the **Keep PostScript** option before you start converting your font.

Using Macintosh and MS-DOS type 1 fonts

Macintosh fonts

Macintosh fonts are generally supplied as a Font/DA Mover document, containing the Macintosh version of the font, and one or more Type 1 files containing the PostScript code for use on the printer. There will be one Type 1 file for each weight and variation of the font.

AFM file

In addition to this you need an AFM (Adobe Font Metrics) file for each weight and variation of the font. The Macintosh does not seem to use this itself, but some fonts are supplied with it anyway. If you do not have the AFM file, contact the font supplier and try to obtain one.

You can convert a font without using an AFM file, however the resultant RISC OS font will lack kerning information.

Transfer the files

You need to copy the Type 1 files from the Macintosh to your computer. The Macintosh stores data and its description separately in what are called the *data fork* and the *resource fork* respectively, so you'll need a way to access these. Copying the files to an MS-DOS formatted removable disc is one way of doing this; this disc can then be read directly by your RISC OS computer.

Transfer the resource fork of the font file to one file on your computer, and set its file type to PoScript (&FF5). Transfer the AFM file (usually in the data fork) to another file and give it the file type Text.

MS-DOS Fonts

Fonts for MS-DOS computers are supplied as a group of files suitable for installing through Control Panel in Windows. Among the files will be one or more Type 1 files containing the PostScript code for the printer. There will be one Type 1 file for each weight and variation of the font. The Type 1 files usually have the extension . PFB.

AFM file

In addition to this you need an AFM (Adobe Font Metrics) file for each weight and variation of the font. If you do not have the AFM file, contact the font supplier and try to obtain one.

You can convert a font without using an AFM file, although the resultant RISC OS font will lack kerning information.

Other files, including the PFM file, are not needed for the conversion.

Transfer the files

Transfer the AFM and PFB files using the methods described in the section *Using DOS and Windows discs* on page 140. Change the file type of the PFB file to PoScript (&FF5) and the file type of the AFM file to Text.

45   HForm

This application is used to format or initialise hard discs, memory cards, and SCSI discs ready for use. Usually you won't need to use this application if your computer has a hard disc as your supplier will have formatted and loaded it with the standard RISC OS applications.

The native disc format in RISC OS is handled by the FileCore module; such discs are said to be *FileCore formatted* and HForm is a *FileCore formatter*. Use HForm to:

- Prepare removable memory cards, such as Secure Digital or MultiMediaCard, for use with SDFS.

- Prepare SCSI discs, including USB connected drives, for use with SCSIFS.

- Prepare hard discs for use with ADFS.

- Initialise a hard disc that has not been formatted by your supplier.

- Clear an existing hard disc if it develops a problem that can only be solved by formatting.

WARNING: Formatting your hard disc will permanently remove all data stored on the disc. It is essential that you copy all the data and applications that you want to keep to another disc (or otherwise back them up) before you reformat the disc.

WARNING: Save your work and quit all applications before using HForm.

You should keep a spare copy of HForm on another disc in case your hard disc becomes unusable.

Formatting your existing hard disc

In the following instructions it is assumed that you have to reformat your existing hard disc because of repeated hard disc errors. In order to carry out the reformatting successfully you should have a record of the disc errors which have occurred and their addresses.

HForm allows you to leave the program at any time by pressing Escape before you start formatting. Additionally, at the end of the Format options you will be asked if you want to proceed with the formatting; answer **No** and HForm will quit without formatting your disc.

Starting the application

HForm is in the `Utilities.Caution` directory on your hard disc or network. To start HForm, double-click on the !HForm icon. The application starts immediately.

Using HForm

Once you've started HForm, the desktop will disappear and be replaced by a blank screen with just text on it. You'll need to reply to certain questions that appear on the screen. Text that you should type in is shown in bold below. You should press ⏎ after anything you type in.

1   First, tell HForm which filing system the drive is connected via:

```
FILECORE HARD DISC FORMATTER 2.72 (28-Feb-16)
Is your drive connected to ADFS, SCSIFS, or SDFS (A/S/M) ? A ⏎
```

This question will be skipped when only one of the filing systems which HForm supports is installed, jumping straight to step 2 below. Otherwise, select:

- **A** for a hard disc connected to the computer's motherboard via an IDE or SATA cable, using ADFS.

- **S** for a hard disc connected to a SCSI expansion card, and any media connected via the Universal Serial Bus either directly or in an external caddy.

- **M** for memory cards in sockets directly mounted on the computer's motherboard, using SDFS. Note that card readers with several different socket sizes are usually USB peripherals and would therefore use SCSI.

2   HForm will then look for drives that the filing system could use. A list will be presented describing each drive found similar to this example:

```
4 : Conner peripherals CP30254    1.00    240 Mbytes
5 : Samsung SV8004H               2.49     80 Gbytes
Format which drive (4 - 7) ? 4 ⏎
```

If you want to accept the default drive number, press ⏎, otherwise type the desired number and press ⏎. HForm displays detailed information about the drive in a message similar to this:

```
Drive 4 is an IDE drive
Drive ADFS::4 identifies itself as :
Description     : Conner peripherals 240MB - CP30254
Firmware version : 0.33
Configuration   : 895 cylinders, 10 heads and 55 sectors/track
```

Some larger capacity drives also support logical block addressing which is easier to understand than Cylinder-Head-Sector notation; you will be shown these parameters too if applicable.

3 Next, tell HForm which hard disc shape to use.

You don't need to know the manufacturer of your hard disc or its specifications, since you can just accept all the defaults offered. If you want to use a different drive shape turn to *Changing the hard disc shape* on page 471, otherwise:

```
This disc was last formatted using the standard shape:
      895 cylinders, 10 heads and 55 sectors/track
      Parking cylinder 894, Initialisation flag 1,
      LBA flag 1(enabled)
Do you wish to retain this shape (Y/N) ? Y ↵
```

4 Decide whether you simply want to format the disc, or whether you want to map out any defects found. HForm gives you the following choices:

```
A: no more changes to defect list
B: add defect by cylinder, head, byte/sector
C: add defect by disc address
D: remove defect
```

If you want to add some defects see *Recording a list of hard disc defects* on page 470. If you are simply formatting a disc:

```
A, B, C or D? A ↵
```

5 Decide whether to format or initialise the hard disc.

```
Format or just initialise the drive (F/I) ? I ↵
```

You only need to format the disc if it has never been formatted before, or if it was previously formatted using the wrong parameters. This example assumes you want to initialise the disc only:

6 Decide whether you want to carry out a soak test.

```
Soak test the hard disc for defects (Long/Short/None) ? S ↵
```

Soak testing checks that the state of the defects on the disc is stable.

L is the long test; the disc is continuously tested until you press the Space bar. S is the short test, which is just one scan of the disc, lasting a few minutes.

7 Tell HForm if this will be the main drive that your computer uses at power on to boot from.

```
Do you wish this to be a bootable disc (Y/N) ? Y ↵
```

8 Choose whether to format the disc with long filenames or not.

```
Do you want long filenames on this disc (Y/N) ? Y ↵
```

In RISC OS 3.71 and earlier FileCore limited filenames to 10 characters. If you need to read the disc with these earlier versions turn off long filenames.

9   HForm will calculate the optimum file allocation unit which is the size that the disc map is divided up into, the larger the drive the larger the unit. Only advanced users will want to alter the value it proposes:

```
Large file allocation unit ? 1024
```

10 You now have a final chance to quit the format process before it starts, or decide to proceed:

```
Are you SURE you want to do this to ADFS::4 (Y/N) ? Y ⏎
```

Entering Y and pressing ⏎ starts the format or initialisation. Entering N will quit from the HForm application without formatting the disc.

If you specified the long soak test, the test continues until you press the Space bar. It is recommended that you carry out the soak test for at least 24 hours.

If you do not perform a soak test, and if the verification process detects any additional defects, HForm will then repeat the formatting and verification process in order to include the new defects. It will display the messages `Formatting` and `Verifying` as it does so.

The formatting process is now complete.

Recording a list of hard disc defects

A defect is a fault that has been detected in part of the disc. The following process marks the defective part of the disc, so that the defective part is no longer used.

HForm lists the current defects (if any) on the hard disc and invites you to change the list by adding any new defects that you may have discovered. You may wish to add a new defect because of a previously returned disc error message, such as:

```
Disc error 10 at :4/00831E00
```

You should make a note of any errors on your hard disc of this type that the computer reports.

When HForm asks you if you want to map out any defects:

1   Type **C** then press ⏎.

2   Type in the defect address exactly as it appeared in the disc error message, but omit anything up to and including the colon (e.g. for the error above, you'd just type **4/00831E00**) then press ⏎. After each addition, the list of current defects will be shown.

3   Add further defect addresses by returning to step 1, above.

4   When you have entered all the defects you wish to, type **A** and press ⏎ to indicate there are no more changes.

Changing the hard disc shape

HForm prompts you to confirm the specifications of the hard disc used (known as the *shape*) of the disc in your computer. Where possible HForm gets this information from the previous FileCore format type.

However, you may need to change the shape if

● you are adding a new hard disc

● the hard disc has not yet been formatted

● you only want to use the first part of a large disc and leave the rest unused

● the information on the hard disc has been corrupted or is incorrect.

If you want to change the disc shape you can answer NO to the following question:

```
Do you wish to retain this shape (Y/N)? N ↵
```

You will be presented with a list of alternative shapes to choose from. If you don't want to use any of these shapes use OTHER. You will have to enter the formatting specifications you require. Consult the manual accompanying your hard disc for its precise specifications or contact your supplier for details.

Note: During this process, if your disc supports it and is connected to ADFS, you'll be given the opportunity to specify Logical Block Addressing (LBA):

```
Drive LBA flag ? 1 ↵
```

LBA provides a faster calculation of disc addresses. If you don't set the LBA flag here, the normal Cylinder-Head-Sector (CHS) addressing will be used.

46   ChangeFSI

ChangeFSI is a useful program for converting and displaying image files of various formats. These images can then be converted into sprites or JPEGs for viewing with RISC OS applications such as Paint and Draw.

ChangeFSI stands for 'Change Floyd Steinberg Integer' (ChangeFSI performs Floyd Steinberg error diffusion dithering).

You should make sure that your conversion and subsequent use of an image does not infringe on any copyright that the image may be under.

ChangeFSI can read image data, scale the data to improve an image, change its width and height, sharpen an image and write the result using error diffusion dithering in one step (so it provides the best possible quality). All operations are carried out with 32-bit fixed-point numbers (three per pixel in the case of a colour picture).

Starting ChangeFSI

ChangeFSI is in the Utilities directory on your hard disc or network. To start the application, double-click on the !ChangeFSI icon.

Using ChangeFSI

1   Display the directory that contains the file for the image to be processed.

2   Choose whether to save the image as a sprite or JPEG file.

3   Change to a desktop screen display mode that you wish to view and store the image in, if you're exporting to a sprite.

    ChangeFSI automatically converts the file to give the best possible screen image for any display mode. For example, if you choose a 32-thousand colour mode ChangeFSI will produce an image with 32 thousand colours; if you only choose a 16-colour display mode ChangeFSI will produce a 16-colour image – if the colours are nearer to the greys than the colours in the 16-colour palette, it may be that the image is displayed in monochrome on a 16-colour display, but this doesn't mean that the colour information has been lost (unless you save the image as a sprite in that mode).

4   Drag the image file's icon onto the ChangeFSI application on the icon bar. ChangeFSI then attempts to convert the file to give a RISC OS sprite, or a JPEG file, displaying the result.

Note: ChangeFSI may not retain transparent sprite pixels during processing. Transparent pixels can be changed to a colour, depending on the screen mode (e.g. transparent pixels in a 16-colour sprite become white in a 256-colour sprite).

Picture formats

ChangeFSI can convert many types of images to a sprite or JPEG file; see page 480 for a full list. These include:

● PC graphics formats TIFF, Targa TGA, ZSoft PCX, Windows BMP and ICO;

● UNIX RLE, Portable Bit Map, Sun Raster;

● Kodak PhotoCD images and contact sheets;

● Common internet image formats PNG, WAP, CompuServe GIF, JPEG;

● Various specialist scientific and raw image capture formats.

ChangeFSI can also convert sprites or JPEGs from one display resolution into another. Be careful, though: every time you recompress a JPEG file it loses some information. Process a file first, and only save it as a JPEG once, right at the end.

Additional information

The information in this chapter gives an overview of how ChangeFSI works from the desktop. Additional information in the form of text files is held within the application. If you want to read these files, Shift double-click on !ChangeFSI to open the application directory, then open its Documents directory and double-click on one of the text files:

File	Description
BTPCInfo	Standard information about Binary Tree Predictive Coding.
CmdBasUse	Syntax for using ChangeFSI from the command line, and for calling it from BASIC programs.
DesktopUse	Instructions for using ChangeFSI from the desktop.
Formats	Details of formats that ChangeFSI can use as input or output.
JPEGInfo	Standard information about JPEG processing (taken from the Independent JPEG Group's JPEG software).

File	Description
Theory	Theoretical explanation of how ChangeFSI works, likely only to be of interest to advanced users.
256sprites	Information for programmers about creating, recognising and displaying a sprite with a 256-entry palette.

A couple of hints on memory usage

If you're short on memory, Drag the **Next** slot (in the Task Manager display window) down to 320kB. If you're converting wide images (e.g. PhotoCD images up to 3072 pixels wide) increase the **Next** slot to 508kB or more.

Icon bar menu options

This section tells you how to use ChangeFSI's menu options.

Scaling options

The **Scaling** options set which scale factor you wish to apply to your image. You can also transform, rotate or mirror the image.

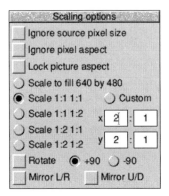

Scale 1:1 1:1 gives a full-sized image (the same dimensions as the original). The other **Scale** options set different preset scaling ratios.

Custom gives you finer control over the size of the output image. You can either set your own scaling ratio by filling in all four boxes, or you can set the size in pixels by filling in the left **x** and **y** boxes only, leaving the right boxes blank.

Scale to fill scales the image so that it covers the entire screen area at the current display resolution; this may distort the aspect ratio.

Ignore source pixel size ignores any source information about the pixel size. This can be useful if you have images that use a non-standard pixel size. The pixels are all considered to be square.

Ignore pixel aspect ignores all the size information in the source file. Both source and output pixels are considered to be square.

Lock picture aspect prevents the Scale to fill and Custom options from stretching the image horizontally or vertically. The output image will fit within the size you specified; it may be smaller than you asked in one direction only, to avoid changing its aspect ratio.

Rotate can shift an image through 90° (+90 is anticlockwise).

Mirror performs left/right and up/down mirror operations on an image.

If you select to both rotate and mirror, the rotation is performed first.

Processing options

The Processing options control the image processing used in the conversion and display of the image. You'll notice that all of these options are 'off' by default; you will not normally need to change these settings.

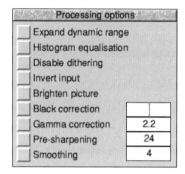

Expand dynamic range will expand the range of colours in the image. This normally brightens the image. It expands the dynamic range of a picture to full scale.

Histogram equalisation will most often result in a worse picture but it can be used to recover detail from an otherwise useless image. Alternatively you can use it to look at information locked in a small part of the input scale.

Disable dithering will disable Floyd-Steinberg dithering. This will usually result in an inferior image.

Invert input will result in the negative version of your image, with colours inverted so black becomes white and white becomes black for example.

Brighten picture will produce a picture that is slightly brighter than it should be. Useful if you have dark pictures. This option only works with monochrome pictures.

Black correction is useful if you want to print the image on a laser printer. You should use a number between zero and 128, though values between 32 and 64 usually give the best result; experiment. Images treated in this way will give a poor result when viewed on screen. This only works for 1bpp (black and white) output.

Gamma correction is used to correct the image quality as displayed on your monitor. Low values of gamma (0 to 1) make colours darker and high values (above 1) make them lighter. Gamma correction is most often used to correct images that have been scanned in with a scanner. Different monitors may need different gamma corrections. A standard value is 2.2 (TV industry standard).

Pre-sharpening is used to sharpen the edges of objects in the image. Values between 10 and 20 can be used to sharpen an image. Values between 20 and 30 can be used to compensate for the blurring introduced by the dithering process.

For example, a value of 24 will counteract the general dither blurring. A value of 20 is noticeably sharp. All values from 1 to 99 can be selected.

Smoothing does the reverse of sharpening; it smoothes the edges of objects in the image. You can use values between 1 and 23, with low values giving the most smoothing. Values between 1 and 3 can be used to blur an image. Values between 3 and 10+ can be used to reduce noise in an image.

Output options

Sprite output options

To output an image in sprite format, choose **Sprite output** from the icon bar menu and set up the output options:

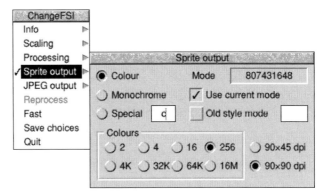

Colour gives a sprite in colour.

Monochrome gives a sprite in shades of grey.

Special allows the use of special file suffixes. These are the same as the <mode> parameter described in the documentation file CmdBasUse.

Use current mode outputs the image for display in the current desktop Display Manager mode.

Old mode allows you to output the image for display in a numbered screen mode from the table in the appendix *Old-type screen modes* on page 533. We don't recommend that you use this method (it is overridden if you set a colour mode and then use the **Monochrome** button).

The **Mode** number is only useful in old-type screen modes. It's an information box (you can't type anything into it). When **Use current mode** is selected, the mode number generated with new style screen displays has no significance.

Colours uses the group of buttons to set the number of colours in the output image to **2**, **4**, **16**, **256**, **4K, 32K, 64K** or **16M** respectively, or for **Monochrome** output to **2**, **4**, **16** and **256** greys. Beside the colour selection buttons is a further option to choose either a square pixel mode (90 × 90dpi) or a non-square (90 × 45dpi) one.

JPEG output options

To output an image in JPEG format, choose **JPEG output** from the icon bar menu and set up the output options:

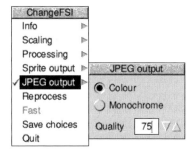

Colour produces a full colour JPEG image in the red/green/blue colour space.

Monochrome produces a JPEG image in shades of grey.

Quality can take any value from 0 to 100 and is passed to the JPEG compression code. The default value is 75, but you can change this using **Save choices**. The default value gives a sensible compromise between quality and compression.

Reprocess

This option reprocesses the file according to any new options you may have set.

Fast

This option speeds up ChangeFSI by blanking the screen during image processing. If there is no benefit to be had from doing this, the option will be greyed out.

Save choices

This option will save any changes you have made to the ChangeFSI options so that you can use these options as your default options next time you run ChangeFSI.

Quit

This quits the application, removing it from the icon bar.

Image menu options

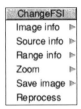

Once your image has been produced you can click Menu over the image to display a menu of information about the input and output images.

Image Info gives you information about the output file.

Source Info gives you information about the source file.

Range Info gives you information about the dynamic range of the image.

Zoom allows you to change the magnification of the image. This is not the same as scaling the source image.

Save image allows you to save the image as a sprite file or JPEG file (this depends on the settings made from *Output options* on page 478).

Reprocess allows you to process the image again using any options you have subsequently changed on the main menu.

Image file conversion

ChangeFSI will convert any of the following image formats into the sprite or JPEG format. You can choose the type of RISC OS sprite that is created by setting the **Output Options**. If no special output mode is chosen, ChangeFSI produces a sprite that is compatible with the current display mode.

Image type	Recognised by
RISC OS sprites	file type FF9
ArVis 15-bit HIP + LOP sprites	file type FF9, and file is beneath a HIP directory, and a similar LOP file exists
Watford digitiser pictures, 512×256, 64 greys	file type DFA
and triple red, green, blue separations	directory of type DFA files named RED, GREEN and BLUE
ProArtisan compressed pictures, 640×256, 256 colours	file type DE2
JPEG 'JFIF' files	'JFIF' in file, or file type C85
Kodak PhotoCD images	file type BE8, or file's name ends /PCD
TimeStep satellite images, 800×800, 256 greys	file type 7A0
PC TGA images	file type 69D, or file's name ends with /TGA or /VDA
MTV 24-bit PIC images	file type 699, or file is beneath a PIC directory
QRT 24-bit RAW images	file type 698, or file's name is RAW
ZSoft .PCX files	file type 697, or &0A,&00|02|03|04|05,&01 at start of file, or file is beneath a PCX directory, or file's name ends /PCX
Degas PI1, PI2, PI3 images	file type 691

Image type	Recognised by
!Translator Clear format files	file type 690
CCIR 601 4:2:2 images	file type 601
!RayShade 'RGB' images	file type 371
TimeStep satellite images, 128×256, 256 greys –	file type 300
and triple red, green, blue separations	directory of type 300 files named RED, GREEN and BLUE
AIM/Wild Vision Hawk V10, 256×256, 256 greys	file type 004
Wild Vision Hawk V12, 512×512, 256 greys	file type 006
Wild Vision Hawk V9, 512×256, 12-bit colour	'MercSoft' or 'SnapShot' at start of file
Wild Vision Hawk V9 Mk II, 16-bit colour	'MercSof1' at start of file
Pineapple 16 bit per pixel images	'FSIfile' at start of file
FITS astronomical format images	'SIMPLE ' at start of file
Irlam Instruments YUV 411 files	'IRLAM YUV 411' at start of file
Irlam Instruments 24-bit files	'Irlam' at start of file
Windows 3 and OS/2 BMP files	'BM' in file
and RIFF files	'RIFF' at start of file and 'RDIBdata' and 'BM' in file
and ICO files containing icons	&00,&00,&01,&00 in file and file type &132 or file's name ends /ICO
and CUR files containing mouse cursors	&00,&00,&02,&00 in file and file type &6A5 or file's name ends /CUR
CompuServe's GIF files up to 8 bit per pixel	'GIF8' at start of file
.PIC 8 bit per pixel files	'AV_VO' at start of file
Sun 'pixrect' raster files	&956AA659 at start of file
GEM .IMG images	&08000100 at start of file, or file is beneath an IMG directory, or file's name ends /IMG
Apollo GPR 16-colour images	&01000100 at start of file
RIX Softworks ColoRIX 8 bit per pixel files	'RIX3' at start of file
Technol video digitiser images	'T-I' in file, or file type &CBE
TIFF pictures	'II*null' or 'MMnull*' at start of file
UNIX rle format files	&CC52 at start of file
Portable Bit Map (pbm) binary encoded formats	'P1', 'P2', 'P3', 'P4', 'P5' or 'P6' at start of file
ChangeFSI packed portable bitmaps	'P15' at start of file
PocketBook I and II PIC format files	'PIC' at start of file
Electronic Art's IFF ILBM pictures	'FORM' at start of file and 'ILBM' in file
MILLIPEDE PRISMA, 768×576, 8-bit colour images	'MILLIPEDE' in file
MacPaint files, 576×720, 1 bit per pixel	'PNTG' in file
MacPICT2 v2 8 and 24/32 bit per pixel	&00,&11,&02,&FF,&0C,&00,&FF,&FE in file
RT 24-bit run length coded IMAGE files	file is beneath an IMAGE directory
PC EGA DSP images, 640×350, 16 colours	file is beneath a DSP directory, or file's name ends /DSP
Alpiar 36 bit per pixel	'ALPIAR12' at start of file

Image type	Recognised by
Alpiar 48 bit per pixel	'ALPIAR16' at start of file
Kodak RGB images, 24 bits per pixel	file's name ends /RGB
BTPC binary tree predictive coding image	'btpc 4.' at start of file
Portable network graphics PNG images	&89,PNG,&0D,&0A,&1A,&0A at start of file
Wireless application protocol bitmaps, 2 colour	&00,&00 in file and file type F8F or file's name ends /WBMP

47   Usage

Usage monitors the amount of time each application is loading the central processing unit (CPU) for, presenting the result as a bar graph of usage.

Starting Usage

Usage is in the Utilities directory on your hard disc or network. To start the application, double-click on the !Usage icon.

Unlike most applications where the icon bar icon looks the same as it does in a directory display, Usage uses its space on the icon bar to show a rolling graph of CPU load. For much of the time the desktop is idle waiting for you to press a key or click a mouse button, but when applications are busy these are shown in black on the rolling graph. If the rectangle is solid black then the CPU is being used 100% of the time and you may notice the desktop being slow or unresponsive.

Detailed display

Clicking Select on the Usage icon bar icon will open the detailed display.

This display should be familiar as it is arranged like the Tasks window in Task Manager as described in the section *Application tasks* on page 74. However, instead of showing the amount of memory each application is using it shows the amount of CPU time each application is using.

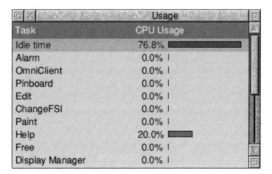

Any spare time is grouped in the *Idle time* bar, shown at the top of the list in red.

483

48 Patch

Patch can be used to apply small updates – patches – to applications which you already have installed. These updates will typically be fixes to minor defects, or improvements in compatibility, rather than major new versions.

Starting Patch

Patch is in the Utilities directory on your hard disc or network. To start the application, double-click on the !Patch icon.

Applying or removing patches

There are a small number of patches built into the utility as supplied, but in most instances your software supplier will have provided you with a Patch file, which is file type &FC3. Double click on the Patch file you have been provided with to register it with the Patch utility.

Drag the application to update on to the Patch icon. The patch window will open listing the application's purpose, its location, along with some information about the nature of the update.

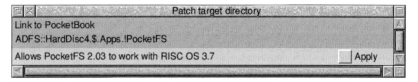

You can repeat this process for several other applications, or even whole directories of applications; only those which have corresponding patches registered will be listed and the other applications will be ignored.

Each application listed can be in one of three states:

- **Unrecognised** – the application is known to Patch, but none of the patches match the version presented. For safety, Patch will not let you apply patches to versions it doesn't recognise.

- **Apply** – this application is ready to be patched.

- **Remove** – this application has previously been patched, and you have the option of removing the patch to restore it to the former, unpatched, state.

485

Work through the list, select the **Apply** option next to each application that you would like to update, select the **Remove** option to restore the original application by removing the earlier updates.

Click Menu on the patch window to choose which operation to perform on the applications listed.

Select all apply

Save time by marking all those in the **Apply** state with a tick.

Select all remove

Save time by marking all those in the **Remove** state with a tick.

Clear selection

Deselect all applications in the patch window.

Patch selected

Perform the patch operation, either **Apply** or **Remove** as determined by the selections made. After applying or removing the patches, you have finished with Patch and can choose **Quit** from the icon bar menu to remove Patch from memory.

49 SparkFS

S parkFS is a universal modular archive filing system for RISC OS. It allows access to the Spark, Zip, and Tar archive file types via a filing system interface.

Archives

An archive file is a special class of file which itself contains other normal files and directories. It appears to the Filer as a single file yet can be opened and manipulated in the same way as a directory can, revealing the original contents that were archived inside.

Aggregating normal files and directories together into a single archive file makes them easier to transfer via long distance communication, and to backup.

Archive files may optionally be reduced in size using data compression techniques. Text and Sprite files especially will be smaller when compressed and hence will be faster to send over a slow communications link, or occupy less space on backup media.

Read-only edition

The edition of SparkFS provided is a special cut down version of the commercial application of the same name. It is limited in that it only handles Spark, Zip and Tar archives and that archives can only be read from; the full edition allows archives to be written to and updated, as well as supporting numerous other archive file types.

The icons for Spark, Zip, and Tar files are shown as stylised directories to remind you that they have properties of both.

Starting SparkFS

SparkFS is in the Utilities directory on your hard disc or network. To start the application, double-click on the !SparkFS icon. SparkFS is a filing system, so its icon appears on the left hand side of the icon bar.

Dragging an archive to SparkFS will open it in the Filer.

Icon bar menu

Info

This gives you information about the application, including how to purchase the full version. With the read-only edition it is not possible to create new archives, so the second menu entry is faded.

Archive

The submenu lists the archives which SparkFS is currently working with.

Choices...

Choosing this option is equivalent to clicking Adjust on the SparkFS icon bar icon, and will open a dialogue allowing settings for SparkFS to be changed.

Quit

Quit removes the SparkFS filer from the icon bar, but leaves the filing system in memory so you can continue to open and read from archives. The submenu includes an option to remove the filing system too; this saves memory and will make all archive files behave like normal files again.

Archive handling

Choosing an archive from the **Archive** menu opens a dialogue describing the archive. Alternatively drag an archive to the icon bar icon while pressing the Ctrl key.

The information presented is similar to that shown by 'About this object' for a normal file in the Filer. There are four additional buttons available:

1   **Test** will extract all of the contents from the archive but not save the result anywhere. This is useful to check the integrity of an archive, because corruption in an archive can make the rest of the contents unreadable.

2 Use **Forget** to finish working with the archive. If the archive is held on removable media this stops SparkFS looking for it again in future.

3 The **Open** button will reopen the archive and bring it to the front of the screen even if you had earlier closed it.

4 The **Find** button is similar to **Open**, except that the parent directory containing the archive is opened and brought to the front of the screen.

Some types of archive will also show an extra section where a password can be entered at the bottom of the dialogue describing the archive. Not all types of archive allow this. To access the contents of a protected archive, type the password then click Select on the method of protection used.

If you do not know the password or type of protection used, contact the person who created the archive, otherwise the contents will remain inaccessible to you.

Converting archives

When archive files are held locally on your disc or network they are in binary format, but some communication protocols can't convey binary files. To work around this the SparkFS filer can convert binary archive files into specially formatted text files which the computer at the far end can then reconstruct back into binary format.

Earlier you read how dragging an archive to SparkFS opens it, and how dragging with Ctrl pressed describes the archive. Lastly, dragging an archive with Shift pressed will open an extended version of a **Save as** dialogue for conversions.

Select the conversion type to create. Both **UUcode** and **BtoA** are common on UNIX systems, with the latter being a more compact form; **Mime** is commonly used for email attachments; **FCET** is used with *Viewdata* systems; and **Boo** will be encountered using the *Kermit* transfer protocol.

The name for the converted text file is derived from the original archive's name, and can be changed if required. Click **OK** or drag the icon to a directory display to perform the conversion. The original archive is not changed in the process.

Choices

The choices dialogue sets options governing the operation of SparkFS.

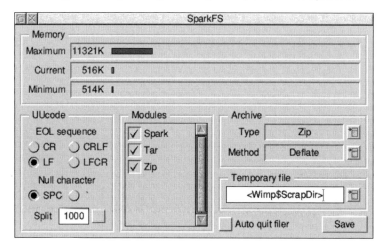

The minimum and maximum memory amounts can be set by dragging the red bars left and right, in a similar manner to the Task Manager in the chapter *Managing the desktop*:

● The amount set by the minimum value will always be reserved by SparkFS even if it currently needs no memory at all. This setting can be small as it is only needed to make sure SparkFS still works when other applications are using up all the memory.

● The maximum value setting can be made larger to speed up archive operations. When working with a large archive more memory will make the operation fast, for sizes beyond the maximum some of the data will be put into a temporary file. Temporary files are much slower than using memory.

● The current value is for information only, it has a green bar and cannot be changed.

The name of the temporary file to use when the maximum memory is exceeded can be set either by typing a name or clicking the pop-up and dragging the file from the **Save as** dialogue.

The **Modules** list shows which of the archive file types is recognised by SparkFS. Unticking a module will stop it from being loaded and save some memory.

The archive type and method, shown as Zip/Deflate above, is for information only in the read-only edition.

When producing a UUcode text file, as described in section *Converting archives* on page 489, there are some settings to determine what the encoder does:

- The *end of line sequence* (EOL seq.) can be changed to one of the four combinations of *line feed* (LF) and *carriage return* (CR) characters. Both RISC OS and UNIX systems use line feed endings, and this is the default selection.

- When a zero byte (Null char.) is encountered, the encoder can either emit a space (SPC) or back tick (') character. Consult the recipient to discover which they are expecting.

- Enabling **Split** will cause the encoder to produce a new file once the number of bytes shown has been reached. For example, when enabled with a value of 1000, encoding a 2500 byte file will produce three files in total: two of 1000 bytes each and the remainder in a third file of 500 bytes.

The **Auto quit filer** option, when enabled, will load the chosen SparkFS modules when an archive is double clicked and then remove the filer from the icon bar straight away. This saves memory and may be preferred since the SparkFS filer icon is mainly used to create new archives, which the read-only edition cannot do.

Click **Save** to confirm the choices made.

If you have enabled **Auto quit filer** it is not possible to get to the choices dialogue any more to change the setting back. To get the SparkFS icon back, double-click on the !SparkFS icon with the Alt key held down; this will temporarily ignore the auto quit option.

Appendices

Appendix A: The command line

Usually you will use the RISC OS desktop for almost all of your computing tasks. However occasionally you may need to use the command line.

The command line is very different from the desktop. Gone are the windows, icons and menus. These are replaced by a set of single line commands that always start with a star, known as *star commands* (or * commands).

All the commands are described, in alphabetical order, in the file `StarComms` in the `Documents.UserGuide` directory. Alternatively, see *Getting Help* on page 500.

Using the command line you can run scripts. Scripts are small programs (which you usually write in Edit) that help you control the computer. The command line is also used to issue operating system commands from BASIC.

This chapter gives you an introduction to the command line. The RISC OS *Programmer's Reference Manual* expands on all the information given in this chapter.

Accessing the command line

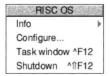

The command line is accessed by choosing **Task window** from the Task Manager icon bar menu, or pressing Ctrl-F12 on the keyboard.

When you open a task window, you will see the * prompt. You can now type operating system commands in the window.

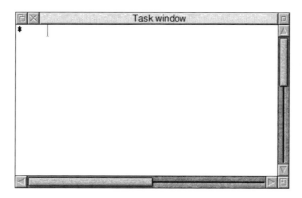

The task window is provided by Edit, so don't be surprised if you see the Edit icon appear on your icon bar.

The amount of memory that the task window uses is controlled by the size of the Next slot in the Task Manager window. If you need a lot of memory for the Task Manager, you can increase the Next slot size.

Command line mode

The star (∗) prompt indicates that you are in command line mode and that the computer is expecting a command to be typed. Note that command line mode is sometimes called 'Supervisor mode' (for example, if the machine starts up in command line mode rather than the desktop).

The commands in this Guide are always preceded by a star. The star is provided as a prompt in command line mode, so you do not have to type it (though it does not matter if you do: any extra stars are ignored). However, if you type a command following some other prompt (at the BASIC > prompt, for example), you must precede it with a star so that the computer knows how to interpret what follows.

Starting BASIC from the command line

Enter BASIC by typing ∗BASIC from the command line. The prompt will change from ∗ to >. To confirm that you are in BASIC, type in the following one-line program (must be typed using capital letters):

FOR N=1 TO 20: PRINT "HELLO": NEXT N (press Return)

This will cause the word HELLO to be printed twenty times.

For information on using BASIC, turn to appendix BBC BASIC on page 523. The BBC BASIC *Reference Manual*, available from your supplier, is a complete reference guide for the BBC BASIC language.

Leave BASIC by typing QUIT or ∗Quit.

Other ways to access the command line

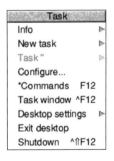

Advanced users can issue commands outside of the desktop by using the Task Manager menu accessed from the Tasks display.

New task

To start a new task, move to the **New task** submenu of the Task menu. This produces a writable icon into which you can type any Command Line command. If the command causes a task that is not a desktop application to run, any output from the task will be displayed in a new window; other tasks will be suspended until this task has completed. If the task is a desktop application, starting it from the **New task** submenu is equivalent to double-clicking on the application.

* Commands

By choosing ***Commands** from the Task menu, or pressing F12, you can enter the shell Command Line Interpreter (ShellCLI). A * prompt appears at the bottom of the screen, where you can type operating system commands. Press Return without entering any text to return to the desktop.

Exit desktop

Choosing **Exit desktop** causes the desktop and all tasks to be closed down and replaced by the command line. You can restart the desktop by typing desktop at the * prompt, and then pressing Return.

Using the task window

The major advantages in entering commands in a task window instead of at the command line prompt are:

● You can have more than one window open at a time.

● Other applications continue to run in their own windows while you run the task (this does mean, though, that the task may run more slowly than it would using other methods of reaching the Command Line).

● Commands that you type, plus the output (if any), appear in a conventional Edit window, and may therefore easily be examined by scrolling up and down in the usual way. When you type into the window, or when a command produces output, the window immediately scrolls to the bottom of the text.

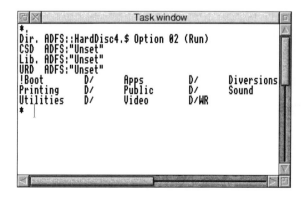

Anything you type in is passed to the task, and has the same effect as typing whilst in command line mode. You can change this by *unlinking* the window: in this case, anything you type in alters the contents of the window in the same way as any other Edit window, even while a task is running. Any output from the task is appended to the end.

You cannot use graphics in a task window. The output of any commands that use graphics will appear as screen control codes.

The menu for a task window contains the following options:

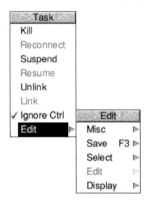

Kill stops and destroys the task running in the window.

Reconnect starts a new task in the window, allocating memory from the Task Manager's **Next** slot.

Suspend temporarily halts the task running in the window.

Resume restarts a suspended task.

Unlink prevents the sending of typed-in characters to the task. Instead, they are processed as if the task window were a normal Edit text window.

Link reverses the effect of **Unlink**.

Ignore Ctrl, when selected, prevents any control characters generated by the program from being sent to the screen. It also intercepts Ctrl-C and Ctrl-V keystrokes so that instead of being passed on to the task they can be used to copy and paste text (see *Task windows and the clipboard*).

Edit leads to the normal Edit menu. Although this makes available most of Edit's features, you cannot use facilities such as the cursor keys or keys such as Page Up and Home while you are using a task window.

Task windows and the clipboard

Text in a task window can be copied to the clipboard in the normal way by selecting it and choosing **Copy** from the **Select** submenu, or by pressing Ctrl-C if **Ignore Ctrl** is selected.

You can paste input to a linked task by selecting **Paste** from the **Select** submenu, or by pressing Ctrl-V when **Ignore Ctrl** is in force. The text on the clipboard is sent to the task as if it was being typed.

Some guidelines and suggestions for using task windows

In order to use a task window, you will need to be familiar with Command Line mode. However, you will also find that nearly all of the commands that affect the configuration of the desktop can also be performed using the Configure application and the Task Manager window **Tasks**.

Here are a few commands:

- `*Cat` gives a directory listing of the current directory.
- `*Show` displays information about your computer. Press Shift to display the next screenful as necessary (or scroll a task window).
- `*Help Modules` shows you which versions of modules are currently loaded.
- `*ROMModules` shows you which modules are stored in the ROM inside the computer.
- `*Status` shows you the status of the computer's CMOS memory defaults.

The command `*Spool` should not be used from a task window. Because its effect is to write everything that appears on the screen to the spool file, using `*Spool` from the desktop will produce unusable files full of screen control characters. There is, in any case, no point in using `*Spool`, since the output from the task appears in the window, and can be saved using Edit as normal.

When you run a command in a task window, the computer divides its time between the task window and other activities running in the desktop. You should note that some time-consuming commands, for example, a `*Copy` of a large file, may prevent access to the filing system that they use until the command is complete.

Note 1: Command line notions such as 'current directory' become relevant when you are using Task Windows.

Note 2: Do not close a task window while a command-line process is still running, or initiate one with little memory available, as internal errors may result.

Getting Help

The command *Help gives brief information about each command in the operating system. *Help *keyword* displays a brief explanation of the keyword and, if the keyword is a command name, the syntax of the command.

If you are not sure about the name of a command:

*Help Commands will list all the available utility commands;

*Help FileCommands will list all the commands relating to filing systems;

*Help Modules will list the names of all currently loaded modules, with their version numbers and creation dates;

*Help Syntax explains the format used for help messages.

The usual use of *Help is to confirm that a command is appropriate for the job required, and to check on its syntax (the number, type and ordering of parameters that the command requires).

The specification of the keyword can include abbreviations to allow groups of commands to be specified. For example,

*help con.

produces information on *Configure and *Continue. You can also use this to establish the current abbreviation for a command. Since RISC OS uses the first command it finds that matches an abbreviation, typing *Con. is equivalent to *Configure. For the *Continue command, the minimum abbreviation must distinguish it from *Configure, and is therefore *Cont. These abbreviations may change as new commands are added.

Using the command line

You'll find many hints in the following sections:

- *Command line syntax*, detailing the syntax you need to use at the command line.

- *System devices*, giving you a summary of useful system devices you can use.

- *System variables*, explaining how variables are used by the operating system.

- *Command and application options and other variables*, explaining how to use variable options with commands and applications.

- *Command scripts*, showing you how to write Command and Obey files to control the computer.

- *Using GS formats in scripts*, showing the formats used to handle control characters.

Command line syntax

The interface to the command line is built into the RISC OS operating system and processes valid commands sent as text strings. The text string is normally terminated by Return.

The syntax of each command in the following chapters is described in a standard way, with examples of its use where these are helpful. The symbols used in syntax descriptions are:

<value>   indicate that an actual value must be substituted. For example, <filename> means that you must supply an actual filename.

[...]   indicate that the item enclosed in the square brackets is optional.

| indicates alternatives. For example, 0 | 1 means that the value 0 or 1 must be supplied.

What are parameters?

RISC OS commands are sometimes followed by one or more *parameters* which tell the computer how you want the command to be modified.

In the following descriptions, the parameters are in italics. You can leave spaces only **between** parameters, since otherwise the operating system cannot tell where you want one parameter to end and the next to begin.

Command line parameters may be optional: in this case they are shown in the syntax within square brackets. Often, when a parameter is specified as optional, the operating system will supply a default value; the value of this is specified for each command.

Numeric parameters

Some commands have one or more numeric parameters. These are interpreted as decimal by default (unless the description of the command specifies otherwise), but it is possible to express them in any base by prefacing the parameter itself with the base followed by an underscore, as in the following examples:

`*Eval 2_1010101`   Returns the integer value of the argument, 85.

`*Eval 16_FFF`   Similarly, returns the value 4095.

An alternative form for hexadecimal uses the & sign to signify base 16:

`*Eval &FFF`

Decimal and hexadecimal are likely to be the most useful bases.

Checks on the command

Before a command is executed, the command line interface carries out a certain amount of pre-processing on the line:

- Stars and spaces are skipped at the start of a command. The command line prompt includes a star, so there is no need to type one, but it doesn't matter if you do.

- Comment lines are ignored. Comments are introduced by typing '|' as the first non-space character on a line.

- Command length is checked. Command lines must be less than or equal to 1024 characters, including the terminating character. Lines which are too long produce an error message.

- Redirection (output to a file, or input from a file) is checked.

- Single-character prefixes are checked, such as '/', equivalent to Run, or '%' which instructs the command line interface to skip alias checking.

- Alias commands are checked (*System variables* on page 507 gives more information on the use of aliases).

- The command is passed for execution. Commands offered to the command line interface are looked up in the OS table, passed to any other modules, the filing system manager, and finally *Run as a file of the name given, in an attempt to execute the command.

Full details of this checking are given in the RISC OS *Programmer's Reference Manual*.

Using pathnames

The anatomy of a pathname was introduced on page 61. You will often need to use pathnames to specify files as Command Line parameters. Technically, a pathname has the following general form:

filing-system::*disc-name*.[*directory-names*.]*filename*

When using a pathname at the command line, most items are optional:

- If a *filing-system* is not specified, the current filing system is used
- If a *disc-name* is not specified, the current disc is used
- If a disc name is specified but no *directory-names* are specified, the root directory of the specified disc is used
- If neither a disc name nor a directory is specified, the currently selected directory is used

Certain characters have special significance when used in a pathname. $ and & have already been introduced elsewhere, and in addition there are:

.	Separates directory specifications, eg $.fred
:	Introduces a drive or disc specification, eg :0, :welcome. It also marks the end of a filing system name, eg ADFS:
*	Acts as a 'wildcard' to match zero or more characters, eg prog*
#	Acts as a 'wildcard' to match any single character, eg $.ch##
@	is the currently selected directory (CSD)
^	is the 'parent' directory
%	is the currently selected library directory (CSL)
\	is the previously selected directory

As mentioned above, a filename on its own is assumed to be in the CSD.

Note that CSD contains the disc name as well as the directory. When a disc is first mounted the CSD is set to point at the root directory of the disc, and each filing system maintains its own CSD. Therefore, a command such as:

```
*Copy CDFS:index ADFS:*
```

would be copying from the CSD on CDFS to the CSD on ADFS.

The following commands alter the currently selected directory:

*Dir   Sets CSD to the specified place

*Up   Moves up the directory tree the specified number of levels. Hence *Up 3 is equivalent to *Dir ^.^.^

*Back Swaps the current and previous directories on the current filing system

Examples

`*Dir :HardDisc4.$.Utilities.Caution`

This selects the specified disc and directory on the current filing system.

`*Dir ^.^.Documents`

Moves up two levels, then selects the 'Documents' directory from that level.

`*Dir UserGuide`

Selects a directory *relative* to the currently selected directory. It is also where the file `StarComms` can be found, which lists all of the commands from these examples.

Wildcards

It is useful in many command line operations to specify objects using 'wildcards'. There are two wildcards:

*	stands for zero or more characters
#	stands for a single character

Examples

`he*`	would stand for *he, help, hello,* or *hencoop*
`he*p`	would stand for *help* or *hencoop*
`he##`	would stand for *help, hens* or *head*, but not *hen* or *health*

File redirection

A powerful feature of RISC OS is the ability to redirect input or output streams (or both) for the duration of the command. By default, output is directed to the screen, but it may be convenient to redirect the output stream to a file so that you can examine it later in more detail, or process it further.

The format of a redirection is:

`<command> { <redirection spec> }`

where the `<redirection spec>` is at least one of:

`> <filename>`	Output goes to `filename`.
`< <filename>`	Input read from `filename`.
`>> <filename>`	Output is appended to `filename`.

Note the following:

- Spaces in the redirection specification are significant.
- The braces are a literal part of the redirection format.

● There must be a single space between each pair of elements for it to be recognised as a redirection.

Examples

```
*Cat { > mycat }
```

This sends a list of the contents in the current directory to a file called mycat.

```
*Help Cat { > CatHelp }
```

This sends all the help information on the command Cat, (elicited by the command *Help Cat) to a file called CatHelp.

Comparison with other operating systems

The Command Line implements a very similar set of commands to those found in other operating systems. The following table lists some of the more common commands and their RISC OS equivalents to those on other systems.

Action	DOS 'command.com'	UNIX 'bash'	RISC OS 'CLI'
Change directory	cd *example*	cd *example*	dir *example*
Go up one directory	cd..	cd ..	dir ^
Clear the screen	cls	Press Ctrl-L	Press Ctrl-L
Copy a file	copy *src dst*	cp *src dst*	copy *src dst*
Delete one file	del *file*	rm *file*	delete *file*
List files in directory	dir	ls	cat
Show a message	echo *msg*	echo *msg*	echo *msg*
Create a directory	md *example*	mkdir *example*	cdir *example*
Rename a file	ren *old new*	mv *old new*	rename *old new*
Delete one directory	rmdir *example*	rmdir *example*	delete *example*
Set a variable	set *var val*	set *var val*	set *var val*
List text file contents	type *file*	cat *file*	type *file*

Through the use of command aliases, described in the section *Changing and adding commands* on page 510, it is even possible for RISC OS to accept the commands from other operating systems. For example, if you are more familiar with the UNIX command ls listing files in the current directory then this can be aliased to the RISC OS equivalent *Cat command if you wish.

System devices

The operating system contains a number of useful system devices, which behave like files in some ways. You can use them anywhere you would normally use a filename as a source of input, or as a destination for output. These include:

System devices suitable for input

kbd: the keyboard, reading a line at a time (this allows editing using Delete, Ctrl-U, and other keys)

rawkbd: the keyboard, reading a character at a time

serial: the serial port

parallel: the parallel port

null: the 'null device', which effectively gives no input

zero: a source of an infinite stream of byte zero

random: pseudo random bytes

urandom: an alternative name for random:

System devices suitable for output

vdu: the screen, using GSRead format (see page 520)

rawvdu: the screen, via the VDU drivers

serial: the serial port

parallel: the parallel port

printer: the currently configured printer

netprint: the currently configured Econet network printer

null: the 'null device', which discards all output

These system devices can be useful with commands such as *Copy, and the redirection operators (> and <):

*Copy myfile printer: Send myfile to the printer

*Cat { > printer: }   List the files in the current directory to the printer

*Cat netprint: Display the currently selected network printer and a list of available network printers.

The system device `null:` is useful to suppress unwanted output from a command script or program:

`*myprogram { > null: }`   Runs `myprogram` with no output

The most useful system devices for the general user are likely to be `printer:` and `netprint:`

!Run and !Boot files within applications

If you Shift-double-click on an application you'll see a !Run file (it has the file type Obey). An application's !Run file is obeyed whenever you start the application. This file sets up the application's environment, loads any resources it requires and then starts the application code (often called !RunImage).

The application also contains a !Boot file; this is run when the application is first 'seen' by the Filer because the directory containing the application is opened on screen.

Using Draw as an example

Most !Boot and !Run files have lines containing Set commands. For example, Draw sets up variables that include a RunType and a PrintType for the normal DrawFile file type, &AFF.

Draw also sets up a variable called `Draw$Dir` which sets up the computer to remember where the Draw application is on the computer. It uses another variable called `Obey$Dir`, this contains the path of the directory in which the current obey file is running.

You will find all these variables explained in greater detail later in this appendix.

If you look at the !Run file of Draw you'll also see some RMEnsure commands. These particular commands are used to make RISC OS check the named module is present in the RMA (relocatable module area). A module is a piece of software that is loaded into the RMA.

System variables

Introducing system variables

System variables are used by RISC OS to store settings that control the behaviour of the computer. For example, they store how you like the time and date to be printed, how you want the `*Copy` command to work, and what prompt you like.

However, unlike configuration features, your settings for system variables are not preserved when you switch the computer off or reset it. When you do this, the computer always goes back to the default values for the standard set of system variables. You can see these default values by typing *Show just after switching on your computer.

In addition to RISC OS system variables, applications commonly use variables of their own, to control their default behaviour. For example, Edit uses variables to store your choices of display font, background colour and so on. Some suggestions for using them are also included later in this chapter.

Setting variables in a Boot file

If the default values are not the ones you want, you can change them using the *Set command. The computer does not remember system variables between sessions, so if you want different default values you must change the variable each time you use your computer. Rather than typing them each time by hand, you can include the *Set commands in a boot file (a file that is run each time you use the computer).

However, although you could create such a boot file 'by hand', typing it in Edit, a much easier way is to use the Task Manager's Desktop settings facility, described in *The Boot application* on page 111. You will then not need to understand anything about system variables as such, since you can simply set up the desktop the way you want it and make a Desktop settings file. Creating your own settings file by editing one created by the Task Manager is the easiest way to start.

Referring to variables

Each variable is accessed by its name, which can contain any character which is neither a space nor a control character. As with filenames, the case of characters is remembered, but is ignored when the names are looked up.

What are variables for?

RISC OS uses the values of variables to make the desktop work. When you double-click on a file (not an application), RISC OS looks up the alias for RUNning that file type in the variable list. If it finds a match, the command stored in the variable (for example RMLoad %*0) is executed, substituting the name of the file in place of the marker %*0. If no match is found an error box is displayed. In general, files which are displayed as white squares (they have no file type icon) will give this error if you try to use them in this way.

Application variables

There are many different system variables provided and used by RISC OS, as well as some which may be added by applications. You can see them all by typing *Show.

The following section gives standard names used for some of the variables that are connected to a particular application.

App$Dir

An *App*$Dir variable gives the full pathname of the directory that holds the application *App*. This is typically set in the application's !Run file by the line:

```
Set App$Dir <Obey$Dir>
```

App$Path and App$Path_Message

An *App*$Path variable gives the full pathname of the directory that holds the application *App*. An *App*$Path variable differs from an *App*$Dir variable in two important respects:

● The pathname includes a trailing '.'

● The variable may hold a set of pathnames, separated by commas.

An *App*$Path_Message variable gives an alternative error message to be used if the path App: cannot be found. This message is then used instead of the default one provided by RISC OS.

It's common to use an *App*$Dir variable rather than an *App*$Path variable, but there may be times when you need the latter.

An *App*$Path variable might, for example, be set in the application's !Run file by the line:

```
Set App$Path <Obey$Dir>.,%.App.
```

if the application held further resources in the subdirectory *App* of the library.

App$PrintFile

An *App*$PrintFile variable holds the name of the file or system device to which the application *App* prints. Typically this will be printer:, and would be set in your application's !Run file as follows:

```
Set App$PrintFile printer:
```

App$Resources

An *App*$Resources variable gives the full pathname of the directory that holds the application *App*'s resources. This might be set in the application's !Run file by the line:

```
Set App$Resources App:Resources
```

Note the use of *App:* to make reference to *App*$Path.

App$Running

An *App*$Running variable shows that the application *App* is running. It should have value 'Yes' if the application is running. This might be used in the application's !Run file as follows:

```
If "App$Running" <> "" then Error App is already running
Set App$Running Yes
```

Changing and adding commands

Alias$*Command*

An Alias$*Command* variable is used to define a new command named *Command*. For example:

```
Set Alias$Now Time
```

By using the name of an existing command, you can change how it works.

Using file types

File$Type_XXX

A File$Type_*XXX* variable holds the textual name for a file having the hexadecimal file type *XXX*. It is typically set in the !Boot file of an application that provides and edits that file type. For example:

```
Set File$Type_XXX TypeName
```

The reason the !Boot file is used rather than the !Run file is so that the file type can be converted to text from the moment its 'parent' application is first seen, rather than only from when it is run.

Alias$@LoadType_XXX, Alias$@PrintType_XXX and Alias$@RunType_XXX

These variables set the commands used respectively to load, print and run a file of hexadecimal type *XXX*. They are typically set in the !Boot file of an application that provides and edits that file type.

For example:

```
Set Alias$@PrintType_XXX /<Obey$Dir> -Print
Set Alias$@RunType_XXX /<Obey$Dir>
```

Note that the above lines **both have a trailing space** (invisible in print!).

The reason the !Boot file is used rather than the !Run file is so that files of the given type can be loaded, printed and run from the moment their 'parent' application is first seen, rather than only from when it is run.

Setting the command line prompt

CLI$Prompt

The CLI$Prompt variable sets the command line interpreter prompt. By default this is '*'. One common way to change this is so that the system time is displayed as a prompt. For example:

```
SetMacro CLI$Prompt <Sys$Time> *
```

This is set as a macro so that the system time is evaluated each time the prompt is displayed.

CLI$Greeting

The CLI$Greeting variable sets the text shown when the ShellCLI command line interpreter prompt first starts. This line is only shown once, unlike CLI$Prompt, and can be used to override the default. For example:

```
Set CLI$Greeting "Welcome to the command prompt"
```

There's more on this in *Creating your own command line prompt* on page 514.

Configuring RISC OS commands

Copy$Options, Count$Options and Wipe$Options

These variables set the behaviour of the *Copy, *Count and *Wipe commands. For a full description type *Help *command* at the command line.

System path variables

File$Path and Run$Path

These variables control where files are searched for during read operations or execute operations. They are both path variables, which means that – in common with other path variables – they consist of a comma-separated list of full pathnames, each of which has a trailing '.'.

If you wish to add a pathname to one of these variables, you must ensure that you append it once, and once only. For example, to add the 'bin' subdirectory of an application to Run$Path, you could use the following lines in the application's !Boot file:

```
If "<App$Path>" = "" then Set Run$Path <Run$Path>,<Obey$Dir>.bin.
Set App$Path <Obey$Dir>.
```

Obey files

Obey$Dir

The Obey$Dir variable is set to the directory from which an Obey file is being run, and may be used by commands within that Obey file.

Time and date

Sys$Time, Sys$Date and Sys$Year

These variables are code variables that are evaluated at the time of their use to give, respectively, the current system time, date and year.

Sys$DateFormat

The Sys$DateFormat variable sets the format in which the date is presented by some commands.

!System and !Scrap

System$Dir and System$Path

These variables give the full pathname of the System application. They have the same value, except that System$Path has a trailing '.', whereas System$Dir does not. You must not change these values.

(There are two versions of this pathname for compatibility with some old applications). System and Scrap are contained in the Boot application.

Wimp$Scrap

The Wimp$Scrap variable gives the full pathname of the Wimp scrap file used by the file transfer protocol. You must not use this variable for any other purpose, nor change its value.

Wimp$ScrapDir

The `Wimp$ScrapDir` variable gives the full pathname of a scrap directory within the Scrap application, which you may use to store temporary files. You must not use this variable for any other purpose, nor change its value.

The desktop

Desktop$File

The `Desktop$File` variable shows the desktop boot file that was used to start the desktop.

Wimp$Font and Wimp$FontSize and Wimp$FontWidth

These variables set the desktop font if the font chosen is not one of the ROM fonts supplied with the computer. The `Wimp$Font` variable holds the name, while the `Wimp$FontSize` and `Wimp$FontWidth` set the size (in $\frac{1}{16}$ths of a point) if the default is not acceptable.

Wimp$State

The `Wimp$State` variable shows the current state of the Wimp. If the desktop is running, it has the value 'desktop'; otherwise it has the value 'commands'.

Wimp$IconTheme

The `Wimp$IconTheme` variable contains the name of the style of icons currently selected for the desktop. It has a trailing '.' which allows the variable to be inserted into the middle of a pathname and still form a valid one overall.

Command and application options and other variables

Some commands, such as *Copy and *Wipe, can operate in a variety of ways. For example, you can effectively turn *Copy into a Move command by setting the D(elete) option, which deletes the source file after copying it to another directory or filing system. You would do this by typing

```
*Set Copy$Options <Copy$Options> D
```

at the command line prompt. These options are described in the entries for each command in the file `StarComms` in the `Documents.UserGuide` directory.

A few applications also use system variables to record their current configuration. Such variables use the format *App$Options*, where *App* is the name of the application in question. These variables will only be listed in the computer's response to the *Show command if you have changed them from their default values.

In addition to 'options', applications may use other variables for a variety of purposes. For example, ChangeFSI allows the resolution of the index image read from a PhotoCD to be set with the variable ChangeFSI$PCDIndex. To avoid having to carry out this action each time you use the application, you can put a *Set command identifying the directory in your boot file, for example:

```
*Set ChangeFSI$PCDIndex 3
```

Creating your own command line prompt

You can use a system variable to change the operating system prompt – normally * – by setting the variable CLI$Prompt to (for example) the character #:

```
*Set CLI$Prompt #
```

You can also set one variable to the value of another:

```
*Set CLI$Prompt <Sys$Time> *
```

This sets the prompt to the system time, but only does so once, when the command is given. However, it would clearly be more useful if the prompt always showed the current time. To do this, change CLI$Prompt from a variable into a macro. A macro is similar to a variable, but is evaluated every time it is used, instead of just once when it is set. Therefore, type the following:

```
*SetMacro CLI$Prompt <Sys$Time> *
```

Each time Return is pressed at the command line prompt a new prompt is given (unless you have not typed anything since the last Return; you will then be returned to the desktop); the current time is worked out and displayed, followed by a space character and an asterisk:

```
12:59:06  *
12:59:07  *
12:59:08  *
```

Passing values between programs

Programmers can use system variables to pass values between programs. One program can create and write to a variable which another program can then read. Such variables should have names starting *App$*, where *App* is your program; this avoids problems caused by different programs using the same system variable names.

Command scripts

Command scripts are files of commands that you would normally type in at the command line prompt. There are two main uses for such files:

- To set up the computer to the state you want, either when you switch on or when you start an application.

  This type of command script is commonly known as a boot file, because it is used to 'boot up' the computer. You can create such a file without needing to know anything about the command line, using the **Desktop settings** facility in the Task Manager, described in *The Boot application* on page 111.

- To save typing in a set of commands you find yourself using frequently.

  For example, if you often want to display information about a file and then print it, you can combine the commands *FileInfo and *Type into a command script.

You may find using an Alias$... variable to be better for the second case. The main advantage of using variables rather than command files is that they are held in memory and so are quicker in execution; however, they are only really suitable for short commands. If you use variables you will probably still want to use a command file to set them up when you switch on.

Command and Obey file types

There are two types of file you can use for command scripts: Command files, and Obey files. The differences between these two file types are:

- An Obey file is always passed to the command line interpreter, whereas a Command file is passed to the current input stream.

- An Obey file is read directly, whereas a Command file is treated as if it were typed at the keyboard (and hence usually appears on the screen).

- An Obey file sets the system variable Obey$Dir to the directory it is in.

- An Obey file can have parameters passed to it.

The differences between Command and Obey files are demonstrated in an example on page 518.

Additionally there are the TaskExec and TaskObey file types. These are very similar to Command and Obey files. Their main advantage is that they multi-task under the desktop:

- A TaskExec file is *Exec'd in a task window.

- A TaskObey file is *Obey'd, opening a task window only if needed for I/O. It quits the window when finished.

It is recommended that you don't use *Copy and related filer commands in TaskObey files in order to make them multi-task – use the Filer instead.

Creating a command script

A command script can be created using any text editor. If you create the file using Edit, you should set the file's type by pressing Menu over the Edit icon on the icon bar and choosing the desired file type, such as Command or Obey.

When you save the file you should consider in which directory you will save it. By default, files are looked for first in the current directory, then in the library. Therefore, if you want to avoid having to type the full pathname of the file every time you run it you should save it in one of the following:

- The directory from which the command script will be run (typically within an application directory).

- The library. The library is typically $.Library, but may be $.ArthurLib on a network, and has the special abbreviation %.

Running the script

Provided that you have set the file type to Command or Obey, the file can then be run in the same ways as any other file, by

- typing its name at the * prompt
- typing its name preceded by a * at any other prompt (some applications may not support this)
- double-clicking on its icon in a directory display.

The same restrictions apply as with any other file. If the file is not in either your current directory or the library, it will not be found if you just give the filename; you must give its full pathname. This assumes you have not changed the value of the system variable Run$Path.

Making a script run automatically

You can make scripts run automatically

- from the network when you first log on
- from a disc when you first switch the computer on
- from an application directory when the application is run.

You'll find information on how to do this in *The Boot application* on page 111.

Using parameters

An Obey file – but not a Command file – can have parameters passed to it, which can then be used by the command script. The first parameter is referred to as %0, the second as %1, and so on. You can refer to all the parameters after a particular one by putting a * after the %, so %*1 would refer to all the parameters from the second one onwards.

These parameters are substituted before the line is passed to the command line interpreter. Thus if an Obey file called Display contained:

```
FileInfo %0
Type %0
```

then the command *Display MyFile would do this:

```
FileInfo MyFile
Type MyFile
```

Sometimes you do not want parameter substitution. For example, suppose you wish to define an alias command called 'WhoRuns' in your file, such as:

```
Set Alias$WhoRuns Show Alias$@RunType_<%0>
```

If you were to include the *Set command in an Obey file, when the file is obeyed the %0 will be replaced by the first parameter passed to the file (if any). To prevent the substitution you need to change the % to %%:

```
Set Alias$WhoRuns Show Alias$@RunType_<%%0>
```

Now when the file is run, the '%%0' is changed to '%0'. No other substitution occurs at this stage, and the desired alias is set up.

Examples

These example files illustrate some of the differences between Command and Obey files:

Example 1

```
*BASIC
AUTO
FOR J= 1 TO 10
  PRINT "Hello"
NEXT J
END
```

If this is a command file, it will enter the BASIC interpreter, and input the file shown. The command script will end with the BASIC interpreter waiting for another line of input. You can then press Escape to get a prompt, type RUN to run the program, and then type QUIT to leave BASIC. This script shows how a command file is passed to the input, and can change what is accepting its input (in this case to the BASIC interpreter).

On the other hand, if this is an Obey file it will be passed to the command line interpreter, and an attempt will be made to run these commands:

```
*BASIC
*AUTO
*FOR I = 1 TO 10
*   PRINT "Hello"
*NEXT I
*END
```

Only the first command is valid, as an Obey file all this does is to leave you in the BASIC interpreter. Type QUIT to leave BASIC; you will then get an error message saying File 'AUTO' not found, generated by the second line in the file.

Example 2

The next example illustrates how control characters are handled:

```
echo <7>
echo |<7>
```

The control characters are represented in GSTrans format (see *Using GS formats in scripts* on page 520). These are not interpreted until the echo command is run, and are only interpreted then because echo expects GSTrans format.

The first line sends an ASCII 7 to the VDU drivers, sounding a beep. In the second line, the | preceding the < changes it from the start of a GSTrans sequence to just representing the character <, so the overall effect is:

```
echo <7>        Send ASCII 7 to VDU drivers – beeps
echo |<7>       Send <7> to the screen
```

Example 3

The last examples are a Command file:

```
*Set Alias$more %echo |<14>|m %type -tabexpand %*0|m %echo |<15>
```

and an Obey file that has the same effect:

```
Set Alias$more %echo |<14>|m %type -tabexpand %%*0|m %echo |<15>
```

The only differences between the two examples are that the Command file has a preceding * added, to ensure that the command is passed to the command line interpreter, and that the Obey file has the %*0 changed to %%*0 to delay the substitution of parameters.

The file creates a new command more by setting the variable Alias$more.

- The % characters that precede echo and type ensure that the actual commands are used, rather than an aliased version of them.

- The sequence |m represents a carriage return in GSTrans format (see *Using GS formats in scripts* below). It is used to separate the commands, just as Return would if you were typing the commands.

- The two echo commands turn scroll mode on, then off, by sending the control characters ASCII 14 and 15 respectively to the VDU drivers.

- The | before each < prevents the control characters from being interpreted until the aliased command more is run.

The command turns scroll mode on, types a file to the screen expanding tabs as it does so, and then turns scroll mode off. The Scroll Lock key also stops the screen from scrolling up while active.

Using GS formats in scripts

The GSTrans and GSRead formats are used by a number of commands that need to be able to handle control characters, and characters whose top bit is set. They enable you to use these characters, which would otherwise cause unpredictable output from your monitor or printer, and which would be difficult to enter directly from the keyboard. The two formats are identical.

The GSRead or GSTrans format is used by some commands to read characters that you type in. The characters are interpreted using the following conventions:

● A character preceded by a | is converted into the relevant control code: |C would become ASCII 3 (which is Ctrl C).

● An integer within angle brackets is converted into the equivalent ASCII code: <7> would become ASCII 7.

● A variable name within angle brackets is replaced by the value held in the variable, or is ignored if the variable does not exist.

● All other characters are unchanged.

A full list of ASCII codes and how to obtain them is given below. Of course, any ASCII code may be obtained by enclosing it in angle brackets as described above, and this may be easier to remember than the symbol encoding.

ASCII code	Symbols used	
0	| @	
1 - 26	| *letter* e.g.	| A (or | a) = ASCII 1
		| M (or | m) = ASCII 13
27	| [or | {	
28	| \	
29	|] or | }	
30	| ^ or | ~	
31	| _ or | '	
32 - 126	keyboard character, except for:	
	"	|"
	|	||
	<	|<
127	| ?	
128 - 255	| ! *coded-symbol* e.g.	ASCII 128 = | ! | @
		ASCII 129 = | ! | A etc

You must use | < to prevent the < from being interpreted as the start of a number or variable name enclosed in angled brackets.

To include leading spaces in a definition, the string must be in double quotation marks, ", which are not included in the definition. To include a literal " character in the string, use | " or " ".

Appendix B: BBC BASIC

BBC BASIC is still one of the most popular and widely-used versions of the BASIC programming language. It consists of special keywords from which the programmer can create sequences of instructions, or programs, to be carried out by the computer. Such programs might perform calculations, create graphics on the screen, manipulate data, or carry out virtually any action involving the computer and the devices connected to it.

The BASIC language operates within an environment provided by the computer's operating system. The operating system is responsible for controlling the devices available to the computer, such as the keyboard, the screen, and the filing system. For example, it is the operating system which reads each key you press and displays the appropriate character on the screen. Operating system commands can be entered directly from within BASIC by prefixing them with an asterisk (*).

If you want to find out more about the BBC BASIC programming language, you need the BBC BASIC *Reference Manual* available from your supplier.

On-line help is available within BASIC; just type HELP (in uppercase) for more information.

BBC BASIC V and VI

There are two variants of BBC BASIC supplied with RISC OS: BASIC V and BASIC VI.

BASIC V is the most commonly used interpreter. BASIC VI is very similar to BASIC V, except that it uses 8 bytes (or 64 bits) to store floating point numbers, and is sometimes known as BASIC64 for this reason. BASIC V only uses 5 bytes, so it is slightly less accurate.

The 8 byte representation used follows the IEEE 754 floating point standard and will make use of a *Floating Point Accelerator* or *Vector Floating Point* hardware floating point unit if it is available.

BASIC VI is used by some applications where the extra precision is important, for example SciCalc, so it may get loaded into memory without you having to take any special action.

BASIC programs saved from both BASIC V and BASIC VI are the same and can be run using either BASIC, however floating point numbers written to data files using the PRINT# keyword are incompatible and will need to be read back in using the INPUT# keyword on the same version of BASIC with which they were written.

Entering BASIC

BASIC V

To start BASIC V, open the Task Manager menu and choose the **Task window** option or press Ctrl-F12. Then type the following:

    BASIC

Press Return, and the BASIC V version and memory will be displayed on the screen.

BASIC can also be started from the **New Task** option on the Task Manager menu or from the command line (press F12).

BASIC VI

To start BASIC VI, proceed as for BASIC V, but instead you would type the following:

    BASIC64

Press Return, and the BASIC VI version and memory will be displayed on the screen.

Leaving BASIC

To leave BASIC, type QUIT (which must be in uppercase) or type *Quit.

Writing and editing BASIC files

Edit will automatically convert BASIC programs to and from BASIC's special tokenised format, so you can do all editing of BASIC using Edit as described in the section *Writing and editing* BASIC *programs* on page 271.

BASIC also includes a simple editor of its own called the ARM Basic Editor (ARMBE). This resides as a module on disc which BASIC will load when you type the command EDIT in immediate mode. Press Ctrl-F5 to show the help for ARMBE, or Shift-F4 to return to the BASIC prompt.

Note that ARMBE will not work from a task window as it uses graphical control codes drawn on the screen. To edit BASIC files in the desktop, use Edit.

Command line syntax for BASIC

The following pages describe in full the command line interface for BASIC V and BASIC VI.

*BASIC

The command to enter the BASIC V interpreter.

Syntax

```
*BASIC [options]
```

Purpose

To activate the BASIC interpreter.

The *options* control how the interpreter will behave when it starts, and when any program that it executes terminates. If no option is given, BASIC simply starts with a message of the form:

```
ARM BBC BASIC V (C) Acorn 1989

Starting with 651516 bytes free

>
```

The number of bytes free in the above message will depend on the amount of memory in your Next slot. The first line is also used for the default REPORT message, before any errors occur.

One of three options may follow the *BASIC command to cause a program to be loaded, and, optionally, executed automatically. Alternatively, you can use a program that is already loaded into memory by passing its address to the interpreter. Each of these possibilities is described in turn below.

In all cases where a program is specified, this may be a tokenised BASIC program, as created by a SAVE command, or a textual program, which will be tokenised (and possibly renumbered) automatically.

```
*BASIC -help
```

This command causes BASIC to print some help information describing the options documented here. Then BASIC starts as usual.

```
*BASIC [-chain] filename
```

If you give a *filename* after the *BASIC command, optionally preceded by the keyword -chain, then the named file is loaded and executed. When the program stops, BASIC enters immediate mode, as usual.

```
*BASIC -quit filename
```

This behaves in a similar way to the previous option. However, when the program terminates, BASIC quits automatically, returning to the environment from which the interpreter was originally called. If you have a variable BASIC$Crunch defined, it also performs a CRUNCH %1111 on the program. This is the default action used by BASIC programs that are executed as * commands. In addition, the function QUIT returns TRUE if BASIC is called in this fashion.

```
*BASIC -load filename
```

This option causes the file to be loaded automatically, but not executed. BASIC remains in immediate mode, from where the program can be edited or executed as required.

```
*BASIC @start,end
```

This acts in a similar way to the -load form of the command. However, the program that is 'loaded' automatically is not in a file, but already in memory. Following the @ are two addresses. These give, in hexadecimal, the address of the start of the in-core program, and the address of the byte after the last one. The program is copied to PAGE and tokenised if necessary.

Note that the in-core address description is fixed format. It should be in the form:

```
@xxxxxxxx,xxxxxxxx
```

where x means a hexadecimal digit. Leading zeros must be supplied. The command line terminator character must come immediately after the last digit. No spaces are allowed.

```
*BASIC -chain @start,end
```

This behaves like the previous option, but the program is executed as well. When the program terminates, BASIC enters immediate mode.

```
*BASIC -quit @start,end
```

This option behaves as the previous one, but when the BASIC program terminates, BASIC automatically quits. The QUIT flag will return TRUE during the execution of the program.

Examples

```
*BASIC
*BASIC -quit shellProg
*BASIC @000ADF0C,000AE345
*BASIC -chain fred
```

*BASIC64

The command to enter the BASIC VI interpreter.

Syntax

```
*BASIC64 [options]
```

Purpose

This has exactly the same purpose as the *BASIC command, and takes the same options, the only difference being that it enters the BASIC VI interpreter instead of the BASIC V interpreter.

If no option is given, BASIC VI simply starts with a message of the form:

```
ARM BBC BASIC VI (FPA) (C) Acorn 1989

Starting with 581628 bytes free

>
```

The text in brackets on the first line of the message shows whether the FPA or VFP version of BASIC VI has been started. This will depend on the type of CPU in your computer. The number of bytes free in the above message will depend on the amount of free space in your Next slot.

Examples

```
*BASIC64
*BASIC64 -quit shellProg
*BASIC64 @000ADF0C,000AE345
*BASIC64 -chain fred
```

Appendix C: RISC OS file types

File types are three-digit hexadecimal numbers. They are divided into ranges:

E00 - FFF	allocated for use with generic data types
400 - DFF	allocated to applications from commercial software houses
100 - 3FF	allocated to applications published by individuals
000 - 0FF	free for personal use in applications not to be distributed

For each type, there may be a default action on loading and running the file. These actions may change, depending on whether the desktop is in use, and which applications have been seen. The system variables `Alias$@LoadType_XXX` and `Alias$@RunType_XXX` give the actions (*XXX* = file type).

Some types have a textual equivalent set, which may be used in most commands (but not in the above system variables) instead of the hexadecimal code. The system variable `File$Type_XXX` provides the textual equivalent.

You should use the hexadecimal file type in command scripts and in programs, otherwise you will find that your files will give an error if you try to run them on a machine that uses a territory in a different language.

The operating system sets up several textual equivalents by default – for example, file type &FFF is set to have the textual equivalent `Text`; these are indicated in the table below by a dagger '†'. Other textual equivalents may be set when an application is booted – for example, Maestro sets up file type &AF1 to be `Music`; these textual equivalents are indicated in the table below by an asterisk '*'.

Files transferred from outside RISC OS may not have a file type. This could be because they arrived from an operating system which doesn't use them, or where a separate message header was used to describe the content type. Examples of this situation that you might encounter are

- the three letter extensions used with DOSFS (see *Transferring files between computers* on page 141);

- the *Multipurpose Internet Mail Extensions* used by MIME compatible emails.

The Internet application, introduced in *The Resources directory* on page 112, contains a database which maps from MIME types to filename extensions to RISC OS file types and back again; this is the MimeMap.

The following types are currently used or reserved by RISC OS. Not all file types used by software houses are shown. This list may be extended from time to time:

Generic file types

Type	Description	Textual equivalent	
FFF	Plain ASCII text	Text	†
FFE	Command (Exec) file	Command	†
FFD	Data	Data	†
FFC	Position independent code	Utility	†
FFB	Tokenised BASIC program	BASIC	†
FFA	Relocatable module	Module	†
FF9	Sprite or saved screen	Sprite	†
FF8	Absolute application loaded at &8000	Absolute	†
FF7	BBC font file (sequence of VDU operations)	BBC font	†
FF6	Outline font	Font	†
FF5	PostScript	PoScript	†
FF4	Dot Matrix data file	Printout	†
FF3	LaserJet data file	LaserJet	
FF2	Configuration (CMOS RAM)	Config	†
FF1	Raw unprocessed data (e.g. terminal streams)	RawData	
FF0	Tagged Image File Format	TIFF	*
FED	Palette data	Palette	†
FEC	Template file	Template	†
FEB	Obey file	Obey	†
FEA	Desktop commands file	Desktop	†
FE6	UNIX executable	UNIX Ex	
FE4	DOS file	DOS	†
FE1	Make commands file	Make	
FDC	Unresolvable UNIX soft link	SoftLink	
FDB	Text using CR and LF for line ends	TextCRLF	
FDA	DOS batch file	MSDOSbat	
FD9	DOS executable file	MSDOSexe	
FD8	DOS command file	MSDOScom	
FD7	Obey file in a task window	TaskObey	†
FD6	Exec file in a task window	TaskExec	†
FD5	DOS picture file	Pict	
FD4	International MIDI Assoc. MIDIfiles standard	MIDI	
FD3	DDE: debuggable absolute application image	DebImage	
FD1	BASIC stored as text	BASICTxt	

Type	Description	Textual equivalent	
FCF	Font cache	Cache	†
FCC	Device object within DeviceFS	Device	†
FCA	Single compressed file	Squash	*
FC9	Sun raster file	SunRastr	
FC8	DOS disc image	DOSDisc	†
FC6	Printer definition	PrintDfn	*
FC3	Patch description file	Patch	*
FC2	Audio interchange file format	AIFF	
FB2	Audio video interleave	AVI	
FB1	Waveform audio data	Waveform	
FB0	DDE: Allocation request	Allocate	
FAF	Hypertext markup language	HTML	
FAE	Toolbox resource	Resource	†
F98	Photoshop picture	PhotoShp	
F96	Generic sound container	GenSound	
F95	Generic code container	Code	†
F91	Universal resource identifier web page link	URI	
F8F	Wireless bitmap picture	WBMP	
F8E	Wireless markup language	WML	
F89	UNIX compressed data	GZip	
F88	Real audio data	F88	
F82	Java archive executable	JAR	
F81	Javascript or ECMAScript program	JSScript	
F80	Extensible markup language	XML	
F7F	XML document type definition	XML_DTD	
F76	Extended display identification data	EDID	†
F75	Javascript object notation	JSON	
F74	YAML data serialisation language	YAML	
F0D	Tab separated values	TSV	
E1F	Executable and linkable format program	ELF	

Commercial software file types

Type	Description	Textual equivalent	
DFE	Comma separated values	CSV	
DEA	Data exchange format (AutoCAD etc)	DXF	*
DDC	Multiple compressed files	Archive	*
DB0	Lotus 123 file	WK1	
CE5	T$_E$X file	TeX	
CAF	IGES graphics	IGES	
CAE	Hewlett-Packard graphics language	HPGLPlot	
C85	JPEG (Joint Photographic Experts Group) file	JPEG	*
C46	UNIX tape archive	Tar	*
BE8	Kodak PhotoCD image	PhotoCD	†
BBC	BBC ROM file (ROMFS)	BBC ROM	†
B60	Portable network graphics	PNG	
AFF	Draw file	DrawFile	†
AFE	Mouse event record	Mouse	
AF1	Maestro file	Music	*
AE9	Alarm file	Alarms	*
AE7	Acorn Replay movie file	ARMovie	
AE6	Microsoft Word document	MSWord	
AE5	Python script	Python	
ADF	Adobe portable document format	PDF	
A91	Phil Katz Zip compressed files	Zip	*
A7E	XML Microsoft Word document	MSWordX	
A7A	Moving JPEG	MJPEG	
A6D	Genealogical Data Communication	GEDCOM	
6A5	Microsoft Windows mouse cursor image	CUR	
69D	TrueVsion Targa image	Targa	
69C	Microsoft Windows bitmap image	BMP	
697	ZSoft PCX image	PCX	
695	CompuServe graphics interchange format	GIF	

Public domain software file types

Type	Description	Textual equivalent
132	Microsoft Windows icon image	ICO

Appendix D: Old-type screen modes

This appendix gives information about the numbered screen modes that were used with earlier versions of the RISC OS operating system. This information is only needed for backward compatibility purposes: for example, you may be using an old software application or game that demands a particular old type screen mode.

Display Manager

This section gives a quick recap on how the screen Display Manager operates and where to find more information.

In the Screen setup plug-in of Configure, the type of monitor used with your computer is defined. This controls the selection of resolutions used by the Display Manager. It is described in *Screen setup plug-in* on page 101.

Use the Display Manager to choose the display resolution and number of colours used by the desktop. The Display Manager is described in *Desktop colours and resolution* on page 62.

The display options that your monitor can use depend upon the characteristics of your monitor. These characteristics are described in a special file called a **M**onitor **D**efinition **F**ile, or MDF. This file is tuned to each monitor type and should not normally be changed. In some cases the MDF will be created automatically by querying the monitor itself using **E**xtended **D**isplay **I**dentification **D**ata, or EDID.

Numbered screen modes

Numbered screen modes were the way colours and resolutions were selected prior to RISC OS 3.50, but they are still understood by your computer.

There are several reasons why you may want to use an old type screen mode:

● To play a game that demands an old type screen mode.

● To use an application that demands an old type screen mode.

● To generate old type sprite files using Paint.

Choosing a numbered mode

You can choose old-type numbered modes from the Display Manager icon bar menu. Choose the Mode window, delete any information in the box, and then type in the mode number you want to use. Click on **OK**.

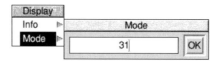

If your chosen mode is not available, the Display Manager will substitute one with the same number of colours.

Old type sprite files

Your computer uses a new sprite file format, the file type used to save Paint pictures. However you cannot use one of these new format sprite files on a computer running versions older than RISC OS 3.50. If you want to use a sprite on a computer running an earlier version of the operating system you should create it while using one of the backward compatible screen modes. Alternatively the graphic translator application ChangeFSI can convert between sprite types.

Mode table

The table of modes on the following pages show:

● The mode number.

● The text resolution in columns × rows.

● The graphics resolution in pixels, which corresponds to the clarity of the mode's display.

● The number of colours available.

● The monitor types, from the list given on page 537, that support that mode.

● Whether the mode can be used to show the desktop or not.

List of screen modes

This is the list of screen modes supplied with RISC OS. Third party suppliers may produce software and hardware that supports different video modes; such modes are not listed here.

Mode	Text resolution	Pixel resolution	Logical colours	Monitor types	Desktop mode?	Notes
0	80 × 32	640 × 256	2	0,1,3,4	Yes	③
1	40 × 32	320 × 256	4	0,1,3,4	Yes	③
2	20 × 32	160 × 256	16	0,1,3,4		③
3	80 × 25	Text only	2	0,1,3,4		③④⑥
4	40 × 32	320 × 256	2	0,1,3,4		③
5	20 × 32	160 × 256	4	0,1,3,4		③
6	40 × 25	Text only	2	0,1,3,4		③④⑥
7	40 × 25	Teletext	16	0,1,3,4		③④
8	80 × 32	640 × 256	4	0,1,3,4	Yes	③
9	40 × 32	320 × 256	16	0,1,3,4	Yes	③
10	20 × 32	160 × 256	256	0,1,3,4		③
11	80 × 25	640 × 250	4	0,1,3,4	Yes	③
12	80 × 32	640 × 256	16	0,1,3,4	Yes	③
13	40 × 32	320 × 256	256	0,1,3,4	Yes	③
14	80 × 25	640 × 250	16	0,1,3,4	Yes	③
15	80 × 32	640 × 256	256	0,1,3,4	Yes	③
16	132 × 32	1056 × 256	16	0,1	Yes	⑤
17	132 × 25	1056 × 250	16	0,1	Yes	⑤
18	80 × 64	640 × 512	2	1	Yes	
19	80 × 64	640 × 512	4	1	Yes	
20	80 × 64	640 × 512	16	1	Yes	
21	80 × 64	640 × 512	256	1	Yes	
22	96 × 36	768 × 288	16	0,1	Yes	①
23	144 × 56	1152 × 896	2	2	Yes	
24	132 × 32	1056 × 256	256	0,1	Yes	⑤
25	80 × 60	640 × 480	2	1,3,4,5	Yes	
26	80 × 60	640 × 480	4	1,3,4,5	Yes	

Mode	Text resolution	Pixel resolution	Logical colours	Monitor types	Desktop mode?	Notes
27	80 × 60	640 × 480	16	1,3,4,5	Yes	
28	80 × 60	640 × 480	256	1,3,4,5	Yes	
29	100 × 75	800 × 600	2	1,4	Yes	①②
30	100 × 75	800 × 600	4	1,4	Yes	①②
31	100 × 75	800 × 600	16	1,4	Yes	①②
32	100 × 75	800 × 600	256	1,4	Yes	①②⑦
33	96 × 36	768 × 288	2	0,1	Yes	①
34	96 × 36	768 × 288	4	0,1	Yes	①
35	96 × 36	768 × 288	16	0,1	Yes	①
36	96 × 36	768 × 288	256	0,1	Yes	①
37	112 × 44	896 × 352	2	1	Yes	①
38	112 × 44	896 × 352	4	1	Yes	①
39	112 × 44	896 × 352	16	1	Yes	①
40	112 × 44	896 × 352	256	1	Yes	①
41	80 × 44	640 × 352	2	1,3,4	Yes	①③
42	80 × 44	640 × 352	4	1,3,4	Yes	①③
43	80 × 44	640 × 352	16	1,3,4	Yes	①③
44	80 × 25	640 × 200	2	1,3,4	Yes	①③
45	80 × 25	640 × 200	4	1,3,4	Yes	①③
46	80 × 25	640 × 200	16	1,3,4	Yes	①③
47	45 × 60	360 × 480	256	1,3,4	Yes	①⑦
48	40 × 60	320 × 480	16	1,3,4	Yes	①⑦
49	40 × 60	320 × 480	256	1,3,4	Yes	①⑦
50	40 × 30	320 × 240	2	0,1,3,4,5	Yes	①⑧
51	40 × 30	320 × 240	4	0,1,3,4,5	Yes	①⑧
52	40 × 30	320 × 240	16	0,1,3,4,5	Yes	①⑧
53	40 × 30	320 × 240	256	0,1,3,4,5	Yes	①⑧

Notes

1   These modes were not available in RISC OS 2.00, nor (except for mode 31) were they available in RISC OS 2.01.

2   These modes are not available on early models of RISC OS computers (i.e. the Archimedes 300 series, 440, and 400/1 series, and the BBC A3000).

3   If you are using a VGA or Super-VGA-type monitor, these modes are all displayed on a screen having 352 raster lines. Where a mode has fewer than 352 vertical pixels, it is centred on the screen with blank lines at the top and bottom. Because of their appearance these modes are known as letterbox modes. The refresh rate is 70Hz.

4   These modes provide compatibility with BBC and Master series computers.

5   In these modes circles, arcs, sectors and segments do not look circular. This is because the aspect ratio of the pixels is not in a 1:2, 1:1 or 2:1 ratio.

6   These are gap modes, where the colour of the gaps is not necessarily the same as the text background.

7   These modes are only available from RISC OS 3.50 and later.

8   These modes are only available from RISC OS 5.06 and later.

Logical colours

In 256-colour modes, there are some restrictions on the control of the colours. Only 64 base colours may be selected; 4 levels of tinting turn the base colours into 256 shades. Also, the selection from the colour palette of 4096 shades is only possible in groups of 16.

When selecting a numbered mode RISC OS 5 may substitute it with one of the same resolution, but with a different number of logical colours, in order to match the capabilities of the graphics hardware in your computer.

Monitor types

The monitor type numbers which RISC OS uses are:

0	Standard 50Hz monochrome or colour television
1	Multi frequency monitor
2	High resolution monochrome monitor
3	VGA-type monitor
4	Super VGA-type monitor
5	LCD panel
8	Standard 60Hz monochrome or colour television

Not all monitors can display all of the old type screen modes. If you attempt to select a mode which is not appropriate to the current monitor type, a suitable mode for that monitor is substituted.

Appendix E: Removing a disc defect

This appendix shows you how to map out a defect in your disc should it develop a problem during normal use.

What is a defect?

There are many types of media available for use with RISC OS, commonly found examples include:

- a spinning hard disc in a sealed metal unit
- solid state drives (SSD)
- memory cards of various form factors
- removable 3.5" floppy discs
- USB flash drives

Regardless of media type, each disc is divided up into small storage units called *sectors* and these sectors can sometimes fail through electrical wear or mechanical damage.

While the filing system is accessing the disc, it may encounter a failed sector and retry the access, ultimately giving up and reporting an error message such as:

```
Disc error 13 at :4/00001C00
```

This suggests that you have found a disc defect. You might also find a disc defect if you are verifying your disc.

Removing a defect

Having encountered such a disc error, it is possible to tell the filing system not to use that sector again in future; you can still use the rest of your disc.

Assuming that you saw an error message such as:

```
Disc error 13 at :4/00001C00
```

write it down.

The number after the colon is the drive number, followed by the disc address as a hexadecimal number. With large capacity media the disc address could be up to 16 digits long.

1 At the command line type `*Defect`, the disc name and the last part of the disc address:

    `*Defect :4 00001C00`

2 If this section of disc is in use you will see a message such as:

    ```
    $.myfile1 has defect at offset 800
    $.myfile2 must be moved
    ```

3 Try to copy the named files to another part of the disc (into another directory) and delete the originals. The affected part of the disc is now unallocated.

4 At the command line type the `*Defect` command again:

    `*Defect :4 00001C00`

The affected part of the disc is now made inaccessible.

Technical details

The `*Defect` command is more formally described on page 541.

*Defect

Reports what object contains a defect, or (if none) marks the defective part of the disc so it will no longer be used.

Syntax

```
*Defect disc_spec disc_addr
```

Parameters

disc_spec	the name of the disc or number of the disc drive
disc_addr	the hexadecimal disc address where the defect exists, which must be a multiple of the sector size (typically 256, 512, 1024 or 4096) – that is, it must end in '00'

Use

*Defect reports what object contains a defect, or (if none) marks the defective part of the disc so it will no longer be used. *Defect is typically used after a disc error has been reported, and the *Verify command has confirmed that the disc has a physical defect, and given its disc address.

If the defect is in an unallocated part of the disc, *Defect will render that part of the disc inaccessible by altering the 'map' of the disc.

If the defect is in an allocated part of the disc, *Defect tells you what object contains the defect, and the offset of the defect within the object. This may enable you to retrieve most of the information held within the object, using suitable software. You must then delete the object from the defective disc. *Defect may also tell you that some other objects must be moved: you should copy these to another disc, and then delete them from the defective disc. Once you have removed all the objects that the *Defect command listed, there is no longer anything allocated to the defective part of the disc; so you can repeat the *Defect command to make it inaccessible.

Sometimes the disc will be too badly damaged for you to successfully delete objects listed by the *Defect command. In such cases the damage cannot be repaired, and you must restore the objects from a recent backup.

Appendix F: Character sets

This chapter shows the character tables for the alphabets available on your RISC OS computer. The Latin1 character set is the alphabet normally used by the desktop, although this can be changed for different territories.

Most alphabets have a number of undefined characters. They are shown in the following character tables by a light grey square.

The character codes 0 - 31 and 127 are not printable characters. They are shown by a dark grey square.

Loading an alphabet

You can load an alternative alphabet using the *Alphabet command which will overlay the previous alphabet. Any undefined characters will leave the previous character definition for that code in effect.

Whilst the alphabets shown in this chapter have at most 256 characters, the Font Manager can also use the Unicode character set (which has up to 2,097,152 characters) by changing to the 8 *bit Unicode Transformation Format*, or UTF-8, alphabet.

How alphabets are initially set up

The default alphabet

The default system alphabet always contains all characters that are defined in the Latin1 alphabet. Note that this definition has been gradually extended by the addition of extra characters in the range &80 - &9F (128 - 159).

In the future some of these undefined characters may be used to further extend the Latin1 alphabet, or their representation may change. Consequently, you must not rely upon their initial representation.

The configured alphabet

The default alphabet is overlaid by the alphabet that is correct for the computer's configured territory, as set by *Configure Territory.

Keyboard shortcuts

There are some useful keyboard shortcuts which you can use to access various characters and alphabets while you are working. You can use these wherever you can use the keyboard: for example, at the command line, in an application like Edit, or when entering a filename to save a file.

Using top bit set characters

Although the easiest way of inserting top bit set characters (those that have a code greater than 127) into your document is using the Chars application (see *Chars* on page 403) you can also insert them by using special key combinations. You enter characters using the Alt key and the numeric keypad. For example:

Alt *<decimal character code typed on numeric keypad>*

enters the character corresponding to the character code typed.

Changing between alphabets

Alt Ctrl F1 Selects the keyboard layout appropriate to the country UK.

Alt Ctrl F2 Selects the keyboard layout appropriate to the country for which the computer is configured (if available).

Switching between other alphabets

The following sequence also switches the keyboard layout:

1   Press and hold Alt and Ctrl together.

2   Press and release F12.

3   Release Ctrl.

4   Still holding Alt, type on the numeric keypad the international telephone dialling code for the country you want (e.g. 49 for Germany, 39 for Italy, 33 for France).

5   Release Alt.

A small number of keyboard layouts exist for which imaginary dialling codes have been assigned so that they may be switched to using this technique:

Country	Alphabet	Dialling code
Wales	Latin1	1222 (former area code for Cardiff)
Wales2	Welsh	2222 (2nd layout for Wales)
Esperanto	Latin3	1100
DvorakUK	Latin1	9944 (99 followed by UK's dialling code)
DvorakUSA	Latin1	991 (99 followed by USA's dialling code)

Typing special characters

Sometimes you need to be able to type special characters that are not apparently on the keyboard, such as accented characters, or symbols like ©. You can in fact get at lots of extra characters using the Alt key. The section *Typing special characters* on page 14 tells you much more about this.

Latin1 alphabet (ISO 8859-1)

This is the default alphabet used by RISC OS.

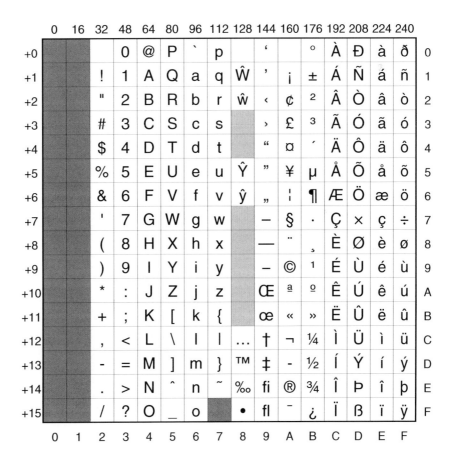

	0	16	32	48	64	80	96	112	128	144	160	176	192	208	224	240	
+0				0	@	P	`	p		'		°	À	Ð	à	ð	0
+1			!	1	A	Q	a	q	Ŵ	'	¡	±	Á	Ñ	á	ñ	1
+2			"	2	B	R	b	r	ŵ	‹	¢	²	Â	Ò	â	ò	2
+3			#	3	C	S	c	s		›	£	³	Ã	Ó	ã	ó	3
+4			$	4	D	T	d	t	"	¤	´	Ä	Ô	ä	ô	4
+5			%	5	E	U	e	u	Ŷ	"	¥	µ	Å	Õ	å	õ	5
+6			&	6	F	V	f	v	ŷ	„	¦	¶	Æ	Ö	æ	ö	6
+7			'	7	G	W	g	w	—	§	·	Ç	×	ç	÷	7
+8			(	8	H	X	h	x	—	¨	¸	È	Ø	è	ø	8
+9			)	9	I	Y	i	y	–	©	¹	É	Ù	é	ù	9
+10			*	:	J	Z	j	z	Œ	ª	º	Ê	Ú	ê	ú	A
+11			+	;	K	[	k	{	œ	«	»	Ë	Û	ë	û	B
+12			,	<	L	\	l	|	…	†	¬	¼	Ì	Ü	ì	ü	C
+13			-	=	M	]	m	}	™	‡	-	½	Í	Ý	í	ý	D
+14			.	>	N	^	n	~	‰	fi	®	¾	Î	Þ	î	þ	E
+15			/	?	O	_	o		•	fl	¯	¿	Ï	ß	ï	ÿ	F
	0	1	2	3	4	5	6	7	8	9	A	B	C	D	E	F	

Latin2 alphabet (ISO 8859-2)

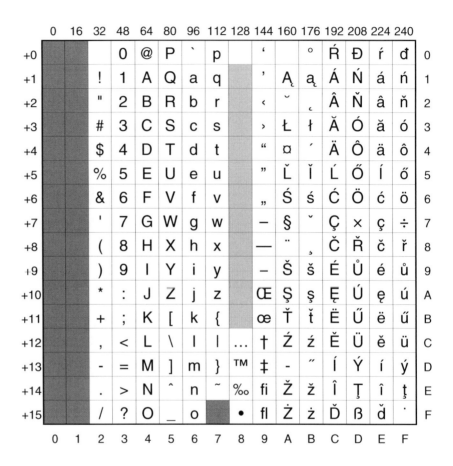

	0	16	32	48	64	80	96	112	128	144	160	176	192	208	224	240	
+0				0	@	P	`	p		'		°	Ŕ	Đ	ŕ	đ	0
+1			!	1	A	Q	a	q		'	Ą	ą	Á	Ń	á	ń	1
+2			"	2	B	R	b	r		‹	˘	˛	Â	Ň	â	ň	2
+3			#	3	C	S	c	s		›	Ł	ł	Ă	Ó	ă	ó	3
+4			$	4	D	T	d	t		"	¤	´	Ä	Ô	ä	ô	4
+5			%	5	E	U	e	u		"	Ľ	ľ	Ĺ	Ő	ĺ	ő	5
+6			&	6	F	V	f	v		„	Ś	ś	Ć	Ö	ć	ö	6
+7			'	7	G	W	g	w		–	§	ˇ	Ç	×	ç	÷	7
+8			(	8	H	X	h	x		—	¨	¸	Č	Ř	č	ř	8
+9			)	9	I	Y	i	y		–	Š	š	É	Ů	é	ů	9
+10			*	:	J	Z	j	z		Œ	Ş	ş	Ę	Ú	ę	ú	A
+11			+	;	K	[	k	{		œ	Ť	ť	Ë	Ű	ë	ű	B
+12			,	<	L	\	l	|	…	†	Ź	ź	Ě	Ü	ě	ü	C
+13			-	=	M	]	m	}	™	‡	-	˝	Í	Ý	í	ý	D
+14			.	>	N	^	n	~	‰	fi	Ž	ž	Î	Ţ	î	ţ	E
+15			/	?	O	_	o		•	fl	Ż	ż	Ď	ß	ď	˙	F
	0	1	2	3	4	5	6	7	8	9	A	B	C	D	E	F	

Latin3 alphabet (ISO 8859-3)

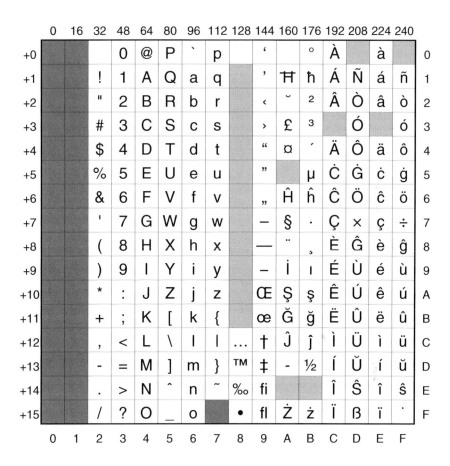

	0	16	32	48	64	80	96	112	128	144	160	176	192	208	224	240	
+0				0	@	P	`	p		'		°	À		à		0
+1			!	1	A	Q	a	q		'	Ħ	ħ	Á	Ñ	á	ñ	1
+2			"	2	B	R	b	r		‹	˘	²	Â	Ò	â	ò	2
+3			#	3	C	S	c	s		›	£	³		Ó		ó	3
+4			$	4	D	T	d	t		"	¤	´	Ä	Ô	ä	ô	4
+5			%	5	E	U	e	u		"		µ	Ċ	Ġ	ċ	ġ	5
+6			&	6	F	V	f	v		„	Ĥ	ĥ	Ĉ	Ö	ĉ	ö	6
+7			'	7	G	W	g	w		—	§	·	Ç	×	ç	÷	7
+8			(	8	H	X	h	x		—	¨	¸	È	Ĝ	è	ĝ	8
+9			)	9	I	Y	i	y		–	İ	ı	É	Ù	é	ù	9
+10			*	:	J	Z	j	z	Œ	Ş	ş	Ê	Ú	ê	ú		A
+11			+	;	K	[	k	{	œ	Ğ	ğ	Ë	Û	ë	û		B
+12			,	<	L	\	l	|	…	†	Ĵ	ĵ	Ì	Ü	ì	ü	C
+13			-	=	M	]	m	}	™	‡	-	½	Í	Ŭ	í	ŭ	D
+14			.	>	N	^	n	~	‰	fi			Î	Ŝ	î	ŝ	E
+15			/	?	O	_	o		•	fl	Ż	ż	Ï	ß	ï	˙	F
	0	1	2	3	4	5	6	7	8	9	A	B	C	D	E	F	

Latin4 alphabet (ISO 8859-4)

	0	16	32	48	64	80	96	112	128	144	160	176	192	208	224	240	
+0				0	@	P	`	p		'		°	Ā	Đ	ā	đ	0
+1			!	1	A	Q	a	q		'	Ą	ą	Á	Ņ	á	ņ	1
+2			"	2	B	R	b	r		‹	Ķ	˛	Â	Ō	â	ō	2
+3			#	3	C	S	c	s		›	Ŗ	ŗ	Ã	Ķ	ã	ķ	3
+4			$	4	D	T	d	t		"	¤	´	Ä	Ô	ä	ô	4
+5			%	5	E	U	e	u		"	Ĩ	ĩ	Å	Õ	å	õ	5
+6			&	6	F	V	f	v		„	Ļ	ļ	Æ	Ö	æ	ö	6
+7			'	7	G	W	g	w		–	§	ˇ	Į	×	į	÷	7
+8			(	8	H	X	h	x		—	¨	̦	Č	Ø	č	ø	8
+9			)	9	I	Y	i	y		–	Š	š	É	Ų	é	ų	9
+10			*	:	J	Z	j	z	Œ	E	ē	Ę	Ú	ę	ú		A
+11			+	;	K	[	k	{	œ	Ģ	ģ	Ë	Û	ë	û		B
+12			,	<	L	\	l	|	…	†	Ŧ	ŧ	Ė	Ü	ė	ü	C
+13			-	=	M	]	m	}	™	‡	-	Ŋ	Í	Ũ	í	ũ	D
+14			.	>	N	^	n	~	‰	fi	Ž	ž	Î	Ū	î	ū	E
+15			/	?	O	_	o		•	fl	¯	ŋ	Ī	ß	ī	·	F
	0	1	2	3	4	5	6	7	8	9	A	B	C	D	E	F	

Cyrillic alphabet (ISO 8859-5)

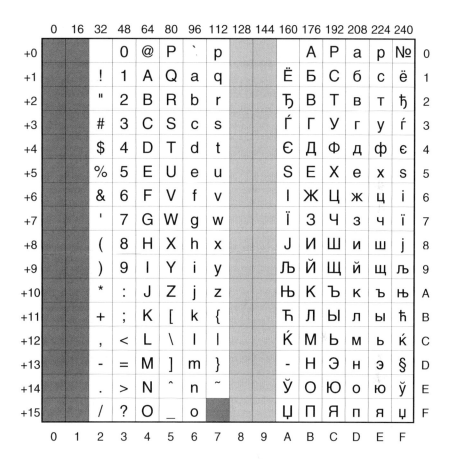

	0	16	32	48	64	80	96	112	128	144	160	176	192	208	224	240	
+0				0	@	P	`	p				А	Р	а	р	№	0
+1			!	1	A	Q	a	q			Ё	Б	С	б	с	ё	1
+2			"	2	B	R	b	r			Ђ	В	Т	в	т	ђ	2
+3			#	3	C	S	c	s			Ѓ	Г	У	г	у	ѓ	3
+4			$	4	D	T	d	t			Є	Д	Ф	д	ф	є	4
+5			%	5	E	U	e	u			Ѕ	Е	Х	е	х	ѕ	5
+6			&	6	F	V	f	v			І	Ж	Ц	ж	ц	і	6
+7			'	7	G	W	g	w			Ї	З	Ч	з	ч	ї	7
+8			(	8	H	X	h	x			Ј	И	Ш	и	ш	ј	8
+9			)	9	I	Y	i	y			Љ	Й	Щ	й	щ	љ	9
+10			*	:	J	Z	j	z			Њ	К	Ъ	к	ъ	њ	A
+11			+	;	K	[	k	{			Ћ	Л	Ы	л	ы	ћ	B
+12			,	<	L	\	l	|			Ќ	М	Ь	м	ь	ќ	C
+13			-	=	M	]	m	}			-	Н	Э	н	э	§	D
+14			.	>	N	^	n	~			Ў	О	Ю	о	ю	ў	E
+15			/	?	O	_	o				Џ	П	Я	п	я	џ	F
	0	1	2	3	4	5	6	7	8	9	A	B	C	D	E	F	

Welsh alphabet (ISO IR-182)

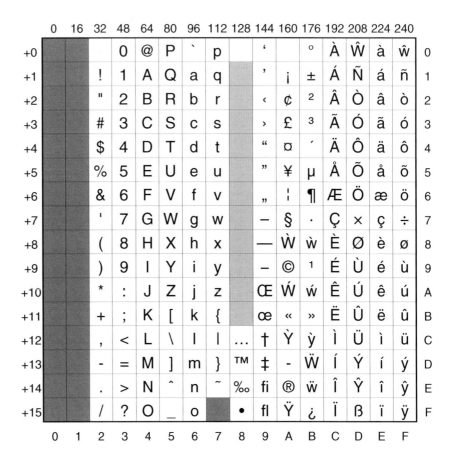

+row	0	16	32	48	64	80	96	112	128	144	160	176	192	208	224	240	hex
+0				0	@	P	`	p	'			°	À	Ŵ	à	ŵ	0
+1			!	1	A	Q	a	q	'		¡	±	Á	Ñ	á	ñ	1
+2			"	2	B	R	b	r	‹		¢	²	Â	Ò	â	ò	2
+3			#	3	C	S	c	s	›		£	³	Ã	Ó	ã	ó	3
+4			$	4	D	T	d	t	"		¤	´	Ä	Ô	ä	ô	4
+5			%	5	E	U	e	u	"		¥	µ	Å	Õ	å	õ	5
+6			&	6	F	V	f	v	„		¦	¶	Æ	Ö	æ	ö	6
+7			'	7	G	W	g	w	–		§	·	Ç	×	ç	÷	7
+8			(	8	H	X	h	x	—		Ẁ	ẁ	È	Ø	è	ø	8
+9			)	9	I	Y	i	y	–		©	¹	É	Ù	é	ù	9
+10			*	:	J	Z	j	z	Œ		Ẃ	ẃ	Ê	Ú	ê	ú	A
+11			+	;	K	[	k	{	œ		«	»	Ë	Û	ë	û	B
+12			,	<	L	\	l	|	…	†	Ỳ	ỳ	Ì	Ü	ì	ü	C
+13			-	=	M	]	m	}	™	‡	-	Ẅ	Í	Ý	í	ý	D
+14			.	>	N	^	n	~	fi		®	ẅ	Î	Ŷ	î	ŷ	E
+15			/	?	O	_	o		fl	•	Ÿ	¿	Ï	ß	ï	ÿ	F

Column hex labels (bottom): 0 1 2 3 4 5 6 7 8 9 A B C D E F

Greek alphabet (ISO 8859-7)

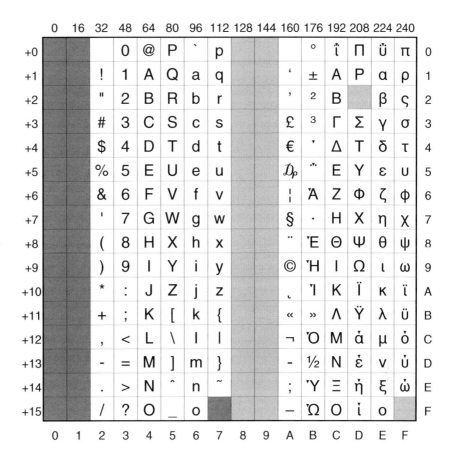

	0	16	32	48	64	80	96	112	128	144	160	176	192	208	224	240	
+0				0	@	P	`	p				°	ῐ	Π	Ϋ	π	0
+1			!	1	A	Q	a	q			'	±	Α	Ρ	α	ρ	1
+2			"	2	B	R	b	r			'	²	Β		β	ς	2
+3			#	3	C	S	c	s			£	³	Γ	Σ	γ	σ	3
+4			$	4	D	T	d	t			€	΄	Δ	Τ	δ	τ	4
+5			%	5	E	U	e	u			₯	῭	Ε	Υ	ε	υ	5
+6			&	6	F	V	f	v			¦	Ά	Ζ	Φ	ζ	φ	6
+7			'	7	G	W	g	w			§	·	Η	Χ	η	χ	7
+8			(	8	H	X	h	x			¨	Έ	Θ	Ψ	θ	ψ	8
+9			)	9	I	Y	i	y			©	Ή	Ι	Ω	ι	ω	9
+10			*	:	J	Z	j	z			ͺ	Ί	Κ	Ϊ	κ	ϊ	A
+11			+	;	K	[	k	{			«	»	Λ	Ϋ	λ	ϋ	B
+12			,	<	L	\	l					¬	Ό	Μ	ά	μ	ό	C
+13			-	=	M	]	m	}			-	½	Ν	έ	ν	ύ	D
+14			.	>	N	^	n	~			;	Ύ	Ξ	ή	ξ	ώ	E
+15			/	?	O	_	o				—	Ώ	Ο	ί	o		F
	0	1	2	3	4	5	6	7	8	9	A	B	C	D	E	F	

Hebrew alphabet (ISO 8859-8)

	0	16	32	48	64	80	96	112	128	144	160	176	192	208	224	240	
+0				0	@	P	`	p				°			א	ן	0
+1			!	1	A	Q	a	q				±			ב	ס	1
+2			"	2	B	R	b	r			¢	²			ג	ע	2
+3			#	3	C	S	c	s			£	³			ד	ף	3
+4			$	4	D	T	d	t			¤	´			ה	פ	4
+5			%	5	E	U	e	u			¥	µ			ו	ץ	5
+6			&	6	F	V	f	v			¦	¶			ז	צ	6
+7			'	7	G	W	g	w			§	·			ח	ק	7
+8			(	8	H	X	h	x			¨	¸			ט	ר	8
+9			)	9	I	Y	i	y			©	¹			י	ש	9
+10			*	:	J	Z	j	z			×	÷			ך	ת	A
+11			+	;	K	[	k	{			«	»			כ		B
+12			,	<	L	\	l	|			¬	¼			ל		C
+13			-	=	M	]	m	}			-	½			ם		D
+14			.	>	N	^	n	~			®	¾			מ		E
+15			/	?	O	_	o				¯			=	ן		F
	0	1	2	3	4	5	6	7	8	9	A	B	C	D	E	F	

Unprintable character 253 is the left-to-right mark, used to set the printing direction in a mixed text containing both script reading orders.

Unprintable character 254 is the right-to-left mark, used to set the printing direction in a mixed text containing both script reading orders.

Latin5 alphabet (ISO 8859-9)

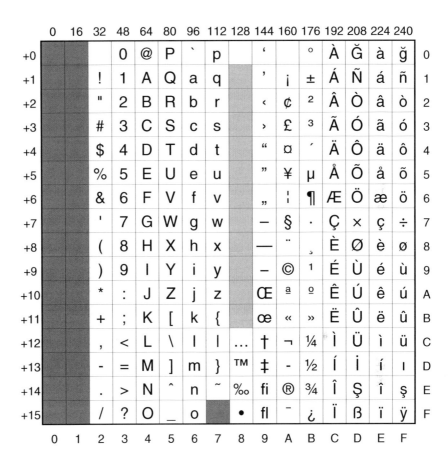

Latin6 alphabet (ISO 8859-10)

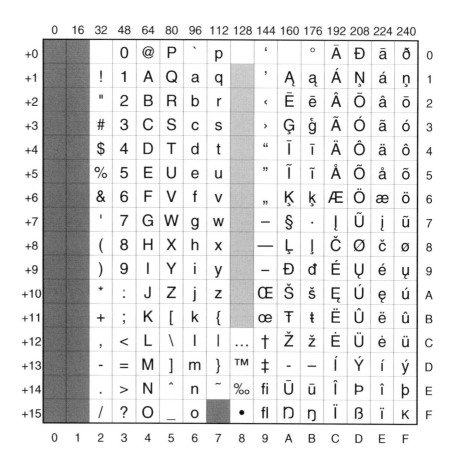

	0	16	32	48	64	80	96	112	128	144	160	176	192	208	224	240	
+0				0	@	P	`	p		'		°	Ā	Đ	ā	ð	0
+1			!	1	A	Q	a	q		'	Ą	ą	Á	Ņ	á	ņ	1
+2			"	2	B	R	b	r		‹	Ē	ē	Â	Ō	â	ō	2
+3			#	3	C	S	c	s		›	Ģ	ģ	Ã	Ó	ã	ó	3
+4			$	4	D	T	d	t		"	Ī	ī	Ä	Ô	ä	ô	4
+5			%	5	E	U	e	u		"	Ĩ	ĩ	Å	Õ	å	õ	5
+6			&	6	F	V	f	v		„	Ķ	ķ	Æ	Ö	æ	ö	6
+7			'	7	G	W	g	w		–	§	·	Į	Ũ	į	ũ	7
+8			(	8	H	X	h	x		—	Ļ	ļ	Č	Ø	č	ø	8
+9			)	9	I	Y	i	y		–	Đ	đ	É	Ų	é	ų	9
+10			*	:	J	Z	j	z		Œ	Š	š	Ę	Ú	ę	ú	A
+11			+	;	K	[	k	{		œ	Ŧ	ŧ	Ë	Û	ë	û	B
+12			,	<	L	\	l	|	…	†	Ž	ž	Ė	Ü	ė	ü	C
+13			-	=	M	]	m	}	™	‡	-	–	Í	Ý	í	ý	D
+14			.	>	N	^	n	~	‰	fi	Ū	ū	Î	Þ	î	þ	E
+15			/	?	O	_	o		•	fl	Ŋ	ŋ	Ï	ß	ï	ĸ	F
	0	1	2	3	4	5	6	7	8	9	A	B	C	D	E	F	

Latin7 alphabet (ISO 8859-13)

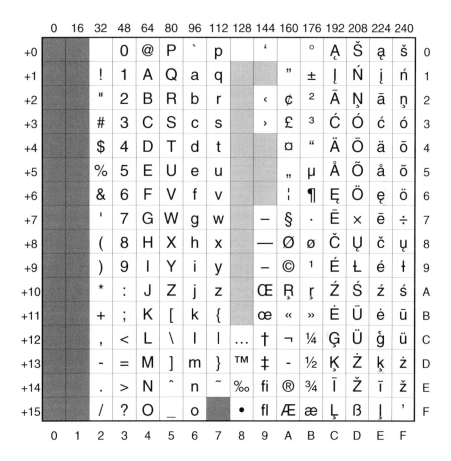

	0	16	32	48	64	80	96	112	128	144	160	176	192	208	224	240	
+0				0	@	P	`	p		'		°	Ą	Š	ą	š	0
+1			!	1	A	Q	a	q			"	±	Į	Ń	į	ń	1
+2			"	2	B	R	b	r		‹	¢	²	Ā	Ņ	ā	ņ	2
+3			#	3	C	S	c	s		›	£	³	Ć	Ó	ć	ó	3
+4			$	4	D	T	d	t			¤	"	Ä	Ō	ä	ō	4
+5			%	5	E	U	e	u			„	µ	Å	Õ	å	õ	5
+6			&	6	F	V	f	v			¦	¶	Ę	Ö	ę	ö	6
+7			'	7	G	W	g	w		–	§	·	Ē	×	ē	÷	7
+8			(	8	H	X	h	x		—	Ø	ø	Č	Ų	č	ų	8
+9			)	9	I	Y	i	y		–	©	¹	É	Ł	é	ł	9
+10			*	:	J	Z	j	z	Œ	Ŗ	ŗ	Ź	Ś	ź	ś	A	
+11			+	;	K	[	k	{	œ	«	»	Ė	Ū	ė	ū	B	
+12			,	<	L	\	l			…	†	¬	¼	Ģ	Ü	ģ	ü	C
+13			-	=	M	]	m	}	™	‡	-	½	Ķ	Ż	ķ	ż	D
+14			.	>	N	^	n	~	‰	fi	®	¾	Ī	Ž	ī	ž	E
+15			/	?	O	_	o		•	fl	Æ	æ	Ļ	ß	ļ	'	F
	0	1	2	3	4	5	6	7	8	9	A	B	C	D	E	F	

Latin8 alphabet (ISO 8859-14)

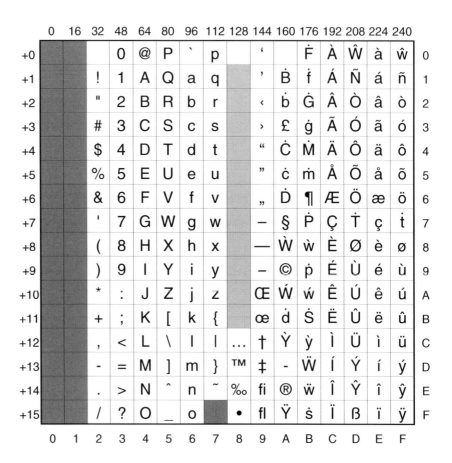

Latin9 alphabet (ISO 8859-15)

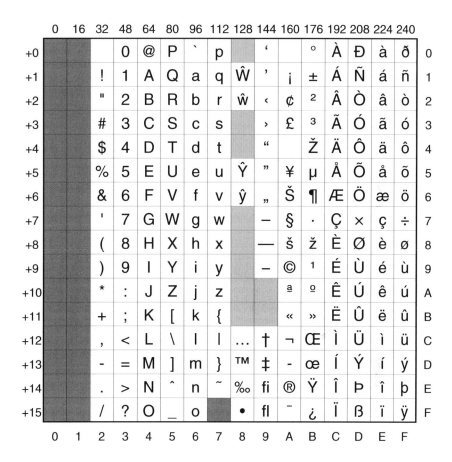

	0	16	32	48	64	80	96	112	128	144	160	176	192	208	224	240	
+0				0	@	P	`	p		'		°	À	Ð	à	ð	0
+1			!	1	A	Q	a	q	Ŵ	'	¡	±	Á	Ñ	á	ñ	1
+2			"	2	B	R	b	r	ŵ	‹	¢	²	Â	Ò	â	ò	2
+3			#	3	C	S	c	s		›	£	³	Ã	Ó	ã	ó	3
+4			$	4	D	T	d	t	"		Ž	Ä	Ô	ä	ô	4
+5			%	5	E	U	e	u	Ŷ	"	¥	µ	Å	Õ	å	õ	5
+6			&	6	F	V	f	v	ŷ	„	Š	¶	Æ	Ö	æ	ö	6
+7			'	7	G	W	g	w		—	§	·	Ç	×	ç	÷	7
+8			(	8	H	X	h	x		—	š	ž	È	Ø	è	ø	8
+9			)	9	I	Y	i	y		–	©	¹	É	Ù	é	ù	9
+10			*	:	J	Z	j	z			ª	º	Ê	Ú	ê	ú	A
+11			+	;	K	[	k	{			«	»	Ë	Û	ë	û	B
+12			,	<	L	\	l	|	…	†	¬	Œ	Ì	Ü	ì	ü	C
+13			-	=	M	]	m	}	™	‡	-	œ	Í	Ý	í	ý	D
+14			.	>	N	^	n	~	‰	fi	®	Ÿ	Î	Þ	î	þ	E
+15			/	?	O	_	o		•	fl	¯	¿	Ï	ß	ï	ÿ	F
	0	1	2	3	4	5	6	7	8	9	A	B	C	D	E	F	

Latin10 alphabet (ISO 8859-16)

	0	16	32	48	64	80	96	112	128	144	160	176	192	208	224	240	
+0				0	@	P	`	p		‘		°	À	Đ	à	đ	0
+1			!	1	A	Q	a	q		'	Ą	±	Á	Ń	á	ń	1
+2			"	2	B	R	b	r		‹	ą	Č	Â	Ò	â	ò	2
+3			#	3	C	S	c	s		›	Ł	ł	Ă	Ó	ă	ó	3
+4			$	4	D	T	d	t		"		Ž	Ä	Ô	ä	ô	4
+5			%	5	E	U	e	u			„	”	Ć	Ő	ć	ő	5
+6			&	6	F	V	f	v			Š	¶	Æ	Ö	æ	ö	6
+7			'	7	G	W	g	w		—	§	·	Ç	Ś	ç	ś	7
+8			(	8	H	X	h	x		—	š	ž	È	Ű	è	ű	8
+9			)	9	I	Y	i	y		–	©	č	É	Ù	é	ù	9
+10			*	:	J	Z	j	z			Ș	ș	Ê	Ú	ê	ú	A
+11			+	;	K	[	k	{			«	»	Ë	Û	ë	û	B
+12			,	<	L	\	l	|		…	†	Ź	Œ	Ì	Ü	ì	ü	C
+13			-	=	M	]	m	}	™	‡	-	œ	Í	Ę	í	ę	D
+14			.	>	N	^	n	~	‰	fi	ź	Ÿ	Î	Ț	î	ț	E
+15			/	?	O	_	o		•	fl	Ż	ż	Ï	ß	ï	ÿ	F
	0	1	2	3	4	5	6	7	8	9	A	B	C	D	E	F	

Appendix G: Error messages

There are many possible error messages; this appendix lists some of the more common ones you might see. It also tells you what the more likely causes of an error message are, and what you can do about it. You may occasionally see other error messages which will usually be self-explanatory. If you have serious problems, especially recurring ones, consult your supplier.

User Errors

These are errors that are mainly caused by you, the user, performing an inappropriate action. Most of these errors are listed in this chapter, together with a way of curing the error.

Internal errors

These errors are not caused by you, but are problems with the system or the application you are using. The most common internal errors are listed here, together with an explanation as to their cause. Most errors of this type start with the word `Internal`.

Error message windows

Standard error boxes

This is what a typical error message window looks like:

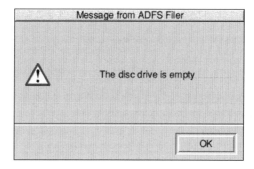

Filer error messages

There is another type of error window you may see. This is generated by the desktop Filer and looks like this:

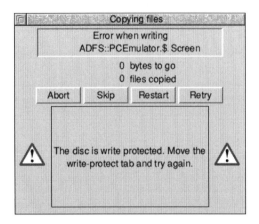

This type of error box is generated when a file operation is not completed. You should clear the fault and then click on the appropriate option. For information about these options, turn to *The Filer* on page 52.

Application error boxes

This type of error box is displayed when one of the applications running on the computer generates an error.

This error box is displayed by the system monitor. It acts like a watchdog and is only activated when something is wrong. The system monitor allows you to selectively remove tasks from the memory of your computer. It is used when you want to remove a task that is misbehaving but you do not want to restart the whole computer system. You'll find out how to use the system monitor in *Managing the desktop* on page 73.

Error messages

Most error messages are self-explanatory; just follow the instructions given in the error message and try again. This section lists the error messages that may need more explanation.

Ambiguous disc name

RISC OS keeps track of removable discs so that you can temporarily remove them from the drive to work with another disc, and will prompt you to insert the original if it is needed again. This error message is caused when the disc that was removed has been modified elsewhere, for example by writing extra files onto it on another computer, meaning it is now ambiguous whether it is the original disc that is inserted or a different one with the same name. Be sure to dismount removable discs before writing extra files onto them on another computer.

An application that loads a file of this type has not been found by the Filer...

Before you can load a file, the application that the file uses must be loaded. The computer cannot find the application unless the operating system knows where it is stored. The easiest way to tell the computer this is to display the application in a directory display, or add it to the list of applications registered at startup using the Boot setup plug-in as described on page 85.

Application is not 32-bit compatible
Module is not 32-bit compatible
Calling standard *xxx* no longer supported by C library

The application you have tried to run, or an extension module which it needs, has been identified as using instructions that your computer can't handle any more. Contact the application author for an updated version.

Chars is unable to display the currently selected outline font

There is not enough memory reserved for the font cache. Use the Task Manager to increase the amount of font cache memory.

Disc error

This may appear for a variety of reasons. The most common explanation is that the media in the drive has a fault on it. You should copy the data onto another disc and then reformat the disc. If you want to try to salvage the disc without formatting it use the command *Defect.

Disc not understood – has it been formatted?

This error message occurs if you put in a disc that has not been formatted or has been formatted in an unknown format. For example an unused and unformatted disc will give this error message and so will a disc formatted to an Apple Macintosh standard since RISC OS does not understand this format.

File not found
Directory not found

The file or directory you have requested has not been found. Make sure that it exists in the directory you have specified and then try again.

This file has been left open from a previous operation

An operation was interrupted by an error, a reset, or similar. Go to the command line by pressing F12 and type in *Close to close all open files. Press Return to return to the desktop and then repeat the operation that previously caused the error. If the error persists, restart your computer. *Close will close all files on the current filing system only. *Shut closes all open files on all filing systems.

File type is unrecognised

An unrecognised file type is usually displayed as a white icon with '?'. Nothing will happen when you double-click on it. You should find the application needed to run it. If you drag the file to Edit you can view the contents of the file in ASCII format (though this may be unhelpful if the file is not a text file).

Free space map full

The data on your disc has become fragmented, and you should compact the disc. This error is only encountered if you are using the old type D or L formats. Use the *Compact command to compact discs. See the file StarComms in the directory Documents.UserGuide.

xxx has tasks active

The User Interface Toolbox keeps a count of how many applications are currently using each of its object types, for example Icon bar or Window objects. This error message is caused by running an application which tries to load an updated module; it is not possible to load the module because the old copy in memory still has tasks using it. Check that the User Interface Toolbox modules installed on your computer are up to date, or contact the application author to find out whether the older version is sufficient.

Illegal window handle
Illegal task handle
Illegal icon handle

This type of message is shown when an application's workspace is damaged and the Window Manager can't find a window/task/icon in the list it keeps. This error may be caused by a bug in the application you are using. Quit the application and then restart the application.

Internal error: undefined instruction

This error may be caused by a bug in the application you are using. Quit the application and then restart the application.

Internal error: abort on data transfer

This error may be caused by a bug in the application you are using. Quit the application and then restart the application.

No reply from the network station

There is a delay on the network, or the Server is not answering; try repeating the command that caused it. If the error happens repeatedly, ask your network manager for help.

Not logged on

You have asked the computer to load a file or application from the network, but you are not logged on. You will see this message if you have just copied an application from the network, logged off, and then tried to load a file straight into the application without loading the application first. The computer tries to load the application from where it first saw it – the network. To avoid this problem, you should first load the application from your disc copy of it, and then load the file.

Printer in use

You are trying to print from more than one application at once. Wait for the first application to finish before printing from the other one.

Printer jammed

The printer is not responding. Check that it is plugged in. If you are using the network printer server, try again later when it may be free; if this error occurs repeatedly, consult your network manager.

System resources cannot be found

The !System application (provided on disc with your computer) cannot be found. Display the directory containing !System and repeat your command. Some applications need to 'see' !System, even though they do not use it.

The access details set for this item do not allow this

Change the access details using the **File/Access** menu so that access is allowed and then try again.

The area of memory reserved for fonts is full

The space reserved for fonts has been used up. Use the Task Manager to reserve more space for the font cache. Alternatively use the Configure application to set the font cache automatically.

The area of memory reserved for relocatable modules is full

The space reserved for modules has been used up. Try quitting some applications, or, if that fails, shutdown and reboot your machine to free up module space.

The disc is write protected

The media you are trying to access is write protected. Move the write-protect tab and try again.

The maximum number of items in a directory has been reached

The number of objects in the root directory of a DOS format disc is fixed when the disc is formatted. Similarly, you cannot have more than 47 objects in a FileCore L format directory, or 77 objects in a FileCore D/E/F format directory.

You should create a new directory to save your work in.

The network is not plugged in

Check the cable from the socket at the back of the computer to the network socket.

There is not enough memory
xxx free memory is needed before the application will start

You need to free more memory before the application will run. You can do this by

● quitting other applications and modules

- using the Task Manager application to reduce the amount of memory used by other things, such as the font cache and system sprite pool

- changing to a screen display with a lower resolution and/or fewer colours

- discarding the RAM disc if you have one. See *Managing memory* on page 79.

There's an upper limit of 512MB on the amount of memory any single application can use and you may see this message if your application reaches this limit.

This item has been locked to stop changes being made to it

You tried to do something forbidden to a locked file, such as delete it. Change the lock access details using the **File/Access/Access** details window so that access is allowed and then try again.

This screen mode is unsuitable for displaying the desktop

You cannot use the proposed mode with the desktop. Change to another mode using the Display Manager.

Index

C

E

H

halftone 195, 197
hard disc 121
    adding applications 238
    backup 128
    defects 132
    DOS partition 142
    formatting 124, 467
    locking 95
    mounting and dismounting 121
    parking heads – *see* switching off the
        computer
    renaming 123
hardware
    configuration 81, 167
    floating point 523
height
    of font 247, 268, 329, 343
    of sprite 356
    paper 205
Help 401
    suspending 402
help
    at the command line 500
    information about applications 54
    on-screen xxi
Helvetica font 246
HForm 467-471
    adding defects 470
    errors 470
    formatting 467
hidden
    mines 451
    mount 185
    objects (network) 164
hinting 248
Home key – *see* keyboard
Homerton font 246
Hopper 439-443
    game keys 440

hourglass
    when displaying screen 252
    when printing 158
HSV colour model 239
    using 243
hue (colour) 240

I

icon
    clicking on 47
    deselecting 51
    on the Pinboard 67
    putting on Pinboard 68
    removing from Pinboard 69
icon bar 4
    bringing to the front 17
iconise
    application windows 68
    configuration 100
    window 46, 67
iconise icon – *see* windows
icons 4
    directories 33
    displaying large or small icons 25
    files 33
    selecting and deselecting 37
ignore
    control characters 498
    control codes and top-bit-set
        characters 198, 200
    pixel size 476
import
    JPEG into Draw 347
    JPEG into Paint 371
    sprite into Draw 304
    text into Edit 264
input focus 419
insert
    special character 403
    special characters 14
internal error 563
</delete>

N

name
disc 122
naming files and directories 35
NetFS 137
network
applications 235
automatic logging on to file server 117
bye 162, 182
downloading fonts 231
errors 165
file ownership 164
file server menu options 161
file servers list 159, 178
logging off 162, 182
logging on 160, 161
manager 159
network printer 209
Open $ 161
overview 149
password 164
printer 202
printing 182, 191
setting password 165
sharing CD and DVD-ROMs 152
time server 108
topology 149
New Century SchoolBook font 246
Newer (Filer option) 59
Newhall font 246
NFS 137
authenticator 180
Boot application 118
case sensitivity 53
printer connection 202
printing over 202
NLQ – *see* printing
non-zero winding rule 327
Num Lock 95
Num Lock key – *see* keyboard
numeric keypad – *see* keyboard

O

obey file
creating 254
see also command/scripts
object
control points 290
convert text to path object 332
Draw 278
editing 330
multi-path Draw object 314
resize handle 303
rotate handle (Draw) 301
selecting (Draw) 314
sending Draw object to front or back of
stack 283
sending to back in Draw 283
snap object control points to grid
(Draw) 311
style 325
OmniClient 177-186
authenticator 180
available file servers 178
discovery 178
mounts file 184
printing 182
startup file 186
open
directory display 47
open submenus automatically 110
Open $ 145, 163, 182
opening files and directories 33
using Adjust button 34
using click-click-hold 90
operating system
entering commands 495
extensions 105
RISC OS xviii, 3
start-up 111
option icon 27
options menu (Filer) 57
OR
Paint colour operator 374

unlink
Task window 498
unsquash 429
urgent alarms 397
Usage 483
starting 483
USB
drives and discs 145
formatting flash drives 124
printer connection 202
see also SCSIFS
user directory 160
user root directory (URD) 161
user name 179
authenticator 180
Econet 159
system variable 186
user privilege on network 161
using applications on removable media – *see*
applications
utilities
ChangeFSI 473
HForm 467
Patch 485
SparkFS 487
T1ToFont 463
Usage 483

V

value (colour) 240
variable 507
Verbose (Filer option) 58
verify
disc 124, 131
video memory – *see* VRAM
volume 104
music CD 139
VRAM 64

W

Wide Area Network (WAN) 149
wide images
processing in ChangeFSI 475
width
of sprite 356
paper 205
wildcard
in * commands 504
in Edit search string 261
in Filer search string 57
Wimp Sprite Pool 75
WimpSlot 117
WimpSymbol font 246
winding rule 325, 327
window
configuration 109
windows 4, 46
adjust size icon 16
back icon 16
close icon 16
closing 19, 46
with Adjust 46
dragging off the screen 17
features 15
iconise icon 16
iconising 46
manipulating 17-22
obscuring the icon bar 17
resizing 17, 46
with Adjust 46
scroll arrows 20
scroll bars 20
scrolling 19-22
with Adjust 22, 46
shuffling 18
slider 20
title bar 16
toggle size icon 16, 18
toggling size 46
with Adjust 46
Windows discs – *see* DOS discs

Reader's Comment Form

RISC OS 5 User Guide, Issue 2

We would greatly appreciate your comments about this Manual, which will be taken into account for the next issue:

Did you find the information you wanted?

Do you like the way the information is presented?

General comments:

If there is not enough room for your comments, please continue overleaf

How would you classify your experience with computers?

☐ **Used computers before**   ☐ **Experienced User**   ☐ **Programmer**   ☐ **Experienced Programmer**

Please send an email with your comments to:

manuals@riscosopen.org

Your name and address:

This information will only be used to get in touch with you in case we wish to explore your comments further